Freedom of Expression in Islam

Freedom of Expression in Islam

Challenging Apostasy and Blasphemy Laws

Edited by
Muhammad Khalid Masud, Kari Vogt, Lena Larsen
and Christian Moe

I.B.TAURIS
LONDON • NEW YORK • OXFORD • NEW DELHI • SYDNEY

I.B. TAURIS
Bloomsbury Publishing Plc
50 Bedford Square, London, WC1B 3DP, UK
1385 Broadway, New York, NY 10018, USA
29 Earlsfort Terrace, Dublin 2, Ireland

BLOOMSBURY, I.B. TAURIS and the I.B. Tauris logo are trademarks of
Bloomsbury Publishing Plc

First published in Great Britain 2021

A catalogue record for this book is available from the British Library.

A catalog record for this book is available from the Library of Congress.

ISBN: HB: 978-1-7845-3857-6
PB: 978-0-7556-3882-6
ePDF: 978-0-7556-3768-3
eBook: 978-0-7556-3767-6

Typeset by RefineCatch Limited, Bungay, Suffolk

To find out more about our authors and books visit www.bloomsbury.com
and sign up for our newsletters.

Contents

List of Contributors vii
Acknowledgements xii
A Note on Transliteration xii

Introduction
Muhammad Khalid Masud, Kari Vogt, Lena Larsen and Christian Moe 1

Part One The Historical Construction

1 Blasphemy Laws in Islam: Towards a Rethinking?
Abdullah Saeed 17

2 Freedom of Religion in Qur'anic Exegesis
Omaima Abou-Bakr 33

3 al-Qadi 'Iyad's Defence of the Prophet and of Scholarly Tradition: *al-Shifā'*
Nora S. Eggen 53

4 Reading Ibn Taymiyya's *al-Ṣārim*: Hermeneutic Shifts in the Definition of Blasphemy
Muhammad Khalid Masud 75

Part Two Present Practices

5 The Crimes of Blasphemy and Apostasy in Iran
Mohammad Mostafaei 101

6 Guarding the Mainstream: Blasphemy and Apostasy in Egypt
Moataz El Fegiery 111

7 Plurality, Dissent and Hegemony: The Story Behind Pakistan's Blasphemy Law
Arafat Mazhar and Syed Zainuddin Moulvi 131

8 Politics of Fatwa, 'Deviant Groups' and *Takfīr* in the Context of Indonesian pluralism: A Study of the Council of Indonesian Ulama
Syafiq Hasyim 157

Part Three New Directions

9 Transgressing All Bounds? Gendering Authority and Engendering Orthodoxy
Kecia Ali 177

10 Re-framing Reform: Lessons from the Apostasy Trials of Hassan Yousefi Eshkevari and Hashem Aghajari
Mahmoud Sadri 195

11 Toward Removing the Punishment of Apostasy in Islam
Mohsen Kadivar 207

Index 237

List of Contributors

Omaima Abou-Bakr is a Professor of English & Comparative Literature at Cairo University. She is a founding member of the Women and Memory Forum and board member of the global organization Musawah (Equality & Justice in the Muslim Family) and of its Knowledge Building team. She specialized in medieval Sufi poetry and comparative topics in medieval English and Arabic literature. Her scholarly interests also include women's mysticism and female spirituality in Christianity and Islam, feminist theology, Muslim women's history and gender issues in Islamic discourses. She has published numerous articles in both English and Arabic on poetry and medieval literary texts, on historical representations of women in pre-modern Muslim societies, women and gender in religious discourses and Islamic feminist issues. Her publications include an edited reader with translations into Arabic of foundational articles in Christian feminist theology and Islamic feminist research, *Al-Niswiyya wa al-Dirāsāt al-Dīniyya* ('Feminism and religious studies', 2012), and two edited volumes of collected articles, *Feminist and Islamic Perspectives: New Horizons of Knowledge and Reform* in English and *al-Niswiyya wa al-Manẓūr al-Islamī* in Arabic (2013).

Kecia Ali (PhD, Religion, Duke University) is Professor of Religion and Chair of the Department of Religion at Boston University. Before joining the BU faculty in 2006, she held research and teaching fellowships at Brandeis University and Harvard Divinity School. Her research addresses Islamic religious texts, especially jurisprudence; women in both classical and contemporary Muslim discourses; and religious biography. She also writes about ethics and genre fiction. Her books include *Marriage and Slavery in Early Islam* (2010), *The Lives of Muhammad* (2014) and *Sexual Ethics and Islam: Feminist Reflections on Qur'an, Hadith, and Jurisprudence* (2nd ed., 2016). Her projects in progress include 'The Woman Question in Islamic Studies', an exploration of the field's gender politics, and 'Women in Muslim Traditions', an introductory survey.

Nora S. Eggen (PhD 2012) is a researcher in Arabic and Islamic studies currently associated with the Faculty of Theology at the University of Oslo. Her research interests include Arabic-Islamic intellectual history, Qur'anic studies and translation studies. Among her recent publications are chapters and articles on the translation of the Qur'an ('On the Periphery', in *Routledge Handbook of Arabic Translation*, 2019; 'Universalised versus Particularised Conceptualisations of Islam in Translations of the Qur'an', *Journal of Qur'anic Studies* 2016); on hermeneutics ('A Multiverse of Knowledge', in *Conceptualizing the World*, 2019); on historiography ('A Book Burner or Not?', *JAIS* 2018); and on the history of Arabic-Islamic studies ('From Handmaiden of Theology to Handmaiden of Area Studies', *Islam and Christian–Muslim Relations*, 2018). Eggen is also a translator from Arabic into Norwegian, and has published translations of al-Nawawi's *Riyāḍ al-Ṣāliḥīn* (2008) and al-Sharif al-Radi's *Nahj al-Balāgha* (2014).

Moataz El Fegiery is Assistant Professor of Human Rights at Doha Institute for Graduate Studies and was Senior Teaching Fellow of Law at the School of Oriental and African Studies (SOAS), University of London. He has extensive experience in human rights research and advocacy in the Middle East and North Africa and has represented international human rights NGOs including Front Line Defenders and International centre for Transitional justice (ICTJ). He was the executive director of Cairo Institute for Human Rights Studies (CIHRS) and is currently a member of its board of directors. El Fegiery is also the treasurer and member of the executive committee of Euro Med Rights and founding board member of the Egyptian Human Rights Forum. He obtained his PhD in Law and his MA in International and Comparative Legal Studies from SOAS, University of London. He is the author of *Islamic Law and Human Rights: The Muslim Brotherhood in Egypt* (2016, Cambridge Scholars Publishing) and contributor to *The Organisation of Islamic Cooperation and Human Rights* (2019, University of Pennsylvania Press).

Syafiq Hasyim is Lecturer and Director of Library and Culture at the Indonesian International Islamic University (UIII), a newly established international graduate university that will start operations in 2021. He is also Lecturer at the Faculty of Social and Political Sciences, UIN Syarif Hidayatullah Jakarta. From March 2020, he is a visiting fellow at the Indonesia Studies Programme of the ISEAS – Yusof Ishak Institute. He obtained DrPhil in Islamic Studies from Freie University, Berlin, Germany, and MA in Islamic Studies from Leiden University, the Netherlands. His research fields include fatwa in Muslim and non-Muslim countries, Islamic commodification, democratic life, political Islam, Islamic feminism and Shari'a life-style. He has published books, international journal articles and commentaries and visual commentaries through TV and YouTube channels. His latest publications include 'Fatwa and Democracy: Majelis Ulama Indonesia (MUI, Council of Indonesia Ulama) and the Rising Conservatism of Indonesian Islam' in *TRaNS: Trans-Regional and -National Studies of Southeast Asia*; 'The Secular and the Religious: Secularization and Shariatization in Indonesia', in Vidhu Verma (ed.), *Secularism, Religion and Democracy in Southeast Asia* (OUP 2019); and *Rising Islamic Conservatism in Indonesia Islamic Groups and Identity Politics* (as co-editor, forthcoming 2021).

Mohsen Kadivar (b. 1959) is a leading public intellectual and a theologian trained in Islamic seminaries in Iran, having earned the certificate of *Ijtihād* (the highest degree of Islamic studies) in Qom and received a PhD in Islamic Philosophy and theology from Tarbiat Modarres University in Tehran, Iran. His criticism of the Iranian regime led to his imprisonment (1999–2000), the banning of his publications and finally to his exile from Iran in 2008. He has been a research professor of Islamic Studies at Duke University (Durham, NC) since 2009. He was a visiting professor at Harvard Law School, University of Virginia and University of North Carolina; a global ethics fellow with the Carnegie Council, research fellow with Wissenschaftskolleg (Institute for

Advanced Study) in Berlin, Germany and a fellow of National Humanities Center in Research Triangle Park, North Carolina. His interests span both classical and modern Islamic thought with a special focus on Islamic philosophy and ethics, Shiʿi theology and jurisprudence, Qurʾanic studies, Shiʿi political thought and Islam and human rights. Author of dozens of books in Persian and Arabic, his forthcoming books in 2020–21 are *Human Rights and Reformist Islam* and *Blasphemy and Apostasy in Islam: Debates in Shiʿa Jurisprudence* (both Edinburgh University Press), and *Islamic Theocracy in the Secular Age: Revisiting Shiʿite Political Thought of Islamic Republic of Iran* (UNC Press).

Lena Larsen is the director of the Oslo Coalition on Freedom of Religion or Belief at the Norwegian Centre for Human Rights, University of Oslo (since 1999). She obtained her PhD in 2011 with a thesis published as *How Muftis Think: Islamic Legal Thought and Muslim Women in Western Europe* (Brill, 2018). She has co-chaired the Oslo Coalition project New Directions in Islamic Thought since 2003, and is co-editor of its previous publications *New Directions in Islamic Thought and Practice* (2009) and *Gender and Equality in Muslim Family Law* (2013). Other publications include *Facilitating Freedom of Religion or Belief: A Deskbook* (2004) and a chapter on economy and gender roles in marriage in *Men in Charge? Rethinking Authority in Muslim Legal Tradition* (2015). She is a member of the advisory committee at the Faculty of Theology, University of Oslo, for a continuing education program for religious leaders. She was awarded a Science and Arts Medal by Egypt in 2008.

Muhammad Khalid Masud (MA, PhD 1973, McGill University) is presently an ad hoc Judge of the Shariat Appellate Bench, Supreme Court of Pakistan. Formerly Director General, Islamic Research Institute, International Islamic University, Islamabad; Chairman, Council of Islamic Ideology, Government of Pakistan, Islamabad; and Professor and Academic Director of the International Institute for the Study of Islam in the Modern World (ISIM), Leiden, the Netherlands. He has published extensively on Islamic law, contemporary issues and trends in Muslim societies. His publications include *Shatibi's Philosophy of Islamic Law* (1995), *Iqbal's Reconstruction of Ijtihad* (1995), *Islamic Legal Interpretation: The Muftis and their Fatwas*, (Harvard, 1996, as co-editor), *Islamic Laws and Women in the Modern World* (1996, editor), *Travelers in Faith, Studies on Tablighi Jamaʿat* (Brill, 2000, editor), *Mafahim-i Qurʾan* (2005, Urdu translation of T. Izutsu's *Ethical Terms in the Qurʾan*), *Dispensing Justice in Islam: Qadis and Their Judgments* (Brill, 2006, co-editor), *Athharwin Sadi Isawi men Barri Saghir men Islami Fikr he Rahnuma* (in Urdu, 2008), *Islam and Modernity: An Introduction to Key Issues and Debates* (University of Edinburgh Press, 2009, co-editor), *Nuqushe Tagore* (2012, transl.) and *Shariʿa Today* (2013).

Arafat Mazhar is Director of the Engage Foundation for Research and Dialogue, where his nine years of research came together in the seminal report 'The Untold Truth of Pakistan's Blasphemy Laws', recognized for its rigor by human rights groups, government and non-government stakeholders. Arafat is also the winner of the Pakistan Debate Society's Malala Yousafzai Award for Courage. He has created multiple online platforms: Shehri Pakistan, which produces civic and legal awareness animations; Hashia, a history channel which explores historical events to understand their impact on our society and culture today; and Soch Videos, an award-winning online news platform. He is currently working on a documentary on the history of Pakistan's blasphemy laws, scheduled for release by end of 2020. In 2019, Arafat also launched an animation film studio, Puffball, where his debut film, the self-described Pakistani dystopian cyber-khilafat short *Shehr e Tabassum*, was praised by critics as 'a treat to behold'. Arafat directed the film and composed the soundtrack for it.

Christian Moe is an independent writer, translator and researcher based in Slovenia. He has written on Islam, human rights and religious affairs in the Balkans, and consulted on religion and foreign policy. He is co-editor of the two previous volumes of the New Directions project, *New Directions in Islamic Thought* (2009) and *Gender and Equality in Muslim Family Law* (2013); the inaugural volume of Brill's *Yearbook of Muslims in Europe* (2009); and two books on religion and representation in the former Yugoslavia, *Religion and Pluralism in Education* (2006) and *Images of the Religious Other* (2008).

Mohammad Mostafaei works as a legal consultant. He studied Law at the Faculty of Law and Political Science at Tehran University, serving as a secretary of the student union, and became a member of the Bar Association in 2001. He established the Hamiyan institution in 2004 and has worked with human rights organizations since then. In 2006, he was appointed as a member of the human rights commission of Iran's Bar Association, and worked as the Commission's secretary. His work has been focused on the death penalty, the stoning punishment, children's rights, specifically execution of juveniles and the rights of women, journalists, minorities and political and human rights activists. His work to defend people against the death penalty and stoning punishment led to the launch of an international campaign. In August 2010, he was forced to leave Iran and move to Norway. There he established the Universal Tolerance Organisation to work for peace, security, freedom and respect for human rights in the world. He has published *I skyggen av Sharia* ('In the shadow of Shariʿa', 2017) in Norwegian.

Zainuddin Moulvi received his BA-LL.B from Lahore University of Management Sciences and is currently a doctoral candidate at the University of Virginia. His research interests include religion and constitutional law, scriptural hermeneutics, legal history, and contemporary issues in the study of Islam, particularly in relation to questions of Islamic law and religious diversity. His current research focuses on the texts and political works of South Asian Muslim thinkers attempting to negotiate the relationship between the modern nation-state and Islamic legal and philosophical traditions.

Syed Mahmoud Sadri is a professor of sociology and an affiliate professor of Women's Studies at Texas Woman's University and the Federation of North Texas Area Universities. He received his BA and MA degrees from the University of Tehran and his PhD from the New School University in New York City in 1988. His major expertise includes Comparative Sociology of Religion, Sociology of Culture and Theoretical Sociology. His area interests are: Middle Eastern and Iranian studies and Islamic Reformation. His books include: *Migration, Globalization, and Ethnic Relations* (Prentice Hall, 2003, with Mohsen Mobasher) and *Reason, Freedom, and Democracy In Islam: The Essential Writings of Abdolkarim Soroush* (Oxford University Press, 2000, with Ahmad Sadri). His last publication, 'Collective Adjustment to Structural Strain', appeared in the *Journal of Sociological Inquiry*, Spring 2020. In addition to his English publications, Mahmoud Sadri frequently speaks in public forums, writes for Iranian reform newspapers and journals and is interviewed by international news organizations concerning developments in Iran, Islam and the Middle East. He is currently working on publishing a collection of his articles.

Abdullah Saeed is currently the Sultan of Oman Professor of Arab and Islamic Studies and Redmond Barry Distinguished Professor at the University of Melbourne, Australia. He is also Advisor to the Studies in Interreligious Relations in Plural Societies Programme and Peter Lim Professor of Peace Studies at the S. Rajaratnam School of International Studies, Nanyang Technological University, Singapore. He is a Fellow of the Australian Academy of Humanities and a Member of the Order of Australia (AM). Among his recent published books are: *Contemporary Approaches to the Qur'an and its Interpretation in Iran* (co-authored with Ali Akbar, 2019); *Islam and Human Rights* (2018); *Reading the Qur'an in the Twenty-First Century* (2014); *Islamic Political Thought and Governance* (edited, 2011); and *The Qur'an: An Introduction* (2008).

Kari Vogt is Associate Professor (Emeritus) at the Department of Cultural Studies and Oriental Languages, University of Oslo. She has published widely on Islamic and Middle East issues, and is co-editor of the previous publications from the Oslo Coalition's New Directions project, *New Directions in Islamic Thought and Practice* (2009) and *Gender and Equality in Muslim Family Law* (2013).

Acknowledgements

The editors would like to acknowledge funding from the Norwegian Ministry of Foreign Affairs for the project New Directions in Islamic Thought at the Oslo Coalition on Freedom of Religion or Belief, which let us hold three workshops in Oslo and Istanbul out of which this book has grown. We would like to acknowledge the many thought-provoking contributions of workshop participants that have not been included here.

A Note on Transliteration

Transliteration of italicized Arabic technical terms and publication titles follows the example of the *International Journal of Middle East Studies*, with diacritics indicating long vowels and emphatic consonants. Arabic book titles are capitalized following the English pattern. For names we have used a simplified transliteration without diacritics, and authors' preferred spellings or common spellings in the English press have been substituted where relevant. Some technical terms are treated as part of the English lexicon, but *ayn* (ʿ) and *hamza* (ʾ) are marked (e.g. Qurʾan, Shariʿa, qadi, hadith, Shiʿi, Sunni). Simplified transliterations have been used for Persian, according to contributors' preference, and Bahasa spellings have been retained for Indonesian names and titles.

Introduction

Muhammad Khalid Masud, Kari Vogt, Lena Larsen and Christian Moe

Asia Bibi, a Punjabi farm worker, was accused of blaspheming against the Prophet Muhammad after a quarrel with Muslim fellow villagers who reportedly refused water to drink from her hand because she was a Christian. In 2010, to global outrage, a Pakistani court sentenced her to hang. The governor of Punjab province, Salman Taseer, called for her pardon and for legal reform. In 2011, he was shot dead by his own bodyguard. In the eyes of his killer, his opposition to the blasphemy laws had made him an apostate from Islam who had to be killed. The bodyguard was eventually tried and executed for the murder, but Pakistani society was divided between those who saw him as a traitor and those who celebrated him as a martyr. A federal minister, Shahbaz Bhatti, was also murdered for his opposition to the blasphemy laws, and Taseer's son was kidnapped. After years in prison Asia Bibi won out on appeal in the Pakistan Supreme Court,[1] a judgement that threw the country into political crisis; for her safety, she has had to leave the country.

While Bibi belongs to a vulnerable minority, the late Nasr Abu Zayd was a Muslim who knew the Qur'an by heart, a professor of Arabic language teaching Islamic sciences at the University of Cairo and a contributor to a previous book in our New Directions in Islamic Thought project.[2] He had to flee Egypt with his wife after the court annulled his marriage on grounds of alleged apostasy, based on his scholarly writings about the Qur'an.

These disturbing stories, which are only two of the most well-known of many around the world, raise a number of issues associated with laws and social norms against blasphemy and apostasy in the Muslim world.

First, blasphemy and apostasy laws can be used both to suppress thought and debate and to harass religious minorities, both inside and outside Islam. They are often used as vicarious arguments to serve political and economic interests, or to settle scores. Local backgrounds can be complex; in the Asia Bibi case, issues of class, caste and purity intertwined with religious notions. Local legal systems can also vary widely: Like Pakistan, Egypt has no criminal penalty for apostasy from Islam, but it has civil-law consequences that were exploited in the Abu Zayd case.[3]

Second, the problem extends beyond law and state practice to attacks by private actors. Accusations of blasphemy or apostasy put people at risk of extrajudicial killings, whether in jail or on the outside.

Third, though it is not our focus here, blasphemy cases also have a transnational reach and have in recent decades become a thorny issue in international politics. Western publics have taken on the causes of individual victims of blasphemy laws in Muslim countries, from the mentioned case of Asia Bibi in Pakistan to Meriam Ibrahim in the Sudan, and have also reacted to violence in their own midst, from Ayatollah Khomeini's 1989 death sentence against Salman Rushdie for the novel *Satanic Verses*, through the 2006 controversy over cartoons of Muhammad in the Danish newspaper *Jyllandsposten*, to the 2015 shooting of staff at the French satirical weekly *Charlie Hebdo*. Below we briefly discuss the international debate as a discourse of identity and a discourse of universal human rights, two aspects that we wish to keep distinct. In this book, however, we are mainly concerned with impacts and debates inside Muslim-majority societies, though these of course do not take place in isolation.

A number of publications on Muslim blasphemy and apostasy laws have appeared in recent years, pointing to the significance of the issue.[4] Relatively little attention has been paid, however, to the diverse responses of contemporary Muslim religious experts and to questions such as: Can religious knowledge be a resource for critical, constructive engagement with those particular modern constructions of Islam that are used to legitimate restrictive state laws and severe sanctions? What different interpretations of the sources are open to Muslim scholars addressing these questions in a changing historical context?

We believe that a knowledge-based approach is needed to criticize this construction of Islam and open a space for public debate, which is hampered by a lack of knowledge of the religious tradition. The challenge of bringing the debate out of deadlock can only be met by Muslim actors in their respective societies, questioning the tradition and its modern interpretations from within and developing a language in which believing Muslim citizens can express their concerns over the injustice and harshness of the laws. In present circumstances, this takes not only knowledge and commitment, but also a great deal of courage.

In this book, an international and diverse group of Muslim scholars rise to the challenge, in a fruitful dialogue between academics, activists and traditional scholars. Brought together by the New Directions in Islamic Thought project of the Oslo Coalition on Religion or Belief, they have spent years developing arguments and case studies to contest restrictions on freedom of religion and expression based on Islamic justifications.

This introduction sets the stage by very briefly surveying the prevalence of blasphemy and apostasy laws, explaining and placing in context some centrally relevant terms and provisions of both Islamic law and international human rights law. We go on to note some recent salient developments in international debate that shift the focus from the unhelpful construct of an East–West conflict over religion, to dialogue on shared concerns for believing human beings. Finally, we outline the contents of the chapters that follow.

Mapping blasphemy and apostasy laws

The problem of blasphemy laws is far from unique to the Muslim world, but it is particularly pressing there. In 2014, according to the Pew Research Center, 'about a quarter of the world's countries and territories had anti-blasphemy laws or policies, and more than one in ten penalized blasphemy.' Twenty-eight Muslim countries made up the bulk of this list.[5] It should be noted, though, that these countries made up only about half the membership of the Organization of Islamic Cooperation (OIC). While most Muslim countries with blasphemy laws punish blasphemy with fines or prison sentences, often lengthy ones, the death penalty and flogging punishments are applicable in several countries.[6]

Today, the criminalization of apostasy *is* a problem unique to the Muslim world (though related problems, such as restrictions on proselytism, are not). In 2014, 23 OIC member states had apostasy laws; India, with its large Muslim minority, was the only non-Muslim country with such a law on Pew's list.[7] Apostasy was expressly a capital offence in Afghanistan, Brunei, Mauritania, Qatar, Saudi Arabia, Sudan, the United Arab Emirates and Yemen. Some countries that do not explicitly criminalize apostasy in their penal codes have nevertheless prosecuted it under religious law, including Iran (see Chapter 5 by Mostafaei) and Jordan. In Muslim countries, leaving Islam can also have grave civil-law repercussions, such as annulling the apostate's marriage and succession rights. Charges of apostasy also put the accused at risk of extrajudicial killing. In a positive development, Tunisia in 2014 introduced a constitutional ban on such attacks.[8]

The full legal effect of blasphemy and apostasy provisions only becomes clear when they are considered together, since Muslims who blaspheme may be charged with apostasy, while countries without explicit apostasy laws may de facto prosecute that offense through blasphemy charges. The degree to which religious offenses have been prosecuted as apostasy, rather than as other crimes, has varied over history.

Repression, freedom and religious justification

The ostensibly religious issue of apostasy and blasphemy is made all the more sensitive by the role it plays in multiple politics of identity that have arisen in response to globalization, colonialism and migration. The role of international relations merits extended study that is not our purpose here, and we only note a few salient points. On the skewed playing field of colonial rule, Muslim societies were exposed to the preaching and proselytizing of Christian missionaries, including polemical arguments that continued a long Western tradition of impugning the credibility of Muhammad and the Qur᾽an;[9] at the same time, conversion from Islam was facilitated by the suspension of Islamic criminal law. On the other hand, some restrictions on expression and belief in the Muslim world are themselves legacies of colonial interests; the original provisions of Pakistan's blasphemy laws, for example, stem from times when Hindu–Muslim polemics threatened to disturb the peace under British rule in India. The unequal position of Muslim countries in post-colonial global power relations continues to inflame the sensitivity of these issues, while culturally defensive reactions are also driven by the contest between various governments and movements for leadership of the Muslim world.

In Muslim countries, apostasy and blasphemy laws are defended on the grounds that they are based on Islamic Shariʿa and intended to protect religion. The religious scholars (*ʿulamāʾ*), as significant actors, are frequently opposed to reform. Harsh penalties have come to be equated with a reassertion of Islam, while critics are accused of serving a Western agenda – or indeed of being apostates themselves, as in the case of the late Punjab governor.

Blasphemy also plays a role in identity politics in liberal Western democracies, where it is defended to protect free speech as a Western value under threat. As noted by Talal Asad, there also occurs an argument that deliberately hurtful blasphemy can serve an emancipatory purpose by shocking Muslims into re-examining their beliefs.[10] The tendency to denounce all critique of religion as blasphemy is mirrored by a tendency to elevate all blasphemy to critique of religion.

The freedoms of religion and expression, however, are not only Western values; they have been affirmed as *universal* human rights in legal documents signed by the world's governments. In current debates, it is often forgotten that these rights are as vital for believing Muslims as for everybody else. They are particularly vital for Muslims who seek political or religious reform, since they often face accusations of blasphemy or apostasy for challenging powerful establishments. It is also forgotten that many Muslims around the world voice their support for democratic rights and freedoms (see Chapter 10 by Sadri), and find support for this view in a liberal reading of their religious sources, such as the Qurʾanic verse 'no compulsion in religion' (2:256, see Chapter 2 by Abou-Bakr). The religious norms and interests that demand repression of blasphemy and apostasy exist in tension not only with international human rights, but with other Muslim religious norms and interests.

The contributions to this book, therefore, do not dwell on colonial history, conflicts between 'Islam' and 'the West', or debates on cultural relativism. Instead, they advance the debate by critiquing the religious legitimation of repressive norms from within the religious tradition itself, grounded in scholarship and moral commitment. They question the power imbalances, ideological narratives and legal constructions underlying blasphemy and apostasy laws in Muslim societies. Some highlight the historically contingent nature of these norms and unravel their connections with political, communal and patriarchal insecurities (see especially Chapters 1, 4 and 9 by Saeed, Masud and Ali respectively). Some seek to locate the freedoms of religion and expression in Islam, explicitly or implicitly exploring the scope for mutual support – rather than tension – between the normative systems of Islamic law and ethics, on the one hand, and international human rights on the other.

Here, we offer the briefest of introductions to key terms in both these normative systems, to help the reader navigate the complexities of the different contributions that we summarize at the end.

Islamic legal terms

Many elements of Islamic tradition are pertinent to this issue. For example, understanding Muslim reactions to blasphemy requires an appreciation of the feelings involved in popular devotion to the Prophet Muhammad. Some chapters in this book review the history of Qurʾanic interpretation (Abou-Bakr) or examine the theology and etiquette of grief (Ali). Here, we focus on traditional Islamic law as a dominant reference in the debate.

Modern legal codes criminalizing blasphemy and apostasy in the Muslim world, as well as the social practices that can lead to violence, rely for their justification on their claim to derive from classical Islamic law and, ultimately, the will of God. They are therefore open to challenge from different readings of the Islamic normative tradition, but to be effective, such challenges must be based on extensive knowledge of that tradition.

By Islamic law, we refer to a tradition of learned opinion on the derivation of norms from religious texts and their application to a wide range of legal, moral and ritual questions as the human understanding (*fiqh*) of the divine law (Shariʿa).

In modern times, nearly all Muslim countries have introduced codes of law enacted by legislatures and have to a large extent replaced Islamic law with laws of Western inspiration in content as well as form. However, a resurgence of political Islam since the 1970s, in combination with the quest of undemocratic regimes for religious legitimacy, caused some countries to pursue the so-called 'Islamization' of law by codifying selected traditional rulings, largely in two areas: gender relations, as we discussed in a previous book;[11] and penal law, including the controversial corporal punishments for certain crimes, the *ḥudūd* ('limits', sg. *ḥadd*).

As these were areas of Islamic law frequently criticized as backward by Westerners, their renewed application served to symbolically reassert the defiantly Islamic identity of the state. So did the reinforcement of blasphemy laws, even when these were, paradoxically, a legacy of colonial rule, as in South Asia.

Blasphemy and apostasy as legal constructions are informed by the history and development of Islamic law schools and their methods of legal reasoning. Without going into details, a brief note explaining key terms may be helpful. Islamic law has its sources in the Qurʾan and in the Sunna, the guidance given by the Prophet Muhammad (and, in Shiʿi legal thought, by his successors, the Imams).

Differences in the jurists' interpretations and methods of reasoning led to the formation of several schools of law (*madhāhib*, sg. *madhhab*) in the ninth century. Sunni Muslims today adhere to four schools: the Hanafi, attributed to Imam Abu Hanifa (d. 767); Maliki, attributed to Imam Malik b. Anas (d. 795); Shafiʿi, attributed to Imam Muhammad b. Idris al-Shafiʿi (d. 820); and Hanbali, attributed to Imam Ahmad b. Hanbal (d. 855); scholars also frequently reference the historical Zahiri school, attributed to Imam Dawud b. Khalaf (d. 884). Among the Shiʿi schools, the largest, and the only one discussed in this book, is the Jaʿfari, also called Imamiyya and Twelver, attributed to Imam Jaʿfar al-Sadiq (d. 765); we also find the Ibadi, Zaydi and Ismaʿili schools.[12]

These schools have continuously developed legal literature employing methods of reasoning (*ijtihād*) on the basis of their respective principles and sources (*uṣūl*). Beside the Qurʾan and Sunna as primary sources, the agreement and consensus (*ijmāʿ*) of jurists in the respective schools has also been generally regarded as a formal source. Schools differ on the definition, nature and history of consensus, and it is problematized in several chapters of this book, but it is a frequently invoked source of legal justification in most schools. Schools differ in other methods of legal reasoning. The method of analogical reasoning, often called *qiyās* (analogy, precedent) or *ʿaql* (human reason) is frequently employed. A number of other principles and methods have been developed in the modern period: interschool borrowings such as *takhyīr* (selection), *talfīq* (combination) and *taṭbīq* (synthesis); taking account of *taysīr* (convenience) and *maṣlaḥa* (common good); and higher principles of the objectives of law or intent of the lawgiver (*maqāṣid al-sharīʿa*). Chapters in this volume have particularly problematized the methods of *ijmāʿ* and the hermeneutics of textual interpretation.

The familiar English terms we use here, blasphemy and apostasy, have a long history in the West, where their meaning has changed over time.[13] They only partly overlap in meaning with the terms used in Islamic legal tradition, which have their own history. Muslim jurists have discussed offenses such as *sabb* (insult), *shatm* (abuse, vilification), *takdhīb* (accusing the Prophet of lying), *zandaqa* (concealed apostasy) and *isaʾa* (vilification), though not the Christian Arabic term *tajdīf* (scoffing at God's name). All of these are at times translated into English as blasphemy. Often the offence at stake is *sabb al-nabī* or *sabb al-rasūl*, vilifying the Prophet.

Apostasy is known as *ridda* or *irtidād*, 'going back', and the apostate as a *murtadd*. The notion arose in the 'wars of *ridda*' in the first years after the death of the Prophet, when his successor, the caliph Abu Bakr, fought tribes of the Arabian peninsula who refused to pay the alms tax. From the beginning, then, there was a tendency to conflate the breach of political allegiance to the Muslim community with abandoning the religious beliefs and practices of Islam. Apostasy is commonly counted among the crimes with fixed penalties (*ḥudūd*), though the Qurʾan does not, in fact, prescribe any punishment for apostasy in this world.

A related concept is *takfīr*, declaring a Muslim to be an unbeliever, i.e. an accusation of apostasy. Such denunciations have a long history and have always been controversial.[14] Recent decades have seen heated debates among Muslims over the tendency of certain modern revivalist movements to charge with unbelief everyone who does not follow their interpretation of Islam, a charge that carries the implied threat of violence and persecution.

Private action against offenders may be justified in terms of *ḥisba*, an obligation incumbent on every Muslim to 'command good and forbid evil' by physical intervention if possible and by verbal denunciation if not. In Egypt, the *ḥisba* doctrine has enabled private persons to bring court proceedings against alleged apostates, as in the case of Professor Abu Zayd. Also involved are religious rulings declaring the offender an outlaw by saying his 'blood' is 'permitted' (*mubāḥ al-damm*). Such doctrines are tempered by a concern that the use of force should be reserved for the legitimate authorities, particularly in Sunni Islam. In the Jaʿfari school, however, there exists a doctrine that the Muslim eyewitness to an act of blasphemy is obliged to kill the offender on the spot.

International standards

Blasphemy and apostasy laws conflict with international human rights standards. In particular, the *freedom of religion or belief*, as set out in international documents signed by nearly all Muslim countries,[15] includes the right to have a religion of one's choice, i.e. the right to keep or to change one's religion. Apostasy laws deny this right to Muslims. Moreover, these laws may be so broadly formulated or applied that even believing Muslims risk being charged with blasphemy or apostasy for voicing religious or political views. Thus, the *freedom of opinion and expression* is also at stake.[16]

Under these standards, criminalizing apostasy is not permissible under any circumstances, as international human rights law recognizes no permissible limitation on a person's beliefs, including the right to change them. There *are* permissible limitations on the freedom to 'manifest' those beliefs, and on the freedom of expression, but only as prescribed by law and as far as necessary in pursuit of the legitimate aims explicitly listed in the human rights treaties, such as public order, public morals and the rights of others.

Different jurisdictions have taken different views on the freedom to express blasphemy. In Europe, where a few countries still have blasphemy laws,[17] the European Court of Human Rights has in several cases upheld certain restrictions on blasphemy, controversially reading a right to the protection of religious feelings into the freedom of religion or belief. Indeed, the year before the Danish cartoon controversy, the Court held that it may be necessary in a democratic society to confiscate a novel insulting the Prophet Muhammad.[18]

However, in 2011, the UN Human Rights Committee concluded that blasphemy laws were incompatible with the freedom of expression, except where the blasphemy amounted to hate speech (incitement to discrimination, hostility or violence). Even in the latter case, the law must not discriminate between religions or beliefs or prevent criticism of religious leaders or commentary on religious doctrine.[19]

At that point, there had been more than a decade of acrimonious international debate over UN resolutions proposed by Muslim countries to combat 'defamation of religions', with broad reference to both Islamophobic hate speech and blasphemous injury to religious feelings. In 2011, however, the debate was transformed by a new UN resolution on combating intolerance, stereotyping, discrimination and violence based on religion or belief, proposed by Pakistan on behalf of the OIC.[20] There followed constructive dialogues between governments in the so-called Istanbul process and between experts who fashioned the Rabat Plan of Action.

This new initiative of Muslim governments involved two crucial conceptual shifts from the 'defamation' debate. First, by focusing on combating intolerance against *persons* based on religion or belief, rather than defamation of *religions*, it reaffirmed the international human right to freedom of religion or belief, which belongs to everyone as a human being and thus protects the *believer* rather than the *belief.*

Second, rather than seeming to pit freedom of religion or belief against the freedom of opinion and expression, it looked for synergies between them.[21] The UN resolution recognized that 'the open public debate of ideas, as well as interfaith and intercultural dialogue, (…) can be among the best protection against religious intolerance'.[22] Experts meeting in Rabat pointed out that the two rights were 'mutually dependent and reinforcing' and that the freedom of expression was 'essential to creating an environment in which constructive discussion about religious matters could be held'.[23] The experts accordingly concluded that states with blasphemy laws should repeal them, due to these laws' 'stifling impact on the enjoyment of freedom of religion or belief.'[24] In a less wide-ranging statement that nevertheless represented a political breakthrough, the UN Human Rights Council in 2017 urged states who had not repealed such laws not to impose the death penalty for apostasy and blasphemy.[25]

The debate is not over, but it is shifting to the problem of how to combat religious intolerance against persons. One strand of this discussion concerns whether and how some expressions formerly prosecuted as 'blasphemy' should be prosecuted on the narrower grounds of 'hate speech', advocacy of religious hatred that constitutes incitement to discrimination, hostility or violence. While some extreme statements may fall under hate speech, though, hate-speech laws will not be a drop-in replacement for blasphemy, as they protect people, not beliefs, and require the element of incitement. Another strand concerns how expressions of intolerance can be met with 'counter-speech' rather than restrictions. In a UN-backed initiative called 'Faith for Rights', for example, faith-based and civil-society actors meeting in Beirut in 2017 stressed the influence and responsibility of religious leaders, called on them to speak with one voice against advocacy of hatred and stressed the need to empower them to do so through training and other support.[26]

Structure of the book

The first part of this book takes a detailed and critical look at the past construction of apostasy and blasphemy as sins and crimes in the scholarly Islamic tradition. The authors trace the development of the law in shifting historical circumstances, survey the interpretations of Qur'anic verses that seem to affirm freedom of religion, place in context the seminal medieval writings that have shaped juristic and popular opinion, and pay attention to the voices and alternative readings that were excluded as threatening to power structures.

Abdullah Saeed's opening chapter sketches a number of themes that recur throughout the book. Saeed argues that blasphemy lacks a firm basis in the Qur'an, the Sunna, or consensus, but rather has its roots in ancient social and political practices. The law has been used by the state and powerful groups against minorities. Its application has changed over time in response to socio-political circumstances; in particular, Saeed traces the relationship of the law with the political power of the Islamic state and its security against outside threats. Acknowledging the challenges that Muslim scholars face today, Saeed argues that the particular socio-political context in which the law of blasphemy developed no longer exists, and that contemporary Muslims are free to rethink this notion in light of their own circumstances.

Further developing the point that interpretations have changed in response to historical contexts, in Chapter 2 Omaima Abou-Bakr examines the exegetical history of verse 2:256 in selected classical and modern *tafsīr* literature. In particular, she looks at how the concepts of freedom and coercion were constructed and developed in religious belief; at how exegetes have oscillated between the hermeneutical methods of generalizing or particularizing the verse and using corroborating evidence from Prophetic tradition; and the thematic connection with two other types of verses, those stressing choice and those urging jihad. Abou-Bakr's discussion highlights the potential for readings of the Qur'an that stress freedom of religion; while tradition followed a different path, this hermeneutic choice was made by exegetes in their social context.

The legal doctrine on blasphemy and apostasy was developed by medieval Islamic scholars. Two scholars whose writings on blasphemy against the Prophet remain influential in contemporary discussions, Qadi ʿIyad and Ibn Taymiyya, are examined in Chapters 3 and 4 by Nora Eggen and Khalid Masud, respectively. In both chapters, biographies are used to shed light on the scholars' motivations for uncompromisingly supporting the death penalty.

Qadi ʿIyad's *al-Shifā'*, a devotional book, vehemently protects the integrity of the Prophet. Eggen presents the *Shifā'* in its wider textual, intellectual and historical context. She argues that it is set within a context of competing views on spiritual, epistemic and political authority, not least the rise of the Almohads, and serves the function of defending a tradition in which scholarly knowledge was valued.

Ibn Taymiyya's *al-Ṣārim al-Maslūl*, which urges the death penalty for blasphemers regardless of whether they are Muslims and whether they repent, has become a basic text in contemporary Muslim discourse on blasphemy. Masud points out that Ibn Taymiyya wrote it, not only in the context of the Crusades, the Mongol invasions and the Shiʿi challenge, but in a situation where the author himself had been punished for falsely accusing a Christian who had apologized and converted to Islam. The *Ṣārim* thus reads more like a heated political comment than a proper theological or legal argument, Masud finds; Ibn Taymiyya's Qur'anic hermeneutics are weak, and his claims to represent a consensus of Muslim jurists are belied by his own discussion of their differing views.

The second part of the book examines the present politics and practices of prosecuting alleged blasphemers and/or apostates in selected Muslim countries – Iran, Egypt, Pakistan and Indonesia – each with their own particular issues and debates. While blasphemy laws can severely infringe the freedoms of non-Muslim minorities, in this book we pay particular attention to their impact on Muslims.

In Chapter 5 Mohammad Mostafaei, an Iranian human-rights lawyer in exile, gives a critical practitioner's perspective on blasphemy and apostasy in Iranian law and legal practice, including one case in which he defended an alleged blasphemer against the death penalty. He discusses the changes in the 2012 penal code. The codified laws are found to be unclear and incomplete, relying on traditional law to fill the gap, and Mostafaei concludes that the system fails to satisfy basic requirements of justice, like legal certainty and procedural safeguards. In the author's view, harsh punishments can only frighten people away from religion.

In Chapter 6 Moataz El Fegiery carefully documents legal developments in Egypt leading up to and including the brief period of civilian rule under Morsi (2012–13), laying a solid ground for further studies. Egyptian law only criminalizes blasphemy, not apostasy, but the latter can have severe civil-law consequences. Egyptian courts have opted for a broad and ambiguous definition of blasphemy and have repeatedly prosecuted writers and other public voices accused of offending against Islamic doctrines, a restrictive line that has been backed by the traditional religious establishment, as well as by political Islam, which has since itself been harshly suppressed. El Fegiery finds that Egyptian courts have used Islam and Shariʿa as a pretext for limiting the scope of religious freedom and freedom of expression, and that the legal debate on blasphemy and apostasy therefore needs to be located within the political and social struggle over the definition of rights in Egypt.

As becomes apparent, the politics of religious authority is central to the contemporary debate on blasphemy and apostasy laws. The remaining two chapters in this part give insight into the contest over the power to define certain positions as Islamic.

Pakistan's harsh blasphemy laws are supposedly based on the Hanafi school of Islamic law. Yet, as Arafat Mazhar and Syed Zainuddin Moulvi carefully argue in Chapter 7, the law departs from Hanafi tradition in key details, following one author's misattribution of Ibn Taymiyya's position to the school, an error already exposed by a nineteenth-century Hanafi scholar. Moreover, Mazhar's and Moulvi's extraordinary study boldly challenges the hypocrisy of religious and public figures who support the existing blasphemy law, well aware of the flaws they point out but unwilling to admit it in public discussion.

In Chapter 8 Syafiq Hasyim examines the 'politics of fatwa' in Indonesia, focusing on a quasi-governmental fatwa body that has taken a lead role in pronouncing various religious groups 'deviant'. Noting the accompanying rise in both blasphemy prosecutions and mob violence against e.g. Ahmadis and Shiʿa, he suggests that this activism against religious deviance is part of a broader agenda to enhance the politico-legal role of religion, 'shariatizing' the secular state. His conclusion that these campaigns are damaging to inter-Muslim unity as well as to the cohesion of a pluralist society, have relevance beyond the specific case of Indonesia as a *pancasila* state.

The third part looks to the future, seeking to provide new perspectives and new directions to the debate.

Kecia Ali's Chapter 9 analyses blasphemy and apostasy laws in broader terms of policing social boundaries and authority structures, as Saeed does, but breaks new ground by shifting the perspective from the dominant voices of tradition to marginalized voices of protest. She sheds new light on the issue by exploring the conjunction of doctrinal and sexual transgression, orthodoxy and patriarchy, through the lens of cases rarely discussed in the present context: the potentially transgressive grief of the bereaved mother; the link between apostasy and divorce; and the modern feminist critic as a threat to the status quo.

Mahmoud Sadri's Chapter 10 is concerned with strategizing change. Based on large-scale surveys, Sadri points out that the harsh and oft-abused penalties for blasphemy and apostasy contradict Muslim publics' express support for democratic rights. Drawing on Gunnar Myrdal's classic *American Dilemma*, Sadri argues that this clash of norms within Muslim polities presents a strategic opportunity for reformers, and shows how it operated in two noted trials of dissident intellectuals in Iran.

Where other chapters in this book primarily approach the issue descriptively through the lens of humanities and social sciences, Mohsen Kadivar's final chapter squarely addresses blasphemy and apostasy from the standpoint of an Islamic legal scholar. Summarizing an argument developed over years of debate with religious leaders in Iran, Kadivar argues passionately for the abolition of the death penalty, and indeed against any criminal liability for blasphemy and apostasy. Though Kadivar favours a thorough reconstruction of Islamic jurisprudence, he adduces many arguments familiar to traditional scholars, particularly in the Shiʿi tradition.

In sum, this book demonstrates how Muslim scholars from different schools and disciplines engage with the issue by showing that religious norms invoked in blasphemy and apostasy laws have been shaped and selected in history by socio-political factors. Repressive norms represent a dominant discourse, wielded by the powerful in different ages, that has marginalized other discourses, obscured the complexity and diversity of interpretations in Muslim history, and limited the imagining of other ways Muslims could deal with religious disagreement, conversion and change.

That dominance is now being questioned, both in response to the repression and exclusion experienced by Muslims themselves in local settings, and in a global conversation on issues of common concern to both Muslims and non-Muslims, including the relationship between cultural identity, international norms and political power. The obstacles to change are not theoretically well-founded, but they are all the more strongly rooted in authoritarian leadership posing as cultural defence against Islamophobic attacks on Muslim sensitivities.

Today, there are diverse methodological approaches to imagining reform from within Islam, and the contributions to this book do not converge on a single road to reform. They do show that historical-critical methods are being brought to bear on constructions of 'Islamic' law that are no longer felt to serve the cause of justice. As in earlier times, political developments will decide whether this new thinking can take root and guide the development of more humane and open societies.

Notes

1 Supreme Court of Pakistan, *Asia Bibi vs. the State*, criminal appeal no. 39-L of 2015, judgment from hearing 8 October 2018.

2 Ziba Mir-Hosseini, Kari Vogt, Lena Larsen and Christian Moe (eds), *Gender and Equality in Muslim Family Law: Justice and Ethics in the Islamic Legal Tradition* (London: I.B.Tauris, 2013).

3 Maurits Berger, 'Apostasy and Public Policy in Contemporary Egypt: An Evaluation of Recent Cases from Egypt's Highest Courts', *Human Rights Quarterly* 25/3 (2003): pp. 720–40.

4 To name but a few, from a variety of both scholarly, polemical and apologetic viewpoints: Shemeem Burney Abbas, *Pakistan's Blasphemy Laws: From Islamic Empires to the Taliban* (Austin, TX: University of Texas Press, 2013); Camilla Adang, Hasan Ansari, Maribel Fierro, and Sabine Schmidtke (eds), *Accusations of Unbelief in Islam: A Diachronic Perspective on Takfīr*, Islamic History and Civilization: Studies and Texts 123 (Leiden/Boston: Brill, 2016); Taha Jabir al-Alwani, *Apostasy in Islam: A Historical and Scriptural Analysis* (London: International Institute of Islamic Thought, 2011); Virginie Andre and John L. Esposito (eds), 'Apostasy and Blasphemy: A Clash of Freedoms – Speech and Religion', special issue of *Islam and Christian-Muslim Relations* 27/1 (1 January 2016); Talal Asad, Wendy Brown, Judith Butler, and Saba Mahmood, *Is Critique Secular? Blasphemy, Injury, and Free Speech,* Townsend Papers in the Humanities 2 (Berkeley, CA: Townsend Center for the Humanities and University of California Press, 2009); Mohamed Badar, Masaki Nagata and Tiphanie

Tueni, 'The Radical Application of the Islamist Concept of *Takfir*', *Arab Law Quarterly* 31/2 (14 June 2017), pp. 134–62; Simon Cottee, *The Apostates: When Muslims Leave Islam* (Oxford: Oxford University Press, 2015); Hossein Esmaeili, Irmgard Marboe, and Javaid Rehman, *The Rule of Law, Freedom of Expression, and Islamic Law* (Oxford; Portland, Oregon: Hart Publishing, 2017); Erich Kolig, *Freedom of Speech and Islam* (Oxon: Routledge, 2016); Göran Larsson, 'Disputed, Sensitive and Indispensable Topics: The Study of Islam and Apostasy', *Method and Theory in the Study of Religion* 30/3 (13 March 2018), pp. 201–26; Elham Manea, 'In the Name of Culture and Religion: The Political Function of Blasphemy in Islamic States', *Islam and Christian–Muslim Relations* 27/1 (2 January 2016), pp. 117–27; Paul A. Marshall and Nina Shea (eds), *Silenced: How Apostasy and Blasphemy Codes Are Choking Freedom Worldwide* (New York: Oxford University Press, 2011); Masaki Nagata, 'Assessing Apostasy, Blasphemy and Excommunication (Takfir) in Islam and Their Modern Application by States and Non-State Actors' (Thesis, Brunel University London, 2016); Patrick Sookhdeo, *Freedom to Believe: Challenging Islam's Apostasy Law* (McLean, VA: Isaac Publishing, 2014); Mark S. Wagner, 'The Problem of Non-Muslims Who Insult the Prophet Muḥammad', *Journal of the American Oriental Society* 135/3 (2015), pp. 529–40.

5 Angelina A. Theodorou, 'Which countries still outlaw apostasy and blasphemy?', 29 July 2016, http://www.pewresearch.org/fact-tank/2016/07/29/which-countries-still-outlaw-apostasy-and-blasphemy/, accessed 3 May 2017.

6 Death penalties for blasphemy are on the books in Brunei, Iran, and Pakistan. Sudan provides for whipping. Several countries rely on uncodified law, which provides for capital punishment; in Afghanistan, death sentences have been given but apparently not carried out; in Saudi Arabia, offenders may be sentenced to hundreds or thousands of lashes meted out over time. Global Legal Research Center, *Blasphemy and Related Laws in Selected Jurisdictions* (Law Library of Congress, January 2017).

7 Theodorou, 'Which countries'.

8 Global Legal Research Center, *Laws Criminalizing Apostasy in Selected Jurisdictions* (Law Library of Congress, May 2014).

9 For instance, William Muir (d. 1905), the Secretary for Frontier Province in India, published *The Life of Mahomet* (London: Smith, Elder & co., 1861), a four-volume work critical of Muhammad's marriages and wars, at the behest of the missionary C.G. Pfander; the leading Muslim modernist of the time, Sayyid Ahmad Khan (1817–98), is said to have sold his property to fund the publication of his rejoinder, *A Series of Essays on the Life of Muhammad and Subjects Subsidiary Thereto* (London: Trubner, 1870). See Christian W. Troll, *Sayyid Ahmad Khan: A Reinterpretation of Muslim Theology* (New Delhi: Vikas, 1978), p. 113.

10 Talal Asad, 'Free Speech, Blasphemy, and Secular Criticism', in *Is Critique Secular? Blasphemy, Injury, and Free Speech*, Townsend Papers in the Humanities 2 (Berkeley: Townsend Center for the Humanities and University of California Press, 2009), p. 39, available from http://escholarship.org/uc/item/84q9c6ft.

11 Mir-Hosseini et al., *Gender and Equality in Muslim Family Law.*

12 The Ibadi school is attributed to Imam Abdullah b. Ibad (d. 708); the Zaydi, to Imam Zayd b. Ali (d. 740); and the Isma'ili, to Imam Isma'il b. Ja'far al-Sadiq (d. 755).

13 Alan Cabantous, *Blasphemy: Impious Speech in the West from the Seventeenth to the Nineteenth Century*, European Perspectives (New York: Columbia University Press, 2002); Leonard W. Levy, *Blasphemy: Verbal Offense against the Sacred, from Moses to Salman Rushdie* (Chapel Hill, NC; London: University of North Carolina Press, 1995);

David Nash, *Blasphemy in the Christian World: A History* (Oxford; New York: Oxford University Press, 2007).

14 Adang et al., *Accusations of Unbelief in Islam.*

15 International Covenant on Civil and Political Rights (CCPR), Art. 18.

16 The freedom of opinion and expression is set out in CCPR, Art. 19.

17 Among Council of Europe member states, Denmark, Greece, Ireland, Italy, Malta, Poland, Russia and Turkey still had blasphemy laws or policies in 2014. Theodorou, 'Which countries'. These included laws that had been recently enacted, such as Article 36 of the Irish Defamation Act of 2009, repealed after a referendum in 2018. Many such statutes are thought to be 'sleeping', but sometimes they wake up, cf. 'Danish man who burned Quran is charged with blasphemy', *New York Times*, 24 February 2017, p. A6, https://www.nytimes.com/2017/02/23/world/europe/denmark-quran-burning.html, accessed 3 May 2017; however, Denmark repealed its blasphemy law in 2017, before this case could come to court.

18 *İ.A. v. Turkey* (app. no. 42571/98), judgment, 13 September 2005; *E.S. v. Austria* (app. no. 38450/12), judgment, 25 October 2018.

19 UN Human Rights Committee General Comment no. 34 on CCPR Art. 19, 12 September 2011, CCPR/C/GC/34, para. 48. The relevant prohibition on hate speech is in CCPR, Art. 20.

20 Human Rights Council resolution 16/18 on Combating intolerance, negative stereotyping and stigmatization of, and discrimination, incitement to violence, and violence against persons based on religion or belief, 21 March 2011, UN doc. A/HRC/16/L.38.

21 On such parallels and synergies, see also the thematic report on the relationship between the two rights by the then UN Special Rapporteur on freedom of religion or belief, Heiner Bielefeldt, 23 December 2015, UN doc. A/HCR/31/18.

22 Resolution 16/18, para. 4.

23 Rabat Plan of Action on the prohibition of advocacy of national, racial or religious hatred that constitutes inducement to discrimination, hostility or violence, adopted by experts at the meeting in Rabat, Morocco, on 5 October 2012, A/HRC/22/17/Add.4, para. 10.

24 Rabat Plan of Action, para. 25.

25 UN Human Rights Council, 'The question of the death penalty', 22 September 2017, UN doc. A/HRC/36/L.6.

26 UN OHCHR, *The Beirut Declaration and its 18 Commitments on Faith for Rights: Report and Outlook*, report of an expert workshop in Beirut, 28–29 March 2017, available from the dedicated web page http://www.ohchr.org/EN/NewsEvents/Pages/FaithforRights.aspx (accessed 15 September 2017).

Part One

The Historical Construction

1

Blasphemy Laws in Islam
Towards a Rethinking?

Abdullah Saeed

This chapter explores the development of the concept of blasphemy in Islam, reflecting on the circumstances, including political and social contexts, surrounding its emergence. The primary focus, however, is to demonstrate that the early Islamic concept of blasphemy may not be viable today, while acknowledging the challenges that Muslim scholars face in reviewing and rethinking it. Therefore, this chapter posits that perhaps the most effective way to argue against blasphemy laws is to show that the concept of blasphemy developed in a particular social and political context and evolved as those circumstances changed. Related to this is the argument that there is no strong textual basis for the death penalty for blasphemy in either the Qur'an or the traditions of the Prophet, and, thus, contemporary Muslims should be free to rethink the concept of blasphemy in light of their own circumstances.

Blasphemy in religious traditions

The signs and symbols of religious traditions serve as identity markers that signal the adherence of their followers to the group. Within each tradition, religious leaders, scholars and thinkers strive to distinguish the manifestation of their faith – including its rituals, beliefs, practices and customs, such as dietary and sumptuary rules – from those of others. In the pre-modern period, these distinctions were important because, in any given society, religion was often at the centre of all aspects of life. Even if there were several religious communities in a society, each tradition clearly demarcated itself from others. Individuals usually had to be part of a religious community, through which they were represented in larger society. Moreover, religious adherence was an important determinant of one's rights and obligations. In most societies, the dominant religion exercized enormous power, and minority confessions had far less.

In the pre-modern period, a society's dominant religion was often closely connected to the apparatus of the state and political power. Thus, religion was used to differentiate the dominant political group from other groups with alternate religious views. The most powerful group often dictated its relationships with other groups, based on the latter's social, political and legal subordination.

Thus, the religious beliefs, symbols and practices of the dominant group often enjoyed absolute supremacy, which minority faiths were forced to recognize in order to survive. This unequal relationship determined what religious symbols were acceptable and how they could be publicly used. Blasphemy laws tended to protect the dominant religious group's symbols and its power. If the sacred symbols of the dominant group were disrespected or denigrated, severe punishment was meted out to the offending party.[1]

This logic of dominance and subordination applied to intra-religious relations as well. Within a religious tradition, there often existed a dominant group with its own distinct institutions, leadership, elites and practices; this may be referred to as the 'mainstream' in a particular place and time. This 'mainstream' orthodoxy was assumed to provide necessary social cohesion. However, the existence of less powerful groups within the tradition challenged – ideologically, and sometimes in reality – the hegemonic concepts and practices of the prevailing group. When such threats were perceived, the dominant group often sought to repress them, dealing with them quickly and harshly. Such dynamics can be identified in many religious traditions, and Islam is no exception. In fact, all the Abrahamic religions (Christianity, Islam and Judaism) have some concept of blasphemy.[2]

However, before a religious tradition attains dominance, it does not necessarily take robust, defensive measures against those mocking, ridiculing or challenging its religious symbols. One obvious reason for this is that the followers of the religious tradition may not be powerful enough to challenge such attacks. They may be concerned with survival and lack the means to counter or repress the disparagement of their beliefs and symbols. Thus, they suffer, struggle and persevere, hoping slowly to gain greater social acceptance. This probably was the case in the first 200 to 300 years of Christianity and the first twelve years of Islam. Blasphemy laws, thus, develop within religious traditions in close connection to their rising political power. Before that power reaches a point where the elite can respond to and suppress any disparagement, blasphemy laws are neither a priority, nor even a possibility, for the group.

When a religious tradition attains political power, it begins to develop ways and means to counter attacks on its symbols. Part of this process involves erecting walls against other religious traditions and then specifying what practices and symbols of other traditions will be tolerated. Penalties, often severe, are developed to defend the dominant religion and its symbols. The charge of blasphemy then becomes a powerful tool in the hands of religious leaders and the political system. It can be used to target and counter any real or perceived threat to the status quo on which the dominant religion's identity, existence and power depend. Therefore, blasphemy should be considered as both a theological and a political issue.

Blasphemy in Islamic tradition: An overview

Blasphemy is derived from two Greek words: *blapto*, meaning 'to injure', and *pheme*, meaning 'to speak'. Thus, blasphemy is considered injurious speech or 'speaking evil'.[3] In Arabic, the term *sabb* is derived from the Arabic root *s-b-b*.[4] Islamic tradition speaks of *sabb allāh* and *sabb al-rasūl*, meaning reviling God or reviling the Messenger.[5] In more specific terms, it refers to '[a]ll utterances expressive of contempt for Allah [God] Himself, for His Names, attributes, laws, commands, or prohibitions [and] all scoffing at Muhammad or any other prophets or apostles of Allah [God]'.[6] Classical Muslim jurists agreed that blasphemy was prohibited by the Shariʿa.[7] Blasphemy was closely connected to the offence of apostasy, since blasphemy was seen as apostasy if committed by a Muslim.[8] This means that a Muslim blasphemer is, by definition, an apostate.

Blasphemy was initially understood in the Islamic tradition as attacks on its core ideas and symbols, centring on God and the Prophet.[9] The Qurʾan provided many details about the nature and quality of such criticism, including ridicule of the Prophet and his message by his enemies in Mecca and Medina. On multiple occasions, the Qurʾan responded to such critiques and ridicule by pointing out the weaknesses in the arguments of opponents and presenting reasoned justifications for the Prophet's teachings.

In its Meccan phase, the Qurʾan's approach to its opponents was to encourage tolerance and perseverance among the Prophet's followers.[10] Muslims were urged to counter evil with good and not to be particularly worried about such ridicule. This approach worked well. The Prophet and his followers undeniably endured high levels of persecution, ridicule and suffering; however, they remained steadfast in their beliefs. This attitude strengthened the moral integrity of the Prophet's followers, which, in turn, attracted more adherents to the new religion.

As with other religious groups, certain penalties for blasphemy developed with the rise of Muslim political power in Medina (from 622). In these changed political circumstances, the Prophet and his followers moved from tolerating ridicule or persecution to actively protecting themselves from it. They had been forced out of Mecca and had settled in Medina, where they sought to create a religious and political community based on the Prophet's teachings. The challenges posed by hostile groups did not cease in the new city, but the Prophet now had access to effective political power, particularly after the first two years. The Muslim community was prepared to defend its new faith and the Prophet. At first, it practiced toleration of ridicule in Medina, but, once the community acquired enough political power and confidence, it was able to confront ridicule and attacks. With the acquisition of power, the Prophet moved to counter the most malicious assaults; yet less threatening opponents were endured.

Blasphemy in the Qurʾan and Sunna

The term *sabb* (in the sense of abuse) occurs twice in the Qurʾan, in 6:108: 'Abuse not those to whom they pray, apart from God, or they will abuse God in revenge without knowledge'.[11] What is noticeable in the Qurʾanic treatment of the issue is that, while there are many references to this kind of abuse in a variety of contexts, using a wide range of terms associated with ridicule and abuse, there is no temporal punishment specified for such blasphemy.[12]

In contrast, the hadith literature does contain references to blasphemy.[13] Some hadith reports make clear references to the killing of certain prominent people, most likely because of their political activities against the Muslim community. One example is the killing of Kaʿb b. al-Ashraf for his extensive anti-Muslim activities and his slander of the Prophet and his followers in Medina.[14]

This famous case is often cited in support of the death penalty for blasphemers. He was most likely targeted, however, not just because he blasphemed, but also because he was perceived as waging war against the emerging Muslim community.[15] Kaʿb was a poet who was known for regularly lampooning the Prophet, his teachings and his symbols. More importantly, he is said to have been involved in a plot to kill the Prophet.[16] Historical sources shed light on two reasons for Kaʿb's killing. The first describes his part in severing the alliance between the Jewish tribe of Banu al-Nadir and the Prophet Muhammad. Subsequently, he was involved in making a treaty with Abu Sufyan (who was then leading the Meccan opposition to the Prophet Muhammad) and a number of Jews, which set forth that 'Quraysh and the Jews should cooperate against Muhammad'.[17] Following these events and the assassination of Kaʿb b. al-Ashraf, the Banu al-Nadir was expelled from Medina.[18] The second reason, reported by ʿIkrima (d. 723), states that the Banu al-Nadir plotted to kill Prophet Muhammad; they spoke to Kaʿb b. al-Ashraf about the matter, and he concurred.[19] This was probably the justification for the Prophet's alleged order of his death. The continued existence of Kaʿb b. al-Ashraf jeopardized the survival of the new religious-political community.

Textual evidence for the 'punishment of blasphemy thus appears to be based on certain incidents during the lifetime of the Prophet',[20] where some non-Muslims, like Kaʿb b. al-Ashraf, who reviled the Prophet, Allah or Islam, were killed. Those killed were among the staunchest opponents of Islam. By abusing and insulting the Prophet, Allah or Islam, 'the transgressors were, in a sense, waging war on Islam'.[21]

However, other examples seem to suggest that verbal abuse perhaps should be tolerated and that no penalties should be imposed for it. An example of this is a report that Abu Bakr, the first caliph, was insulted and abused by an unidentified person in the presence of the Prophet Muhammad:

> Abu Bakr is puzzled by the Prophet's behaviour, since Muhammad refrains from defending his Companion against the stranger's abuse and, at one point, appears to be amazed and smiles without any discernible reason. When Abu Bakr starts to return the abuse to the anonymous person, Muhammad becomes angry and, finally, rises to his feet. After the dispute between Abu Bakr and his adversary has come to an end, Abu Bakr asks Muhammad why he did not support him, but, instead, became angry when he, Abu Bakr, attempted to defend himself. Muhammad replies that an angel had been with Abu Bakr replying in the latter's place. But when Abu Bakr returned some of the abominable words to his adversary the devil entered the scene and he, Muhammad, could not remain in a place where the devil was present.[22]

Much like the Qur'anic treatment of blasphemy, this report does not specify any punishment for the abuse. Importantly, there is no indication in this report that the

Prophet declared the incident blasphemy. There is also the famous case of ʿAbd Allah b. Ubay b. Salul, considered to be the leader of the religious hypocrites (*munāfiqūn*) in Medina, who, though Muslim, was strongly opposed to the Prophet Muhammad. The Qurʾan mentions a range of his supposed statements of abuse and ridicule against the Prophet, but does not specify any worldly punishment.

The development of blasphemy laws in Islam

Legal scope and punishment

The concept of blasphemy as an offence was developed by Muslim jurists in the post-prophetic period.[23] Blasphemy against the Prophet was considered a greater legal offence than blasphemy against God. This stemmed from the idea that blasphemy was the violation of a 'right of man (*ḥaqq al-ʿabd*)', for which repentance (by itself) was insufficient to absolve the offender.[24] Since the Prophet had passed away and was not able to personally protect himself against denigration, jurists reasoned, it became the community's responsibility to guard his honour by imposing the punishment of death.[25]

Subsequently, the offence was extended by Sunni jurists to cover foul language against the Companions of the Prophet and to silence dissenting voices, such as those of the Kharijis and Shiʿa.[26] The 'view that vilifying the companions of the Prophet [...] was tantamount to blasphemy' arose in the context of the civil wars of the first and second centuries of Islam (seventh and eighth centuries CE), and, according to Takim, the extension of the offence was, in all likelihood, 'part of the Sunni polemic against the Shiʿa'; however, 'not all scholars agreed that vilification of the companions' should result in punishment.[27]

The four leading Sunni schools of Islamic legal thought all recognize the offence of blasphemy; however, there are differences between them on the question of whether perpetrators of the offence should be given the opportunity to repent. For Hanafis, Hanbalis and Malikis, even if a blasphemer repents, he should be executed (though it has been disputed whether this was the original Hanafi position)[28]; Shafiʿis, in contrast, affirm that the repentance of a blasphemer is acceptable.[29]

Interestingly, in the formative texts of the various schools of law, 'blasphemy against the Prophet or the *Ṣaḥāba* is not mentioned among the punishable acts that constitute *ridda* [apostasy] or *kufr* [unbelief]'.[30] Wiederhold finds no mention of the offences of *sabb al-rasūl* or *sabb al-ṣaḥāba* as apostasy (*ridda*) in Malik's *Muwaṭṭaʾ*, Sahnun's *Mudawwana*, al-Shafiʿi's *al-Umm*, or al-Shaybani's *Kitāb al-Aṣl*.[31] However, the notion that 'blasphemy against the Prophet was regarded as an intolerable act by the second/eighth century' is corroborated by the *Muwaṭṭaʾ* of ʿAbd Allah b. Wahb (d. 812).[32] According to Wiederhold, the chapter on *al-muḥāraba* 'contains a paragraph on the blasphemer in which one who insults (*sabb*) the Prophet Muhammad is threatened with the death penalty'.[33] In the same passage, the caliph ʿUmar b. ʿAbd al-ʿAziz (r. 717–20) 'is reported as having stated that the vilification of Prophet Muhammad, but not of any other person, is to be punished'.[34]

According to Wiederhold, some of the most important Shafiʿi works suggest that awareness of *sabb* as an offence that must be punished by the law emerged around the end of the third and the beginning of the fourth centuries of Islam. For instance, he states that Ibn al-Mundhir (d. 930) briefly discusses insults against the Prophet Muhammad in the chapter of his book on *ijmāʿ* that deals with the apostate and that from his point view, anyone 'who insults the Prophet should be put to death'.[35] In Muslim Spain, blasphemy against the Prophet was considered apostasy (*ridda*) in the third century of Islam (ninth century CE).[36]

Historical development

The need to develop detailed blasphemy laws and to protect the sacred began with the consolidation of political power, with the Umayyads and early ʿAbbasids at the helm, and a strong, growing sense of the new religion's superiority over other religions. During this period, the emergence of a range of restrictions on non-Muslims in Muslim communities was reflected in the so-called 'Pact of ʿUmar'. By this time, the differences between those who followed Islam and those who did not became much sharper, as a new Muslim identity was in the making. The Muslim community now had the confidence that came partly from a century or so of political power and partly from theological debates between Muslims and people of other faiths, particularly those under Muslim rule (*dhimmīs*). This confidence was reflected in heightened concern for the 'honour' of the Muslim community and state.

Thus, a clear boundary line was drawn between Muslims and non-Muslims who were dhimmis. Under the terms of the agreements from the time of the Muslim conquest of the then Byzantine and Sassanid empires, non-Muslims accepted their subjugated status in a new Muslim polity. This approach immediately created a hierarchical society in which Muslims were the dominant faction. In the early stages of this conquest, Muslims did not maintain firm religious boundary lines in the political and social spheres. However, towards the beginning of Islam's second century, some restrictions on non-Muslims began to emerge regarding religious manifestations and the abuse or denigration of Islamic symbols. Gradually, the idea took hold that, if non-Muslim dhimmis committed blasphemy, their right to protection could be rescinded.

The basis of this view from a juristic perspective appears to be that blasphemy constituted a violation of the non-Muslims' pact with the Muslim state. If non-Muslims were found guilty of the offence, they lost the protection of the pact and, therefore, deserved capital punishment. For the jurists, the reason behind this came from the Qurʾan (9:29). Non-Muslims may 'be killed if they refuse to remain subjugated and subservient under Muslim rule'; therefore, if a dhimmi is sacrilegious or disrespectful towards the Prophet Muhammad, that means he or she 'has rebelled against Muslim sovereignty and does not accept his subjugation'.[37] In the ninth century, for example, both ʿAbd al-Rahman II (r. 822–52) and Muhammad I (r. 852–86), who succeeded him in Muslim Spain, treated the blasphemy of the Christians who courted martyrdom in Córdoba as 'an act of political defiance against the rule of law' and 'a violation of the *ʿahd al-dhimmah* [pact of protection]'.[38] According to Fierro, this line of juristic argument most likely began with the statement of ʿAbd Allah b. ʿAbbas: '...[I]f anyone from amongst non-Muslims protected under pact becomes hostile by openly blaspheming against God or the Prophet (SWS) or any of God's messengers, he is guilty of violating the pact; you shall kill him too'.[39] What constituted the offence of blasphemy remained, however, a point of contention among Muslim scholars.

The belief that Islam was a superior religious tradition (to other monotheistic traditions, for example) also accounts for the evolution of blasphemy laws. This conviction appears to have strengthened alongside the growth of Islam's religious identity and political power. It perhaps emerged as a political issue towards the end of the first century of Islam but continued to develop over time, and was most likely linked to the idea that one should not dishonour the Muslim community through attacks on its sacred symbols, practices and ideas. The consolidation of Muslim power and identity in its first 200 years also aided the development of stronger statements about religion and authenticity, which defined what were 'orthodox' and what were heretical beliefs. The Muslims saw themselves as the exclusive holders of divine truth. Externally, claims that other religious traditions had corrupted their scriptures and distorted the fundamental beliefs taught by the prophets were used as arguments to support the idea that these other religions were misguided or inferior. Internally, the 'orthodox' positions were used to label a range of Muslim groups as 'heretical'. This combination appears to have led to consolidation of the punishments related to blasphemy, which were applied to both Muslim and non-Muslim critics of Islam and its symbols. Parallel to these developments, the number of protected, sacred symbols also significantly increased. Although blasphemy initially concerned God and the Prophet, it became attached to new symbols, some of which became more important than others.

From the eleventh through the thirteenth centuries, new challenges arose in Muslim communities, which extended the ideas and punishments related to blasphemy. In part, this development was a response to threats against the very foundation of Muslim society from a wide range of groups, both Muslim and non Muslim. This was the period of the Crusades, the collapse of the ʿAbbasid Caliphate, the Mongol invasion of the Muslim East and the Christian counterattacks on Muslims in Spain. Combined, these factors aided the development of much stricter ideas and broader notions of blasphemy. Several harsh measures were implemented to protect what was left of Muslim power, superiority, identity and honour.

In the blasphemy debates of this period, the Prophet again became a central symbol requiring 'protection'. After the Prophet's death, a trend arose within the Muslim tradition to elevate him from the status of a human being who became a prophet to something much more. The Prophet came to be considered more than human, the 'Perfect Man', the reason for the existence of the universe and the centre of creation; he was not conceived of as God-like, but was considered as perfect as one can be in relation to God.[40] In this context, al-Nawawi (d. 1276) 'discusses the question of Muhammad's singularity among the prophets in one of his fatwas. According to him, a Muslim may not treat the pre-Islamic prophets and Muhammad as equals'.[41] This tradition grew and expanded towards the fourteenth century CE.

This view of the Prophet Muhammad, which appears to have influenced also the development of blasphemy laws, contrasts with a widespread, modern Muslim view that emphasizes the humanness of the Prophet, arguing that the Qurʾan presents the

Prophet Muhammad as a human being who received a message from God. Emphasis is placed on the role of the Prophet Muhammad as a messenger, rather than on his personality: 'Muhammad is not the father of any of your men, but the Messenger of God and the Seal of the Prophets' (33:40). The Qur'an portrays the Prophet as chosen and unique, speaking of him as 'a Mercy for the worlds' (21:107), and elevates his authority, declaring, 'Whoever obeys the Messenger obeys God' (4:80). However, the Qur'an also emphasizes that he was human: 'Say: I do not say: "With me are the treasures of God and I do not know the Invisible, and I do not say that I am an angel, I only follow that which is revealed to me"' (6:50). It portrays the Prophet as a faithful servant, who patiently awaits God's help, who is susceptible to lapses (80:10).

Today, the practices surrounding blasphemy laws vary across the Muslim world, but formerly non-controversial issues or subjects have also come under the scope of blasphemy. For example, for centuries, Arabic-speaking Christians have used 'Allah' to refer to God. However, in Malaysia, the Christian use of this appellation has become deeply problematic and is seen by some Muslims as blasphemous. Early conceptions of blasphemy did not extend to, for example, the *ʿulamāʾ* or religious authorities; however, in the modern period, some Muslim countries, such as Malaysia, have made the criticism of religious authorities blasphemous.[42] Thus, some Muslim-majority countries have defined blasphemy very differently from the classical Islamic legal tradition. Today, in a number of countries, blasphemy laws have been codified and are applied with the power of the modern state, and they are being contested under the human rights provisions of an international legal order that includes modern Muslim states. The issue has been globalized through migration, modern media and international politics. As an example, we will consider the blasphemy law in Indonesia.

Blasphemy laws today: the Indonesian example

In Indonesia, blasphemy is an offence under Law No. 1/PNPS/1965 and provisions are incorporated into Article 156a of the penal code. The penalties include up to five years in prison for anyone who deliberately gives expression, in public, to feelings or commits acts:

> (1) which principally have the character of being at enmity with, abusing or staining a religion, adhered to in Indonesia; or (2) with the intention to prevent a person to adhere to any religion based on the belief of the almighty God.[43]

Government-funded bodies for each of the six officially recognized religions in Indonesia determine the accepted beliefs of each religion. The law 'establishes civil and criminal penalties for violators who deviate from the government-sanctioned interpretations of each religion'.[44] In 2010, Indonesia's Constitutional Court ruled that this law did not contradict Indonesia's constitution or the provisions for freedom of religion enshrined in the national principles of *Pancasila*.

The Indonesian blasphemy law has been applied many times. Amnesty International reports 106 such convictions between 2005 and 2014.[45] In 2008, the Indonesian Minister of Religious Affairs, the Attorney General and the Minister of Interior issued a Joint Decree on the Ahmadiyya, which ordered Ahmadiyya adherents 'to discontinue the promulgation of interpretations and activities that are deviant from the principal teachings of Islam'.[46] In 2009, the leader of the Sion City of Allah Christian sect and several of his followers were arrested for straying from 'correct Christian teachings'. Since the sect is founded only on the Book of Jeremiah, the government deemed it to be 'an unacceptable branch of Christianity'.[47] In 2012, Alexander Aan, an atheist, stood trial in West Sumatra for blasphemy against the Prophet Muhammad. In the same year, Tajul Muluk, the leader of a Shiʿi boarding school, was tried for asserting that the currently disseminated version of the Qurʾan is not the original one.[48] In 2017, Basuki Purnama ('Ahok'), a Christian and former governor of Jakarta, was sentenced to prison for blasphemy after referring to a Qurʾanic verse in the election campaign.

Naturally, there has been much criticism of Indonesia's blasphemy law. Asma Uddin has argued that the law 'puts the coercive power of the state into the hands of certain religious groups and government officials, who then decide what a particular group may believe and what it should be allowed to propagate'; that if religion is 'so tightly regulated and defined by the state, it is necessarily politicized' and used by state officials to protect and legitimate their own power; and that religious contents 'become intertwined with national security and public order, rather than remaining' the free convictions of individuals within a community.[49]

The rethinking of blasphemy laws

In contemporary Muslim states, blasphemy laws have become a topic of debate. Critics call attention to the constraints that these laws place on the rights of freedom of expression, thought and religion, and to their susceptibility to misuse by powerful individuals and groups. For Mashood Baderin, blasphemy laws sit in tension with the broader principle of freedom of speech and expression, which he regards as an acknowledged right in early Islamic law, prophetic practice and other traditions.[50] For Baderin, freedom of expression is a natural right under Islamic law, confirmed by the Qurʾan (55:1–4).[51]

Another critic, Mohammad Hashim Kamali, believes that freedom of expression is an 'extension and logical consequence' of freedom of religion, which the Shariʿa validates and upholds, despite allowing some limitations.[52] Individuals were permitted a broad range of public expressions, including the utterance of opinions; the support of a cause; the defence of decency, justice or the truth; and the denunciation of conduct or speech contrary to this right.[53] Kamali believes that intellectual debate and religious discussions were not historically prohibited in Islam[54] and that individuals had the right to point out the shortcomings of political leaders, government officials and public servants.[55]

Currently, blasphemy laws have become a serious problem for the advancement of Islamic thought and even research, including a rational assessment of early Islamic history and Islam's central figures. These laws have become a powerful tool of authoritarian regimes and their religious establishments against political opponents, intellectuals and independent scholars. They can also be used to manipulate the emotions of Muslims in support of a particular cause, as has been seen in the case of the Danish cartoon controversy of 2005.

Given the many problems and abuses associated with blasphemy laws, Muslim thinkers and communities are expected to directly address this issue and rethink the laws. The following section will suggest some ideas. There are four crucial issues in rethinking blasphemy laws:

(a) blasphemy laws have a weak textual basis;
(b) significant differences exist among jurists on many details relating to blasphemy laws;
(c) these laws developed in, and in response to, particular socio-political contexts; and
(d) one context was the extreme veneration of the Prophet.

Weak textual basis

First, blasphemy laws have a weak textual basis. No Qur'anic text or authentic hadith clearly stipulates the death penalty for blasphemy. Some scholars who have strongly influenced Muslim discussions of blasphemy, such as Ibn Taymiyya (d. 1328) and Qadi ʿIyad (d. 1149), employ texts from these sources as evidence to substantiate their argument for harsh measures to punish this crime, although these texts are not directly concerned with a temporal penalty for blasphemy (see also Chapters 2 and 4).

Juristic works from the first two centuries of Islam (seventh and eighth centuries CE) generally differ markedly from those of the late third century of Islam onward. In the early period, there were scant discussions of punishment for blasphemy. The focus in this period was on apostasy. However, from the third century of Islam, the death penalty appears to have been specified for blasphemy, and it was discussed as a subset of apostasy.

References to the crime of, and punishment for, blasphemy apparently are non-existent in the earliest *fiqh* sources. As discussed earlier, based on Wiederhold's work, in Malik's *Muwaṭṭaʾ* or Shafiʿi's *al-Umm*, occasional reference is made to the idea that insulting the Prophet is intolerable, but no punishment is discussed. Importantly, given the political nature of the crime, al-Mawardi might have included this topic in his major work on Muslim governance, but does not. The legal text *Bidāyat al-Mujtahid* of Ibn Rushd also does not specify blasphemy as a separate crime. This absence is curious, suggesting that some jurists had difficulty in seeing blasphemy as criminal in nature.[56]

Differences between schools of law regarding the nature of the crime

Second, there are some differences between the schools of law regarding blasphemy. In their established forms, they agree that, if a Muslim insults or reviles God or the Prophet, he or she becomes an apostate and must suffer the punishment of death. Disagreement concerns specific details, such as whether such punishment extends to blasphemy against the companions or wives of the Prophet, whether the punishment is prescribed (*ḥadd*) or discretionary (*ta ʿzīr*); whether the crime is a form of apostasy; whether a female blasphemer should be put to death; whether a person should be given an opportunity to repent; and whether the punishment for a non-Muslim should differ from that of a Muslim.

Socio-political context

Third, as previously discussed, blasphemy laws often develop in conjunction with the development of a religious tradition in general. In Islamic tradition, particularly during and just after the time of the Prophet, relatively few ideas and symbols were considered beyond critique or questioning. Early on, the political and religious contexts required a focus on fundamental beliefs and convincing the Meccan and Medinan populations of the truth of the Prophet's message. In the context of the new faith's implantation, criticism had to be tolerated. The Qur'an makes reference to how both God and the Prophet were ridiculed and were openly rejected. God was characterized as weak, lacking in omnipotence and partisan. The Prophet was labelled a madman, a magician and a liar, who introduced foreign teachings and attributed them to God. On a number of occasions when the Prophet went about in Mecca and its surrounding regions, he was chased, beset with profanities, physically abused and stoned by children. Although the denigration of God and the Prophet continued also in Medina, no specific worldly punishments against offenders appear either in the Qur'an or the Sunna. While certain people in Medina, including some Muslims and certain non-Muslim leaders, were openly critical of the Prophet and his role, they do not seem to have attracted his ire, as is reflected in the Qur'an and in his actions. A clear distinction was made between verbal abuse and denigration, which were tolerated, and plots or political manoeuvring against Muslim society that were accompanied by such verbal acts.

In the post-prophetic period, political concerns also came to influence how blasphemy was sanctioned or punished in some cases. For instance, according to Safran, in some blasphemy cases in Muslim Spain, which were made against Muslims in the Umayyad period in the last years of ʿAbd al-Rahman II's reign, 'the ruler made the final decision' according to political considerations.[57] In one case, the nephew of a relative of ʿAbd al- Rahman II was charged with blasphemy and the death penalty was supported by the ruler. In this case, dominant political interests coincided with the accused's death.[58] In blasphemy and heresy cases available from the past, it is possible to suggest that partisan and political considerations played a role in such cases, generally 'privileging the interests of the regime'.[59]

Extreme veneration of the Prophet

Fourth, the more developed form of blasphemy laws, as seen in the works of Ibn Taymiyya and Qadi ʿIyad, stems, in part, from extreme reverence towards the Prophet. After the Prophet's death, his image and authority were venerated and augmented; this exaltation often exceeded the Qur'an's depiction of the Prophet Muhammad as a human being, as considerable emphasis was placed on miracles as proofs of prophesy. In the Sufi literature, the Prophet became the eternal patron of saints, the 'divine light', the first created being, the Perfect Man and almost God-like. This extreme veneration became part of popular culture in Muslim societies. Such veneration can often play a significant role in accusations of blasphemy against people who say or do something that can be interpreted as belittling the status of the Prophet Muhammad.

In summary, blasphemy laws in Islam developed in response to specific circumstances and contexts, such as responses to internal or external threats to the stability of the community; as expressions of the superiority of Islam within the Muslim state; and as a means to protect the honour and position of the Prophet, the Muslim community and its symbols.

Concluding remarks

Although blasphemy laws have no strong basis in the Qur'an or in the traditions of the Prophet, particularly as far as applying the death penalty is concerned, it is challenging to approach this legal tradition in the modern period. Laws against blasphemy exist in some Muslim states and are often used by the state or powerful religious and political authorities against political opponents and dissenters, curtailing freedom of expression and religion, intellectual activity and academic discussion. They are useful tools for those in positions of power in these societies, where even criticism of such laws themselves can be considered blasphemy. Many critics of blasphemy laws have, thus, been punished with fines, imprisonment or even death.

There are many challenges to understanding and changing these blasphemy laws. There is a basic lack of intellectual freedom in much of the Muslim world. In many countries, where blasphemy laws are maintained and actively in force, the collaboration of political and religious establishments serves to maintain classical sanctions, and the institutions involved are often very resistant to reform.[60] There is also a view that freedom of religion and freedom of expression undermine the governmental control of religion and may result in social or religious upheaval.

More broadly, many Muslims see arguments for change or greater freedom of expression as a threat to their identity – as something that is being imposed from other cultures or from the 'West'. Those who argue against blasphemy laws, even amongst Muslims, are considered enemies of Islam, 'agents' of the West, Orientalists, 'modernists,' suspect Muslims or naïve followers of human rights activists. This 'siege' mentality sees freedom of expression as a threat to the survival of Muslim communities, and discussions generate strong emotions around the issue.

Given these challenges, can blasphemy laws be countered through rational arguments that refer to the most important textual sources of Islam, the Qur'an and the Sunna? One way forward may be to retain the concept of blasphemy in Islamic tradition in some significantly revised form but to remove the punishment associated with it: the death penalty. The death penalty can be set aside because there is no Qur'anic instruction or hadith suggesting in unmistakable terms that this punishment should be applied. Moreover, as there is no clear definition of blasphemy in the Qur'an or hadith, existing definitions of blasphemy can be rethought considering contemporary social and political circumstances, just as they have been in the past.

The redefinition of blasphemy and rethinking of its punishment is a critically important task for Muslim scholars today. Indeed, there is no reason why Muslims cannot accept a concept of freedom of expression informed by contemporary human rights standards and the vast array of Qur'anic verses that seem to support such a freedom.

Notes

1 Riaz Hassan, 'Expressions of religiosity and blasphemy in modern societies', *Asian Journal of Social Science* 35/1 (2007), pp. 111–25, at p. 114.
2 Hassan, 'Expressions of religiosity', p. 111.
3 Ibid., p. 114.
4 Lutz Wiederhold, 'Blasphemy against the Prophet Muḥammad and his Companions (*sabb al-rasūl, sabb al-ṣaḥāba*): The introduction of the topic into Shāfiʿī legal literature and its relevance for legal practice under Mamluk rule', *Journal of Semitic Studies* 42/1 (1997), pp. 39–70, at p. 41.
5 Mashood A. Baderin, *International Human Rights and Islamic Law* (Oxford: Oxford University Press, 2005), p. 128.
6 Ibid., p. 128.
7 Ibid., p. 128.
8 Ibid., p. 128.
9 Ibid., p. 128.
10 Wiederhold, 'Blasphemy against the Prophet Muhammad', p. 41.
11 Ibid., p. 41.
12 Liyakat Takim, 'Blasphemy' (n.d.), unpublished article previously available on Takim's personal website, http://www.ltakim.com/Articles.htm, accessed 31 March 2017.
13 Wiederhold, 'Blasphemy against the Prophet Muhammad', p. 41.
14 Takim, 'Blasphemy'.
15 Ibid.
16 Uri Rubin, 'The assassination of Ka'b b. al-Ashraf', *Oriens* 32 (1990), pp. 65–71, at p. 65. See also M.J. Kister, 'The market of the Prophet', *Journal of the Economic and Social History of the Orient* 8/3 (1965), pp. 272–76, at p. 272.
17 Rubin, 'The assassination of Ka'b', p. 66. See also references there.
18 Ibid., p. 66.
19 Ibid., p. 67. See also references there.
20 Takim, 'Blasphemy'.
21 Ibid.
22 Wiederhold, 'Blasphemy against the Prophet Muhammad', pp. 41–2, citing Ahmad b. Hanbal, *Musnad* (Cairo, 1913), vol. 2, p. 436.
23 Abdullah Saeed and Hassan Saeed, *Freedom of Religion, Apostasy and Islam* (Burlington, VT: Ashgate, 2005), p. 38.
24 Ibid., p. 39.
25 Ibid., p. 39.
26 Ibid., pp. 38–39.
27 Takim, 'Blasphemy'.
28 See Masud's and especially Mazhar's and Moulvi's contributions to this volume.
29 Saeed and Saeed, *Freedom of Religion*, p. 55.

30 Wiederhold, 'Blasphemy against the Prophet Muhammad', p. 44.
31 Ibid., p. 44.
32 Ibid., p. 43.
33 Ibid., p. 43.
34 Ibid., p. 43.
35 Ibid., p. 45.
36 Ibid., p. 42.
37 Javed Ahmad Ghamidi, 'Punishment for blasphemy against the Prophet (SWS)', *Renaissance (A Monthly Islamic Journal)* 21/3 (2011), p. 3.
38 Janina M. Safran, 'Identity and Differentiation in Ninth-Century al-Andalus', *Speculum* 76/3 (2001): pp. 573–98, at p. 591, https://doi.org/10.2307/2903880.
39 Ghamidi, 'Punishment for blasphemy', p. 3.
40 The Prophet Muhammad is referred to as the perfect human being (*al-insān al-kāmil*). This concept is discussed in Ibn ʿArabi's *Fuṣūṣ al-Ḥikam*: See Muhi-e-Din Ibn Arabi, 'The Seal of the Unique Wisdom in the Word of Muhammad' in *Fusus al-Hikam* [The Bezels of Wisdom] (undated), ch. 27, available at *www.sufi.ir/books/download/english/ibn-arabi-en/fusus-al-hikam-en.doc, accessed 1 April 2017.*
41 Wiederhold, 'Blasphemy against the Prophet Muhammad', p. 42, n. 10.
42 'Articles 295–298A of the Malaysian Penal Code provide penalties for those who commit offenses against religion. The penalties include up to three years in prison or a large fine. Prosecutions for blasphemy usually target those who offend Islam, but an insult to any religion can give rise to prosecution.' See end-blasphemy-laws.org, 'Malaysia', available at http://end-blasphemy-laws.org/countries/asia-central-southern-and-south-eastern/malaysia, accessed 1 April 2017.
43 Law No. 27 of 1999, Penal Code of Indonesia (19 May 1999), art. 156(a), available at http://www.wipo.int/wipolex/en/text.jsp?file_id=181078, accessed 1 April 2017.
44 Asma T. Uddin, 'Blasphemy laws in Muslim majority countries', *Review of Faith & International Affairs* 9/2 (Summer 2011), pp. 47–55, at p. 49.
45 Amnesty International, 'Indonesia: Drop blasphemy case against Jakarta governor', 16 November 2016, https://www.amnesty.org/en/latest/news/2016/11/indonesia-drop-case-against-jakarta-governor/
46 Asma Uddin, 'Indonesian blasphemy act restricts free religious expression', *The Huffington Post*, 27 June 2010, available at http://www.huffingtonpost.com/asma-uddin/the-indonesian-constituti_b_554463.html, accessed 1 April 2017.
47 Ibid.
48 Amnesty International, *Prosecuting Beliefs: Indonesia's Blasphemy Laws* (2014), available at https://www.amnesty.nl/sites/default/files/public/blasphemy_report_indonesia_web.pdf, accessed 31 March 2017.
49 Uddin, 'Blasphemy laws', p. 50.
50 Baderin, *International Human Rights and Islamic Law*, p. 127.
51 Ibid., p. 126.
52 Ibid., p. 127, citing Mohammad Hashim Kamali, *Freedom of Expression in Islam* (1997 ed.), p. 6.
53 Mohammad Hashim Kamali, *Freedom of Expression in Islam* (Kuala Lumpur: Berita Publishing, 1994), p. 243.
54 Ibid., p. 243.
55 There are many examples from the time of the *rāshidūn* caliphs, ʿUmar and ʿAli. See Sultanhussein Tabandeh, *A Muslim Commentary on the Universal Declaration of Human Rights*, transl. Frances J. Goulding (London: FJ Goulding, 1970), pp. 73–4.

56 See also Intisar A. Rabb, 'Negotiating speech in Islamic law and politics: flipped traditions of expression', in Mark S. Ellis, Anver M. Emon and Benjamin Glahn (eds), *Islamic Law and International Human Rights Law* (Oxford: Oxford University Press, 2012), pp. 144–67, at p. 162. Also, jurists noted several exceptions to criminal liability. '[I]f there were doubt (*shubha*) about the nature of a potentially blasphemous statement or act, or if there were a legitimate cause or plausible non-blasphemous interpretation (*ta'wīl*)–even if erroneous–no criminal sanctions would attach'. Ibid., p. 163.

57 Safran, 'Identity and Differentiation', p. 592. Isabel Fierro, 'Andalusian "fatāwā"', pp. 103–17.

58 Safran, 'Identity and differentiation', p. 596.

59 Ibid., p. 591.

60 Since 1994, Amnesty International has reported the misuse of blasphemy laws in Pakistan for political and/or sectarian purposes. For instance, allegations of blasphemy were made against the Islamic studies lecturer Hafiz Imam Bukhsh, who was allegedly sympathetic to Jamiat Ulema-i Pakistan, by an official from a rival group. In other instances, complaints have been filed under pressure from local clerics or members of Islamist parties. See Amnesty International, 'Pakistan: Use and abuse of the blasphemy laws' (1994), available at https://berkleycenter.georgetown.edu/publications/pakistan-use-and-abuse-of-blasphemy-laws, p.10, accessed 31 March 2017.

2

Freedom of Religion in Qur'anic Exegesis

Omaima Abou-Bakr

There is no coercion in religion. Sound judgment has become clear from error. So whosoever disavows false deities and believes in God has grasped the most unfailing handhold, which never breaks. And God is Hearing, Knowing.

Qur'an 2:256

Introduction

This chapter will examine the exegetical history of verse 2:256 of the Qur'an through selected representative classical and modern *tafsīr* works. The objective is an analysis of the following aspects: (1) the construction and development of the concept of freedom/coercion in religious belief, as well as the evolving attitude towards the religious 'other'; (2) the hermeneutic methods of either generalizing or particularizing the verse, the implications of the oscillation between the two methods, and the use of corroborating evidence from the Prophetic tradition or historical anecdotes; and (3) whether exegetes perceived a thematic or a semantic connection with two other types of verses: those urging choice (e.g. 10:99, 18:29 and 109:6) and those urging jihad (e.g. 9:73 and 66:9). In the analysis, attention will be paid to the interpreter's own voice, method of deduction and selectiveness. This research aims to demonstrate the nature and dynamics of concept-building in the literature of Qur'anic exegesis, observing the extent to which the historical and political context shaped the interpretive views presented.

The Qur'anic interpretive tradition of *tafsīr* has over the centuries produced a huge corpus of commentaries (both published and in manuscript form), making it difficult to have a complete account of all exegetical works or to undertake comprehensive studies of their full content. Needless to say, there have been valuable scholarly studies that outline the development and evolution of this genre and its different schools, such as John Wansbrough's *Qur'anic Studies: Sources and Methods of Scriptural Interpretation* (1977), Andrew Rippin's edited volume, *Approaches to the History of the Interpretation of the Qur'an* (1988) and Herbert Berg's *The Development of Exegesis in Early Islam* (2000). As for studies or surveys by modern Muslim scholars, the most well-known are Muhammad al-Dhahabi's *al-Tafsīr wa-al-Mufassirūn* (1961) and Muhammad al-Fadil ibn ʿAshur's *al-Tafsīr wa-Rijāluh* (1970). Despite the vastness and diversity of the *tafsīr* literature, it is of central significance to both religious and intellectual history, as Walid Saleh has noted:

> All generations of Muslims in nearly every Islamic land have consistently produced Quranic commentaries that reflect their outlook on fundamental issues confronting Muslim societies, making this genre a continuous record of what Muslims of different lands and different ages have thought on various topics.[1]

However, it should also be considered a two-way interaction, in which the conceptual and discursive trends themselves constructed by the exegetes' understandings also shape social views and cultural practices. This is because, in general, these works consist in explications, the generation of meaning and the development of attitudes towards issues and topics.

In a 2009 article, Patricia Crone provides a very thorough survey of the verse's interpretations across the different sects and divisions. She begins her study with a focus on two particular Muʿtazili theologians, followed by non-Muʿtazilis and the sectarian groups of the Khawarij, the Ismaʿilis and the Zaydis.[2] The second part, dealing with the nineteenth and twentieth centuries, presents another classification into Shiʿi interpreters and Sunni Islamists, followed by an exposition of the related sub-topics and how they were discussed. In structuring her presentation around factions and ideologies, Crone aims to show the utter complexity, irregularity and divergence in past understandings of the issues involved, of which, she maintains, present Muslims are unaware. She criticizes contemporary attempts by 'believers' to re-formulate and re-construct the verse's notions of free choice and tolerance, considering them 'backprojection' and a historical 'misrepresentation' of the tradition, rather than reflecting reformist motives.[3] She sees a tension between historians, who view all interpretations as historically conditioned and devoid of perennial truths, and modern believers, who naively project their changed views upon past tradition and ignore its difference. Unlike Crone, however, I see a value in current interpretive efforts, as well as in objective evaluations of exegetical discourses, which recover and reinforce positive values in the Islamic message that may have been downplayed in past historical stages.

This presentation will only focus on the first part of the verse – 'There is no compulsion/coercion in religion' – and on a rendition and textual analysis of the various passages that contain the exegetes' explications and commentaries, not on jurisprudence or ideology. This systematic following of one particular chronological path shows clearly the cumulative, almost intertextual, nature of this genre. Exegetes tend to be guided and strongly influenced by previous interpretive views and arguments, interweaving their own modifications or additions. Hence, a consecutive reading of this literature allows us to see the genealogy and roots of certain ideas and their formulations. As one scholar noted, the genre of *tafsīr* became the main mediator between the Qurʾan and believers, to the extent that 'much of what Muslims believe the Quran is stating is actually what *tafsīr* says it is.'[4]

Classical exegetical works

Al-Tabari's (d. 923) discussion of the verse establishes and determines the mainstream classical trajectory. The topics comprise the specific occasions of revelation as initial historical context, the issue of *jizya* (the poll tax paid by non-Muslims) and the issue of abrogation. An analysis of Tabari's sequence of presentation and the logic of his arguments shows early attempts to limit the unqualified, unspecified prohibition against 'compulsion'. In keeping with his method, Tabari cites variant or repeated views from the tradition first, then concludes with his own interpretation, which he usually introduces with the phrase *wa-awwala hādhihi al-aqwāl bi al-ṣawāb 'indī* ('the most adequately correct of these views in my opinion is'). He then proceeds to either favour a certain view, arguing for and building on it, or to refute and disagree with all previous opinions, citing reasons and evidence.

The first of these interpretive views that Tabari presents refers to the historical context of the revelation and expresses accordingly the simple, direct understanding of the prohibition in the verse:

> This verse was revealed in reference to some people from the *anṣār* [. . .] who had children whom they had converted to Judaism or Christianity; when God revealed Islam, they wanted to enforce it on them, but God prohibited them from doing this, so that it is they who choose (*yakhtārūn*) entering Islam.[5]

What follows are three detailed variant narratives of how this situation came about. The first mentions the pre-Islamic custom that a wife whose male infants did not survive, would vow that if one of them lived, she would offer him to the 'people of the Book', the Jewish community in Medina. Hence, when the Jewish tribe Banu al-Nadir evacuated the city and these families wanted to take back their children by converting them to Islam by force, the verse was revealed to indicate that those who left would be choosing Judaism and those who willingly stayed would be choosing Islam. No coercion was to be practiced. Another citation mentions a Muslim man (Salem bin 'Awf) from the *anṣār* consulting the Prophet whether he should force his two Christian sons to adopt Islam, though they refused to leave Christianity.[6] The answer was a prohibition from doing so. A third narrative, similar to the first, again cites the situation where Jewish women had nursed children from a Muslim tribe in Medina, so when the Jews were leaving the city, these sons also wanted to accompany them and adopt Judaism, whereas the families objected, wanting to keep them by forcing them to become Muslims. This section of Tabari's explanation of the background to the verse concludes that this instance together with the revelation at hand was considered a 'distinction (*fasl*) between those among them who chose the Jews and those who chose Islam [. . .], so those who left with Banu al-Nadir belonged to them, and those who stayed' chose to belong to Islam.[7]

The second interpretive opinion that Tabari presents deals with more particularities and qualifies this freedom of choice by indicating to what groups and under what conditions it applies. He cites traditions that distinguished between People of the Book, who had *dīn* (belief in a religion) and a *kitāb* (a book of revelation), and the idolaters/disbelievers, who were illiterate and had no Book[8] or religion. It was only the first group who were not to be coerced if they paid the *jizya*, not the latter, who had no option but either to accept Islam or to be fought. A third opinion cited is that this verse has been abrogated, as it was revealed before the divine injunction to fight.

In the end Tabari gives his preferred interpretation: 'This verse was revealed concerning a particular group of people [...] those of the two Books and the Magians, and all whose religion was acknowledged—though different from the religion of truth—paying the *jizya*'.[9] He does not accept abrogation (a method often used by commentators to rationalize apparent contradictions between verses). Instead, he sees no contradiction between two dimensions of meaning: 'when a commandment/prohibition is outwardly general and particular on the inner level'.[10] This interpretive distinction allows him to add the condition of paying the poll tax, though it is not mentioned on the explicit level of the verse. Further, he corroborates this view, that the verse is specified and not unconditional, by claiming that the Prophet fought the idolaters/infidels and did not accept from them a tax as a settlement or alternative to entering Islam. Hence, 'no compulsion in religion means no compulsion of anyone whose tax is allowed and paid, and who thus accepts the sovereignty of Islam'.[11] Following this settlement, there should be no coercion of the People of the Book to convert to Islam, as 'he who deviates from truthfulness after it has become clear to him, will be judged and punished by God when the time comes'.[12] It may be noticed that there is a subtle, yet significant, distinction assumed between enforcing doctrinal belief as an inner personal faith (that is, forcefully converting people from one religion to another) and enforcing a mainstream religious system based on a political settlement that allows non-Muslim communities to co-exist. The statement that the religion of the People of the Book is to be allowed and accepted, with the awareness that it is not truthful according to Muslims, is repeated several times throughout the segment, an attitude of religious acceptance and tolerance to be distinguished from social and political dominance. Moreover, communal co-existence is possible only with Jews and Christians, not with the idolaters.

Tabari's final comment on the concluding segment of the verse – 'and Allah hears and knows all things' – provides an understanding of belief as a personal inner conviction known only to God, who has the power to repay by punishment or reward accordingly. After all that has been inferred and discussed, this seems to be the most appropriate clincher to the argument, as it directs attention to the ultimate, decisive Arbitrator. Tabari expresses this view clearly and emphatically:

> And God hears the faith of the believer in God alone, the disbeliever in false gods or tyrants, when he affirms the oneness of God and is innocent of worshipping idols and false divinities. God is all-knowing of a believer's determination and resolve concerning His oneness, as well as the sincerity of his heart. God also clearly knows a person's innocent conscience of other gods, idols, tyrants, or other hidden attachments within every human soul – He from Whom no secret is kept or matter hidden. Then He repays each group [believers and unbelievers] on Judgment Day according to what every person's tongue has uttered, and what he

harboured in his conscience. If it's good, then good repayment, and if it's bad, then bad repayment.[13]

This understanding of God, the All-Hearing and All-Knowing, as the only One privy to a person's true inner conviction is indeed the most appropriate and sensible capstone of this major verse on free choice of religion. It should have led Tabari and later exegetes who commented on this particular phrase (e.g. al-Razi), to go on to note the contradiction between this conception and their preceding discussions of enforcing the poll tax or fighting the disbelievers, as well as to consider the historicity of these practices and subordinate them to the fixed principle of free choice, not vice versa. Moreover, the implication that this is a personal matter between an individual and God is a very significant principle that should have continued to frame the whole issue and set its criteria. Interestingly, four centuries later the Andalusian exegete and scholar, Muhammad ibn Ahmad ibn Juzayy al-Kalbi al-Gharnati (d. 1357), alluded in his commentary to this chronological aspect by maintaining that the verse was Medinan (revealed in Medina *after* the conquest of Mecca and final triumph) and so commanded 'leaving fighting behind in Mecca', that is, ceasing to fight altogether after that stage. Hence, the claim that the verse was abrogated by the injunction to fight is, according to him, weak because it's rather the opposite. He calls the verse *āyat al-musālama* (the verse of peacefulness) and explains that it means 'gentleness/mildness (*muwāda'a*) by not forcing anyone through fighting to enter Islam'.[14]

As for the next exegete after Tabari, Zamakhshari (d. 1144), he begins his commentary with a straightforward, succinct statement about the nature of belief that 'God did not base faith on force and coercion, but on enabling and choice',[15] followed by quoting another verse that also uses a derivative from *ikrāh* (coercion) negatively in order to prove this element of free will. He is the first exegete who attempts, as a starting point, to extend the range of meaning of the verse by making a thematic/logical connection with other verses to strengthen the argument against compulsion. The verse he quotes is 10:99, 'And had thy Lord willed, all those who are on the earth would have believed all together. Wouldst thou compel men till they become believers?'[16] Zamakhshari paraphrases and stresses further the hypothetical element of the verse: 'Had He wanted, He would have forced them to belief, but He did not do this and rather based the matter on choice (*ikhtiyār*).'[17] Only after foregrounding the above explanation does Zamakhshari include the other traditions: the opinion that the verse is abrogated by 9:73, which urges struggling hard against the disbelievers and the hypocrites; that 2:256 concerns People of the Book who 'are protected by means of the *jizya*'; and the occasion of revelation regarding the man whose two sons were Christian and who was ordered to leave them alone. He does not go to any length concerning those points.

Al-Razi (d. 1209), however, in keeping with his exegetical method of interest in various facets (*wujūh*) of meaning, enumerates and explains these levels of the verse's interpretation. The first is a direct reference to Zamakhshari's statement on volition, though Razi does not mention him by name, but references other Mu'tazili scholars, whose views he reproduces, adding more reasoning to their argument: Since this world is a place of trial and affliction (*ibtilā'*) for humankind, any forceful imposition or oppression for the sake of faith annuls the meaning of this divine test in which people are supposed to earn the merit of arriving at God's truth.[18] Following Zamakhshari's example, al-Razi quotes, in addition to 10:99, two more relevant verses that further emphasize human volition as part of God's plan: 'So whosoever will, let him believe, and whosoever will, let him disbelieve [...]' (18:29); 'If We will, We will send down a sign from Heaven and their heads would remain bowed before it in humility' (26:4). He concludes this segment by referring to the part of the verse which stresses that all proofs and evidence have been made clear and manifest to all; this would supposedly only leave compulsion as a means of leading people to belief, but that, according to al-Razi, is 'illegitimate because it contradicts divine obligation/injunction (*taklīf*)'.[19] In other words, this interpretation is based on an argument from the logical contradiction between compulsion and the human moral achievement of freely striving towards faith or not, for which God will reward or punish accordingly. This basic divine principle would have no meaning if there were no human volition or personal responsibility.

The second facet of meaning presented by al-Razi pertains to the political context. He distinguishes between the disbelievers (*kuffār*) and the People of the Book and the Magians. If the latter group accepts paying the tax, the obligation to fight them is dropped. As for the unbelievers who convert to Judaism or Christianity, jurists differ: Some say not to fight them if they also pay the tax, meaning the statement 'no compulsion in religion' is general to all; others maintain that this situation should not be accepted and so compulsion is allowed. In other words, this view seems to distinguish between those who are already believing Jews and Christians and those who convert as a political tactic to avoid fighting. It is not clear, however, what would constitute 'permissible' enforcement of Islam (according to the latter group of jurists) in the case of those disbelievers who promptly announce their conversion, joining the People of the Book.

The third facet of the notion of compulsion is its social dimension – that of forbidding Muslims from stigmatizing those who entered Islam only after fighting. They should not be considered 'forced' anymore if they have accepted the religion and have become truly Muslim. This situation, according to al-Razi's explanation, is similar to 'And say not unto him who offers you peace, "You are not a believer"' (4:94), which forbids Muslims from calling someone who greets them with the Islamic salutation – *al-salām ʿalaykum* – a non-believer. Whereas one can derive from this a positive meaning against labelling or discrimination based on false assumptions and social judgment, this partial interpretation is not connected with the rest of the verse, and it ignores the fact that the issue of commandment against compulsion points to the initial stage of entering the religion in the first place, not after.

As for the concluding segment of the verse – 'And God is Hearing, Knowing' – al-Razi, following Tabari's example, makes a similar comment, juxtaposing 'believers' and 'disbelievers': only God almighty 'hears the one who utters the two *shahāda*s and the one who speaks of disbelief, and knows what pure faith dwells in the believer's heart and what foul belief in the unbeliever's heart'.[20] This brief comment, however, dilutes the importance and significance of this part of the verse even more than Tabari's does. And similarly, al-Razi perceives no disconnect between the basic ethical import of the verse (that forced faith is no faith, and that it is a matter between God and every individual's heart) and the issues of *jizya* or fighting the *kuffār*.

Al-Qurtubi (d. 1273) reviews and summarizes all the previous interpretations thus far, but focusses on the practical rulings and political practice, not on the dimension of free choice of religion. He enumerates six views: First, that the verse has been abrogated by verse 9:73 and by the fact that the Prophet fought Arab tribes to force them to accept Islam. Second, that the verse is not abrogated, and it is meant for the People of the Book who pay the *jizya*, but not for the idolaters, who may be forced. Here, Qurtubi inserts a new anecdote to prove the distinction: it is narrated that Caliph ʿUmar once called on an old Christian woman to enter Islam, and when she insisted on refusing, he recited 'There is no compulsion in religion' and said, 'God be my witness'.[21] The third and fourth views repeat Tabari's contextual references: to childless women offering their infants to the Jews, the children being suckled by the Jewish tribe of Banu al-Nadir, and their families wanting to force them to come back when the latter evacuated; and to the story of the man who had two sons who were converted to Christianity by Syrian merchants and wanted to leave with them. The fifth view is borrowed from al-Razi, but phrased differently and briefly: 'Do not call those who entered Islam by the sword forced or coerced'.[22] Al-Qurtubi does not comment on the apparent contradiction within the statement, perhaps because it is one of the well-known opinions by now and has been previously explained by al-Razi.

As the *tafsīr* works progress, there is gradually diminishing interest in the general guiding principle of human responsibility as part of God's scheme of repayment, in the point that God could have easily made all people believers if he would, as well as in the details of the 'occasions of revelation'. Al-Baydawi (d. 1286) simply presents a semantic definition of the term *ikrāh* and comments on the clear and evidenced distinction between belief – being proper, truthful and sensible (*rushd*) – which leads to eternal bliss, and disbelief – being in error (*ghayy*) – which leads to eternal wretchedness. Hence, 'a reasonable person, once this is clear to him, will voluntarily seek faith to gain happiness and salvation, and will not need compulsion or force.'[23] Then, he moves to the other levels of the interpretation by stating that this injunction is either a general commandment abrogated by 9:73, or a specific one that concerns only People of the Book. As for the final segment of the verse, God hears 'all sayings' and knows 'all intentions'. In this edition of al-Baydawi's work, the commentary *Tafsīr al-Jalālayn* (completed by Jalal al-Din al-Suyuti, d. 1505) is also included in the bottom margin; it is the most brief and concise of all commentaries so far, sacrificing a lot of nuance and debatable issues. Al-Suyuti presents a superficial paraphrase of the verse and selects one cause of the revelation – it 'was revealed for the one who had Christian sons and wanted to force them to enter Islam'.[24]

Ibn Kathir's (d. 1373) commentary represents an interesting case and a significant stage in the interpretive development of the verse. He continues to follow the previous pattern and material, but adds new evidence. The pattern so far has been an initial paraphrase or exposition of the direct meaning, followed by a section on the various narratives of the 'occasions of revelation', another on restrictions and limitations of scope, and finally – in a few cases – connecting with the final portion of the verse. Ibn Kathir's first part reads:

> Do not force anyone to enter Islam, for it is plain and clear, with manifest evidence and proofs, and does not need enforcement. Those whom God has guided to Islam,

> whose hearts He has opened to faith and whose vision was enlightened, embrace Islam in awareness and fully convinced. For those whose hearts were made blind, hearing and insight blocked, there is no use in being coerced and forced to join the religion. It is mentioned that the occasion of the verse is related to a group from the *anṣār*, yet its ruling is general.[25]

The second part of the commentary repeats the established 'occasions of revelation' in the tradition so far, replacing the previous anecdote – that of the Caliph ʿUmar calling upon an old Christian woman to convert and her refusal – with another in which ʿUmar urges his Christian slave, who refuses, which ʿUmar simply accepts and responds to by reciting 'No compulsion in religion'.

The third part mentions some of the previous views of other scholars, such as that the verse refers to the Christians who pay the tax, and that it is abrogated by the 'fighting' verses. Ibn Kathir explains: 'All peoples and communities should be called upon to enter Islam, and those who refuse to follow or do not pay the *jizya* will be fought until they are killed'.[26] He quotes three different verses that have not been discussed before – 48:16, 9:123 and 66:9 – to corroborate the view of the necessity of combat. As Ibn Kathir groups them here for the purpose of interpreting this verse, they are intended to strengthen the argument for fighting and almost to reverse the verse's original, direct meaning of prohibiting compulsion. However, each of these verses belongs to a specific textual and historical context. Both 48:16 and 9:123 refer to the enemy/disbelievers 'near you' (meaning those among the Arabs), or to certain idolatrous tribes who were indeed defeated later (Banu Hanifa, Banu Hawazin, Banu Thaqif), or they foreshadow future battles against the Byzantine and Persian armies. In other words, these refer to political conquests and may not be apt cross-references of the verse in question. As for 66:9, 'strive against the disbelievers' is understood to mean with the sword as well as through preaching and calling them to God, while striving against 'the hypocrites' is understood to mean by applying the legal punishments for their transgressions.[27] In other words, Ibn Kathir here drops the particular nuances of these other verses and ignores their historical specificity in order to utilize them in a generalized manner.

Additionally, he quotes two hadiths, again included in the interpretation for the first time, mentioning that they are authenticated (*ṣaḥīḥ*). The first describes a group of people entering Heaven in chains, who are explained to be the captives of war who later convert to the religion and become good Muslims. The second hadith, claimed to be narrated by Imam Ahmad ibn Hanbal, narrates a presumed conversation between the Prophet and an unnamed man, in which the Prophet asks the man to become Muslim; the man replies that he feels 'averse' (using the adjective form *kārih*, derived from the same root as *ikrāh*), and the Prophet says: 'Even if you are averse, for God will provide you with good intention/will and sincerity.'[28] Ibn Kathir comments that the Prophet did not force the man, but simply called or summoned him to embrace Islam; that is, he differentiates between 'physical' *ikrāh* (force, violence) and the attempt to persuade people who still feel 'an inner lack of acceptance' (*nafsuh ghayr qabila*) of Islam, but who may later grow convinced. Apart from the question of whether the hadiths are truly authentic or not, they are put to use here to encourage coerced conversion or at least aggressive persuasion, hoping that such people might later become true believers.

To conclude, Ibn Kathir's exposition is a good representation of the established pattern so far: (1) an initial section on the straightforward and theoretical meaning of the verse; (2) historical context in the form of the occasions for revelation and anecdotes; (3) interpretive means (such as abrogation) that introduce exceptions from and limitations on the general rule; (4) the practical, political section on dealing with non-believers and People of the Book, both those accepting the rule and protection of Muslims and other combative, hostile nations; and (5) cross-references to other verses and hadiths to corroborate the above views.

Whereas Ibn Kathir refers to the verses that urge fighting the disbelievers, he does not use the relevant verses that emphasize free will, as was done only by Zamakhshari and al-Razi so far. Perceiving a connection, the former quoted 10:99, and the latter quoted 18:29 and 26:3–4. We have to wait for the nineteenth-century exegete Shihab al-Din al-Sayyid Mahmud al-Alusi (1802–54) for these verses to be referenced again. In his *Rūḥ al-Maʿānī*, he states that this first part of the verse appears in the grammatical form of *ikhbār* (a statement of fact), but it carries the meaning of *nahy* (a prohibition). However, it is either a generalized rule, abrogated by the injunction in 66:9 to strive against disbelievers and hypocrites, or specific to the People of the Book who accepted paying the tax. Then he ends the passage by:

> Some people have said that the intended meaning is that there is no compulsion or coercion by God Almighty in religion, as it is based on enabling and choice, or else trials (*ibtilāʾ*) and tests would be invalidated: 'So whosoever will, let him believe, and whosoever will, let him disbelieve (18:29).'[29]

This shows Zamakhshari's and al-Razi's influence.

Modern exegetes

The influential *Tafsīr al-Manār*, which recorded the interpretive views of Egyptian scholar and modern Muslim reformist Muhammad ʿAbduh (d. 1905), is widely considered as the work that initiated modern Qur'anic commentaries and marked a shift in style and interpretive discourse, appearing after the last of the conventional exegetical works by al-Alusi in the preceding century. Reflecting the influence of modernity and its pressing social and political issues, as well as the context of apologetics vis-à-vis the colonial Orientalism of the time, the discussion of this particular verse has a strong defensive tone. Following the mention of the established occasions of revelation, ʿAbduh begins his commentary by arguing against the prevalent accusation by 'Islam's enemies' that Islam was founded and spread by 'the sword'.[30] He reminds us that the verse was revealed in Medina at the height of Islam's victory and dominance and after the treacherous Jewish tribe of Banu al-Nadir had evacuated, so it was natural for the issue of forcing Islam upon the defeated to come up, but the Revelation's prohibitive response was clear. Then he differentiates between political motives (*siyāsa*) and religion: Although it might be the customary historical practice of other nations to force people to convert to their religions, true religious faith is based on a willing 'surrender of the soul', and this cannot happen through coercion, but only by means of 'demonstration and evidence'.[31] That is why after negating compulsion, the verse states 'sound judgment has become clear from error', meaning that the righteous religion has become manifestly distinct from erroneous paths.

In the following section of cross-references to other verses, 'Abduh quotes 10:99 as a verse similar in meaning, maintaining that there are numerous other verses to support this idea that 'religion is an optional path of guidance offered to people and supported by proofs and illustrations'.[32] Prophets were not sent to be oppressors, but simply messengers, either bringing good news of future reward or delivering a warning. As for the verses commanding fighting (*al-qitāl*), the motive behind them was 'safeguarding the religion and averting the evil/harm of the disbelievers from the believers, so as not to shake the faith of weak-hearted believers, or oppress strong believers by tempting them away from the religion as they used to do publicly in Mecca'.[33] Noteworthy is the new perception of the threat of polemical arguments turning people away from the religion through persuasion, rather than physical attack. This must be a reflection of the intellectual anxiety of the times concerning the advent of modernity and scientific thinking, on one hand, and Orientalist denigration and de-sanctifying of Islam, on the other.

That is why 'Abduh at this point quotes 2:193: 'And fight them until there is no strife (*fitna*), and religion is for God. But if they desist, then there is no enmity save against the wrongdoers.' 'Abduh discusses the concept of *fitna* at some length. The word has a range of meanings and usages – trial, temptation, sedition, persecution, oppression, discord, civil strife – and so has been variously rendered by translators and understood in different senses by both classical and modern exegetes. Its interpretation determines the legitimate causes for fighting: Many classical commentators considered *fitna* in this context to specifically mean idolatry, and so ending *fitna* is overcoming idolatry; 'desist' would mean that they stop being idolaters and become Muslims. Others state that what they should desist from is aggression and hostility. The plain sense of the verse seems to support this latter meaning, as is also corroborated by other verses (e.g. 9:6, on granting asylum to non-combative idolaters) that clearly distinguish between those who attack and expel Muslims and those who do not. However, classical interpreters especially may have understood the point about resisting and fighting aggression and expulsion, but also assumed that these hostilities could only be brought to an end through the idolaters' repentance and conversion to Islam, not just by ending the very real and physical danger they posed to the existence and livelihood of Muslims.[34] An exception is al-Razi, who considered that *fitna* (also occurring in 8:39) referred to the persecution and oppression Muslims endured at the hands of the Meccan idolaters before and after the Hijra, and so they were ordered to fight until they could end this state of tribulation by overcoming the forces of disbelief. More importantly, al-Razi understood this injunction as pertaining only to the historical context and situation of Mecca at the time, not to the whole world.[35]

As for 'Abduh, he interprets *fitna* in 2:193 as aggressive temptation challenging faith in the heart of the believer, who has a right to feel secure and unshaken in the face of such impositions. He states that tribulations (*fitan*) can be stopped through either of two measures. The first is exposing Islam's opponents so as to establish Muslims' viewpoints as superior, thus keeping Muslims from being tempted to turn away from their religion, without preventing them from calling people to it. The second is accepting *jizya* in return for 'our' protection of 'them' following 'their surrender', which safeguards us against their aggression.[36] 'Abduh does not mention specifically in this passage who 'they' are, nor does he mention Christians or Jews, but leaves it vague and generalized. In fact, he seems to be less interested in the issue of obtaining the tax than he is in the idea of fending off attacks that affect Muslims' self-confidence and strength. He maintains:

> No compulsion in religion is one of Islam's grand rules [...], and to be able to uphold this pillar, we should possess power and resistance to defend ourselves and our religion against those trying to tempt us to turn away as a form of aggression while they are totally secure that we are not able to return the attack in a similar way.[37]

Yet, he continues, we have been ordered to call others to God's path by means of wisdom and good advice and to dispute with those who differ religiously in a good, decent manner, relying on the clear distinction between truth and error through demonstrating proofs of faith and the freedom of *da'wa* (proselytizing). Hence, 'jihad in religion is to be considered in this way, not as part of its essence or objectives – only as a protective [measure], for it is a political matter of necessity.'[38] Again he refutes the clichéd accusation that Islam was spread by means of the sword or that 'jihad is required for its own sake'.

One can discern that 'Abduh's goal is mainly defensive in the face of a number of contemporaneous challenges, such as the colonial Orientalist view of Islam as inherently violent; the resultant distortions of Islam's message, values and tradition; and the negative effects on Muslims' self-image and confidence, particularly in the context of the push towards modernisation, progress and scientific reasoning. In an attempt to rationalize or legitimize the Qur'anic idea of jihad, 'Abduh first distinguishes between the political necessity of self-protection and the original religious objectives of peaceful exhortation; second, he represents the act of jihad as self-defence against being considered inferior and made to feel that way; that is, he perceives the conflict between Muslims and non-Muslims as mostly in the arena of disputation and persuasion, rather than armed warfare. Hence, in comparison to the previous classical discourse, he was able to identify and name the divide between the 'political' and the 'religious' in a way that the classical exegetes did not fully articulate; yet, in a similar manner, it was the historical and political context of his times that mostly determined his focus and tone. Whereas medieval scholars spoke from a position of power and territorial dominance vis-à-vis the religious other, Muhammad 'Abduh reveals an awareness of the colonial disempowerment of modern-day Muslims. Scholars studying 'Abduh's contribution to Islamic thought at the turn of the century have always noted this interactive aspect of Islamic reformism that directly addressed the emerging needs of Muslims and current issues at the time and attempted to justify reformist ideas through an Islamic frame of reference.[39]

Many of the following twentieth-century interpreters could be also viewed in this light of responding to the requirements of the age for reform and re-thinking of the tradition. The next significant figure to consider is Mahmud Shaltut (1893–1963), rector of al-Azhar, who wrote a treatise on the subject of jihad, *al-Qur'ān wa-al-Qitāl* (1948), and produced a *tafsīr* of only the first ten parts of the Qur'an (1965). He seems to be directly influenced by 'Abduh in maintaining that the permission to fight was governed by the historical context of the early Muslims defending themselves against the harm inflicted by the Meccans, and he completely rejects abrogation of 2:256.

The above tendencies in both Abduh and Shaltut to ignore or reject abrogation, as well as to argue for a defensive jihad, are characteristic features of modern exegetes. Sayyid Qutb in his *Fī Ẓilāl al-Qur'ān* (1952) praises this great principle of freedom of belief as a form of divine honouring of human beings' will and sense of responsibility, and hence sees it as 'the most specific characteristic of human liberation'. He continues: 'The freedom of belief is the primary human right', and so this is an Islamic call to 'the liberation of human conscience'.[40] Grammatically, the negation in 2:256 is directed at the act of compulsion itself, which is more powerful than a simple prohibition directed at the believers using the second person plural (e.g. *lā tukrihu*, 'don't force'). This expression excludes the act from existence altogether, and the second part of the verse that talks about the clear distinction of sound judgment from error is proof that 'choice is left to human beings'.[41] It is typical of Qutb's method that he completely ignores the previous interpretive details and discussions of the tradition in favour of a free interaction with the ethical dimension of a given verse or verse-passage and how they reveal aspects of the total Qur'anic message of truth. This approach can be faulted for a simplistic hermeneutics that does not take account of the tradition and the issues it has raised; yet, paradoxically, in evading all previous references, the *tafsīr* sets out an uncomplicated response and a most direct interpretation, modern in spirit and style, and one that implies the lasting validity of the divine message. In the particular case of this verse, Qutb does not refer to any relevant historical context, nor does he raise the issues of abrogation, the poll tax, forced conversion, dealing with non-Muslims and disbelievers, or the matter of jihad; he presents only his almost impressionistic outlook on the verse.

However, a more innovative interpretation of this verse appears in the work of the Tunisian Islamic scholar al-Tahir ibn 'Ashur (1879–1973), *al-Taḥrīr wa al-Tanwīr* (*Verification and Enlightenment*, 1984). He applies a number of significant strategies: First, he begins the commentary on the verse with a lengthy passage featuring his own views and argument *before* citing the established traditional references. Second, he begins his commentary by linking 2:256 to the preceding verse 255 – the well-known *āyat al-kursī* (Throne Verse) – which constitutes the ultimate statement of God's oneness and supremacy and the very core of Muslim belief. Ibn 'Ashur notes that there is a logic of textual continuity: after this intensified yet clear identification of the basics of the doctrine in 2:255, verse 256 follows to affirm that people 'with sound minds and thinking' are bound to be guided towards this straight path 'by their choice without enforcement or coercion'.[42] However, because this religion is so manifest, but some nations and people still disbelieve, the question may arise: 'are they to be left in this condition or coerced to enter Islam?'[43] According to this new 'coherence-related'[44] approach that takes the textual context of verses (the flow of verses) into consideration, verse 2:256 is described by Ibn 'Ashur as an 'illustrative resumption' of thought, clarifying the right attitude to those who do not accept the doctrine, even after it is explained.[45] Then follows the familiar explanation that the negation of compulsion is in the form of a statement of fact, yet prohibitive in meaning. This grammatical form demonstrates that the prohibition of religious enforcement is meant to be generalized for 'all kinds of coercion'.[46]

Third, in tackling the issue of historicity, he presents a new point of view. If it had been decided in the early period to fight the idolaters (*mushrikūn*) in order to free Arabia from idolatry and establish monotheism, this verse apparently was revealed *after* the conquest of Mecca and the triumph of Islam. Now that the whole Arabian Peninsula had surrendered willingly to the sovereignty of religion, as huge tribal delegations marched to the Prophet in acceptance ('expressed by the term *dhimma*'), God's purpose had been achieved, namely 'saving the Arabs from idolatry, returning them to the original doctrine of Ibrahim, and purifying the Ka'ba from the disgrace/filth of the idolaters'.[47] From that time on, the truthfulness of Islam was made clear to all with no impediments or obstinacy, and a fine community of believers was formed and prepared to continue upholding this religion and protecting it. When all this was achieved, 'God abolished fighting with the aim of enforcing the religion (*al-qitāl 'ala al-dīn*) and upheld fighting for the expansion of its sovereignty'.[48] (Ibn 'Ashur thus differentiates, like 'Abduh, between religious creed and political dominance.) Hence, it is verse 2:256 that abrogates the previous verses of warfare, such as 66:9, not the opposite.[49] Here Ibn 'Ashur is the first to use the traditional hermeneutical method of abrogation introduced by the classical exegetes but to reverse its purpose by invalidating the jihad of forced conversion and highlighting the issue of the historicity of some Qur'anic injunctions.

In the following segment of the commentary, Ibn 'Ashur identifies three other kinds of related verses that mention fighting: (1) verses on defensive fighting that fends off aggression begun by the disbelievers, such as 2:194 and 9:36; (2) verses restricted by the particular aim of making others accept paying *jizya*; (3) the verse on fighting with the aim of preventing *fitna*, 2:193, which must be abrogated by 2:256 and the *jizya* verse.[50] Ibn 'Ashur does not explain his specific definition of *fitna* in this context, though the implication is that its time has been over since the triumph of Islam; nor does he dwell on the issue of dealing with non-Muslims and other religions, though again paying the tax seems to resolve the situation and prevent warfare. He quickly moves to citing a few of the previous views of the tradition and the occasions for revelation. As for the part of the verse that distinguishes between sound judgment and error, it operates as the 'cause' of 'no compulsion in religion', and so it 'has elaborated that statement'.[51]

The final work to consider is the standard and official 1978 edition of *al-Muntakhab fī Tafsīr al-Qur'ān al-Karīm*, a simplified and accessible commentary produced by the Higher Council of Islamic Affairs of Egypt and intended for the non-specialist average Muslim reader and user looking for a straightforward meaning or explication. It presents a brief paraphrase of the surface meaning of verse 2:256, stating that 'there is no forcing of anyone to enter into religion', and in a footnote makes a cross-reference to the commentary on the related verses of 2:190–5.[52] Thus, they are considered here as one unit or passage, as they comprise the whole range of the so-called 'fighting verses' that have been cited and discussed by successive exegetes from the start. Footnotes, in general, are rarely used in this work; however, a lengthy note to the first verse of the unit, 2:190 – which permits the believers to fight specifically 'those who fight against you' but not to transgress limits – provides an educational, detailed narrative of the preceding historical circumstances, which necessitated a change to a defensive *qitāl*. The passage begins with a refutation of the 'sword' accusation, showing how this particular verse, 2:190, contains the order not to initiate fighting until attacked, and how 22:39 mentions that 'permission is granted to those who are fought because they have been wronged'.[53] It goes on to present evidence of the different stages and events that early Muslims underwent and had to endure before the permission to fight: thirteen years of persecution in Mecca, the immigration to Ethiopia, expulsion and threats, attempts to murder the Prophet, boycott and starvation, and finally the immigration to Medina. Finally, the verses of 22:39–41 were revealed issuing a 'license to the Muslims to fight' as a result of the disbelievers' aggression and initiation of warfare – as is clearly stated and recorded within the verses themselves. As for the wars in Syria, again they were only in response to the violence initiated by the Ghassanid prince, Sharhabil bin ʿAmr, a follower of the Byzantines. Other than that, God ordered the Prophet to call/proselytize for Islam using wisdom, kind advice and appealing to people's minds (*al-ʿaql*), as well to dispute with the People of the Book gently.[54] The passage concludes with a reference to 2:256 as the most decisive verse in the matter. Hence, the interpretation avoids the hermeneutical technicalities of abrogation or the legal/political issues of paying the *jizya*, and misses the opportunity to articulate and develop a succinct discourse on the freedom of conviction in the modern world and the rights of non-Muslims.

Contemporary Muslim views

Especially since the beginning of the 2000s, Muslim thinkers and scholars have been under great pressure to address the globalized demands for freedom of religion, choice of conviction and tolerance, as well as to explain the religious concepts of jihad and apostasy. There have been many responses in the form of scholarship produced in both English and Arabic, revisiting and re-framing verses like 2:256, 10:99, 18:29 and 109:6. One of the earliest such responses is *The Place of Tolerance in Islam* (2002), a small and accessible volume in the form of a conversational roundtable, structured in three parts around a lead essay by Khaled Abou El Fadl, followed by eleven respondents' pieces and a final reply by Abou El Fadl. It is intended to be a simplified exposition of diverse approaches or points of view regarding the issue of tolerance and acceptance of religious plurality in Islam.

Abou El Fadl defines his main approach as one determined by both moral and historical guidance, in the sense of understanding many of the institutions and practices mentioned in the Qurʾan – such as the poll tax – in the light of the historical circumstances surrounding the revelation of the text. Secondly, a Qurʾanic discourse that clearly supports an ethic of diversity and tolerance does exist, and was missed or ignored by classical theologians, also due to their own pre-modern political culture and milieu: 'The classical commentators on the Qurʾan did not fully explore the implications of this sanctioning of diversity, or the role of peaceful conflict resolution in perpetuating the type of social interaction that would result in people "knowing each other."'[55] Though the Qurʾan accepts this human diversity – the plurality of religious beliefs and nations – and even though the Islamic civilization on the whole showed pluralistic and tolerant attitudes for its age, 'pre-modern Muslim scholars did not have a strong incentive to explore the meaning and implications of the Qur'anic endorsement of diversity and cross-cultural intercourse.' Abou El Fadl continues: 'This is partly because of the political dominance and the superiority of the Islamic civilization, which left Muslim scholars with a sense of self-sufficient confidence.'[56] He subjects the matters of jihad and *jizya* to an historical reading and also pays attention to the totality of the relevant Qur'anic injunctions, concluding that the Qur'an also prohibits unjust transgression and unlimited warfare and that the poll tax is not a fixed theological principle with the aim of subordinating or coercing the nonbeliever, but was only endorsed as a common historical practice and as a response to a specific set of circumstances.

This same Qur'an-centered reformist approach, critical of the classical jurists' imperialist orientation and intending to restore the original ethical message, was also argued by Gamal al-Banna (1920–2013), an Egyptian Islamic thinker and reformist, as early as 1977 in the forgotten publication *Ḥurriyyat al-I'tiqād fī al-Islām* (The Freedom of Conviction in Islam), which I have not been able to access. However, a 1998 pamphlet entitled 'The freedom of thought and conviction in Islam' was issued. Al-Banna cites and classifies Qur'anic verses according to a five-point argument against religious coercion: (1) faith and disbelief is a personal matter that does not allow intervention or enforcement; (2) prophets are only messengers sent to inform people about belief, with no coercive authority; (3) true spiritual guidance or enlightenment can come only from God; (4) difference and human diversity are part of the divine plan for this world, as Islam acknowledges the existence of past religions too, and God will be the judge in the Hereafter; (5) there is no worldly legal punishment (*ḥadd*) for apostasy.[57] He also enlists documented historical cases of persons who publicly abandoned the faith during the lifetime of the Prophet Muhammad, yet he left them alone.[58] In 2002, al-Banna published a separate book entitled *al-Jihād*, explaining and discussing all aspects of jihad as a theological and juristic concept as well as a historical phenomenon. Mention should also be made of Taha Jabir al-'Alwani's (1935–2016) more recent study of the issue of apostasy, that uses the first portion of verse 2:256 as part of the title: *Lā Ikrāh fī al-Dīn: Ḥadd al-Ridda fī al-Islām* (2006). An English abridged translation was made available in 2012.[59]

There is also abundant contemporary scholarship in English tackling this web of connected topics in the Islamic theological tradition and their relation to the international demands of human rights, personal freedoms, religious pluralism and multiculturalism, which cannot be covered here. Two significant items, though, should be mentioned: Abdul Aziz Sachedina's chapter on 'Freedom of religion and conscience' in his 2009 book, in which (like other contemporary reformists) he does not shy away from criticizing the mainstream traditionalist outlook on collapsing the political and the religious: 'Whereas the Qur'an treats the diversity of religions as a divinely ordained system, and the unification of all humanity under one confessional tradition as beyond any human power, the Islamic juridical tradition empowers Muslim governments to impose restrictions and discriminate against non-Muslim minorities by reducing them to second-class citizens.'[60] Second, there is Jerusha Lamptey's (2014) important study of the Islamic discourse on religious Otherness and her simultaneous attempt to construct an alternative theological conceptualization of religious difference and plurality, based on a reinterpretation and a close reading of the Qur'anic text.[61]

Conclusion

This has been a selected chronological outline of an idea – the prohibition of religious coercion – as it has occurred in Qur'anic exegetical works, and a consideration of the various interpretive voices and methods used to negotiate its related issues and contradictions. A certain development and variance in either emphasis on or disregard of particular dimensions of the argument can be discerned. From the beginning, however, there have been related issues and references in other verses that caused anxiety or a perceived contradiction for the exegetes and were almost always present in the context of interpreting verse 2:256, namely the fighting verses and the poll-tax. In order to make the verse consistent with these two main references, classical exegetes initiated the hermeneutical strategies of abrogation (*naskh*) and specification (*takhṣīṣ*); in other words, (1) using history to prioritize political goals over the fixed standard principle and to maintain the continuity of the expansion of Islam, rather than to acknowledge the historical contingencies of its early emergent period; (2) restricting and narrowing a generalized principle, so as to theologically fix and canonize the time-bound institution of the *jizya*. In other words, they eternalized what should have been subject to change and considered changeable what should have been a fixed guiding principle. Throughout, however, they never failed to include a discussion of the direct, essential meaning of freedom of belief (the verse in theory), before turning to the practicalities of their age.

Twentieth-century interpreters have mainly been driven by either defensive attitudes or reformist motives. They have aimed at reviving and applying the higher Qur'anic ethical criteria in modern contexts, while historicizing the textual commandments of both jihad and *jizya*, along with their traditional, outdated interpretations by classical theologians and jurists. We have seen the tendency, starting with Muhammad 'Abduh, either to argue for justifying the need for self-defensive confrontation in some cases or to reject the validity of abrogation that discards the essential principle of religious freedom. Both pre-modern and modern treatments of the subject matter show the influence of contemporaneous historical and political context on the interpreters' understanding, emphasis and conceptualizing of religious difference and freedoms.

Perhaps one can observe that present-day apostasy and blasphemy laws in Muslim countries that purport to be religious and Shari'a-based are a product of this historical development of politicization and a departure from the universal principle of the freedom of conscience and belief, especially since there is no Qur'anic legal punishment (*ḥadd*) for leaving Islam. A recent article that presents this disconnect between state laws, on one hand, and Qur'anic injunctions and *fiqh* nuances and flexibility, on the other, cites a survey showing that 70 per cent of nations in the Middle East and North Africa criminalize blasphemy, and that there is widespread social support for the death penalty for what is believed to be *ridda*.[62] However, recent posts on the official site of the Egyptian state religious institution Dar al-Ifta' al-Misriyya's official site feature notable expositions of the issue of punishable apostasy or *ridda*, which it defines, not as disbelief, but as either waging war against Muslims in order to separate them from their religion or a political offense against public order tantamount to treason. This is how 'executing apostates' is to be understood and applied. Hence, the matter falls under the domain of a ruler's authority (*waliyy al-ʿamr*) and is subject to administrative laws, not religious punishment. The posted piece also mentions the cases of apostasy that went unpunished in the time of the Prophet and the rightly guided caliphs.[63] Attempts at publicizing and disseminating such religious opinions can be a sign of a positive change in the discourse of religious institutions regarding this issue.

A more fundamental approach, and a means of getting out of this relativistic, fluid outlook shaped by the political context towards an Islamic conception that can be adopted in the post-modern age, is Abou El Fadl's project of building upon the core ethical criteria of the Qur'an as a corrective to the marginalization of these criteria by either legal and juristic technicalities or the historical practices of Muslim generations. 'In many ways', he argues,

> the Islamic principle of noncoercion was ahead of its time, and being a product of their historical contexts, premodern Muslims were not always able to live up to this ideal. . . .[D]uring the military expansion of Islam, every time there were forced conversions this represented a failure to live up to the Qur'anic ideal. . . .[I]t also ought to be admitted that the Islamic law of apostasy, which punishes conversions out of the faith by death, is a major failure and even a betrayal of the Qur'anic teachings.[64]

Indeed, several aspects of Qur'anic morality were ahead of their time in the seventh century, and so earlier generations of Muslims did not even come close to realizing their full moral potential. Hopefully, researching and sifting through the Islamic tradition with its diverse aspects and views will simultaneously enable a critical outlook and the re-construction of a knowledge that fulfils this potential of the original message.

Notes

1 Walid Saleh, 'Qur'anic commentaries', in Seyyid Hossein Nasr (ed.), *The Study Qur'an: A New Translation and Commentary* (New York: HarperOne, 2015), p. 1645.
2 Patricia Crone, 'No compulsion in religion: Q. 2:256 in medieval and modern interpretation', in M.A. Amir-Moezzi, M.M. Bar-Asher and S. Hopkins (eds), *Le shīʿisme imāmite quarante ans après: Hommage à Etan Kohlberg* (Turnhout, Belgium: Brepols, 2009), pp. 131–78.
3 Ibid., p. 161.
4 Saleh, 'Qur'anic commentaries', p. 1657.
5 Ibn Jarir al-Tabari, *Jāmiʿ al-Bayān ʿan Taʾwīl Āy al-Qurʾān*, 15 vols (Beirut: Dar al-Fikr, 1999), vol. 3, p. 21.
6 Ibid., p. 22.
7 Ibid., p. 23.
8 Ibid., p. 24.

9 Ibid., p. 25.
10 Ibid., p. 25.
11 Ibid., p. 25.
12 Ibid., p. 26.
13 Ibid., p. 31.
14 Muhammad ibn Ahmad ibn Juzayy al-Kalbi al-Gharnati, *al-Tashīl li-ʿUlūm al-Tanzīl*, 2 vols (Beirut: Dar al-ʿArqam, 1995), vol. 1, p. 132.
15 Mahmud ibn ʿUmar al-Zamakhshari, *al-Kashshāf*, 3 vols (Riyadh: Maktabat al-ʿUbaykan, 1998), vol. 1, p. 487.
16 All translations of Qurʾanic verses will be taken from Nasr, *The Study Qurʾan.*
17 Zamakhshari, *al-Kashshāf*, Vol. 1, p. 487.
18 Fakhr al-Din al-Razi, *al-Tafsīr al-Kabīr,* 30 vols (Cairo: Muʾassasat al-Matbuʿat al-Islamiyya, 1934), vol. 7, p. 14.
19 Ibid., p. 14.
20 Ibid., p. 15.
21 Al-Qurtubi, *al-Jāmiʿ li-Aḥkām al-Qurʾān*, 20 vols (Cairo: Dar al-Kutub al-Misriyya, 1936), vol. 3, p. 280.
22 Ibid., p. 281.
23 Nasir al-Din ibn ʿUmar al-Baydawi, *Anwār al-Tanzīl wa-Asrār al-Taʾwīl*, 2 vols (Cairo: Matbaʿat al-Halabi, 1968), vol. 1, p. 135.
24 Ibid., p. 134.
25 Ismaʿil ibn ʿUmar Ibn Kathir, *Tafsīr al-Qurʾān al-ʿAẓīm*, 8 vols (n.p.: Dar Tiba, 2002), vol. 1, p. 682.
26 Ibid., p. 683.
27 Nasr, *The Study Qurʾan*, p. 1391.
28 Ibn Kathir, *Tafsīr al-Qurʾān al-ʿAẓīm*, p. 683.
29 Mahmud al-Alusi, *Rūḥ al-Maʿānī,* 30 vols (n.p.: Dar Ihyaʾ al-Turath al-ʿArabi, n.d.), vol. 3, p. 13.
30 Muhammad ʿAbduh, *Tafsīr al-Manār*, 12 vols (Cairo: al-Hayʾa al-Misriyya al-ʿAmma lil-Kitab, 1973), vol. 3, p. 31.
31 Ibid., p. 31.
32 Ibid., p. 33.
33 Ibid., p. 33.
34 Nasr, *The Study Qurʾan*, p. 84.
35 Nasr, *The Study Qurʾan*, p. 492.
36 ʿAbduh, *Tafsīr al-Manār*, vol. 3, p. 33.
37 Ibid., p. 33.
38 Ibid., p. 34.
39 See for example: Stephane Dudoignon, Komatsu Hisao and Kosugi Yasushi (eds), *Intellectuals in the Modern Islamic World* (New York: Routledge, 2006).
40 Sayyid Qutb, *Fī ẓilāl al-Qurʾān*, 30 vols (Cairo: Dar Ihyaʾ al-Kutub al-ʿArabiyya, 1952), vol. 3, p. 13.
41 Ibid., p. 14.
42 Muhammad al-Tahir ibn ʿAshur, *al-Taḥrīr wa-al-Tanwīr*, 15 vols (n.p.: Dar Sahnun, n.d.), vol. 3, p. 25.
43 Ibid., p. 25.
44 See Nevin Reda, 'Holistic approaches to the Qurʾan: a historical background', *Religion Compass* 4/8 (2010), pp. 495–506.
45 Ibn ʿAshur, *al-Taḥrīr wa-al-Tanwīr*, vol. 3, p. 25.

46 Ibid., p. 26.
47 Ibid., p. 26.
48 Ibid., p. 26.
49 Notice how this interpretation is similar to, and almost builds on, the view of the Andalusian exegete, Ibn Juzayy al-Kalbi al-Gharnati, mentioned above.
50 Ibn ʿAshur, *al-Taḥrīr wa-al-Tanwīr*, vol. 3, p. 27.
51 Ibid., p. 28.
52 *Al-Muntakhab fī Tafsīr al-Qurʾān al-Karīm* (Cairo: al-Majlis al-Aʿla lil-Shuʾun al-Islamiyya, 1978), p. 61.
53 Ibid., p. 44.
54 Ibid., p. 44.
55 Khaled Abou El Fadl, *The Place of Tolerance in Islam*, ed. Joshua Cohen and Ian Lague (Boston: Beacon Press, 2002), p. 16. The reference is to verse 49:13.
56 Ibid., p. 16.
57 Gamal al-Banna, *Ḥurriyyat al-Fikr wa-al-Iʿtiqād fī al-Islām* (*Rasāʾil* series, no. 3) (Cairo: Dar al-Fikr al-Islami, 1998), pp. 7–16.
58 Ibid., pp. 22–23.
59 Taha Jabir Alalwani, *Apostasy in Islam: An Historical and Scriptural Analysis,* transl. Nancy Roberts (London; Washington: International Institute of Islamic Thought, 2011).
60 Abdulaziz Sachedina, 'Freedom of religion and conscience', in *Islam and the Challenge of Human Rights* (Oxford: Oxford University Press, 2009), p. 192.
61 Jerusha Tanner Lamptey, *Never Wholly Other: A Muslima Theology of Religious Pluralism* (Oxford: Oxford University Press, 2014).
62 Faisal Kutty, 'Blasphemy and Apostasy "Laws" in the Muslim World: A Critical Analysis', in Nadirsyah Hosen (ed.) *Research Handbook on Islamic Law and Society* (forthcoming), also available as Valparaiso University Legal Studies Research Paper No. 18-8 (September 14, 2018) at SSRN: https://ssrn.com/abstract=3249693. Kutty cites the survey by Pew Research Center, 'Beliefs about Sharia' (Pew Forum on Religion and Public Life, 30 April 2013), available at www.pewforum.org/2013/04/30/the-worlds-muslims-religion-politics-society-beliefs-about-sharia.
63 "The Reality of Apostasy in Islam." http://eng.dar-alifta.org/Foreign/ViewArticle.aspx?ID=101&text=apostasy. Accessed December 27, 2018.
64 Khaled Abou El Fadl, *Reasoning with God: Reclaiming Shari'ah in the Modern Age* (Lanham, MD: Rowman & Littlefield, 2014), p. 400.

3

al-Qadi ʿIyad's Defence of the Prophet and of Scholarly Tradition: *al-Shifāʾ*

Nora S. Eggen

Among the medieval scholars routinely referred to in contemporary debates on blasphemy and apostasy is the medieval judge and scholar, al-Qadi ʿIyad (d. 544 H/ 1149 CE).[1] In part four of his book *al-Shifāʾ bi-Taʿrīf Ḥuqūq al-Muṣṭafā* (The Healing in Knowing the Rights of the Chosen One),[2] ʿIyad discusses norms concerning individuals who denigrate or insult the Prophet. He holds that it is prohibited, and even a capital offense, to harm the Prophet by ridicule, derogation or insult. The book was widely disseminated, and it has been influential far beyond the temporal, geographical and doctrinal boundaries of this early twelfth-century Maliki scholar in the North African coastal city of Ceuta. In academic literature, the *Shifāʾ* has been construed in various ways. Tor Andræ (d. 1947) suggested in the early twentieth century a mystically inspired interpretative frame, while Annemarie Schimmel (d. 2003) indicated that the title of the book suggests that it has healing powers.[3] Tarif Khalidi has suggested that the title of the book hints at a pre-existing malady, an ignorance for which knowing or defining the truths or rights of the Chosen One is the healing remedy,[4] while Javier Albarrán Iruela highlights the importance of the *Shifāʾ* as a polemical text, addressing Christian views on prophethood as well as contested theological views internal to Islam.[5]

This chapter will revolve around the following questions: How are the discussions on insulting the Prophet framed in ʿIyad's *al-Shifāʾ*? How are the normative questions of beliefs, attitudes, and actions concerning him construed? And how can we understand this book in view of its historical context? To approach these questions, I situate al-Qadi ʿIyad in his time and place and his book *al-Shifāʾ* in its wider textual and intellectual context. ʿIyad lived and worked in times of turmoil, in a period of constant shifts between political fragmentation and consolidation in the Far West and the Iberian Peninsula, and in the transitional phase between the Almoravid and Almohad reigns. The Maliki-dominated scholarly establishment was to be replaced by new elites grounded in the personal authority of the Almohad founder Ibn Tumart, and I argue that ʿIyad's book is set within this context of competing views on spiritual, epistemic and political authority.[6]

Al-Qadi ʿIyad

Abu al-Fadl ʿIyad b. Musa b. ʿIyad b. ʿAmrun b. Musa b. ʿIyad b. Muhammad b. ʿAbd Allah b. Musa b. ʿIyad al-Yahsubi al-Sabti was born in 1083 into a notable and scholarly Arab family in Ceuta. His ancestors, who were of a Himyari Yemeni tribe, had migrated to the Andalusian city of Baza (Ar. Basta) and then moved to al-Qayrawan and Fez before settling in Ceuta around the turn of the fifth/eleventh century.[7] Ceuta (al-Sabta), situated on the northern coast of Africa straight across from Gibraltar, was in the medieval period a flourishing cultural and intellectual centre of political and military importance. Shortly after his takeover of the city in 1084, the Almoravid leader Yusuf b. Tashufin used Ceuta to enter and gain control of al-Andalus, which had been fragmented into city-state kingdoms after the fall of the unifying Caliphate of Córdoba in the early eleventh century. The Almoravids pledged allegiance to the ʿAbbasid caliph in Baghdad and sought to unify the legal framework with Maliki *fiqh*, which already had a long history in the region.[8]

ʿIyad received his training primarily at the hands of the local scholar Abu ʿAbd Allah al-Tamimi (d. 1111), whom ʿIyad praises highly.[9] ʿIyad studied the practical and theoretical skills of a *muḥaddith* and *faqīh* within Maliki jurisprudence, and by the age of thirty he went on a year's journey to al-Andalus (during 1113–14), sponsored by the Almoravid emir ʿAli b. Yusuf (r. 1106–43). There he met and studied with prominent scholars in Córdoba, Murcia, Almeria and Granada. Back in Ceuta, ʿIyad publicly disputed on Sahnun's (d. 854/5) *fiqh* manual *al-Kutub al-Mudawwana*, and he was thereafter appointed as member of the legal council (*shūra*). This was the customary stepping stone to judicial service, which he entered some seven years later, in 1121. He remained the chief qadi of Ceuta for fifteen years.

In 1136 ʿIyad served a period as qadi in Granada, but after a conflict with the local emir of Granada, Tashufin b. ʿAli,[10] he was dismissed from public service until 1145. At this point, the Almohad movement, the followers of the proclaimed Mahdi Ibn Tumart (d. 1130), had begun to seriously challenge Almoravid military, political and ideological dominion, a dominion which relatively recently had succeeded in consolidating Ifriqiya, al-Maghrib and al-Andalus into a unified zone in theological and legal terms.[11] ʿIyad was reappointed a judge in Ceuta in 1145 by the Almoravid emir Ibrahim b. Tashufin (r. 1145–7), when the Almohad movement had already gained control in some areas in the region. The next couple of years were full of drama. The Almoravid political leadership was weak, and ʿIyad may have served as the de facto ruler of Ceuta for a while.[12] The Almohads had gained control on both sides of the Mediterranean, and in 1146 Ceuta had to surrender. ʿIyad is reported to have sworn allegiance to the new rulers in a public sermon,[13] while other accounts suggest that he in this period brought the Almoravid emir Yahya b. al-Sahrawiyya from Algeciras in the hope of restoring Almoravid fortunes.[14] Nevertheless, when the capital Marrakech finally fell under Almohad rule the following year, ʿIyad was exiled there. Two years later he died, in a destitute state.[15]

Many scholars from the far Maghrib and al-Andalus passed through and spent time in Ceuta on their way to or back from the East. A chief judge and important personality in the city, ʿIyad met many of these travellers, learning from them, teaching them and exchanging views on different legal and scholarly issues. In his autobiographical catalogue (*fahrasa*) the *Ghunya* he describes how he met some scholars as they travelled through Ceuta, and others during one of his two sojourns in al-Andalus. There was also extensive written contact between ʿIyad and his fellow scholars in al-Andalus, not least Ibn Rushd al-Jadd (d. 1126),[16] as attested in the collection of his *fatāwā* recorded by ʿIyad's son and scholarly heir Muhammad.[17]

The *Shifāʾ*

ʿIyad wrote several books in fields such as jurisprudence, hadith and *ʿulūm al-ḥadīth,* as well as a biographical dictionary[18] and books on piety.[19] He was a scholar of some repute, but none of his other works attained the popularity of the *Shifāʾ*. More than twenty individuals are known to have heard this text read first hand from ʿIyad, and Muhammad al-Manuni identifies 22 different transmissions,[20] some even from doctrinally rival camps.[21] The transmitters included ʿIyad's son Muhammad and people from Ceuta, as well as people from different cities in the region, some of whom travelled east to Mecca and to cities such as Alexandria and Cairo.[22]

The *Shifāʾ* cannot be decisively dated. If the Andalusians heard the text read by ʿIyad in Andalus, he must have composed it either before his first trip in 1113–4 or before the second sojourn in Granada in 1136. But if they heard it from him in Ceuta, he may have composed it after 1136, which I will argue is likely. After having stepped down from public service, ʿIyad most likely spent the next decade writing and teaching. By now the turmoil in the region was about to reach its peak, with the Almoravid government weakened and the Almohad movement on the rise. ʿIyad, on the other hand, would at this point have had time on his hands, and most importantly, he would have reached the scholarly, intellectual and moral maturity necessary to write a work like the *Shifāʾ*, which brings together knowledge from a variety of fields and genres, and which weaves a comprehensive message serving different purposes: offering consolation to the faithful in troubled times, confirming and reinforcing them in their faith, reminding them of their proper guidelines and path, and disputing and polemicizing against groups and forces that threatened to undermine this path.

The *Shifāʾ* has been transmitted in writing in a large number of manuscripts.[23] It has been a valuable source for later works of *sīra* (life of the Prophet) and seems to have been the most common *sīra* manual in West Africa and the Bilad al-Sudan.[24] It likewise reached a variety of influential scholars, such as the Shafiʿi Ibn Hajar al-ʿAsqalani (d. 1449).[25] It was commented upon by dozens of later scholars from different schools and affiliations,[26] among others al-Suyuti (d. 1505), who concentrated on textual criticism.[27] Finally, the *Shifāʾ* was cited in the earliest extant works which were dedicated to the question of insults to the Prophet,[28] written respectively by the Hanbali scholar Ibn Taymiyya (d. 1328),[29] and the Shafiʿi Taqi al-Din al-Subki (d. 1355).[30] The *Shifāʾ* was widely disseminated in the Iberian Peninsula and was particularly important in Muslim–Christian polemics, as well as in the development of the *mawlid* as a practice of popular veneration.[31] Since the first printing in 1847 in Egypt,[32] a number of printed editions have appeared, as well as translations into English,[33] Urdu,[34] French[35] and Spanish,[36] and two recent abridged English editions.[37]

The title, structure and content of the *Shifā*ʾ

The title, 'The healing (*shifā*ʾ) in knowing (*taʿrīf*) the rights (*ḥuqūq*) of the chosen one (*al-muṣṭafā*)', suggests a link between knowledge, practice and redemption. The Chosen One is a common epithet for the Prophet Muhammad, as ʿIyad points out in his lengthy discussion of the names of the Prophet.[38] He connects the participle *muṣṭafā* to the cognate verb *iṣṭafā* and refers to the Qurʾanic notion of chosenness as a particular quality granted to the Prophet by God.[39] Later on ʿIyad cites a narration which places this chosenness within a genealogical framework: 'God chose the Kinana from the offspring of Ismaʿil, and chose Quraysh from the Kinana, and chose Banu Hashim from Quraysh, and chose me from the Banu Hashim.'[40] Notwithstanding the excellence (*faḍl*) of Muhammad, his chosenness is thus framed within a prophetic lineage that is both spiritual and genealogical. This lineage is in turn linked to the idea of a transhistorical light transferred from a primordial state through Adam and the prophets to Muḥammad.[41] The motif of the Muhammadan Light (*al-nūr al-muḥammadī*) is central to the image of the Prophet in the *Shifā*ʾ, and in the opening section ʿIyad introduces this idea by explaining the light of God in the Light Verse (*āyat al-nūr*, 24:35) as a blessed tree; a parable for the light of Abraham. However, in compliance with scholarly prudence, ʿIyad carefully states that there are other ways to understand this verse, and 'God knows best'.[42]

The *Shifā*ʾ consists of four parts, each with two to four chapters containing from five to thirty-five sections. In part one, almost half the book, ʿIyad elucidates the elevated standing of the Prophet and writes about his miracles. In part two he considers the duties of the believers towards the Prophet, including believing in him, following him, loving him, praying for him and visiting his grave. The topic of part three is the traits and characteristics of the prophets and the Prophet Muhammad in particular, with discussions on the concepts of infallibility (ʿ*iṣma*) and humanity (*bashariyya*). Finally, in part four, ʿIyad raises the issue of how to deal with those who denigrate (*tanaqquṣ*) or insult (*sabb*) the Prophet.

In his introduction, ʿIyad emphasizes part three as 'the secret of the book, and the essence of the fruits of these chapters. What precedes this part is principles, introductions and arguments for clarifying the points in it, and this governs what comes after it.'[43] In other words, ʿIyad posits the discussion of the infallibility of the Prophet as the pivotal point for the whole book, as what will make 'the reasonable person grant the Prophet his due', which points back to his rights (*ḥuqūq*): to be loved and followed (part two) and to be protected against insulters (part four).

ʿIyad's sources for the *Shifā*ʾ

As noted by Amira K. Bennison, ʿIyad 'represented the Maliki–Ashʿari synthesis that valued the authoritative literature of the Maliki school, but also accepted the merit of hadith study and *kalām* methods of argumentation.'[44] He was obviously very well versed in the relevant material. For most topics in the book he refers extensively to the Qurʾan, to narrations from the Prophet and the *ṣaḥāba*, and not least to viewpoints from earlier scholars. Among the most often cited *fuqahāʾ* in the *Shifāʾ* is Malik (d. 795) as transmitted in Sahnun's *al-Mudawwana*, but there are references to scholars of most *madhhabs* and affiliations, and ʿIyad often cites narrations to the same effect from such different sources. He frequently resorts to general references like 'the Andalusians' or 'the exegetes', and although some of the narrations are thoroughly documented, most of the time he neither verifies the narrations nor cites the *isnāds* in this book. This is somewhat surprising, in view of the fact that ʿIyad had read and worked extensively on hadith and hadith criticism.

In *Ikmāl al-Muʿlim fī Sharḥ Ṣaḥīḥ Muslim*, ʿIyad commented on the collection of Muslim (d. 875), and in the work *Mashāriq al-Anwār*, he commented on Malik's *Muwaṭṭa* and the *Ṣaḥīḥ* collections of al-Bukhari (d. 870) and Muslim. For the *Shifāʾ* he may have taken inspiration from a chapter on *dalāʾil al-nubuwwa* (proofs of prophecy) in al-Bukhari's collection. We also know from ʿIyad's *fahrasa* that he read al-Tirmidhi's (d. 892) *Shamāʾil al-Nabī*, which contains a very detailed account of the physical, personal and moral characteristics of the Prophet.[45] According to Ibn Khayr (d. 1179), ʿIyad wrote a *Kitāb Ikhtiṣār Sharaf al-Muṣtafā*, apparently an abridged version of a *Sharaf al-Muṣtafā* by Abu Saʿd al-Kharkushi (d. 1016).[46] These sources touch upon the central topics in the first half of the *Shifāʾ*, where ʿIyad details his doctrine on the Prophet: his standing with God, his personal characteristics pertaining to religion and to mundane affairs (*faḍāʾil dīniyya wa-dunyawiyya*), and his divinely granted miracles (*muʿjizāt wa-karamāt*) and power of blessing (*baraka*). With this lengthy theological argument for the Prophet Muhammad's outstanding position, ʿIyad prepared the reader for the next stage in his exposition: exhorting the believer to right conduct.

The rights of the Prophet: On faith, love and obedience

Conventionally invoking a readership request, ʿIyad presents the *Shifāʾ* as a response clarifying the standing (*qadr*) of the Prophet, the reverence (*tawqīr*) and respect (*ikrām*) he is entitled to, and the judgement (*ḥukm*) on those who fail to observe this.[47] Thus, ʿIyad's ambition in the book was not to verify historical facts or anchor them geographically. His biography addresses another level in the reading of the life of the Prophet, a reading in which the ethical value of history was highlighted. Rather than constructing a comprehensive collection of narratives, the narrative elements were evoked to serve as guides to moral conduct. In this endeavour, emphasis on love as a motivational force emerges as more central in the *Shifāʾ* than it had been in earlier *sīra* literature. Loving Muhammad, having faith in him and following his moral example are construed as interconnected and interdependent attitudes and actions.

Love is defined as an inclination towards what a human being finds agreeable either because of delight in perception of the object, or delight in mental apprehension of the virtue of the object, or because the object may offer a favour or benefaction. All these reasons combine to foster love for Muhammad.[48] ʿIyad then states that faith (*imān*) in the Prophet is obligatory and a prerequisite for Islam, with reference to the Qurʾan 48:13.[49] This faith consists in confirmation of his prophethood (*nubuwwa*) and messengerhood (*risāla*), by heart and tongue. ʿIyad goes far in equating *imān* and *islām*,[50] but goes on to distinguish between the two concepts in that faith is for God to evaluate in the hereafter, whereas in this life people are judged on what is apparent, *islām*, because 'man has no access to secrets, and he is not ordered to search for them'.[51] The obligation to follow the Prophet by following his Sunna is a necessary consequence of the obligation to faith, ʿIyad holds, with reference to the Qurʾan 8:20.[52] Obedience to the Prophet is obedience to God,[53] but following him is also a sign of true love, here with reference to the Qurʾan 3:31.[54] Love for the Prophet manifests itself in exalting him (*taʿẓīm*) and praying for him, which is obligatory without any temporal limitations,[55] and in visiting his grave, which is commendable.[56]

There is, however, no mention in the *Shifāʾ* of the celebration of the *mawlid* that would later become so popular, and which possibly represented a development towards a greater emphasis on ritual veneration. These festivities on the occasion of the birth of the Prophet are known from Fatimid North Africa in the eleventh or twelfth century, and they were introduced in the Far West by Abu al-ʿAbbas al-ʿAzafi (d. 1236) in Ceuta.[57] Marion Katz notes that ʿIyad is credited with one of the earliest *mawlid* texts: *Risāla Badīʿa fī Mawlid al-Nabī ʿAlayhi al-Salām wa-Ajdādihi wa-Miʿrājihi wa-Baʿḍ Muʿjizātihi*.[58] Underlying many *mawlid* texts emerging in the subsequent decades and centuries, according to Katz, is the kind of love for the Prophet which is described and prescribed in ʿIyad's *Shifāʾ*, although she emphasizes that she does not 'suggest that the *mawlid* genre was shaped specifically in view of the work of al-Qādī ʿIyāḍ', but that it does suggest a certain 'continuity and consistency in ideas about devotion to the Prophet'.[59] The *Risāla* is reportedly preserved in two manuscripts.[60] A preliminary study of one of these manuscripts reveals a versatile text, with content ranging from a linguistically oriented *tafsīr*, through a creation narrative clearly inspired by non-canonical textual material, to more conventional accounts of the birth, ascension into Heaven (*miʿrāj*) and death of the Prophet.[61] Although some of these topics are treated in the *Shifāʾ*, the manuscript does not appear to be a copy of parts of the *Shifāʾ*. The bibliographical sources do not mention this title,[62] and there is no evidence to corroborate that this late manuscript, dated 1001 H (1593 CE), is transmitted from a text from ʿIyad's hand, but it cannot be ruled out at this stage.

Mercedes García-Arenal argues that ʿIyad's writings, and in particular the way he identifies love of the Prophet with love of his family and descendants, had direct influence on the development of the *mawlid* as a practice of popular veneration; it was no coincidence, she states, that the practice was introduced in ʿIyad's city Ceuta at a time when the *shurafāʾ* (descendants from the Prophet) gained increased influence.[63] Exalting the Prophet (*taʿẓīm*) extended to honouring him after his death by faithfully transmitting his message. In this his family and followers were instrumental, and consequently honouring his family and followers as his outstandingly loyal and faithful heirs was in ʿIyad's view a way to honour the Prophet himself.[64] His family here includes his wives, descendants and immediate family (specified as the families of ʿAli, Jaʿfar, ʿAqil and al-ʿAbbas).[65] In this way ʿIyad contributed to the popularity of the 'house of the Prophet' in the Maghrib.[66] Additionally, the *Shifāʾ* was the most cited book in Morisco polemics, in which the motif of light, the miracles of the Prophet and the veneration of his descendants inspired ideas of a triumphal past and even of crypto-Islamic practices.[67]

Rights of the Prophet: On denigration and insult

In part four of the *Shifā'*, which makes up slightly less than one fifth of the text, 'Iyad deals with the issue of those who denigrate or insult God, the prophets and the Prophet Muhammad in particular and, by extension, his family and companions.[68] According to 'Iyad, there is no difference between the prophets in this matter, although most of the sources and examples given pertain to insults of Muhammad.[69]

The discussions start off from the Qur'anic condemnation of those who harm (*yu'adhūna*) God and His Prophet (33:57; 9:61; 33:53).[70] Such harm is done in a number of ways: by ridicule (*istihzā'*), exemplified by twisting of words to give them a denigrating meaning; by causing embarrassment (*al-izrā' bihi*), such as calling out to him by his nickname (*kunya*) and then telling him 'no, not you'; disrespectfully putting him on the spot (*ta'nītan lahu*) or belittling his rights (*istikhfāfan li-ḥaqqihi*); disgracing him (*'ābahu*); causing damage to him (*alḥaqa bihi*); derogation (*al-ghaḍḍ minhu*); or insult through improper similes (*tashbīh*).[71] Generally, the legal norm for these actions is prohibition (*taḥrīm*), and they are punishable by death, 'Iyad says. This also applies to related actions, such as cursing (*la'na*), swearing at him (*al-du'ā 'alayhi*) and mockery (*'abath*), foolishness (*sukhaf*) or obscene language (*hujr*).[72]

'Iyad attributes this view to a variety of early authorities, among them Ibn Mundhir (d. 930), al-Layth (d. 971), Ahmad (d. 855), Abu Bakr al-Siddiq (d. 634), Abu Hanifa (d. 767), al-Thawri (d. 778) and Ishaq b. Rahwayh (d. 853). He holds that the general norm for insults is grounded in both the Hanafi and Shafi'i, as well as the Maliki *madhhab*.[73] There is no discussion on insulting the Prophet in Malik's *Muwaṭṭa'*.[74] 'Abd Allah b. Wahb's (d. 812) recension of the *Muwaṭṭa'* includes a '*Kitāb al-muḥāraba*' which has a section on *sabb al-nabī*,[75] but there is no evidence to suggest that 'Iyad read this particular recension.[76] Among the earlier authorities 'Iyad refers to, there are Maliki scholars like Ibn al-Qasim (d. 806), Sahnun and Ibn Habib (d. 853).[77] The two latter also quote from Anas b. Malik, who is stated to have said that 'Whoever among the Muslims insults the Prophet will be killed, and he will not be asked to repent.'[78] In the entry on Ibn Habib in 'Iyad's bibliographical dictionary *Tartīb al-madārik*, a fuller quote is provided: 'Whoever kills, is killed; whoever insults God and his prophets, is killed; whoever changes his religion, is killed. . .'[79] But then 'Iyad goes on to say that there are those who do not prescribe capital punishment, and who hold that heavy imprisonment or beating will suffice. What is first presented as a categorical prescription, without quoting any sources, is modified in the next sentence, likewise without quoting any sources.

'Iyad draws on a vast repository of transmitted material, but in this context, he is not concerned with evaluating the material. He presents one alleged, but unverifiable, quote from the Prophet to support capital punishment for insult: 'Whoever insults a prophet, kill him and whoever insults my companion, hit him.'[80] Otherwise, 'Iyad's sources on this topic are scholarly tradition and interpretations of incidents in the life of the Prophet. He refers to a number of such incidents and discusses how the Prophet dealt with them, sometimes with strictness, as in the famous case of Ka'b b. al-Ashraf,[81] and at other times with lenience. In the case of a Jew who greeted the Prophet with a pun on the Qur'anic greeting: 'Death be upon you' (*al-sām ʿalaykum*), ʿIyad holds that this is no clear insult nor supplication, except with what naturally will befall all human beings.[82] ʿIyad does not seem to feel any need to explain the strict reactions, whereas he explains in more detail the reasons for lenience: the Prophet's wish to draw people close by showing forbearance and his reluctance to be seen as one who attacked his followers.[83] ʿIyad refers to a narrative according to which ʿA'isha said that the Prophet would only react harshly to attacks on the sanctity of God.[84] He would also distinguish between serious attacks and what he viewed as bad manners (*sū' adab*): words and actions spoken or done in ignorance or heedlessness, not intended to harm, although hurtful. However, there is no excuse for foul language about the Prophet, ʿIyad says, as one is held responsible for one's actions as long as one has not lost one's senses and there is no coercion involved.[85]

ʿIyad provides a detailed exposition of different circumstances and various views with regard to actual and hypothetical cases. He cites a whole host of scholars, not always clarifying his own position. But he seems to most often side with a general Maliki view, or what he presents as the majority opinion (*jumhūr*). According to him, scholarly consensus ordains capital punishment for the Muslim insulter, although he reports a difference of opinion as to whether it should be categorized as apostasy (*ridda*), concealed apostasy (*zandaqa*) or disbelief (*kufr*).[86] Later in the text, he specifies that it is to be classified as a *ḥadd* punishment, and the judgement is the same as for concealed apostasy, not as for disbelief.[87] This is the reason why a possible repentance is not taken into consideration. Insulting the Prophet is not like other private acts but a matter of public interest. Yet another view is that the insulter has effectively changed his religion through his behaviour, in which case the judgement for the insulter resembles the judgement for the apostate (*murtadd*), whom some scholars grant the option to repent, while others do not.[88]

ʿIyad emphasizes that there is no difference between prophets when it comes to the offence of insult, nor between angels.[89] Insulting Muhammad's family and companions is likewise forbidden and a crime, but not punishable by capital punishment,[90] with the exception of ʿA'isha; Malik is reported to have prescribed capital punishment for insulting her.[91] ʿIyad also touches upon the important question of the integrity of the Qur'an and specifically the *muṣḥaf* (the written and bound text), and he states that whoever disavows the Qur'an is considered an unbeliever, and reportedly he should be 'struck by the neck'.[92] In this connection he discusses the status of and judgement on an insulter who is a non-Muslim subject (*dhimmī*), in which there is an important distinction between insulting God and insulting his prophets. A Christian or a Jew who insults God is potentially subject to the same capital punishment as the Muslim,[93] but the non-Muslim who insults any of the prophets may escape punishment by repenting and embracing Islam.[94] ʿIyad warns against using inauthentic sources and against what he perceives as the distorted images of the Prophet presented by the *ahl al-kitāb*.[95] However, he does not discourage exploring the historical knowledge about the prophets, including their human traits and weaknesses, as long as the subject is treated with knowledge and wisdom.[96] For instance, ʿIyad says, being a herdsman is used as a denigrating description, although it was common practice among the Arabs as well as earlier prophets.[97] Likewise, being unlettered is considered a shortcoming in other people, but in the Prophet, it is a divine sign.[98]

Legal discourse and practice

The *Shifā*ʾ neither represents nor replaces formal legal discourse. ʿIyad assembles many viewpoints and often repeats the arguments several times, but decisive conclusions on the different questions he raises are seldom presented in part four of the book, other than in broad terms. The discussions on insult refer to historical cases, although in a theoretical manner. Of the known legal cases dealing with charges of blasphemy or insult to the Prophet in al-Maghrib and al-Andalus, none refer to ʿIyad's courtroom,[99] and in the fatwas collected by his son Muhammad, insult is a minor topic. The collection contains two fatwas dealing with insult, both in the chapter on *ḥudūd* punishments. One deals with someone abusing (*shatm*) a virtuous and learned person, which warrants punishment without further specification.[100] The other deals with the case of a non-Muslim subject belittling (*istakhaffa*) the Prophet, the Muslims or their Book. ʿIyad refers to the opinion of his Andalusian contemporary, Muhammad b. Ismaʿil (Ibn Furtish, d. 1136),[101] who holds that such a person should be imprisoned for scrutiny and then receive capital punishment.[102] Ibn Furtish served as judge in turbulent times in Zaragoza until the definite Christian reconquest of the town (1118), after which he transferred to Granada. The short text does not give us any contextual evidence, but a political backdrop for Ibn Furtish's fatwa is certainly plausible. Ibn Rushd did treat the same issues,[103] but although ʿIyad constantly refers to his fatwas, he does not do so in these particular cases.

In ʿIyad's biographical work, *Tartīb al-Madārik*, there are a few references to the question of insult. There is for instance an uncorroborated narrative about a certain al-Marawidi who was imprisoned for insulting the Prophet, and ʿIyad tells us that at a certain point insulting the Prophet was a widespread practice in Qayrawan.[104] In the *Shifā*ʾ, ʿIyad refers to some better substantiated historical cases. One case is that of Ibn Hatim al-Tulaytuli who was sentenced for 'belittling the rights of the Prophet' (in al-Andalus, between 1064 and 1072).[105] In the second case, the Qayrawanians sentenced the poet and polymath Ibrahim al-Fazari for 'ridiculing God, his prophets and our Prophet'.[106] In a third case, that of Harun b. Habib during the reign of ʿAbd al-Rahman II (822–52), there was difference of opinion both as to whether the words spoken could amount to insult, whether the witnesses were sufficient in number, and about his health condition.[107] These historical cases show that the personal integrity and authority of the Prophet had been attacked in the Islamic West, and that some such attacks had resulted in legal judgements.[108] Janina M. Safran suggests that it was these events that raised the interest and more elaborate debate on blasphemy in Maliki circles in the ninth century.[109] This may have helped spur ʿIyad to write a book in defence of the Prophet. But all the cases date from one to several centuries back in time. ʿIyad suggests that the contemporary attitude towards insult to the Prophet was rather lenient, but he signals a new urgency in his particular historical situation: 'Today we are not allowed this forbearance with them over [insulting] him.'[110] I consider this statement vital to a contextual understanding of his work.

Socio-political context and possible functions of the text

The *Shifāʾ* is often considered a text of *al-sīra al-nabawiyya*. But, as Tarif Khalidi holds, it represents a new development in this vast literary field.[111] Khalidi sees ʿIyad as a representative and a founding father of an Andalusian group of writers who gave new shape and content to the *sīra*. Earlier biographers such as Ibn Saʿd (d. 845), specialized historians such as Ibn Ishaq (d. 768), Ibn Hisham (d. 833) and al-Wakidi (d. 822/3), as well as writers of universal history such as al-Baladhuri (d. 892) and al-Tabari (d. 923), had collected a body of accumulated narratives. In the subsequent centuries, this corpus was subjected to critical assessment, and different kinds of textual materials were selected from it to fit into new interpretative frames and serve new ends. In the ninth through eleventh centuries, proofs of prophecy had become more important than imperial history. Superhuman qualities like miraculous powers and sinlessness were asserted in order to fortify the faith, yet at the same time, the Prophet remained humanly imitable as an object of love and devotion.[112] Khalidi emphasizes the cosmological framework of ʿIyad's portrait of an eternal prophet.[113] Even though ʿIyad positions himself in the theological debates on questions such as miracles, and selects from the pool of historical materials to serve his purposes, Khalidi sees the *Shifāʾ* primarily as a tribute of love, where the Prophet is portrayed as the miraculous prophet, the moral paragon, the supreme object of love.[114] Khalidi's approach is to read the *Shifāʾ* in view of a particular literary tradition, but situating the book in its historical context may offer a different perspective. ʿIyad clearly speaks *to* his fellow believers, admonishing and inspiring them, but whom is he speaking *against*?

As we have seen, ʿIyad is speaking against non-believers, nominal believers he considers to be hypocrites and believers on the wrong path.[115] If any of these were to insult the Prophet, the case would be clear. Tantamount to insulting the Prophet are also subtler and less clear-cut actions, such as trying to elevate oneself or others (*al-tarfīʿ li-nafsihi aw li-ghayrihi*) through comparisons with the Prophet, not in the praiseworthy sense of emulating his Sunna, but in the sense of claiming for oneself some of his unique characteristics. In ʿIyad's view, this amounts to denigration or insult.[116] As argued above, I suggest that the *Shifāʾ* was written in the late 1130s or early 1140s, when the Almohad movement was gaining momentum, among a series of other theologically and politically oppositional movements. As Linda Jones suggests, although ʿIyad writes about the poets in this context, 'his real target was probably the cult surrounding the founder of the Almohads, Ibn Tumart'.[117]

Ibn Tumart had done more than compare himself to the Prophet; he had ventured to surpass the Prophet by describing himself as a cosmic pole (*al-ʿamūdu*), holding up the heavens and the earth.[118] The sources do not decisively resolve the question of whether Ibn Tumart proclaimed himself the infallible Mahdi or was proclaimed so by his followers, but at the very least he prepared the way for such a proclamation.[119] The term Mahdi had a wide range of usages: the excellent example, the religio-political leader and the revolutionary and apocalyptic Mahdi proclaiming the beginning of a new area and heralding the coming of the Day of Judgement (*al-qāʾim*), and Ibn Tumart was considered to be the latter type.[120] Although the terminology differs slightly, the imaginary recalls both Shiʿi discourse of the sinless Mahdi who will arise (*mahdī ma'ṣūm* and *qā'im*) and Sufi discourse of the Pole (*quṭb*), without Ibn Tumart subscribing to any of those traditions in theological or legal terms. He likewise rejected Ash'ari doctrine on the Imamate,[121] disowned the traditional Maliki heritage and prescribed direct engagement with foundational sources: the Qur'an and the Sunna. Thus, the Almohad period has been perceived as bringing a renewed interest in rational and empirical thinking. However, Ibn Tumart also had esoteric orientations, and the emphasis on human reasoning, paired with a notion of mystical knowledge, enabled him to carve out for himself a space of absolute authority.[122] This legacy was carefully passed on. Whereas Ibn Tumart was proclaimed *al-mahdī al-ma'lūm* and *al-imām al-ma'ṣūm*, his successor from 1130, 'Abd al-Mu'min, took the title *khalīfa*, and became the first Almohad caliph (r. 1147–63). 'Abd al-Mu'min thus terminated the Almoravid allegiance to the 'Abbasids, sought a break with the Maliki-dominated tradition in the legal as well as the political field, and established a new elite, the *ṭalaba*, meant to replace the traditional Maliki *'ulamā'* and become institutional preservers of the Almohad doctrine.[123]

Epistemic authority, judicial reasoning and infallibility

This break with the Maliki-dominated tradition had implications for the very crucial question of interpretational and epistemic authority, which is an underlying topic throughout the *Shifā'* and is dealt with above all in 'Iyad's discussion on revelation (*waḥy*), infallibility (*'iṣma*),[124] and judicial reasoning (*ijtihād*). *Ijtihād* as a method for normative argumentation and reasoning pertains to the field of presumption (*ẓann*), allowing for disagreement and opposing views, and the question of whether the Prophet performed *ijtihād* or not is linked to the relationship between human reasoning and revelation as well as the status of prophetic versus non-prophetic moral and epistemic authority. The later legal scholar al-Shawkani (d. 1839) sums up the many scholarly discussions on the issue of *ijtihād* of the prophets by first distinguishing between questions pertaining to mundane needs (*maṣāliḥ al-dunyā*) and normative and religious questions (*al-aḥkām al-shar'iyya wal-umūr al-dīniyya*).[125] With regard to the first type of questions, the scholars unanimously agree that the prophets performed *ijtihād*. With regard to the second type, however, there is a difference of opinion. One group holds that the prophets did not perform *ijtihād*, because they had access to certain knowledge through revelation (*li-qudratihim 'alā l-naṣṣ bi-nuzūl al-waḥy*). However, al-Shawkani held that according to the majority of scholars, the Qur'anic statement that what the Prophet received was revelation (53:4), only applied to the Qur'an; there was textual evidence that the Prophet actually exercized *ijtihād*, but in a qualitatively different way from others, in view of the infallibility of the Prophet *qua* prophet.

This is the view adopted by 'Iyad in the *Shifā'*. He holds that the metanorm asserting the uniqueness of legal truth (*al-ḥaqqu fī ṭarafin wāḥid*) was valid in the time of the Prophet only,[126] and thus the question of infallibility was vital to 'Iyad's project of constructing and maintaining a scholarly tradition.[127] The *'iṣma* of the prophets protected Muhammad and placed him in a separate and unique position in questions pertaining to theology, and his *ijtihād* on mundane questions would be sanctioned by revelation in his lifetime. As revelation ended with the Prophet, so did this unique access to final truths, according to ʿIyad. Consequently, with regard to all subsequent, post-prophetic normative thought, ʿIyad subscribed to the metanorm of multiplicity of legal truths (*taṣwīb al-mujtahidīn*). ʿIyad does not specify who his opponents are in this question, but as Maribel Fierro holds, he may well have directed this statement at Ibn Tumart, who had rejected the possibility of there being more than one valid answer to a normative question, and who had claimed this absolute interpretational and epistemic – and by extension, political – authority for himself.[128] ʿIyad had dedicated his life to scholarly work, both as a *muḥaddith*, a jurist, a judge and a teacher; and to a scholarly tradition, not least as a biographer consolidating the Maliki scholars in his immense *Tartīb al-Madārik*. Fierro argues that the *Shifāʾ* and the *Madārik* complement each other and together contribute to the defence of the prophecy of Muhammad and of his heritage, mounted by the *ʿulamāʾ* according to the Sunni point of view, against the early Almohad rejection of the Maliki teachings and the traditional religious elites.[129]

Similarly opposed to the Almoravids, but doctrinally different from Ibn Tumart's followers and their rivals in politics, were groups with mystical and esoteric leanings that emerged around Ibn Barrajan (d. 1141) and his younger associate Ibn al-ʿArif (d. 1141).[130] Ibn Barrajan was a traditional Sunni *muḥaddith* and *mufassir* whose writings at the turn of the twelfth century took a drastic turn toward mysticism. Ibn Barrajan claimed a spiritual authority that indicated a pre-eminence over the political leadership and sought to supersede the traditional scholarship he himself was part of.[131] Chiefly operating in Seville, these Sufi movements were also distinctively anti-Almoravid. The conflict with the Almoravid ruler eventually caused Ibn Barrajan and Ibn al-ʿArif to be summoned to emir ʿAli b. Yusuf's court in Marrakech, where they were accused of innovation in religious matters (*bidʿa*), and where they both died under unclear circumstances in 1141.[132]

There is no known evidence that ʿIyad met Ibn Barrajan or Ibn al-ʿArif, and he was not one of the scholars at court involved in the hearing against them. There is, however, evidence to suggest that he had written contacts with Ibn al-ʿArif,[133] although the nature and topics of this written contact is not known. Ibn al-ʿArif was originally from Ceuta, but he moved to Almeria at an early stage in life. He was a traditionalist Sufi and had studied among others with al-Sadafi,[134] with whom ʿIyad had also studied.[135] ʿIyad's life and teachings were imbued with pious ideals (*zuhd*). These two rival movements were, however, not only leaning towards traditionalist piety, they were also given to the more esoterically oriented paths of the Sufi traditions and they often opposed the Maliki scholars.[136] As José Bellver suggests, to the Almoravids, the Sufi movements were not perceived as a political threat in the same way that the ardent Almohads were.[137] Ibn Barrajan and Ibn al-ʿArif had some, albeit loose, connections to a more explicitly political figure, Ibn Qasi (d. 1151).[138] Like Ibn Tumart's movement, the Sufi movements have been described as Mahdist,[139] and Ibn Qasi proclaimed himself Mahdi in 1144, in the revolt of the Muridun in the Algarve. This revolt was defeated, and Ibn Qasi later paid allegiance to the Almohad rulership.[140]

Concluding remarks

In view of the content and reception of the *Shifāʾ*, construing it solely as a polemical writing may seem reductionist. As demonstrated above, the readership of the *Shifāʾ* has extended far beyond ʿIyad's fellow Malikis, and the work has been cited and referred to in diverse discourses. The book celebrates the Prophet and calls for the protection of his heritage. ʿIyad presents a comprehensive argument on the impeccability of the Prophet and the centrality of his person to faith and practice. Safeguarding the integrity of Prophet becomes equal to safeguarding the integrity of the faith, and ʿIyad holds that it must be upheld by the strictest possible means, including the threat of capital penalty for violations. Although his descendants are granted a certain privilege, the Prophet remains unique in terms of spiritual and epistemic authority. However, this understanding of the Prophet and his privileged position is grounded in scholarly discourse throughout. Traditional scholarly authority is evoked, and, I argue, advocated.

In the years of turmoil following Ibn Tumart's death, before the Almohad success was complete, and amid the threatening although ultimately unsuccessful moves of Ibn Barrajan's movement, ʿIyad's purpose in writing the *Shifāʾ* may have been to build an intellectual Sunni bulwark against what he perceived as dangerous forces: forces threatening to compromise Maliki, and by extension Sunni, doctrine; to disintegrate the Almoravid political order and the unity with the ʿAbbasid rulership; and to destabilize the hegemony of traditional scholarship. To this end, he formulated mystical elements of the faith, the miracles of the Prophet and the love for him, within the framework of an inclusive scholarly learning surpassing his own Maliki affiliation. The vehement protection of the integrity of the Prophet put forward in the *Shifāʾ*, in addition to being devotional, also serves the function of defending the value of scholarly tradition and production of knowledge, and thus of defending ʿIyad and his intellectual peers against decreasing authority and prestige. To this end, the *Shifāʾ* manifests itself as a combined tribute to the Prophet and a defence of traditional scholarly learning, and somewhat paradoxically, as a polemic against the esoterically based spiritual authority and reliance on rationality that paved the way for the authoritarian and exclusivist truth claims of the Almohads.

Notes

1 ʿIyad was for instance referenced by the former Saudi Chief Mufti ʿAbd al-ʿAziz b. Baz (d. 1999): Mark S. Wagner, 'The problem of non-Muslims who insult the Prophet Muḥammad', *Journal of the Americal Oriental Society* 135/5 (2015), pp. 529–40, at p. 531. Reference has also been made to ʿIyad and Ibn Taymiyya's work by Al Qaeda/ISIS-affiliated individuals, e.g. in connection with the Danish cartoon controversy 2005–2006: *Usama bin Ladin, al-Arshīf al-Jāmiʿ lil-Kalimāt wa-Khaṭabāt Imām al-Mujāhidīn Usāma bin Muḥammad bin Lādin* (2006), Jihadi Document Repository at FFI/UiO, Oslo, p. 295. This has led others to insist that this reading is not valid today and that neither ʿIyad nor Ibn Taymiyya sanctioned terrorism or the death penalty outside of a strictly legal order: Rashad Ali, *Blasphemy, Charlie Hebdo, and the Freedom*

of Belief and Expression (London: Institute for Strategic Dialogue, February 2015), available at http://www.strategicdialogue.org/publications (accessed 17 May 2016).

2 Abu l-Fadl ʿIyad bin Musa bin ʿIyad al-Yahsubi, *al-Shifāʾ bi-Taʿrīf Ḥuqūq al-Muṣṭafā lil-Qādī ʿIyāḍ*, ed. ʿAli Muhammad al-Bajawi, 2 vols (Beirut: Dar al-Kitab al-ʿArabi, 1984).

3 Annemarie Schimmel, *And Muhammad is his Messenger: The Veneration of the Prophet in Islamic Piety* (Chapel Hill, NC and London: The University of North Carolina Press, 1985), p. 33. Schimmel refers to Tor Andræ's influential work on Muhammad in Islamic piety, in which he argued that the *Shifāʾ* was a main source for later treatments on the topic of Muhammad's miraculous powers, and also asserted that the *Shifāʾ* was considered to have such miraculous power in its own right: Tor Andræ, *Die person Muhammeds in Lehre und Glaube seiner Gemeinde* (Stockholm: Norstedt, 1918), p. 60.

4 Tarif Khalidi, *Images of Muhammad: Narratives of the Prophet in Islam Across the Centuries* (New York: Doubleday, 2009), p. 209.

5 Javier Albarrán Iruela, *Veneración y polémica: Muḥammad en la obra del Qāḍī ʿIyāḍ* (Madrid: Ediciones de la Ergástula, 2015).

6 This perspective is inspired by my on-going work on ʿIyad's autobiographical catalogue *al-Ghunya*, and by Maribel Fierro's article 'El tratato sobre el profeta del Cadi ʿIyāḍ y el context almohade', in Raif Georges Khoury, Juan Pedro Monferrar-Sala and María Jesús Viguera Molins (eds), *Legendaria Medievalia: En honor de Concepción Castillo Castillo* (Cordoba: Ediciones El Almendro, 2011), pp. 19–34.

7 On ʿIyad's life and work, see M. Talbi, 'Introduction', in [al-Qadi ʿIyad], *Tarājim aghlabiyya mustakhrija min madārik al-qāḍī ʿIyāḍ/Biographies aghlabides: Extraites des Madārik du Cadi ʿIyāḍ*, ed. Muhammad al-Ṭalbi (doctoral thesis, Tunis: Université de Tunis, 1968); Camilo Gómez-Rivas, 'Qāḍī ʿIyāḍ (d. 544/1149)', in Oussama Arabi, David Stephan Powers and Susan Ann Spectorsky (eds), *Islamic Legal Thought: A Compendium of Muslim Jurists* (Leiden: Brill, 2013), pp. 323–38; Camilo Gómez-Rivas, *Law and the Islamization of Morocco under the Almoravids: The Fatwās of Ibn Rushd al-Jadd to the Far Maghrib* (Studies in the History and Society of the Maghrib) (Leiden: Brill, 2014); M. Talbi, 'ʿIyāḍ b. Mūsā', in P. Bearman, Th. Bianquis, C.E. Bosworth, E. van Donzel and W.P. Heinrichs (eds), *Encyclopaedia of Islam,* 2nd ed., (Leiden: Brill), available through Brill Online at www.brillonline.nl (accessed 2 September 2014).

8 On the history of formation and consolidation of Maliki law in North Africa and al-Andalus, see Christopher Melchert, *The Formation of the Sunni Schools of Law: 9th-10th Centuries C.E.* (Leiden: Brill, 1997), pp. 156–63; Yasin Dutton, *The Origins of Islamic Law: The Qurʾān, the Muwaṭṭaʾ and Madinan ʿAmal* (Surrey, UK: Curzon, 1999); Umar F. Abd-Allah Wymann-Landgraf, *Mālik and Medina: Islamic Legal Reasoning in the Formative Period* (Leiden: Brill, 2013).

9 ʿIyad b. Musa, *al-Ghunya: Fihrist Shuyūkh al-Qāḍī 'Iyāḍ*, ed. Mahir Zuhayr Jarrar (Beirut: Dar al-Gharb al-Islami, 1982), 27–46. Here ʿIyad listed and described his own intellectual pedigree. The *Ghunya* is the earliest account we have of ʿIyad's life and work, together with a biographical account that his son wrote about his father; Muhammad b. ʿIyad, *al-Taʿrīf bil-Qāḍī ʿIyāḍ*, ed. Muhammad b. Sharifa (Rabat: Wizarat al-Awqaf wal-Shuʾun al-Islamiyya, 1982). The *fahrasa,* a rather formalized biographical or autobiographical catalogue of scholarly learning, was a genre of growing popularity in this period, cf. ʿAbd al-Aziz al-Ahwani, 'Kutub barāmij al-ulamāʾ fī l-Andalus', *Majallat Maʿhad al-Makhṭūṭāt al-ʿArabiyya / Revue de l'institut des manuscrits árabes* 1/1 (1955), pp. 91–120; ʿAbd al-Hayy b. ʿAbd al-Kabir al-

Kattani, *Fihras al-Fahāris wal-Athbāt wa-Muʿjam al-Maʿājim wal-Mashaykāt wal-Musalsalāt* (Beirut: Dar al-Gharb al-Islami, 1982).

10 Tashufin b. ʿAli was later to become Almoravid emir between 1143 and 1145.

11 Amira K. Bennison, *The Almoravid and Almohad Empires* (Edinburgh: Edinburgh University Press, 2016), pp. 241–2.

12 The historical evidence is not decisive on this point. The rulership is argued in Hanna E. Kassis, 'Qadi Iyad's Rebellion against the Almohads in Sabtah (A.H. 542–543/A.D. 1147–1148): New Numismatic Evidence', *Journal of the American Oriental Society* 103/3 (1983), pp. 504–14. The theory is discussed in Maribel Fierro, 'Sobre monedas de época almohade: I. El dinar del Cadí ʿIyāḍ que nunca existió. II. Cuándo se acuñaron las primeras monedas almohades y la cuestión de la licitud de acuñar moneda', *al-Qanṭara* 27/2 (2006), pp. 457–76.

13 Linda G. Jones, "A Case of Medieval Political 'Flip-Flopping'? Shifting Allegiances in the Sermons of al-Qāḍī ʿIyāḍ," in Franco Moranzoni (ed.), *Preaching and Political Society from the Late Antiquity to the End of the Middle Ages* (Turnhout, Belgium: Brepols, 2013), pp. 65–110.

14 Maribel Fierro, 'The Almohads (524–668/1130–1269) and the Ḥafṣids (627–932/1229–1526)', in Maribel Fierro (ed.), *The New Cambridge History of Islam*, Vol. 2, *The Western Islamic World Eleventh to Eighteenth Centuries* (Cambridge: Cambridge University Press, 2010), pp. 66–104 at pp. 71–2; Bennison, *Almoravid and Almohad*, p. 73.

15 Ibn ʿIyad, *al-Taʿrīf*, p. 113.

16 Delfina Serrano Ruano, 'Ibn Rushd al-jadd (d. 520/1126)', in Oussama Arabi, David Stephan Powers and Susan Ann Spectorsky (eds), *Islamic Legal Thought: A Compendium of Muslim Jurists* (Leiden: Brill, 2013), p. 295–322.

17 Muhammad Ibn ʿIyad, *Madhāhib al-Ḥukkām fī Nawāzil al-Aḥkām*, ed. Muḥammad b. Sharīfa (Beirut: Dar al-Gharb al-Islami, (1990/1997). See also Spanish translation in Muhammad Ibn ʿIyad, *Madhāhib al-Ḥukkām fī Nawāzil al-Aḥkām (La actuación de los jueces en los procesos judiciales)* (Fuentes arábico-hispanas 22), transl. Delfina Serrano (Madrid: Agencia Española de Cooperación Internacional, 1998).

18 Al-Qadi ʿIyad, *Tartīb al-Madārik wa-Taqrīb al-Masālik li-Maʿrifat Aʿlām Madhhab Mālik*, ed. Muḥammad Bin Tawit al-Ṭanji (vol. 1), ʿAbd al-Qadir al-Ṣahrawi (vol. 2–4), Muhammad Bin Sharifa (vol. 5) and Saʿid ʾAhmad ʾAʿrab (vol. 6–8) (Rabat: Wizarat al-Awqaf wal-Shuʾin al-Islamiyya, 1983). See Gómez-Rivas, 'Qāḍī ʿIyāḍ', for translation of an extract, and see a fuller discussion of the work in the introduction to al-Ṭalbi, *Tarājim Aghlabiyya*. For the *Madārik* as a source for Maliki thought, see Dutton, *The Origins of Islamic Law*; Wymann-Landgraf, *Mālik and Medina*.

19 See a comprehensive survey over extant and lost works in Hasan Waragili, *Abū al-Faḍl al-Qāḍī ʿIyāḍ al-Sabtī* (Beirut: Dar al-Gharb al-Islami, 1994), pp. 19–25, and a short overview in Gómez-Rivas, 'Qāḍī ʿIyāḍ'. See also the HATA databases under the direction of Maribel Fierro, at http://kohepocu.cchs.csic.es/.

20 Muhammad al-Manuni, 'Kitāb al-shifā lil-qāḍī ʿIyāḍ min khilāl ruwātihi wa-riwāyātihi', *al-Manāhil* 22 (1982), pp. 305–423 at pp. 313–40.

21 For instance, a famous linguist often associated with the Zahiri school and a qadi close to the Almohad rulership, Ibn Madaʾ (592/1196), read the *Shifāʾ* when he studied hadith with ʿIyad in Ceuta, and he passed it on (al-Manuni, 'Kitāb al-shifā', pp. 309, 322).

22 One of the transmitters instrumental in spreading the *Shifāʾ* was the Andalusian travelling scholar and man of letters Ibn Jubayr (d. 1217), who had heard it in Ceuta in 1183 before he travelled east. On the way, he read the *Shifāʾ* to a number of people who in turn passed it on widely. Muhammad al-Manuni, 'Riwāya mashriqiyya li-kitāb

al-Shifāʾ min ṭarīq al-raḥḥala al-andalūsī Abī l-Ḥusayn b. Jubayr', *al-Manāhil* 19 (1980), pp. 392–9 at p. 393.

23 Al-Manuni registered 37 manuscripts ('Kitāb al-shifā', pp. 342–62) and ʿAli Muhammad al-Bajawi, who investigated the holdings in the Egyptian al-Azhar and Dar al-Kutub, says he 'never saw anything like the numbers of manuscripts for this book', respectively 49 and 4 manuscripts (ʿIyad, *al-Shifāʾ*, Introduction, p. 15). The HATA databases list more than 200 manuscripts (http://kohepocu.cchs.csic.es, Section 5: Ascetismo Mistica, pp. 118–126).

24 Ousmane Oumar Kane, *Beyond Timbuktu: An Intellectual History of Muslim West Africa* (Cambridge, MA: Harvard University Press, 2016), p. 86.

25 Al-Manuni, 'Kitāb al-shifā', p. 318.

26 See a comprehensive list in Badri Muhammad Fahd, 'Kitāb *al-shifāʾ* bi-taʿrif ḥuqūq al-muṣṭafā', *al-Manāhil* 19 (1980), pp. 488–535 at pp. 527–34.

27 Jalal al-Din al-Suyuti, *Manāhil as-Safāʾ fi Takhrīj Aḥādīth al-Shifāʾ bi-Taʿrīf Ḥuqūq al-Muṣṭafā lil-Qāḍī ʿIyāḍ* (Beirut: Muʾassasa l-Kutub al-Thaqafiyya; Dar al-Jinan, 1988).

28 ʿIyad mentioned in his *Tartīb al-Madārik* that Muhammad b. Sahnun (d. 870) wrote a *Risāla fi-man Sabba al-Nabī* (ʿIyad, *Tartīb al-Madārik*, Vol. 4, p. 207). This work is apparently lost.

29 Ibn Taymiyya cites ʿIyad in several instances. Ibn Taymiyya, *al-Ṣārim al-Maslūl ʿalā Shātim al-Rasūl*, ed. Muhammad b. ʿAbd Allah b. ʿUmar al-Halwani and Muhammad Kabir Ahmad Shawdari (Dammam: Ramadi lil-Nashr, 1997), 14–15 and passim. See Abdelmagid Turki, 'Situation du "Tributaire" qui insulte l'Islam, au regard de la doctrine et de la jurisprudence musulmanes', *Studia Islamica* 30 (1969), pp. 39-72. See also Chapter 4 in this volume by Muhammad Khalid Masud.

30 Al-Subki cites ʿIyad extensively, cf. Taqi al-Din ʿAli b. ʿAbd al-Kafi al-Subki, *al-Sayf al-Maslūl ʿalā man Sabba al-Rasūl*, ed. ʿIyad Ahmad al-Ghawj (Amman: Dar al-Fath, 2000), passim. See Lutz Wiederhold, 'Blasphemy against the Prophet Muḥammad and his Companions (*sabb al-rasūl, sabb al-ṣaḥābah*): The introduction of the topic into Shāfiʿī legal literature and its relevance for legal practice under Mamluk rule', *Journal of Semitic Studies* 42/1 (1997), pp. 39–70.

31 Mercedes García-Arenal, '*Shurafā* in the last years of al-Andalus and in the Morisco period: *Laylat al-mawlid* and genealogies of the Prophet Muḥammad', in Kazuo Morimoto (ed.), *Sayyids and Sharifs in Muslim Societies: The Living Links to the Prophet* (Oxon: Routledge, 2012), pp. 161–84; Albarrán, *Veneración y polémica*, pp. 100–8.

32 Al-Manuni, 'Kitāb al-shifā', p. 339.

33 Qadi ʿIyad ibn Musa al-Yahsubi, *Muhammad Messenger of Allah: Ash-Shifa of Qadi ʿIyad*, transl. Aisha Abdarraham Bewley (Inverness, UK: Madinah Press, 1991).

34 Qadi ʿIyad, *Kitāb al-Shifāʾ*, transl. ʿAbd al-Hakim Sahib (Lahore: Maktaba Nabawiyya, 1997).

35 Bilingual edition: al-Qadi ʿIyad al-Yahsobi, *al-Shifāʾ bitaʿrīf ḥuqūq al-mustafā = Déclaration parfaite des obligations de vénération envers l'élu Prophète (qu'Allah le benisse et le salue)*, transl. J.F. Kayale (Beirut: Dar al-Kutub al-ʿIlmiyya, 2007).

36 Qadi ʿIyad, *ash-Shifá*, transl. ʿAbd al-Ghani Melera Navío (Granada: Madrasa Editorial, 2016).

37 Supreme Justice Eyad, *The Cure: Ash-Shifa: The Healing (of the Reader) by Defining the Rights of the Chosen Prophet, Praise and Peace be Upon Him*, transl. Anne Stephens and

Ahmad Darwish (n.p., 2011); Qadi Iyad ibn Musa al-Yahsubi, *Loving Rasul Allah: An Extract from Qaḍī ʿIyāḍ's Shifāʾ*, transl. Abu Hasan (n.p.: Ridawi press, 2015).

38 ʿIyad, *al-Shifāʾ*, pp. 311–22, especially p. 320.

39 Ibid., p. 48, with reference to Q 93:3; 79.

40 Ibid., p. 108, also pp. 215–17. Hadith no. 2276, narrated by Wathila b. al-Asqaʿ, in Abu al-Husayn Muslim b. al-Hujjaj al-Qushayri al-Nisaburi, *Ṣaḥīḥ Muslim* (Beirut: Dar al-Kutub al-ʿIlmiyya, 2008), ch. 43/1, p. 897. ʿIyad notes that al-Tirmidhi vouched for the authenticity of this narration. He also cites Q 3:33, in which the progeny of Ibrahim are mentioned among the chosen ones (ʿIyad, *al-Shifā*, p. 179).

41 ʿIyad, *al-Shifāʾ*, p. 109. *Al-Nūr* is also noted as one of Muhammad's epithets (ʿIyad, *al-Shifāʾ*, p. 320).

42 Ibid., pp. 20–1.

43 Ibid., p. 10.

44 Bennison, *Almoravid and Almohad*, p. 241.

45 ʿIyad, *al-Ghunya*, p. 132.

46 Abu Bakr Muhammad b. Khayr b. ʿUmar b. Khalifa al-Umawi, *Fahrasat Ibn Khayr al-Ishbīlī*, ed. Muhammad Fuʾad Mansur (Beirut: Dar al-Kutub al-ʿIlmiyya, 1998), p. 257. Al-Kharkushi's text seems to be lost.

47 ʿIyad, *al-Shifāʾ*, pp. 4–5.

48 Ibid., p. 579, cf. Khalidi, *Images of Muhammad*, p. 213.

49 Ibid., p. 538.

50 This ties in with recurrent debates on the two concepts. See a brief overview in Nora S. Eggen, 'Universalized versus particularized conceptualizations of Islam in translations of the Qurʾan in Scandinavia', *Journal of Qurʾanic Studies* 18/1 (2016), pp. 49–91 at pp. 51–52.

51 ʿIyad, *al-Shifāʾ*, p. 540.

52 Ibid., p. 542.

53 Ibid., p. 544.

54 Ibid., p. 571.

55 Ibid., p. 627.

56 Ibid., p. 666. This was a prominent topic in ʿIyad's literary production as well, both in poetry and in letters in rhymed prose, addressing the Prophet and expressing his longing to visit his grave (ʿAbd al-Salam Shaqqur, *al-Qāḍī ʿIyāḍ al-Adīb: al-Adab al-Maghribī fī Ẓilli l-Murābiṭīn* (N.p.: Dar al-Fikr al-Maghrabī, 1983).

57 James A.O.C. Brown, 'ʿAzafid Ceuta, Mawlid al-Nabī and the Development of Marīnid Strategies of Legitimation', in Amira K. Bennison (ed.), *The Articulation of Power in Medieval Iberia and the Maghrib*, (Oxford: Oxford University Press, 2014), pp. 127–51.

58 Marion Holmes Katz, *The Birth of The Prophet Muhammad: Devotional Piety in Sunni Islam* (New York: Routledge, 2007), pp. 51, 121.

59 Ibid., p. 121.

60 The two manuscripts are located in the manuscript section of the Central Library of Al-Imam Muhammad Ibn Saud Islamic University in Riyad, see ʿAbd al-ʿAziz b. Rashid al-Sunaydi, *Muʿjam mā ʾullifa ʿan Makka* (Riyadh, 1420/1999), pp. 165, 172, as cited in Katz, *Birth of The Prophet Muhammad*, pp. 51 and 230 n. 166.

61 MS 1752, in 36 folios. The index card suggests that it is a reproduction of a manuscript located in the Amin Damj-library in Beirut, but there is a possibility that the physical manuscript was obtained by the library with the Khayr al-Din al-Zarkali-library. I would like to thank librarian ʿAmmar Talmal at the King Faisal Center for Research

and Islamic Studies, Riyadh for providing me with the facsimiles and Laila Makboul for helping out.

62 See Ibn ʿIyad, *al-Taʿrīf*, pp. 116–18, and al-Waragili, *Abū al-Faḍl*, who has collected information from all the relevant bibliographical sources.

63 García-Arenal, '*Shurafā*', p. 165. García-Arenal does not consider the pseudo-ʿIyad *Risāla*.

64 ʿIyad, *al-Shifā*ʾ, p. 595.

65 Ibid., pp. 604–5.

66 David Powers, *Law, Society, and Culture in the Maghrib, 1300–1500* (Cambridge: Cambridge University Press, 2002), p. 172.

67 García-Arenal, '*Shurafā*', pp. 172–4; Albarrán, *Veneración y polémica*, p. 107–8; Maribel Fierro, 'How do we know about the circulation of books in al-Andalus? The case of al-Bakrī's Kitāb al-Anwār', *Intellectual History of the Islamicate World* 4/1–2 (2016), pp. 152–69.

68 ʿIyad, *al-Shifā*ʾ, pp. 926–1116.

69 Ibid., p. 937.

70 Ibid., pp. 926, 944. The verb *adhā* is polysemous, and in the Qurʾan, according to Ibn al-Jawzi (d. 1200), it carries as many as ten different aspects of meaning, among them 'disobedience' (*ʿiṣyān*), 'hardship' (*shidda*), 'abuse' (*shatm*) and 'insult' (*sabb*). Jamal al-Din Abu'l-Faraj ʿAbd al-Rahman b. ʿAli Ibn al-Jawzi, *Nuzhat al-ʿUyūn al-Nawāẓir fī ʿIlm al-Wujūh wal-Naẓāʾir*, ed. Khalil al-Mansur (Beirut: Dar al-Kutub al-ʿIlmiyya, 2000), pp. 53–4.

71 ʿIyad, *al-Shifā*ʾ, pp. 928–32.

72 Ibid., p. 932.

73 Ibid., p. 933.

74 Isabel Fierro, 'Andalusian 'fatāwā' on blasphemy', *Annales Islamologiques* 25 (1991), pp. 103–17, at p. 103 n. 5.

75 Schacht, J. 'On some manuscripts in the libraries of Kairouan and Tunis', *Arabica* 14/3 (1967), pp. 225–58; Dutton, *The Origins of Islamic Law*, p. 24; Wymann-Landgraf, *Mālik and Medina*, p. 59. The differences between Wahb's *Muwaṭṭa*ʾ and the other recensions of Malik's *Muwaṭṭa*ʾ prompted Jonathan E. Brockopp to suggest that it may be considered a separate text: Jonathan E. Brockopp, *Early Mālikī Law: Ibn 'Abd Al-Ḥakam and His Major Compendium of Jurisprudence* (Leiden: Brill, 2000), p. 74.

76 According to his own record, ʿIyad read Malik's *Muwaṭṭa*ʾ in the transmission of Yahya Ibn Yahya al-Laythi (d. 234/848) (ʿIyad, *al-Ghunya*, pp. 29–31).

77 ʿIyad does not mention in the *Ghunya* having studied the *Risāla fī-man Sabba al-Nabī* written by Sahnun's son, Muhammad b. Sahnun (ʿIyad, *Tartīb al-Madārik*, vol. 4, p. 207).

78 ʿIyad, *al-Shifā*ʾ, p. 936.

79 ʿIyad, *Tartīb al-Madārik*, vol. 4, p. 137. ʿAbd al-Malik b. Habib al-Sulami is described as outstanding in Maliki *fiqh*, but not well versed in *ḥadīth* and in discerning the strong from the weak (ʿIyad, *Tartīb al-Madārik*, vol. 4, p. 123). His brother, Harun b. Habib, was accused of insult, see below.

80 ʿIyad, *al-Shifā*ʾ, p. 948. The narration is attributed to ʿAli b. Abi Talib through his son al-Husayn.

81 Ibid., p. 949.

82 Ibid., p. 966.

83 Ibid., pp. 960, 964.

84 Ibid., p. 969.

85 Ibid., p. 973.

86 Ibid., pp. 934–8. On these notions in the Andalusian context, see Maria Isabel Fierro Bello, 'Accusations of "zandaqa" in al-Andalus', *Quaderni di Studi Arabi* 5/6 (1987–1988), pp. 251–258; Maribel Fierro, 'Religious dissension in al-Andalus: Ways of exclusion and inclusion', *al-Qanṭara* 22/2 (2001), pp. 463–87.
87 ʿIyad, *al-Shifāʾ*, p. 1015
88 Ibid., p. 975.
89 Ibid., p. 1096.
90 Ibid., p. 1106.
91 Ibid., p. 1110.
92 Ibid., pp. 1101–2.
93 Ibid., p. 1087.
94 Ibid., p. 1098. ʿIyad holds that insult violates the pact of protection (*ʿahd al-dhimma*). ʿIyad, *al-Shifāʾ*, pp. 1034–6; cf. Janina M. Safran, *Defining Boundaries in al-Andalus: Muslims, Christians, and Jews in Islamic Iberia* (Ithaca; London: Cornell University Press, 2013), p. 97. As noted by John Tolan, the Shafiʿi jurist al-Mawardi (d. 1058) specified among the conditions for the protection of the *dhimmī* subjects that they do 'not talk of the Apostle, God bless him and grant him salvation, in terms of denial or disparagement': John Tolan, 'Blasphemy and protection of the faith: Legal perspectives from the Middle Ages', *Islam and Christian-Muslim Relations* 27/1 (2016), pp. 35–50).
95 ʿIyad, *al-Shifāʾ*, p. 1010.
96 Ibid., p. 1003.
97 Ibid., p. 1004.
98 Ibid., p. 996. ʿIyad dedicates a separate section to the miracles (*muʿjizāt* and *karamāt*) of the Prophet: ʿIyad, *al-Shifāʾ*, pp. 341–536.
99 Fierro, 'Andalusian "fatāwā"'; Declan Patrick O'Sullivan, *Punishing Apostasy: The Case of Islam and Shari'a Law Re-Considered*, PhD thesis (Durham University, 2003), vol. 2, pp. 375–98; Delfina Serrano, 'Twelve court cases on the application of penal law under the Almoravids', in Muhammad Khalid Masud, Rudolph Peters and Davis S. Powers (eds), *Dispensing Justice in Islam: Qadis and their Judgements* (Leiden: Brill, 2006), pp. 473–93.
100 Ibn ʿIyaḍ, *Madhāhib al-Ḥukkām*, p.77; cf. Ibn ʿIyaḍ, *La actuación*, p. 208.
101 ʿIyad, *Tartīb al-Madārik*, vol. 8, p. 95; Ibn ʿIyāḍ, *La actuación*, 557.
102 Ibn ʿIyad, *Madhāhib al-Ḥukkām*, p. 81; cf. Ibn ʿIyad, *La actuación*, p. 212.
103 Ibn Rushd, *Masāʾil Abī al-Walīd b. Rushd (al-Jadd)*, ed. Muhammad al-Habib al-Tajkani (Beirut; Morocco: Dar al-Jil; Dar al-Afaq al-Jadida, 1978), pp. 274, 1268.
104 ʿIyad, *Tartīb al-madārik*, vol. 5, pp. 292, 303–5.
105 ʿIyad, *al-Shifāʾ*, p. 940; see also Maribel Fierro, 'El proceso contra Ibn Ḥātim al-Ṭulayṭulī (años 457/1064–464/1072)', in Manuela Marín (ed.), *Estudios onomástico-biográficos de al-Andalus* VI (Madrid: Consejo Superios de Investigaciones Científicas, 1994), pp. 187–215.
106 ʿIyad, *al-Shifāʾ*, p. 941. I have not been able to verify this incident in other sources, but according to ʿIyad it took place during the qadiship of Abu al-ʿAbbas b. Talib (d. 888 or 889) and Yahya b. ʿUmar (d. 902), who resided at the Qayrawan court in the late ninth century (ʿIyad, *Tartīb al-Madārik*, vol. 4, pp. 308–31).
107 ʿIyad, *al-Shifāʾ*, pp. 1048–49, see also Fierro, 'Andalusian "fatāwā"', pp. 106–9; Safran, *Defining Boundaries*, pp. 48–9. Harun b. Habib was the brother of the above-mentioned scholar ʿAbd al-Malik b. Habib al-Sulami. ʿIyad does not mention other well-known cases, like the case of Yahya b. Zakariya al-Khashshab during the same

period (Fierro, "Andalusian 'fatāwā"', pp. 104–5; Safran, *Defining Boundaries*, pp. 73–6), or the Christian martyr movement in Córdoba in the 850s, cf. Kenneth Baxter Wolf, *Christian Martyrs in Muslim Spain* (Cambridge: Cambridge University Press, (1988/2014), p. 23. See also Safran, *Defining Boundaries*, pp. 91–9.

108 That these cases were relatively few may be due to a reservation against issuing capital punishment judgement in cases of doubt, although as Intisar A. Rabb has shown, these practices were also embedded in socio-political considerations. Intisar A. Rabb, 'Islamic legal maxims as substantive canons of construction: *Ḥudūd*-avoidance in cases of doubt', *Islamic Law and Society* 17 (2010), pp. 63–125; Intisar A. Rabb, *Doubt in Islamic Law: A History of Legal Maxims, Interpretation, and Islamic Criminal Law* (Cambridge: Cambridge University Press, 2014), pp. 88–93.

109 Janina S. Safran, 'Identity and differentiation in ninth-century al-Andalus', *Speculum* 76/3 (2001), pp. 573–98 at p. 590.

110 ʿIyad, *al-Shifāʾ*, p. 959.

111 Khalidi, *Images of Muhammad*, p. 18.

112 Ibid., p. 18.

113 Ibid., p. 210.

114 Ibid., p. 213.

115 His list of groups and points of view leading to disbelief (*kufr*) fills many pages: ʿIyad, *al-Shifāʾ*, pp. 1066–87.

116 ʿIyad, *al-Shifāʾ*, p. 985.

117 Linda G. Jones, 'The Shifaʾ of al-Qadi ʿIyad', in Coeli Fitzpatrick and Adam Hani Walker (eds), *Muhammad in History, Thought, and Culture* (Santa Barbara; Denver; Oxford: ABC - Clio, 2014), vol. 1, p. 58.

118 Ibn Tumart, *Kitāb aʿazz mā yuṭlab: Le livre de Mohammed Ibn Toumert*, ed. I. Goldziher (Alger: Imprimerie Orientale Pierra Fontana, 1903), p. 246; cf. Allen J. Fromherz, *The Almohads: The Rise of an Islamic Empire* (London; New York: I.B.Tauris, 2010), p. 153; Mercedes García-Arenal, *Messianism and Puritanical Reform: Mahdīs of the Muslim West* (Leiden: Brill 2006), pp. 181–3. According to García-Arenal, citing Tilman Nagel, the term used is *quṭb*, but in Goldziher's edition the term *ʿamūd* occurs.

119 García-Arenal, *Messianism*, pp. 180–84; Fromherz, *The Almohads*, pp. 237–8 n. 1 and 4.

120 Fromherz, *The Almohads*, pp. 139–40; García-Arenal, *Messianism*, p. 182.

121 Paradoxically, Ibn Tumart would claim spiritual and intellectual affinity with Abu Hamid al-Ghazali (d. 1111), who had fiercely opposed the claims to infallibility of the Fatimid *imām/mahdī* (García-Arenal, *Messianism*, p. 179; Fromherz, *The Almohads*, pp. 30–5). On the controversial position of al-Ghazali in Almoravid al-Andalus, see Delfina Ruano Serrano, 'Why did the scholars of al-Andalus distrust al-Ghazāli? Ibn Rushd al-Jadd's *Fatwā on Awliyāʾ Allah*', *Der Islam* 83 (2006), pp. 137–56; Nora S. Eggen, 'A book burner or not? History and myth: Revisiting al-Qāḍī ʿIyāḍ and the controversies over al-Ghazālī in the Islamic West', *Journal of Arabic and Islamic Studies* 18 (2018), pp. 87–109.

122 Maribel Fierro, 'The legal policies of the Almohad caliphs and Ibn Rushd's *Bidāyat al-mujtahid*', *Journal of Islamic Studies* 10/3 (1999), pp. 226–48, at p. 233.

123 Josep Puig Montada, 'Ibn Rušd and the Almohad Context', in Resianne Fontaine, Ruth Glasner, Reimund Leicht and Giuseppe Veltri (eds), *Studies in the History of Culture and Science: A Tribute to Gad Freudenthal* (Leiden: Brill, 2010), pp. 189–208, at p. 190. See also Emile Fricaud, 'Les ṭalaba dans la société almohade (le temps d'Averroès)', *Al-Qanṭara* 18/2 (1997), pp. 331–87. In the long run, however, the Maliki tradition

proved persistent, and eventually Almohad caliphs were forced to reach a compromise with it. Fierro, 'The Legal Policies,' p. 239; David S. Powers, *Law, Society and Culture in the Maghrib, 1300–1500* (Cambridge: Cambridge University Press, 2002), p. 100.

124 ʿIyad, *al-Shifāʾ*, p. 734.

125 Muhammad b. ʿAli b. Muḥammad al-Shawkani, *Irshāb al-Fuḥūl ilā Taḥqīq al-ḥaqq min ʿIlm al-Uṣūl* (N.p.: Dar al-Fikr, n.d.), pp. 255–6. See also Mohammad Hashim Kamali, *Principles of Islamic Jurisprudence* (Cambridge: Islamic Texts Society, 1991), pp. 381–3; Bernard G. Weiss, *The Search for God's Law: Islamic Jurisprudence in the Writings of Sayf al-Dīn al-Āmidī* (Salt Lake City: University of Utah Press, 1992), pp. 690–4; Éric Chaumont, 'La problématique classique de l'Ijtihâd et la question de l'Ijtihâd du prophète: Ijtihâd, Waḥy et ʿIṣma', *Studia Islamica* 75 (1992), pp. 105–39.

126 ʿIyad, *al-Shifāʾ*, pp. 732–3, at p. 888.

127 Albarrán, *Veneración y polémica*, pp. 152–59.

128 Fierro, 'El tratato', pp. 32–3. See also Maribel Fierro, 'The legal policies of the Almohad caliphs', pp. 226–48; Maribel Fierro, 'Le mahdi Ibn Tûmart et al-Andalus: l'élaboration de la légitimité almohade', *Revue d'Etudes sur le Monde Musulman et la Méditerranée* 91/4 (2000), pp. 107–24.

129 Fierro, 'El tratato', p. 34.

130 José Bellver, '"Al-Ghazālī of al-Andalus": Ibn Barrajān, Mahdism, and the emergence of learned Sufism on the Iberian Peninsula', *Journal of the American Oriental Society* 133/4 (2013), pp. 659–81.

131 Gerhard Böwering and Yousef Casewit (eds), *A Qurʾān Commentary by Ibn Barrajān of Seville (d. 536/1141): Īḍāḥ al-ḥikma bi-aḥkām al-ʿibra (Wisdom Deciphered, the Unseen Discovered) - a critical edition and analytical introduction* (Leiden: Brill, 2015), pp. 7, 20.

132 Böwering and Casewit, *A Qurʾān Commentary*, p. 19.

133 Ibn Khallikan, *Wafayāt al-aʿyān wa-anbāʾ abnāʾ az-zamān (Deaths of Eminent Men and History of the Sons of the Epoch)*, transl. Mac Guckin de Slane (Beirut: Librarie du Liban, 1970), vol. 2, p. 148; vol. 1, p. 150.

134 Bellver, '"Al-Ghazālī of al-Andalus"', p. 669.

135 ʿIyad, *al-Ghunya*, p. 129.

136 Ibid., Introduction, p. 13.

137 Bellver, '"Al-Ghazālī of al-Andalus"', p. 676.

138 Ibid., p. 671.

139 Maribel Fierro, 'Le Mahdi Ibn Tûmart et al-Andalus', pp. 107–24; Tilman Nagel, 'Le Mahdisme d'Ibn Tûmart et d'Ibn Qasî: une analyse phénoménologique', *Revue des mondes musulmans et de la Méditerranée* 91–4 (2000), pp. 125–36; Brett, 'Le Mahdi dans le Maghreb médiéval', *Revue des mondes musulmans et de la Méditerranée* 91–4 (2000), pp. 93–106; García-Arenal, *Messianism*, pp. 134–9.

140 Apparently Ibn Qasi did not fully abandon his own politico-religious aspirations, cf. Michael Ebstein, 'Was Ibn Qasī a Ṣūfī?', *Studia Islamica* 110/2 (2015), pp. 196–232 at p. 198. Ebstein discusses in this article how the content of Ibn Qasi's message significantly differed from classical Sufism.

4

Reading Ibn Taymiyya's *al-Ṣārim*: Hermeneutic Shifts in the Definition of Blasphemy

Muhammad Khalid Masud[1]

Ibn Taymiyya's book *al-Ṣārim al-Maslūl ʿalā Shātim al-Rasūl*[2] (The Sharp Sword Drawn Against Those Who Insult[3] the Messenger) has become the basic text in contemporary Muslim discourse, particularly on the issue of blasphemy[4] in Pakistan.[5] To understand Ibn Taymiyya's impact on modern Muslim religious and political thought since the nineteenth century[6] and on the continuing Muslim discourse on blasphemy[7] and freedom of religion, it is imperative to study *al-Ṣārim*, not least because its author, Taqi al-Din Ahmad ibn Taymiyya (1263–1328), wrote this book to defend himself against the accusation that he had wrongly incited the public against a Christian for insulting the Prophet.[8] Recently, most of his works have been studied, edited and published, but there are only a few studies that focus on *al-Ṣārim*.[9] Ibn Taymiyya opened *al-Ṣārim* by stressing the centrality of the Prophet Muhammad in the religion of Islam and examining the issue of blasphemy from an ontological perspective.[10] Defining consensus as the majority view and developing a new legal methodology, Ibn Taymiyya shifted the hermeneutics of the definition of blasphemy from the meanings of apostasy and breach of pact to that of 'insulting the Prophet'. This chapter is divided into five parts: 'Historical context' describes the political and religious conditions in which he wrote this book. 'Personal context' reviews Ibn Taymiyya's personal life and the events that led him to write it. 'Doctrinal context' surveys the problematic development of Muslim jurists' discourse on blasphemy before Ibn Taymiyya. 'Reading *al-Ṣārim*', the fourth part, summarizes his arguments presented in this book and describes his style, hermeneutics and legal methodology. The final section reviews Ibn Taymiyya's impact on the later development of the doctrine.

Historical context

Ibn Taymiyya lived in a period of immense political turmoil and religious crisis. The Mongols had destroyed the ʿAbbasid caliphate and captured Baghdad in 1258, and were continuously conquering other Muslim areas. The Mamluks, who arose as a warrior dynasty in Egypt, began ruling in the name of the ʿAbbasids after defeating the Mongols in the Battle of Ayn Jalut in 1260. Despite repelling the attacks of the French crusaders in 1270 and the Mongols in 1271 and 1281, the Mamluks lacked the general support of the religious groups.[11] Facing a crisis of legitimacy, they chose to focus on jihad. The Mamluk sultan Malik Mansur Lajin appointed Ibn Taymiyya to preach jihad during his expedition against the kingdom of Armenia in 1297. By 1300, Ibn Taymiyya had emerged as the public leader of jihad. He was sent to speak to the Mongol leader Ilkhan Ghazan, who had converted to Islam. In 1301, he travelled to Cairo to seek Sultan Qalawun's support for jihad against the Mongols in the battle of Shaqhab in 1303. It was in this battle in the month of Ramadan that Ibn Taymiyya gave a fatwa exempting Muslim soldiers from the duty of fasting during jihad.[12] The Mongols were defeated, and Ibn Taymiyya rapidly gained popularity among the masses as well as the trust of most of the Mamluk sultans.

Religious politics had become increasingly intense in that period due to fierce Sunni–Shiʿa controversy, not only because the Shiʿa had allegedly supported the Mongols in the destruction of Baghdad,[13] but also because some Mongol factions in central Asia had converted to Shiʿi Islam and were accused of attacking the Sunni Muslim lands. Ibn Taymiyya was part of the expedition in 1300 against the Shiʿa of Kasrawan, who were accused of helping the Mongols and the Franks. With reference to the Shiʿa, insulting the Prophet's Companions had been a serious politico-religious issue. The Sunnis considered *sabb al-ṣaḥāba* (insulting the Companions of the Prophet) to be *kufr* (renouncing Islam, apostasy).

Personal context

Life

Ibn Taymiyya belonged to a well-known family of Hanbali scholars in Harran, a city in present-day Turkey. He was six years old when a Mongol attack on their native town forced his family to migrate to Damascus. Ibn Taymiyya completed his education there in 1284 at the Madrasa Sukkariyya, where his father was the principal, and began teaching after his father died that year. The next year he began teaching at the Umayyad Mosque, the central religious institution in Damascus.

His opponents raised objections about his anthropomorphic statements about God, and Shafiʿi and Hanafi qadis (judges) indicted him for making statements against majority views. His controversial statements were regarded as *kufr* and punishable by death. He also produced polemical writings, like *Manāsik al-Ḥajj*, written in 1293 denouncing certain Hajj rituals as heretic innovations (*bidʿa*); *al-Ḥamawiyya al-Kubrā*, a Hanbali critical theological response to his opponents, especially the followers of orthodox Ashʿarism; and *al-Wāsiṭiyya*, a theological treatise. He personally led violent physical attacks on Sufi shrines and orders in 1305. As a result, he faced a series of trials in Damascus and Cairo, and he was repeatedly imprisoned in the citadel in Cairo in the years 1306–1307, 1308, 1309, 1320 and 1326. His book *al-Ṣārim al-Maslūl* was also written in response to one of these trials. He died in prison in 1328.[14]

Ibn Taymiyya's biographers never fail to mention his radical views, aggressive style and sharp tongue, which got him more enemies than friends among the religious scholars of his time. In an article titled 'Did Ibn Taymiyya have a screw loose?', Donald Little wrote that Ibn Taymiyya's student Shams al-Din al-Dhahabi (d. 1348) counselled his teacher to give up 'his pride, his vanity and his pretensions... and his love for publicity'.[15] Abu al-Hasan Ali Nadwi, who regarded Ibn Taymiyya as one of the eminent reformers, also complained that his style made his writings inaccessible, 'as if his mind and pen cannot concentrate on one point'.[16] Ibn Taymiyya wrote in a scholastically polemical style full of rejoinders. His arguments were not logically structured; the mass of evidence made his style imposing, but not necessarily convincing. Sudden digressions, lengthy details and proliferation of citations made his writings difficult to follow.[17] Rapoport and Ahmed remark that his assertive style reflected his bold and proud personality. According to them, a narrow focus on his staunch puritanism has distracted from his pragmatic approach to social practices, and Ibn Taymiyya has remained generally misunderstood to this day. His popularity in modern times stands in contrast to his marginality in the pre-modern period.[18]

Why Ibn Taymiyya wrote *al-Ṣārim al-Maslūl*

In his introduction to *al-Ṣārim*, Ibn Taymiyya wrote that a specific recent event had compelled him to write this book.[19] He did not provide details, but his remarks allude to the event that I analyse below. This helps the reader to understand not only why he wrote this book, but also the contents and the line of argument he developed in it.

Most of the later sources rely on Ibn Kathir (d. 1373), but I have chosen Ibn Athir al-Jazari (d. 1337), because he was closer than Ibn Kathir to the event and, more importantly, because he provided a more detailed day-by-day report.[20] These details help us to grasp the gravity of the event, its complexity and the impact of the public rage against the blasphemer. Ibn Kathir's account also differs from al-Jazari's in some details.[21] Both versions, however, clearly point to the tension between the ruling and the religious elite and to the politics of blasphemy in that period.

According to al-Jazari, a large group of people from Suwayda came to Damascus on 27 Rajab 692 H (4 July 1293 CE), complaining that the Christian secretary[22] of the Amir ʿAssaf b. Amir Shihab al-Din Ahmad b. al-Hajji had insulted the Prophet Muhammad. Al-Jazari did not mention the name of the Christian secretary, but Ibn Kathir and others erroneously call him ʿAssaf. The deputy governor, Amir Shams al-Din al-Aʿsar, did not entertain the complaint, in deference to his friend the Amir ʿAssaf. The next morning, a group of jurists and other people, led by Ibn Taymiyya and Shaykh Zayn al-Din al-Fariqi, came to speak to the Deputy Governor about this matter. He assured the group that he would summon the Christian and deal with him in accordance with the Shariʿa. Meanwhile, a large crowd had gathered at the Nasr Gate. They were protesting that Amir ʿAssaf had granted asylum to the Christian. When ʿAssaf came out, the crowd threw stones at ʿAssaf and injured him. ʿAssaf ran to take refuge in the house of one of the officials.

The news reached the Deputy Governor, and he sent the chief of police with a troop of soldiers to rescue ʿAssaf and the two shaykhs from the protestors. When the police chief reported what had happened, the Deputy Governor was furious and summoned the two shaykhs. He scolded them for what they had done; both were flogged and detained in the Madrasa al-ʿAdhrawiya. The Deputy Governor then ordered a charge on the protesting mob. Some were struck down, some hanged, and some were arrested and detained in the same Madrasa.

Two days later, the Governor sent four members of the judiciary from Damascus to Suwayda to investigate. In the meantime, the Christian had converted to Islam in humility. The group of protestors remained detained in the Madrasa. After the Friday prayer, the Deputy Governor called for the Shafiʿi qadi and prominent Shafiʿi jurists,[23] who affirmed that the death sentence could be waived, as the Christian had converted to Islam. Shaykh Zayn al-Fariqi was released after he endorsed the fatwa written by the Shafiʿi jurists. The Deputy Governor received Ibn Taymiyya with due deference and released him and the other detainees. The former Christian was brought to the Governor's office and was put in one of the houses there. A few days later, the Governor called a council in his office, attended by the jurists, the four chief qadis and several scholars. The discussion went on for hours and ended without any clear decision.

After several months, the Deputy Governor quietly released the former Christian in the night. The jurists continued debating whether the Christian could be pardoned after converting to Islam. Husam al-Din al-Razi, the Hanafi chief qadi, wrote an emotional poem condemning his release. He insisted that there was a consensus of all the schools that his acceptance of Islam could not spare him from a *ḥadd* punishment, and lamented that even 'the swords of God in Syria and the lions in every battle' had not been able to protect the religion. He feared the end of the world because Muslims had not fulfilled their obligation to Muhammad.[24] Al-Jazari's report illustrates the scale of the event and the charged public emotions. The religious elite were furious with the authorities for failing to act against a violation of the honour of the Prophet. As will be discussed below, the Shafiʿi and Hanafi jurisprudence differed on several points, such as the nature and legal consequences of blasphemy by a protected Christian. As Al-Jazari mentioned, even the Hanafi chief qadi, whose school was known to differ with other schools on these points, called for the death sentence.

Having converted to Islam, the Christian went to Hijaz on pilgrimage, but was killed by somebody. According to Ibn Kathir, he was killed by his nephew in the neighbourhood of Medina.[25] It is unclear whether the killing was motivated by the jurists' fatwas that he must be sentenced to death even after accepting Islam.

Ibn Taymiyya titled the book 'The Sharp Sword . . .', stressing the significance of this event in the following words:

> The event demanded that I state the punishment that the Law prescribes for those, Muslims or non-Muslims (*kāfir*), who insult (*sabb*) the Prophet [. . .] as the least that I owe to the Prophet, in view of the fact that God obliges us all to honour and to protect him by all means [. . .].[26]

Consequently, Ibn Taymiyya stated, he wrote the book to explain the divine law (*sharʿ*) which the muftis should follow in their fatwas and the qadis in their judgments. He considered it an obligation for the rulers and the Muslim community to enforce this law to the extent possible.[27] Ibn Taymiyya considered *al-Ṣārim al-Maslūl* his most important and original contribution.[28]

Al-Ṣārim is divided into two parts: an introduction and four issues which are phrased as code statements:

1. Whoever insults the Prophet (peace be on him) must be sentenced to death, be he Muslim or infidel.
2. The death sentence is fixed; it is not lawful to enslave him, or release him mercifully, or take ransom for him.
3. He must be sentenced to death and not invited to recant, regardless whether he is Muslim or infidel.
4. Explanation of the above-mentioned term 'insulting' and the difference between this term and plain apostasy.

Al-Ṣārim is hard to read due to its repetitive and expansive style of discussion. He may have chosen this style for three reasons. First, because it was written extemporaneously from memory. Second, as related above, Ibn Taymiyya wrote it to defend himself against the accusation that he had wrongly incited the public against a Christian for insulting the Prophet in 1292–3. Third, as he mentioned in the introduction, he was addressing the qadis and muftis. That is why, after the introduction, he goes straight to discussing the contentious four issues.

Doctrinal context

Ibn Taymiyya was not the first to write on the issue of blasphemy,[29] *shatm al-rasūl* or *sabb al-nabī*, insulting the Prophet Muhammad. The Maliki jurist Muhammad b. Sahnun (d. 878) was arguably the first,[30] and Qadi ʿIyad (d. 1149) wrote a very comprehensive treatise on this subject before Ibn Taymiyya.[31] The word *sabb* in Arabic denotes the following meanings: abuse, calling names, cursing, insulting, reviling, scolding, swearing and vilifying. As a technical term, it is synonymous with *shatm* (reviling) and *laʿn* (cursing). It may also mean scorn (*istikhfāf*) and false accusation (*qadhf*), though the latter originally refers to false accusation of adultery. It also includes insulting God, any of the Prophets, the Prophet Muhammad, his companions, other revered persons and so on.[32] The offence of apostasy (*ridda*, *irtidād*) attracted jurists' attention very early, but it took blasphemy (*sabb al-nabī*) some years to dominate the jurists' discourse.[33] Earlier, blasphemy was discussed mostly in chapters on apostasy, war, international relations and dhimmis (non-Muslims 'under protection', *dhimmī*). The shift from apostasy to blasphemy as the dominating issue complicated the legal discourse and generated diverse angles of reasoning and interpretations. The main points of discussion, then as later, were whether apostasy was punishable by death in all cases, and whether the offender could be pardoned if he recanted or repented. Similar and further questions arose with reference to blasphemy, but in the case of non-Muslims, additional questions concerned the nature of the offence, the grounds for punishment and whether punishments could be averted by converting to Islam.

The discursive development of Islamic jurisprudence generated a huge diversity of opinion among the jurists, both between and within the schools of law. Attempts to analyse this development are also complicated by the fact that the juristic texts often attributed well-known accepted opinions in a school to the founders, apparently to reduce this diversity. Sometimes, even the explanation or clarification in commentaries was mistaken for part of the authors' opinions.[34] The following analysis is not exhaustive; it only aims to underscore the diversity and complexity of the subject, which reveals the sensitivity of the issues and the intricacies of the reasoning in Islamic legal discourse.

Nature of the offence

Defining blasphemy (*sabb al-nabī*), some jurists likened it in gravity with the offence of apostasy committed by a Muslim, but some distinguished between the two offences. Among the Hanafis, for instance, Abu Jaʿfar al-Tahawi (d. 933), Abu Bakr al-Jassas al-Razi (d. 980), Abu al-Hasan al-Sughdi (d. 1069) and Burhan al-Din al-Marghinani (d. 1197)[35] associated blasphemy with apostasy; so did Imam Ahmad b. Hanbal's son Abu ʿAbdallah (d. 903) among the Hanbalis.[36] The Maliki jurists Ibn Wahb (d. 813), Muhammad b. Sahnun (d. 870) and Abu Zayd al-Qayrawani (d. 996)[37] distinguished between apostasy and blasphemy; according to Ibn Wahb, Imam Malik also made a distinction, yet treated blasphemy as part of apostasy.[38]

Some jurists, for example, the Shafiʿi jurists Abu Bakr al-Saydalani (d. *c.*1044) and Imam al-Haramayn al-Juwayni (d. 1085),[39] the Maliki jurists Ibn Wahb,[40] Abu al-Qasim al-Khiraqi (d. 945),[41] Ibn ʿAbd al-Barr (d. 1071),[42] and Qadi ʿIyad (d. 1149), the Hanbali jurist Shams al-Din al-Maqdisi (d. 1362);[43] and the Jaʿfari jurists[44] Shaykh Tusi (d. 1067), Ibn Zahra al-Halabi (d. 1190), Al-Muhaqqiq al-Hilli (d. 1277) and Al-Fadil al-Abi (d. 1291) distinguished between blasphemy and apostasy, seeing the former as a violation of a right of human beings and the latter as violation of the rights of God. Al-Juwayni considered it *qadhf*. Abu Ishaq al-Shirazi al-Shafiʿi (d. 1003) considered both blasphemy and apostasy pardonable after repentance.[45] Later Maliki jurists like Abu Muhammad ʿAbd al-Wahhab Nasr (d. 1030) held that a blasphemer publicly disclosed his hidden disbelief, and an apostate disavowed his belief in reverence for the Prophet.[46]

Qadi ʿIyad developed the whole doctrine from the perspective of protecting the rights of the Prophet Muhammad, 'because protection from harm is the right of the Prophet, and hence the right of the Muslim community. As with all the rights of humans, repentance is not acceptable in this case either.'[47] This raised the question whether the offenders might be forgiven as the Prophet forgave some persons who had insulted him. Qadi ʿIyad explained that those were exceptional cases that happened while the Islamic polity was still in its nascence, and that the Prophet preferred to give his fellows a chance to mend their ways. According to him, the Prophet had the right to forgive those who offended him, and he did so, but in his absence, no one had authority to pardon such offenders.[48] Muslim hearts were wounded each time the Prophet was hurt, he elaborated. They could be healed only by punishing those who insulted him. Hence the title of his book, *Healing by Recognizing the Rights of the Chosen One*.

Ja'fari jurists ruled that a Muslim who heard someone insulting the Prophet was directly and personally obliged to kill the offender. Shaykh Tusi, however, exempted the listener from this duty if it put his life at risk. Ibn Zahra al-Halabi, al-Muhaqqiq al-Hilli and al-Fadil al-Abi ruled that those who had not personally heard the blasphemous words were not obliged to kill the offender. They further clarified that the offender could not be killed without the permission of the authorities. Some of the Ja'fari (Shi'i) jurists uniquely held that when a Muslim heard someone insulting the Prophet, it was his personal obligation to kill the offender immediately.

While the Malikis counted apostasy as a crime of *ḥudūd*, Hanafis did not do so.[49] The Hanafi jurist Abu Bakr Al-Sarakhsi (d. 1096) problematized blasphemy like apostasy, probably because both were punishable by death. He did not, however, count it among the crimes of *ḥudūd*, because the Hanafis distinguished between the rights of God and the rights of humans. They used the term *ḥadd* (singular of *ḥudūd*) for the death penalty and allowed it in exceptional cases beyond the specific *ḥudūd* crimes. They justified this penalty in the public interest (*siyāsa*), as a prerogative of the ruler. To appreciate this nuanced Hanafi reasoning, let me translate the relevant lines by Al-Sarakhsi:

> The true *kufr* is the greatest sin, but it is between the man and his God. The punishment for this sin is postponed until the day of judgment. Legitimacy for hastening (preponing) punishments in this world is rationalized as public interest (*siyāsa*). The *qiṣāṣ* (retribution) is lawful for protecting lives, the *ḥadd* (punishment) for *zinā'* (unlawful sexual relations) is to protect lineage and the marital bed [. . .P]ersistence in *kufr* means that the offender is at war with Muslims. He is sentenced to death in defence during war. Nevertheless, in some places, God has also mentioned war as a legal cause ('. . .if they fight against you, then kill them. . .' Qur'an 2:191).[50]

Punishment and repentance

As mentioned above, Malikis generally regarded blasphemy as violation of the right of the Prophet and hence of the Muslim community. Was this offence pardonable? Jurists' opinion in response to this question was divided. Maliki jurists Ibn 'Abd al-Barr, Ibn Wahb and Nasr; the Hanbali jurist Ibn Qudama (d. 1223); and the Shafi'i jurists Abu Bakr al-Farisi (d. *c.*960), Abu Bakr al-Afzal (d. 975), al-Juwayni and Sharaf al-Nawawi (d. 1277) considered both blasphemy and apostasy non-pardonable.[51] On the other hand, the Shafi'i jurist Abu Ishaq Shirazi (d. 1003) considered both pardonable.[52] Abu Bakr al-Saydalani considered only apostasy pardonable. Hanafi jurists considered apostasy pardonable. Abu Hanifa (d. 767) and Abu Yusuf (d. 798) regarded it as obligatory to give respite for repentance thrice. No respite was allowed the fourth time.[53] Muhammad b. Hasan al-Shaybani (d. 805)[54] and Al-Sarakhsi[55] ruled that respite was allowed only if an apostate asked for it; if he recanted and reverted to Islam, he would not be punished. Abu al-Husayn Ahmad al-Quduri (d. 1037) considered the respite obligatory; the apostate must be imprisoned for three days and invited to revert to Islam. If he refused, he must be executed.[56] Al-Sarakhsi clarified that the ground for the death sentence for apostasy was not disbelief but insisting on disbelief; since repentance removed that ground, the death sentence was cancelled.[57] Commenting on this diversity of opinions, al-Juwayni observed that capital punishments could not be decided by jurists' interpretive opinions; they must be sanctioned by the primary sources.[58]

Non-Muslims

Breaching the pact deprived the dhimmis of the protection. The jurists differed as to whether the death sentence could be averted, and the pact restored, if the offender converted to Islam. These were real questions also in the episode that led Ibn Taymiyya to write *al-Ṣārim*, in which the accused Christian was killed even after converting to Islam. On this matter, too, jurists held diverse views. Maliki jurist Abu al-Walid Ibn Rushd (d. 1126) held that a non-Muslim would be absolved only if he converted to Islam.[59] The Hanafi jurists ʿAlaʾ al-Din al-Kasani (d. 1191) and Al-Marghinani did not consider the offence of blasphemy a breach of pact.[60]

Muhammad b. Idris al-Shafiʿi (d. 820) discussed this issue as a condition of the pact of protection, and in fact drafted a *jizya* pact stipulating it. He made no mention of *sabb al-nabī*; instead, he used the general term 'improper mention' (*bi-mā lā yanbaghī ʿan yadhkuruhu bihi*) as a clause in the proposed draft: 'if any non-Muslim living under the pact made improper mention of God's Prophet, Book and religion, Muslims would be absolved of the duty to protect them, and the pact of peace would be cancelled.'[61] Otherwise, he counted only refusal to pay the *jizya* tax as violation of the pact (*lā yakūnu al-naqḍu li al-ʿahdi illa bi-manʿ al-jizya*); the offences of highway robbery, murder of a Muslim, rape of a Muslim woman and spying on Muslims were crimes, but even those did not constitute violation of the pact.[62] Imam al-Shafiʿi clarified that apostasy was defined by the Prophet as 'disbelief after belief' (*kufr baʿda imān*), meaning that that the blood of a non-believer became inviolable after his conversion to Islam, but apostasy made it violable again.[63] A born Muslim, on the other hand, was governed by the laws of Islam, including *ḥudūd*.[64]

Al-Sarakhsi explained that unlike a Muslim apostate, a dhimmi was originally a disbeliever. An apostate must be sentenced to death if he did not revert to Islam; a dhimmi, on the other hand, could be punished by death only if he went to war against Muslims or joined the enemy camp after breaching the pact.[65] Al-Marghinani held the same views; blasphemy did not constitute breach of the pact.[66]

The Jaʿfari jurist Sharif al-Murtada (d. 1046) observed that the punishment of death applied to both Muslim and dhimmi offenders. While agreeing with the Hanafis that a non-Muslim could not be called an apostate, al-Murtada held that the act of insulting constituted a breach of the pact of *dhimma*. By insulting Shariʿa, the offender withdrew himself from the protection of the law. Thus, his blood became lawful (i.e., he could be killed with impunity).[67]

Qadi ʿIyad claimed a total consensus among Muslim jurists on the death sentence for blasphemy, supported by the Qurʾan, hadith and Sunna;[68] he did mention juristic differences, but dismissed them as insignificant.

Reading *al-Ṣārim al-Maslūl*

The above summary review of juristic differences underscores how careful the jurists were with details and how difficult it was for muftis and qadis to reach clear judgment. Ibn Taymiyya wrote *al-Ṣārim* to present a coherent and clear law that could be applied confidently. It was to be a concise and comprehensive but simplified treatise on the subject, like a code of law, prescribing rules and supporting them with selected relevant texts and the claimed consensus of the jurists. Recognizing the historical, theological and juridical complexity, however, he concluded:

> On the whole there are several categories of blasphemy (*sabb*); some are undoubtedly considered apostasy, some cannot be so classified, and there are still others that are unclear. This is not the place for a thorough examination of all terms. I have mentioned them at the end because they are relevant to the point of the discussion.[69]

Unlike a mufti who presents the relevant evidence and answers the question, Ibn Taymiyya dealt with the major possible questions and developed his answers in three steps. First, he claimed consensus and analysed the opinions of Sunni jurists. Second, he cited texts from the Qur'an and hadith and offered his interpretations. Third, he referred to the views of the Companions and precedents from the practice in early Islam.

Overall, the book argued that insulting the Prophet was a capital crime punishable by death, regardless of whether the offender was Muslim or non-Muslim, and even if the offender repented, converted or reverted to Islam. As mentioned earlier, Ibn Taymiyya problematized blasphemy and apostasy as four issues and sought clarity to achieve juridical certainty.

The view of insulting the Prophet as grave offences of blasphemy and apostasy was informed by the increasing centrality of the Prophet Muhammad in the faith, the assumption of a perpetual state of war between Islam and *kufr*, and Muslim concern for religious, political and social cohesion. Ibn Taymiyya developed a theological and legal methodology to redefine consensus, a method of reasoning and hermeneutics for reading the Qur'an and hadith. It is significant that he added to the juristic analysis of the laws of apostasy and blasphemy a theological discussion of the concepts of *sabb/shatm* (insult), the death sentence, and the criminal intent of *istiḥlāl* (considering lawful what was forbidden).

To avoid repetition and to keep it short, I review Ibn Taymiyya's discussion of the first issue in detail, but outline only briefly the other three issues because he repeats the same citations from the Qur'an and Sunna and jurists' views while discussing the other issues.

The first issue: Death penalty for blasphemy – insulting (*sabb*) the Prophet

Ibn Taymiyya ruled, 'Whoever insults the Prophet, Muslim or non-Muslim (*kāfir*), shall (*yajibu*) be sentenced to death'. He stated that 'This is the opinion held by scholars in general (*ʿāmmat al-ʿulamāʾ*)'.[70] To justify his claim, Ibn Taymiyya developed five sets of argument, referring respectively to jurists' views, relevant Qurʾanic verses, hadith and the consensus among the Companions of the Prophet.

First, to claim consensus on this point, he referred to the following leading jurists who held this view: Layth b. Saʿd (d. 791), Malik b. Anas (d. 795), Muhammad b. Idris al-Shafiʿi, Ahmad b. Hanbal (d. 855) and Abu Dawud Sulayman b. al-Ashʿath al-Sijistani (d. 899). He mentioned Muhammad b. Sahnun, Abu Bakr Muhammad b. Ibrahim Ibn al-Mundhir al-Nishapuri (d. 930) and Qadi ʿIyad for Maliki views, and Ishaq b. Rahuwayh[71] (d. 853), Abu Sulayman Hamd b. Muhammad al-Khattabi (d. 998) and Abu Bakr al-Farisi (d. 961) for Shafiʿi views. These jurists used different terms for 'consensus' and specified it as the majority of the scholars and the Muslim community (*ajmaʿa ʿawāmm ahl al-ʿilm, ijmāʿ al-muslimīn* and *ajmaʿat al-umma*). After citing statements of jurists who supported his above rule, Ibn Taymiyya concluded this preliminary discussion as follows.

> These statements confirm that if a Muslim insulted the Prophet, he committed apostasy and there is no disagreement that he must be sentenced to death. That is the agreed opinion of the founders of the four schools and others. This consensus is reported by Ishaq b. Rahuwayh and others in the following words: If it is committed by a dhimmi, he must also be punished by death, according to the opinion of Maliki school and the people in Medina; their statements will be discussed subsequently. That is also the opinion of Ahmad b. Hanbal and the jurists of the Hadith school.[72]

Ibn Taymiyya also referred to other jurists like Imam Abu Hanifa – mentioned by his first name, Nuʿman – who disagreed with the above view. According to the Hanafi school, capital punishment for a Muslim was for apostasy, not for blasphemy. A non-Muslim could not be punished for expressing the words of disbelief because he was protected despite his disbelief. The act of expressing the words of disbelief also did not count as breach of the pact of protection in Hanafi jurisprudence. This punishment was due only in case of public defiance of the pact or violation of the terms of contract.[73]

Ibn Taymiyya relied mostly on Qadi ʿIyad, who discussed differences among the jurists in detail and rarely claimed complete consensus. Ibn Taymiyya, on the other hand, marginalized juristic differences. Why? Probably, as suggested above, he wanted to codify laws on blasphemy to remove the ambiguity and uncertainty that diversity of views allowed. This short chapter does not allow me to explore this suggestion further. I must, however, give a few examples to illustrate how he reduced differing opinions into agreement to claim the authority of consensus (*ijmāʿ*), a serious issue with Ibn Taymiyya's legal methodology.

For example, what Ibn al-Mundhir simply mentioned as the majority opinion, Ibn Taymiyya called a consensus.[74] Abu Bakr al-Farisi used a term meaning 'consensus' and qualified it by adding that 'consensus' either referred to that of the first two generations in early Islam, or to the point that they all agreed that the death sentence was only prescribed for a Muslim and not for insulting others than the Prophet. Abu

Sulayman al-Khattabi's statement as cited in *al-Ṣārim* is incomplete: 'I do not know any Muslim who disagreed with the obligatory punishment of death',[75] as the full statement cited in *al-Shifā'* included the phrase 'if he was a Muslim',[76] making it clear that Khattabi's reference to consensus related to a Muslim offender, not to a non-Muslim. Similarly, Ibn Taymiyya cited Muhammad b. Sahnun only in part, excluding the phrase 'whoever doubts his apostasy and divine punishment commits apostasy'.[77] This missing phrase clarifies that Ibn Sahnun meant a Muslim offender, not a non-Muslim.[78] Similarly, he missed Ishaq b. Rahuwayh's qualifying statement that 'A Muslim offender born to Muslim parents must be sentenced to death, but if he was born a pagan and converted to Islam, he must be invited to recant'.[79] Ibn Taymiyya treated other juristic differences in a similar manner. According to the Hanbali jurist Abu al-Qasim Umar b. Husayn al-Khiraqi (d. 945), a Muslim apostate must be given three days to recant his blasphemous statement and could be sentenced to death only if he did not do so.[80] Qadi Abu Ya'la Muhammad ibn al-Farra' (d. 1131) held that a dhimmi wrongfully accusing a Muslim of *zinā'*, for instance, did not commit breach of pact; he would be punished only for *qadhf* (the offence of wrongful accusation). The Qadi's colleagues Al-Sharif Abu Ja'far (d. 1077), Abu al-Fath al-Halawani (d. 1112), Abu al-Khattab Mahfuz b. Ahmad al-Kalwadhani (d. 1116), Abu al-Wafa 'Ali b. 'Aqil (d. 1119) and Abu Muhammad Abd al-Rahman al-Halawani (d. 1151) agreed with him. Ibn Taymiyya criticized the above jurists for not following the principles of the Hanbali school; hence, he argued, their difference did not challenge the consensus.[81] Contrary to Ibn Taymiyya, Shafi'i was very cautious about charging a dhimmi with breach of pact. He explicitly stated that a dhimmi committing the crimes of highway robbery, murder, adultery with a Muslim woman or spying would be punished for these offences under regular laws, but none of those offences constituted breach of pact. Similarly, if a dhimmi converted to Islam after committing a crime falling under the categories of *ḥudūd* and *qiṣāṣ* (e.g. murder) in Muslim law, he would be punished for that crime, not for breach of pact.[82] Apparently, Ibn Taymiyya regarded Shafi'i's assiduous method of legal reasoning as unnecessary, since he had prescribed in *al-Umm* that the pact with non-Muslims must include the following stipulation: 'If one of you speaks about God, His Prophet, His Book, or His religion in an improper manner he shall have no protection by God, the ruler or the Muslim community, and the pact will be annulled.'[83] Shafi'i clarified that 'even if he [the dhimmi] committed one of the offences that I described as breach of the contract and converted to Islam, he will not be sentenced to death [for breach of pact, but for that specific crime of *ḥadd* or *qiṣāṣ*]'.[84] Again, Ibn Taymiyya advised the Hanafis to adopt the death sentence for breach of pact, since they held that the ruler could award death punishment to non-Muslim offenders under the Hanafi principle of *siyāsa* in the best interest of the state and society.[85] Why did Ibn Taymiyya choose to focus on consensus rather than diversity despite recognizing the existence of opposing views? Most probably, to justify the validity of his prescribed rules.

Ibn Taymiyya's second set of arguments pertained to the Qur'anic verses justifying the death penalty for insulting God, or His Book, or His religion or His Prophet. The act of insulting constituted breach of pact for a dhimmi and apostasy for a Muslim;

both were to be sentenced to death. He cited fifteen Qur'anic verses[86] relating to Muslims, including apostates (2:217) and hypocrites (2:217; 4:65; 9:58, 61, 64–6, 101; 33:53, 57–8, 60–1; 24:4, 63–4; 58:5, 20); and non-Muslims, including idolaters (9:7–8), People of the Book (9:29–32), dhimmis (9:12–14) and opponents (9:61–3; 58:5, 20–1; 33:57). Ibn Taymiyya explained that the legal status of these different categories was defined correspondingly.[87] He nevertheless collapsed different categories into that of insulting (*sabb* or *shatm*) the Prophet. I need not repeat the juristic differences. It is, however, important to add that he developed a particular hermeneutics to justify that all the various terms used in these verses referred to the heinous nature of the offence of hurting the Prophet and, therefore, deserved capital punishment.[88] He argued that all those who raised their voice against, faulted, slandered, hurt, harmed, vilified, or insulted the Prophet, in fact disobeyed and defied his authority and declared war against him. Similarly, Ibn Taymiyya interpreted the Qur'anic descriptions of various punishments – like divine vengeance, curse, disgrace, deeds becoming worthless – to mean the death sentence. For instance, he cited the following verses with reference to breach of pact:

> But if they violate their oaths after their covenant and taunt you for your Faith, – fight ye the chiefs of Unfaith: for their oaths are nothing to them: that thus they may be restrained. Will ye not fight people who violated their oaths, plotted to expel the Messenger, and took to aggression by being the first (to assault) you? Do ye fear them? Nay, it is Allah Whom ye should more justly fear, if ye believe! Fight them, and Allah will punish them by your hands, cover them with shame, help you (to victory) over them, heal the breasts of Believers. (Qur'an 9:12–15)

He argued that these verses obliged Muslims to wage war against those who violated the pacts, making *qitāl* (fighting) synonymous with *qatl* (in the sense of the death sentence).[89] He concluded that the verses about tolerance and mercy were revealed in Mecca and abrogated in Medina.[90] Third, he cited fifteen hadiths and precedents from the practice of the Prophet that mentioned the death sentence for the offender, whether he was under the pact or not. He used three terms to qualify them as evidence, clear text (*naṣṣ*), evident proof (*dalīl*) and logical conclusion (*ḥujja*), as three categories of his strong approval.[91] Some, according to Ibn Taymiyya, meant to say that whoever insulted or harmed the Prophet, in fact intended to kill him or instigated others to do so.[92] In some cases, the Prophet forgave the offender out of his habit of showing mercy.[93] Fourth, citing examples,[94] Ibn Taymiyya concluded that the 'Companions of the Prophet unanimously agreed that the people under the pact had no right to criticize the Muslim religion in public. If they did so, it made their blood violable.'[95] Fifth, Ibn Taymiyya explained that whenever the Prophet waived punishment, it was for specific reasons: either because the offender had repented before his arrest, or because the person was not protected (a *ḥarbī*, not a *dhimmī*), but had gone on to accept Islam. Ibn Taymiyya provided ten examples of application of such principles. He called this method of discovering reasons in the text *i'tibār*.[96] I will discuss it below in connection with his jurisprudence.

The second issue: The death sentence supersedes other punishments

Ibn Taymiyya ruled: 'The punishment of death is established. It is not permitted to make [the offender] a slave or release him on grace or for ransom [i.e., instead of killing him].'

In this rule, the mention of enslaving, release and ransom as punishments refers to the Qur'anic reforms in the laws about prisoners of war.[97] Juristic discussions about the punishment of blasphemy and apostasy within the framework of laws of war reveals also how the criminal nature of these offences was conceived legally. Abdelmagid Turki summarized Ibn Taymiyya's reasoning as follows: There is no pact without a battle; peace and the pact come into effect after the war. Breach of the pact takes the person back to the pre-pact state of *ibāḥa* (violability, war).[98] Ibn Taymiyya clarified that the death penalty was prescribed both for *ḥudūd* crimes and for breach of pact. He supported this rule with three sets of arguments. He referred to the discussions among the Hanafi and Shafiʿi jurists about resolving their differences on the options between death, enslavement, ransom or release on grace in certain cases.[99] After analysing their arguments he found those views weak that did not support the death sentence. This conclusion is questionable because, on the same pages, he mentions the contrary views of Malik, al-Shafiʿi and Abu Hanifa about the options for the ruler in cases of breach of pact by the protected non-Muslims.[100] Ibn Taymiyya provided fifteen proofs from the Qur'an and hadith as evidence that disallowed the option of treating those who reviled the Prophet and violated the pact of protection as prisoners of war, who could be enslaved or released for ransom or for free; and that instead prescribed death for breach of pact and for finding fault with religion.[101] Ibn Taymiyya commented that it was extremely disappointing that Muslims hesitated to support and honour the Prophet against an offender who was in their custody and whose killing was legally justified.[102]

The third issue: Invitation to repentance

Ibn Taymiyya ruled: 'Whoever insults the Prophet shall not be invited to repent, regardless of whether he is a Muslim or not.' In support, he cited a saying of Imam Ahmad b. Hanbal narrated by his cousin Hanbal b. Ishaq b. Hanbal al-Shaybani (d. 886/7): 'Whoever insulted the Prophet or faulted him, be he Muslim or disbeliever, will be sentenced to death. In my opinion, he should be sentenced without invitation to repent.'[103] As Ibn Taymiyya's further discussion on this issue shows, jurists differed hugely over the details of this issue, e.g. over the definition and scope of apostasy and repentance, Muslims and dhimmis, born Muslims and converts, and whether this rule applied only to insulting the Prophet or included others, like the Prophet's mother and wives. For instance, regarding the specific question whether a dhimmi who repented after insulting the Prophet should be punished by death, Hanbali and Shafiʿi jurists generally ruled that he should. Malik held that capital punishment would not apply if he repented after the arrest. Malik and Ibn Hanbal also held that the death sentence would be waived if the dhimmi converted to Islam. Shafiʿi jurists waived the death sentence if he repented and accepted reverting to the pact of protection.[104] *Al-Ṣārim* mentions three different positions in the Hanbali School on the issue of repentance:

(1) Repentance was not at all acceptable. (2) Repentance was acceptable in all cases. (3) It was acceptable in case of a Muslim offender reverting to Islam, but in case of a dhimmi only if he converted to Islam.[105] To Ahmad b. Hanbal, the punishment of death for changing religion did not apply when a Muslim repented and returned to Islam.[106]

Three different opinions were attributed even to Imam Ahmad b. Hanbal on this issue. The first statement mentioned above, as narrated by his cousin Hanbal, is not conclusive; the Imam expressed it as his opinion, and Hanbal clarified that the rejection of repentance and death sentence for a Muslim and a dhimmi were based on different grounds. The Imam's second opinion was reported by his son ʿAbdullah. He asked his father, 'Should a person who insulted the Prophet be invited to repent?' Ibn Hanbal replied, 'He must be sentenced to death and not asked to repent' and explained that Khalid b. Walid, a Companion of the Prophet, killed a person who had insulted the Prophet, without inviting him to repent. Probably anticipating a possible objection, ʿAbdullah explained that this opinion did not differ from his father's principal view (*madhhab*), that a 'simple apostate' (*al-murtadd al-mujarrad*) must be invited to repent three times. He also clarified that the Imam's authoritative view (*mashhūr*), in which he followed major Companions of the Prophet, required inviting all apostates to repent.[107] Distinguishing the various categories of apostasy, ʿAbdullah described the 'simple apostate' as 'one who was not born a Muslim' (*mawlūd ʿala ʾl-fiṭra*).[108]

Ibn Taymiyya distinguished the 'simple apostate' from the heretic, the rebel, the one who insulted the Prophet and the one who left the Muslim community after apostasy.[109] Having clarified that the point at issue was not repentance (*tawba*) but inviting the offender to repent (*istitāba*), Ibn Taymiyya dismissed the idea of invitation because the Prophet administered the death sentence in cases of apostasy and breach of pact and did not invite the offender to repent.[110]

The fourth issue: Defining *sabb*, *kufr* and *istiḥlāl*

Ibn Taymiyya ruled: 'It is established that every act of *sabb* and *shatm* (blasphemy, insulting) that attracts the death punishment signifies apostasy (*kufr*, disbelief), even if every case of apostasy is not considered blasphemy (*sabb*).'[111] He developed this general rule in view of juristic differences about the application of the two terms in the cases of Muslims and dhimmis and in determining punishments for the various categories of apostasy and blasphemy. According to him, the concepts of apostasy, blasphemy and breach of pact were closely associated with belief (*imān*), and distinguishing between the legal application of belief to Muslims and dhimmis required both theological and hermeneutical as well as legal and juridical analysis of the implications of belief in these offences. Ibn Taymiyya considered this analysis so critical that he added a preamble to this section on the fourth issue.[112] He explained that faith in Islam required confirmation of Muhammad as prophet; insulting him negated that verification in case of Muslims. Some deviant theologians like the Jahmiyya argued to the contrary; they said that some acts might be sinful but could not be considered denial of belief. Ibn Taymiyya refuted this argument and clarified that the act of insulting falsified belief. The requirement of confirmation in the heart was witnessed in practice. Faith in the Prophet meant respect for and obedience to him; faith would not be complete without compliance. To insult a person whom one claims to believe in as Prophet of God would be an act of disbelief.[113] Ibn Taymiyya felt the need to add this preamble in the discussion on the fourth issue, probably to reproach the Hanbali jurist Qadi Abu Yaʿla b. al-Farraʾ, who suggested distinguishing between public (*ẓāhir*) and private (*bāṭin*) expression of apostate belief. The Qadi's comments stood opposed to Ahmad b. Hanbal, Muhammad b. Sahnun, Qadi ʿIyad and Abu Ishaq b. Rahwayh, according to Ibn Taymiyya, who believed that all the Sunni jurists maintained that faith pertained to both belief and action.[114] Consequently, the jurist community unanimously regarded insulting as apostasy in the case of a Muslim, regardless of whether the speaker uttered the insults in public or in private, whether he regarded them as forbidden or permissible, or whether he uttered them deliberately or in forgetfulness or by mistake.[115] Qadi Abu Yaʿla, as cited in *al-Ṣārim* on this point, agreed with Ibn Taymiyya's view. He elaborated that if a Muslim insulted God and his Prophet in public, yet claimed that he did not consider his act lawful, his testimony would be set aside and he would be judged according to what was evident. This was because, according to him, public expression of disbelief in God and his Prophet was motivated only by apostasy. To clarify his point, he compared it with the case of a thief who pleaded that he did not consider his act lawful; his faith would be judged by his private belief, but he would be punished for his evident act, because there was some personal gain for him in committing that act. Qadi Abu Yaʿla added that according to some jurists, if a person insulted the Prophet and considered it lawful, he would be regarded as an apostate, but if he did not consider it lawful and still committed that act, he would be regarded as sinful (*fāsiq*). He also cited some reports about the Iraqi jurists who ruled for punishment of lashes in some cases of insulting the Prophet.[116] Ibn Taymiyya reproached Abu Yaʿla for bringing up irrelevant theological issues like the Jahmiyya,[117] who defined belief as faith at heart even if the person might not express it in words or deeds. He faulted the Qadi for contradictory arguments, rejecting evidence and stories of dissenting jurists that were contrary to his own views.[118]

After clarifying the theological implications, Ibn Taymiyya proceeded to develop his hermeneutics on the meaning of *sabb*, the central term in *al-Ṣārim*. The word had a broad semantic field that covered words/speech actions (*kalām*) and religious practices and included cursing (*laʿn*) and rebuking (*taqbīḥ*), words and actions with the intent to disparage (*intiqāṣ*) or ridicule (*istikhfāf*). He clarified that the following categories of insulting (blasphemy) were also to be considered apostasy in case of Muslims: allusion (*taʿrīḍ*), disparagement (*tanaqquṣ*), insinuation (*lamz*), mockery (*istihzāʾ*), faulting (*ʿayb*), resistance (*ḥaraj*), hurt (*īdhāʾ*), etc.,[119] and the words and actions which common people regard as insults. Ibn Taymiyya considered it erroneous to assume that *sabb* was not punishable apostasy if the speaker did not consider it forbidden at heart. He clarified that *istiḥlāl*, believing the forbidden to be lawful, is another form of apostasy.

Defining *istiḥlāl* as believing that the matter in question was not really forbidden by God,[120] Ibn Taymiyya described it as the secret (*sirr*) to grasping the gravity of the issue.[121] Accordingly, to believe that public expression of apostasy was lawful if one believed that it was forbidden would also be *istiḥlāl* constituting apostasy; mere belief that insulting was not forbidden in one form or other sufficed to convict a person for apostasy. No distinction was allowed between insulting the Prophet, his Companions and Muslims in general. Insulting was forbidden even when the words were spoken in a fit of anger or as a joke. Ibn Taymiyya, however, distinguished between blasphemy and apostasy when he distinguished between the disbelief (*kufr*) of a non-Muslim (which he called *kufr mujarrad*, simple disbelief) and the apostasy of a Muslim (*tabdīl dīn*, changing religion).[122] Simple apostasy meant denying Muhammad as prophet. In case of Muslims, some jurists recommended that the offender should be invited to repent; Ibn Taymiyya disagreed. In case of dhimmis it did not count as breach of pact, nor did it attract the death sentence; they were not, however, allowed to express it publicly, and were liable to discretionary punishment.[123] Ibn Taymiyya provides a detailed list of the various categories of *sabb*; while the punishment unanimously prescribed for insulting the prophets was death, the majority supported the death penalty for insulting God and the Prophet's wives, but differed over its application in the case of insulting the Companions.

Ibn Taymiyya's jurisprudence

In *al-Ṣārim*, Ibn Taymiyya referred to the following four sources of evidence (*dalīl*) in this order: consensus (*ijmā ʿ*), Qur'an, hadith and *i ʿtibār* (interpretation), replacing *qiyās*. His theorization of these sources differed from other jurists due to his hermeneutical approach.

Ijmā ʿ

Ibn Taymiyya presented *ijmā ʿ*, consensus, as the definitive source of legal authority, but as explained above, he did not mean by it the total agreement of all the jurists. He regularly mentioned the names of jurists who differed with what he claimed was the consensus. Ibn Taymiyya referred to Abu Hanifa and al-Shafi ʿi disagreeing with his views; he mentioned Hanafi jurists, often not by their school affiliation.[124] To dismiss the differences among the jurists, Ibn Taymiyya employed the scholastic method of resolving contradictions and differences: listing objections, offering rebuttals and drawing definitive conclusions.

The Qur'an and Sunna

Ibn Taymiyya developed a unique hermeneutic method to define the meaning of the Qur'anic verses connecting with other semantic fields of the words used. In this way, he managed to equate 'annoyance' with 'hostility' and 'disobedience' and to derive capital punishment in this world from the otherworldly punishment promised in the Qur'an. For instance, look at the following four verses. I have added emphasis to show offences in bold and punishment in italics.

1. And among them are men who **hurt (*yū ʾdhūn*) the Prophet (Muhammad)** . . . But those who **hurt Allah's Messenger** (Muhammad) will have *a painful torment*. (9:61).

2. Verily, those who **annoy (*yū'dhūn*) Allah and His Messenger** – Allah has *cursed* them in this world, and in the Hereafter, and has prepared for them a *humiliating torment* (33:57).
3. Know they not that **whoever opposes (*yuḥādid*) and shows hostility to Allah and His Messenger**, certainly for him will be the *Fire of Hell* to abide therein. That is *extreme disgrace* (9:63).
4. I will cast terror into the hearts of those who have disbelieved, so *strike them over the necks, and smite over all their fingers and toes.* This is because they **defied and disobeyed (*shāqqū*) Allah and His Messenger**. And whoever **defies and disobeys (*yushāqiq*)** Allah and His Messenger, then verily, Allah is severe in *punishment.* (8:12–13).

Ibn Taymiyya used the hermeneutic method of parallelism to determine the meaning of these verses by looking at patterns of word substitution in the Qur'an. These verses contain parallel statements about punishment for offences against God and the Prophet. Ibn Taymiyya concluded that by using hurting, annoying, opposing and disobeying (the highlighted terms) as substitutes for each other, God demonstrated that they were synonyms. Consequently, an insulting statement implies hostility, disobedience and defiance. As to the punishment, the substituted words are painful torment (*'adhāb*), the fire of hell (*nār Jahannam*), curse (*la'n*), extreme disgrace (*dhilla*), severe punishment and striking over the neck (*ḍarb 'ala al-a'nāq*). Thus, he concluded that the punishment prescribed for the offence of insulting the Prophet was striking over the neck. Therefore, *īdhā'* (hurt, curse, insult) = *kufr* (renouncing Islam) + *muḥaraba* (treason).[125]

He cited different sets of verses to justify the punishment. One set was presented to argue that since the Muslim community was hurt by such offences, they could only get satisfaction by fighting and sentencing the offenders (9:14–15, 20). Another set of verses was cited to argue that insulting the Prophet was synonymous with challenging God and defying Him (4:65; 9:58, 61–6; 24:63; 33:53, 57–8; 49:1–5). He cited several Qur'anic verses (3:21; 9:6–14, 28–9) dealing with diverse subjects not directly related to the subject of *sabb* and the death sentence (like fighting the non-Muslims, violation of the treaties and the etiquette of visiting the Prophet) to argue that insulting and hurting the Prophet was synonymous with apostasy, denial of belief in Islam by a Muslim. The same act, in the case of a dhimmi, amounted to a breach of the pact of protection. In both cases, apostasy and blasphemy meant declaring war against the Muslim community (9:62–3, 33:57). He laid down a principle of interpretation: 'When a protected person publicly faults our religion, he breaks the pact and the generality of the verse applies to him, in word and meaning. This kind of generality reaches the level of clear text.'[126]

I'tibār

It is significant that Ibn Taymiyya chose *i'tibār* ('consideration') in place of *qiyās* (syllogistic reasoning). *I'tibār* (*ta'bīr*, 'interpretation') is technically hermeneutic and broader than syllogism (*ta'līl*), on which juristic *qiyās* is based. Ibn Taymiyya strongly criticized the use of Greek logic[127] and the *qiyās* based on Greek logic[128] commonly applied in *uṣūl al-fiqh*. He frequently also used the term *qiyās*, but in the meaning of 'measuring', i.e. equality in reason (*ḥikma*) in both the branch (*far*ʿ, the given case) and the root (*aṣl*, the precedent) as well as equality in the 'evidence of reason'.[129] He called it *al-qiyās al-jalī* when this equality or similarity was quite evident. Apparently, *qiyās jalī* and *i*ʿ*tibār* both refer to this method of discovering reason in the legal text.

Conclusion

Ibn Taymiyya wrote *al-Ṣārim* to defend himself after he was convicted and punished for falsely accusing a Christian. Ibn Taymiyya's polemical discussion is juristic in structure, but the structure of his reasoning is more rhetorical than legal.

He offers extensive evidence from the Qur'an, Sunna, Islamic law and early Muslim history. The hermeneutic method of his interpretation of Qur'anic verses, however, is quite subjective. He claimed consensus among Muslim jurists of all schools that the punishment for blasphemy was death, regardless of whether the offence was committed by a Muslim or non-Muslim. This claim of consensus is incorrect. Ibn Taymiyya himself stated the Hanafi school's position that a Muslim apostate must be given the opportunity to recant his blasphemy, or rather, he must be invited to do so. A non-Muslim could be punished for blasphemy, but it did not constitute breach of the pact, as Ibn Taymiyya claimed. Ibn Taymiyya developed a peculiar type of hermeneutics to reduce the differences of opinion between various schools and jurists into agreement. Subsequently even the Hanafi jurists, who differed with other schools, began to be influenced by Ibn Taymiyya's reasoning.

Ibn Taymiyya addressed the issue in the context of the Crusades and the Mongol invasions in the thirteenth and fourteenth centuries. It was in this war context that he appealed to the centrality of the Prophet Muhammad in Muslim theology and referred to the consensus of the community of scholars as decisive. The above analysis shows that the thrust of his argument reflects Muslim sensibilities about political and social cohesion, rather than Islamic jurisprudence. The roots of Muslim sensibilities about the freedom of religion and expression can be traced to the early history of Islam, when the community came to be divided into various conflicting groups due to political, ethnic, theological and juristic differences. The jurists later came to believe that unity in this diversity could be achieved only through consensus based on adherence (*taqlīd*) to schools of law (*madhāhib*). In this environment, the collective interest of the community regulated individual freedom and autonomy of the self. More significantly, political preferences began to define collective interests. Heresy, apostasy and insulting the Prophet were perceived to threaten community cohesion and transgress the limits on freedom of religion and expression. Ibn Taymiyya's restrictions on the public expressions of one's belief are more likely political comments than theological arguments.

Ibn Taymiyya's arguments assumed a perpetual state of war. Apostates and blasphemers were assumed to be enemies, or it was feared that they would join the enemy camp. Laws based on these arguments call for revision in the modern context, when international law is based on pacts and treaties and a state of war is not the norm.

Notes

1 I must express my gratitude to several colleagues who read this chapter and made valuable suggestions, particularly to my fellow editors who commented on several drafts.

2 This chapter refers to the edition Ibn Taymiyya, *al-Ṣārim al-Maslūl ʿalā Shātim al-Rasūl*, ed. Muhyi al-Din ʿAbd al-Hamid (al-Hirs al-Watani al-Mamlikat al-Saʿudiyya, 1983), hereafter cited as 'Ibn Taymiyya, *al-Ṣārim*'. For this and many other texts I refer to the electronic collection al-Maktaba Al-Shāmila, version 3.64 (2016), hereafter '*al-Shamila* 2016 edition'. See also Ibn Taymiyya, *al-Ṣārim al-Maslūl ʿalā Shātim al-Rasūl*, ed. Muhammad b. ʿAbdullah b. ʿUmar al-Halwani and Muhammad Kabir Ahmad Shawdari (al-Dammam: Dar al-Maʿali, 2007). I have also benefited from the Urdu translation by Ghulam Ahmad Hariri, revised and annotated by Hafiz Shahid Mahmud using the above 2007 edition (Lahore: Maktaba Quddusiya, 2011), PDF: www.kitabosunnat.com, accessed 20 July 2018, hereafter cited as 'Mahmud, *al-Ṣārim*'. Thirteen manuscripts existing in various libraries of the world, a considerable number of commentaries and abridgements before its first printing in 1904, fourteen prints since then and more than one translation in Urdu illustrate *al-Ṣārim*'s continuing impact. See the editor's introduction in the above-mentioned edition of *al-Ṣārim* about commentaries and abridgements.

3 I prefer to translate the Arabic word *shatm* as 'insulting' to cover its several meanings and to convey a sense of offence. *Shatm* is translated in English to mean to abuse, revile and vilify. These meanings do not convey the full sense of the Arabic word. Abuse is more often used in the meaning of abusing one's power, hence implying a certain legitimacy. To revile conveys a sense of criticism, finding fault. Vilifying refers to defaming and disparaging, and also includes the sense of insulting. Ibn Taymiyya uses the words *shatm* and *sabb* (abusing, calling names and insulting) almost synonymously, but focuses more on *sabb* than *shatm* in this book.

4 The term 'blasphemy' in this chapter refers to the terms *sabb al-nabī* and *shatm al-rasūl* used in *al-Ṣārim* and other Islamic legal texts. For a discussion of its juristic meanings, see the section 'Doctrinal context' in this chapter.

5 Muhammad Ismail Qureshy, *Muhammad, the Messenger of God and the Law of Blasphemy in Islam and the West* (Lahore: Nuqoosh, 2008).

6 See Yossef Rapoport and Shahab Ahmed (eds), *Ibn Taymiyya and His Times* (Oxford: Oxford University Press, 2010), 'Introduction', pp. 4–20, at pp. 16–17. Also, Henry Laoust, 'Ibn Taymiyya', *Encyclopaedia of Islam, New Edition* (Leiden: Brill, 1979), vol. 3, p. 954 for his posthumous influence on later scholars and references therein for manuscripts; and David Thomas and Alex Mallett (eds), *Christian–Muslim Relations: A Bibliographical History*, vol. 4, *1200–1350* (Leiden: Brill, 2012), p. 583.

7 Rapoport and Ahmed, *Ibn Taymiyya and His Times*, 'Introduction'. Ibn Qayyim counts 350, al-Dhahabi, 500; others mention as many as 700.

8 Ibn Taymiyya, *al-Ṣārim*, p. 2.

9 Thomas and Mallett, *Christian–Muslim Relations*, p. 855 mentions the following five studies on this book: Hasan Qasim Murad, '*Miḥan* of Ibn Taymiyya: A narrative account based on a comparative analysis of sources', unpublished M.A. Thesis (Montreal, Canada: McGill University, 1968), http://digitool.library.mcgill.ca/webclient/StreamGate?folder_id=0&dvs=1508038755332~914&usePid1=true&usePid2=true (accessed 15 October 2017); Murad, 'Ibn Taymiyya on trial: A narrative account of his *Miḥan*', *Islamic Studies* 18 (1979), pp. 1–32, at pp. 1–2, 26 n. 4; Abdelmagid Turki,

'Situation du "Tributaire" qui insulte l'Islam, au regard de la doctrine de la jurisprudence musulmane', *Studia Islamica* 30 (1969), pp. 39–72; Thomas F. Michel (ed./transl.), *A Muslim Theologian's Response to Christianity: Ibn Taymiyya's al-Jawāb al-Ṣaḥīḥ* (Delmar, New York: Caravan Books, 1984); Yochanan Friedmann, *Tolerance and Coercion in Islam: Interfaith Relations in the Muslim Tradition* (Cambridge: Cambridge University Press, 2003), pp. 149–52; and al-Halwani and Shawdari, *al-Ṣārim al-Maslūl*, pp. 165–82, 211–51.

10 Ibn Taymiyya, *al-Ṣārim*, p. 2.

11 Abu Zahra, *Ibn Taymiyya: Ḥāyatuhu wa ʿAṣruhu wa Ārāʾuhu wa Fiqhuhu* (Cairo: Dar al-Fikr al-ʿArabi, 1977), p. 147.

12 H. Laoust, 'Ibn Taymiyya', p. 951.

13 Abu Zahra, *Ibn Taymiyya*, pp. 127, 134.

14 Murad, '*Miḥan* of Ibn Taymiyya'; Murad, 'Ibn Taymiyya on trial'; and Laoust, 'Ibn Taymiyya'. See note 47.

15 Donald P. Little, 'Did Ibn Taymiyya have a screw loose?', *Studia Islamica* 41 (1975), pp. 93–111, at p. 103. The title refers to the famous remark reportedly made by Ibn Taymiyya's contemporary Ibn Battuta (d. 1369), '*illā anna fī ʿaqlihi shayʾan*' ('except that there was something wrong with his intelligence'), which Little analysed. Little doubted if Ibn Battuta actually met Ibn Taymiyya. Little, p. 103.

16 Abu'l Hasan ʿAli Nadwi, *Tarikh Da'wat o ʿAẓīmat* (Azamgarh: Matbaʿa Maʿarif, 1957), p. 141.

17 Ibid.

18 Rapoport and Ahmed, *Ibn Taymiyya and His Times*.

19 Ibn Taymiyya, *al-Ṣārim*, p. 2.

20 Almost all later sources, including modern scholars like Henri Laoust, rely on Ibn Taymiyya's student Ibn Kathir for this story, but David Thomas finds Shams al-Din al-Jazari's fuller account more reliable. Thomas and Mallett, *Christian–Muslim Relations*, p. 853.

21 In Ibn Kathir's report, ʿAssaf is the name of the Christian who insulted the Prophet. Contrary to Ibn Kathir, Al-Jazari mentioned ʿAssaf as the name of the Amir (ʿAssaf b. al-Amir Shahab al-Din Ahmad b. Hajji) whom the Christian served as secretary. Further, Ibn Kathir reported that a group of people testified that they had witnessed the offence of blasphemy committed by the Christian. Ibn al-Jazari reported that certain persons from al-Suwayda came to Damascus and reported the event. But Amir ʿAssaf interceded, and the Christian was not arrested. According to Ibn Kathir, the Christian surrendered himself to the investigating council and converted to Islam. He provided evidence of the witnesses' hostility against him. He was acquitted and travelled to Hijaz, where his nephew killed him in the neighbourhood of Medina. Ibn Kathir, *Al-Bidāya wa al-Nihāya*, Urdu translation (Karachi: Nafis Academy, 1989), vol. 13, p. 551.

22 Mark S. Wagner describes the Christian as a priest. Mark S. Wagner, 'Time to argue for Islam's humane view of blasphemy', *Christian Science Monitor*, 17 September 2012, http://www.csmonitor.com/Commentary/Opinion/2012/0917/Time-to-argue-for-Islam-s-humane-view-of-blasphemy (accessed 26 December 2012).

23 The jurists included al-Khatib Sharaf al-Din b. al-Maqdisi, Safi al-Din al-Hindi, Jamal al-Din al-Bajiriqi and Ibn al-Wakil.

24 Shams al-Din Abi ʿAbd Allah Muhammad b. Ibrahim b. Abi Bakr Ibn al-Jazari, *Tārīkh Ḥawādith al-Zamān wa Abnāʾihi wa Wafayāt al-Akābir wa'l-Aʿyān min Abnāʾihi* (Beirut: al-Maktaba al-ʿAsriyya, 1998), *al-Shamila* 2016 edition, pp. 202–5.

25 Ibn Kathir, *Al-Bidāya wa al-Nihāya*, p. 551.
26 Ibn Taymiyya, *al-Ṣārim*, pp. 2–3.
27 Ibid.
28 'I composed a big book that I titled *al-Ṣārim al-Maslūl* [...]. I have discussed this issue in that book. I do not know anyone who wrote on this issue before me.' Ibn Taymiyya, *Majmū' al-Fatāwā* (Madina: Majma' al-Malik Fahd li-Taba'at al-Mushaf, 1998), *al-Shamila* 2016 edition, vol. 3, p. 515.
29 The *Concise Oxford English Dictionary* (2008) defines the term 'blasphemy' as 'profane or sacrilegious talk about God or sacred things'. Article 298 in the Penal Code of Pakistan defines it as a religious offence as follows: 'Whoever, with the deliberate intention of wounding the religious feelings of any person, utters any word or makes any sound in the hearing of that person or makes any gesture in the sight of that person or places any object in the sight of that person, shall be punished with imprisonment [...] for a term which may extend to one year, or with fine, or with both.' Article 295 c (amended in 1986) defines the offence of insulting the Prophet as follows: 'Whoever by words, either spoken or written, or by visible representation, or by any imputation, innuendo, or insinuation, directly or indirectly, defiles the sacred name of the Holy Prophet Muhammad [...]'. The term 'blasphemy' in this chapter refers, therefore, to *sabb al-nabī*, or *shatm al-rasūl*, translated as insulting the Prophet Muhammad.
30 His work *Risāla fī Man Sabb al-Nabī* is still in manuscript. See Sha'ban Muftah Isma'il, 'Muḥammad Ibn Saḥnūn: an educationalist and faqih', *Muslim Education Quarterly*, 12/4 (1995), pp. 37–54, at p. 40.
31 Qadi 'Iyad b. Musa, *al-Shifā' bi-Ta'rīf Ḥuqūq al-Muṣṭafā* (Amman: Dar al-Fayha', 1986).
32 *Al-Mawsū'a al-Fiqhiyya al-Kuwaytiyya*, vol. 24 (2006), pp. 133–44.
33 The term *sabb al-nabī* is rarely mentioned in early texts like *al-Muwaṭṭā'*, *al-Mudawwana* or *al-Umm*; first mention is mostly under the headings of apostasy, jihad and *siyar*.
34 For instance, Mulla Khusru (*Durar al-Ḥukkām*, commentary on *Ghurar al-Aḥkām*, *al-Shamila* 2016 edition, vol. 1, p. 300) concludes his arguments on the death sentence for blasphemy with a general statement that it was the legal position of Abu Hanifa, the jurists in Kufa and Malik and his followers. He also refers to the Maliki jurists Ibn Sahnun, al-Khattab and Taqi al-Din al-Subki as well as the Hanafi jurist al-Bazzazi, who claimed complete consensus by Muslim jurists on this position. See the section on 'Ibn Taymiyya's impact'.
35 Al-Razi, *Mukhtaṣar al-Ṭaḥāwī* (2010, *al-Shāmila*), vol. 6, p. 141–2; Al-Sughdi, *al-Natf fī al-Fatāwā* (Beirut: Mu'assasat al-Risala, 1984), vol. 2, p. 694; al-Marghinani, *al-Hidāya* (Beirut: Dar Ihya al-Turath al-'Arabi, n.d.), vol. 2, p. 405.
36 Abu 'Abdallah b. Hanbal, *Mas'ala Aḥmad b. Ḥanbal* (Beirut: Al-Maktab al-Islami, 1981), vol. 1, p. 431.
37 Al-Qayrawani, *al-Risāla* (Dar al-Fikr, *al-Shamila*), vol. 1, p. 127.
38 Ibn 'Abd al-Barr, *al-Kāfī fī Fiqh Ahl al-Madīna* (Riyadh: Maktabat al-Riyad al-Haditha, 1980), vol. 2, p. 1091.
39 Al-Juwayni, *Nihāya al-Maṭlab fī Dirāya al-Madhhab* (Dar al-Minhaj, 2007), *al-Shamila* 2016 edition, vol. 18, p. 47.
40 Ibn 'Abd al-Barr, *al-Kāfī*, vol. 2, p. 1091.
41 Ibn Qudama, *al-Kāfī fī fiqh al-Imām Aḥmad* (Beirut: Dar al-Kutub al-'Ilmiyya, 1994), vol. 4, p. 62.

42 See Qadi ʿIyad b. Musa, *al-Shifāʾ*, vol. 2, p. 551.
43 Al-Maqdisi, *Kitāb al-Furūʿ* (Beirut: Muʾassasat al-Risala, 2003), vol. 10, p. 94.
44 Ibn Zuhrah al-Halabi, *Ghunyat al-Nuzūʿ* (Qum: Iʿtimad, 1417/1997), p. 429; al-Muhaqqiq al-Hilli, *Sharāʾiʿ al-Islām* (Tehran: Istiqlal, 1988), vol. 4, p. 948; al-Fadil al-Abi, *Kashf al-Rumūz* (Qum: Muʾassassat al-Nashr al-Islami, 1410/1990), vol. 2, p. 567.
45 Al-Juwayni, *Nihāya*, vol. 18, pp. 46–7.
46 Ibid.
47 Qadi ʿIyad, *al-Shifāʾ*, vol. 2, p. 550.
48 Ibid., pp. 496–8.
49 See *al-Mawsūʿa al-Fiqhiyya al-Kuwaytiyya*, *al-Shamila* 2016 edition, vol. 17, pp. 129, 131.
50 Sahl al-Sarakhsi, *al-Mabsūṭ* (Beirut: Dar al-Maʿrifa, n.d.), *al-Shamila* 2016 edition, vol. 10, p. 110.
51 Ibn ʿAbd al-Barr, *al-Kāfī*, *al-Shamila* 2016 edition, vol. 2, p. 1091; Nasr, *al-Māʿūna*, vol. 1, p. 1408; Ibn Qudama, *al-Kāfī*, vol. 4, p. 62; Juwayni, *Nihāya*, vol. 18, pp. 46–7.
52 Juwayni, *Nihāya*, vol. 18, pp. 46–7.
53 Sarakhsi, *al-Mabsūṭ*, vol. 10, pp. 98–9.
54 Muhammad b. Hasan al-Shaybani, *al-Siyar al-Ṣaghīr* (Beirut: Dar al-Muttahida li al-Nashr, 1975), p. 197.
55 Sarakhsi, *al-Mabsūṭ*, vol. 10, pp. 98–9.
56 Abu al-Husayn Quduri, *Mukhtaṣar al-Qudūrī* (Beirut: Dar al-Kutub al-ʿIlmiyya, 1997), p. 237.
57 Sarakhsi, *al-Mabsūṭ*, vol. 10, p. 110.
58 Juwayni, *Nihāya*, vol. 18, pp. 46–7.
59 Abu al-Walid ibn Rushd, *al-Bayan*, *al-Shamila* 2016 edition, vol. 16, p. 398.
60 Al-Kasani, *Badāʾiʿ al-Ṣanāʾiʿ* (Beirut: Dar al-Kutub al-ʿIlmiyya, 1986), vol. 7, p. 113.
61 Al-Shafiʿi, *al-Umm* (Beirut: Dar al-Maʿrifa, 1990), *al-Shamila* 2016 edition, vol. 4, pp. 208–9.
62 Ibid., p. 198. Ibn Qayyim stated that Shafiʿi regarded insulting as a breach of the pact and punishable by death, but I was not able to find that in *al-Umm*. Ibn Qayyim, *Aḥkām Ahl al-Dhimma* (Al-Dammam: Rumadi li al-Nashr, 1997), *al-Shamila* 2016 edition, vol. 3, p. 1371.
63 Shafiʿi, *al-Umm*, vol. 6, p. 169.
64 Ibid., p. 178.
65 Sarakhsi, *al-Mabsūṭ*, vol. 10, p. 116.
66 Al-Marghinani, *al-Hidāya*, *al-Shamila* 2016 edition, vol. 2, p. 404.
67 Murtada, *al-Intiṣār* (Qum: Muʾassasat al-Nashr al-Islami, 1415/1994), pp. 480–1.
68 Qadi ʿIyad, *al-Shifāʾ*, vol. 2, p. 467.
69 Ibn Taymiyya, *al-Ṣārim*, p. 587.
70 Ibid., p. 3.
71 Also spelled 'Rahawayh' and 'Rahwayh'.
72 Ibn Taymiyya, *al-Ṣārim*, p. 4.
73 For detailed analysis, see ibid., p. 10.
74 Ibid., p. 3, Qadi ʿIyad, *al-Shifāʾ*, vol. 2, p. 205. Also, Ibn al-Mundhir, *al-Awsat*, vol. 2, p. 682; Ibn al-Mundhir, *al-Ijmāʿ*, p. 153 (cited in Mahmud, *al-Ṣārim*, p. 38). Ibn al-Mundhir mentions Malik, Layth b. Saʿd, al-Shafiʿi, Ahmad, Ishaq and his followers. He does not include Abu Hanifa. Ibn al-Mundhir, *Al-Iqnāʿ*, edited by ʿAbd Allah b. ʿAbd al-ʿAziz al-Jibrin, published in 1408/1987, *al-Shamila* 2016 edition, vol. 2, p. 584.

75 Ibn Taymiyya, *al-Ṣārim*, p. 4. Al-Khattabi's full statement cited in *al-Shifāʾ*, 'I do not know any Muslim who disagrees with the obligatory death punishment in case of a Muslim', clarifies that he was referring to a Muslim insulting the Prophet, not to a non-Muslim. His fuller statement in *Maʿalim al-Sunan* makes it clearer: 'It explains that one who insults the Prophet is sentenced to death because his act of insulting the Prophet constitutes apostasy from Islam. I do not know any Muslim disputing that his death punishment is legally obligatory. However, in the case of a *dhimmī* (non-Muslim), the jurists disagreed. Malik b. Anas ruled that a Jew or a Christian who insulted the Prophet should be sentenced to death if he did not accept Islam. Ahmad b. Hanbal held the same view. Shafiʿi ruled that a dhimmi who insulted the Prophet must be sentenced to death and his protection be withdrawn. He derived this rule from the story of Kaʿb b. al-Ashraf. It is narrated that Abu Hanifa held that dhimmis must not be sentenced to death for insulting the Prophet, because they were protected despite believing in more than one God, which was a graver offence than insulting.' *Maʿalim al-Sunan* [commentary on *Sunan Abī Dāʿūd*] (Aleppo: al-Matbaʿa al-ʿIlmiyya, 1932), vol. 3, p. 296.

76 Qadi ʿIyad, *al-Shifāʾ*, vol. 2, p. 216.

77 Ibn Taymiyya, *al-Ṣārim*, p. 4.

78 The punishment mentioned in the Qurʾan refers to Muslim offenders ('And if any of you turn back from their faith and die in unbelief, their works will bear no fruit in this life and in the Hereafter; they will be companions of the Fire and will abide therein', 2:217).

79 Ibn Taymiyya, *al-Ṣārim*, p. 314.

80 Ibid., p. 5. Al-Khiraqi, *Mukhtaṣar* (n.p: Dar al-Sahaba li al-Turath, 1993), *al-Shamila* 2016 edition, pp. 132–3.

81 Ibn Taymiyya, *al-Ṣārim*, p. 6.

82 Ibid., p. 8, Shafiʿi, *al-Umm*, vol. 6, p. 150.

83 Ibn Taymiyya, *al-Ṣārim*, p. 8.

84 Ibid., p. 8.

85 Ibid., pp. 10–11.

86 Ibid., pp. 11–59.

87 Ibid., p. 15.

88 Ibid., p. 57.

89 Ibid., pp. 11–18.

90 Ibid., p. 217.

91 Ibid., pp. 61–200.

92 Ibid., p. 153.

93 Ibid.

94 Ibid., pp. 200–5.

95 Ibid., p. 202.

96 Ibid., pp. 206 ff.

97 Ibid., p. 253. This concerns the following verse: 'When you meet the unbelievers, smite their necks, then, when you have made wide slaughter among them, tie fast the bonds; then set them free, either by grace or ransom, till the war lays down its loads. So it shall be; and if God had willed, He would have avenged Himself upon them; but that He may try some of you by means of others. And those who are slain in the way of God, He will not send their works astray.' Qurʾan 47:4, Arberry's translation. Pickthall also translates it as grace. Others use the terms generosity (Yusuf Ali) and favour (Shakir).

98 Turki, 'Situation du "Tributaire"', pp. 42–3.

99 For Ibn Taymiyya's analysis of *al-fidā'*, see *al-Ṣārim*, pp. 276–84.
100 Ibn Taymiyya, *al-Ṣārim*, vol. 1, p. 256 (Imam Ahmad); p. 258 (al-Shafi'i, Malik); p. 259 (Abu Hanifa).
101 Ibid., pp. 274–99.
102 Ibid., p. 300.
103 Ibid., p. 300.
104 Ibid., p. 330.
105 Ibid., p. 330.
106 Ibid., p. 306.
107 Ibid., p. 301.
108 The Urdu version of the book translates it as 'born by nature as Muslim'. This is in view of the hadith that every child is naturally born a Muslim; the parents make him Christian . . . This translation is not befitting the Imam's argument. Mahmud, *al-Ṣārim,* p. 393.
109 Ibn Taymiyya, *al-Ṣārim*, pp. 319, 320, 342.
110 Ibid., p. 300.
111 Ibid., p. 525.
112 Ibid., pp. 512–25.
113 Ibid., pp. 515–25.
114 Ibid., pp. 512–13.
115 Ibid., pp. 512–13.
116 Ibid., pp. 514.
117 Followers of Jahm b. Safwan, executed in 746 during the Umayyad period.
118 Ibn Taymiyya, *al-Ṣārim*, p. 515.
119 Ibid., pp. 525–7.
120 Ibid., p. 515.
121 Ibid., p. 512.
122 For his usage of the word *al-murtadd al-mujarrad*, see Ibn Taymiyya, *al-Ṣārim*, p. 301.
123 Ibid., p. 532.
124 Ibid., pp. 304, 313, 321, 344.
125 Ibid., pp. 20–6.
126 Ibid., p. 16.
127 Ibn Taymiyya, *Majmū' al-Fatāwā*; Wael Hallaq (ed./transl.), *Ibn Taymiyya against the Greek Logicians* (New York: Oxford University Press, 1993).
128 Ibn Taymiyya, *al-Qiyās fī al-Shar' al-Islāmī* (Beirut: Dar al-Afaq al-Jadida, 1978).
129 Ibn Taymiyya, *al-Ṣārim*, p. 371.

Part Two

Present Practices

5

The Crimes of Blasphemy and Apostasy in Iran

Mohammad Mostafaei

Blasphemy and apostasy are serious crimes under traditional Islamic law, and persons faced with such accusations risk severe punishment in today's Iran, ranging from fines and prison to lashes and death. They may be prosecuted by the judicial system under a complex mix of penal law and other codes of law, as well as uncodified religious law. They may also be persecuted by private actors, who find legitimacy for their threats or acts of violence in the legal opinions of religious scholars.

Blasphemy and apostasy are controversial issues in both international and national debates. With human progress, peace and prosperity, people have come to reject the use of cruel, inhuman or degrading punishments, such as stoning to death. The continued use of such punishments in formerly remote places has become widely publicized with the rise of global media and new technologies and provokes strong reactions. The issue has been widely discussed in Iran's legal system, as well as among ordinary citizens. Perhaps in response to such public pressure, Iranian lawmakers shelved a proposal to write a crime of apostasy into the new penal code of 2012, but as we will see, this does not mean the crime has been abolished.

In this chapter, I explore how apostasy and blasphemy are handled in the legal system of the Islamic Republic of Iran today: What is the relationship between codified and traditional law? What has changed with the penal code of 2012? Does the system satisfy basic requirements of justice?

I address these questions as a lawyer and human rights advocate who has defended young people against the death sentence in Iranian courts. I begin by presenting three cases, one drawn from my own practice and two that have been widely discussed in social media, to exemplify how these laws affect Iranian lives. I go on to discuss the definitions of the crimes and the various relevant legal provisions, and then return to the cases to see how the law has been applied in practice.

Cases

The case of Ruhollah Tavana

Ruhollah Tavana, an engineer born in Mashad in 1984, was arrested on 24 August 2011, after his friends had pressed charges against him. Ruhollah's computer was confiscated at the time of his arrest, and on its hard disk, investigators discovered a private video in which Ruhollah appeared to insult a prophet, though it is not even clear which prophet he referred to. The intelligence service accused him of many crimes, among them blasphemy – insulting the Prophet and the Imams – as well as drinking alcohol.

During his process, Ruhollah declared: 'I made a mistake and insulted the Imams and the Supreme Leader Ayatollah Khamenei at a time when I was under great mental pressure, because I didn't have a good life, and suffered from poverty.' He reaffirmed that he was a Shiʿi Muslim and a servant of the Prophet Muhammad. He also said that he had been reading the Qurʾan for many years.

Ruhollah was notified about the accusations against him on 25 October 2011. He stated during the process that the stresses in his life drove him to consume alcohol, and that when he was drunk, he would speak nonsense without being conscious of it. He rejected the accusations of blasphemy, defending himself by saying:

> I used to sometimes drink alcohol and take pills. I was not conscious when I had taken them. I made insults when I was not sober. I didn't mean to insult anybody. I have repented for the last year for what I said, but take into consideration that I'm not mentally well.

The Forensic Medicine Organization has certified that Ruhollah suffers from a personality disorder and should receive psychological treatment.

In his last defence statement (7 May 2013), Ruhollah said: 'I was an ordinary employee at the oil company. The documents you have found in my computer are from ten years ago, when I was so young.'

Despite Ruhollah's repentance and the fact that the alleged crime had been committed a decade earlier, the judges of the criminal court sentenced Ruhollah to lashes for drinking alcohol and to death by hanging for committing blasphemy. In other words, the judges acknowledged that Ruhollah had not been sober when he made the insulting statements. Ruhollah's lawyers – including myself, working on the case from Norway – filed an appeal to the Supreme Court, but unfortunately, the judges confirmed the order of the criminal court.

After this case received publicity in the media, many human rights activists and organizations condemned the decision and protested against it. With the judiciary under pressure, Iran stayed the execution and the Supreme Court issued an order to review this case carefully one more time. The case was sent to a new court in Mashhad, where it remained pending.

The case of the Imam Naghi campaign

On 11 May 2011, a Facebook page named 'Reminding Shiʿa Muslims of Imam Naghi' was launched.[1] In a very short time, the page drew the attention of Iranians, and some 35,000 people joined it. It also drew a great deal of criticism. Imam Naghi, also known as ʿAli al-Hadi, is the tenth Imam of the Imami Shiʿa, and the Facebook campaign used the name satirically. The members of the campaign, who called themselves Naghavis, said they chose Naghi as the name for their page as a mark of their great respect for him, and on their Facebook page, they asked why Iranians had not paid as much attention to him as to other Imams. The Naghi character created by the campaign, however, was very different from the traditional depiction. It should be said that the Facebook page was not created to mock Shiʿi Imams, but to criticize the Iranian clergy and the religious rulers of the Islamic Republic. The owners of the page introduced themselves as comedians who believed nothing was so sacred that it should be safe from comedy. In their view, the Iranian people would not benefit from change as long as they lived in superstition and poverty. They were opposed to religion, which they said was destructive. The campaign, started by a coalition of young Iranians, may be seen as a creative form of social resistance against fundamentalism and prejudice.

Others rejected the campaign and demanded respect for religious values. The campaign faced a great deal of criticism from other blogs, such as *Vay bar hatakin* ('Shame on the insulters'), run by Armin Alavi, which threatened to release personal details of the members of the campaign if they did not abandon it. The members of the campaign used their real names in the beginning, but later changed them to fake ones on the Facebook page. The Fars and Raja News websites also threatened to reveal their identities.

The campaign induced some people to ask Ayatollah Safi Golpayegani's opinion of the matter: 'In the name of God: Some Iranians, mainly counter-revolutionaries living outside Iran, have regretfully insulted our humble Imam Hadi [Naghi] and have abused him in cyberspace (drawings, jokes, caricatures, swearing and slandering). What is the ruling?' In response, Ayatollah Golpayegani issued a fatwa stating: 'If they have insulted the Imam, they are subject to the punishment for apostasy. God knows best.'[2]

Several young persons were arrested for their connections with the campaign and subsequently convicted to prison and lashes.[3] The judges did not sentence them to the death penalty.

The case of Shahin Najafi

Shahin Najafi is an Iranian singer, songwriter and anarchist based in Germany. A Qurʾan reciter in his youth, he began singing pop and rock as an underground musician in 2000.[4] His songs are banned in Iran. After being expelled from the university, where he had studied sociology, he migrated to Germany in 2005. In 2012, Shahin sang a song named after Imam Naghi.[5] This led to a backlash from Imami Shiʿa who believed he insulted the Imam.

As Shahin Najafi does not live in Iran, the prosecutor cannot reach him. Therefore, the alternative is to convict him by fatwa, encouraging zealots to execute the death sentence by their own hands, outside the legal system of the state.

As seen above, Ayatollah Golpayegani told his followers that if Iranians abroad had insulted Imam Naghi, they were punishable as apostates. Ayatollah Naser Makarem Shirazi, in his response to his followers, claimed that Shahin Najafi had insulted several Shiʿi Imams and went on to say: 'Any form of affront towards the Shiʿi Imams from a Muslim person is considered apostasy.'[6] By saying that Shahin Najafi may be regarded as an apostate, the fatwas imply that he is subject to the death penalty and may be killed by any Muslim who finds him. Activists of the militant Hezbollah group have claimed they are planning to kill Shahin Najafi based on Ayatollah Golpayegani's fatwa. A $100,000 bounty for his murder was posted on the Shia-Online.ir website.[7]

Apostasy and blasphemy in Iran's legal system

Iranian law deals with blasphemy and apostasy in several ways: through the penal code and the press law, as well as through uncodified law. The penal code distinguishes between *ḥadd* punishments, supposed to be specifically fixed in the Shariʿa (art. 15); *qiṣāṣ* retribution or *diya* compensation for murder and bodily harm; and *taʿzir* punishments determined by law, where courts shall take the circumstances into account when sentencing (art. 18). The *ḥadd* crimes are listed in Book Two of the penal code. They include insult to the Prophet (*sabb-e nabi*, Ar. *sabb al-nabī*), as well as sexual offenses (adultery, homosexual acts, pandering); false accusation of sexual offenses (*qazf*, Ar. *qadhf*); consuming alcohol; theft; and illegal armed activities, rebellion and 'sowing corruption' (*moharebeh*, *baqy*, *efsad-e fel-arz*; Ar. *muḥāraba*, *baghy*, *ifsād fī al-arḍ*). Absent from this comprehensive list is apostasy. *Taʿzīr* crimes, with punishments including fines, imprisonment and flogging, are dealt with in Book Five of the code and include insult to religious sanctities.

Insulting the sacred

Iranian lawmakers use the general term 'insult to the sanctities' (*tohin be moghadasat*) without a precise definition. This has led judges to interpret the phrase in different ways. *Tohin* or *ihanat* is the Persian form of an Arabic term, derived from *wahn*, which means to belittle.[8] In the *Dehkhoda* Persian dictionary, the word *tohin* means to weaken, slow down, despise and humiliate. In legal texts, the word is used to convey the meaning of despising and humiliating.

The sacred (*moghadas*, Ar. *muqaddas*) is defined as 'clean' and 'purified' in the *Dehkhoda* and other Persian dictionaries.[9] The plural *moghadasat* connotes purity, cleanness and piety. The law has to some extent defined the word, which has a variety of applications relevant to the Islamic state: the sacred realm of clergy, sacred places, sacred Imams, Islamic saints, the sacred robe of the clergy, the sacred goals of the Islamic state. If a person disrespects any of these categories, which have special value to the Iranian government, he or she can be deprived of certain rights, such as the right to stand for election. However, the law has not specifically declared the act of disrespect a crime. For example, the law has not criminalized the act of affront to the Islamic state, but in practice, any government employee who insults the Islamic state will be fired.

Insult (*tohin*) is classified into different types, each of which has a specific legal definition and specific punishments. The general term therefore has different implications, depending on the importance of the act.

Insult to the holy persons of Islam and religious sanctities is dealt with in the Islamic criminal code, Article 513:

> Anyone who insults the sacred values of Islam or any of the Great Prophets or [twelve] Shi'ite Imams or the Holy Fatima, if considered as Saab ul-nabi [i.e. as

> having committed actions warranting the *hadd* punishment for insulting the Prophet], shall be executed; otherwise, they shall be sentenced to one to five years' imprisonment.[10]

The difference between execution and imprisonment, then, turns on the notion of *sabb al-nabī*. *Sabb* means 'swearing', and *nabī* means 'prophet'. *Sabb al-nabī* specifically refers to swearing at the Prophet Muhammad. In books of Islamic law (*fiqh*), however, it has been expanded beyond its literal meaning, with narratives confirming that it is not limited to Muhammad. For example, a narrative of the Prophet says that swearing at any prophet is a punishable act.[11] Another narrative from Imam ʿAli states that he sentenced a person to 160 lashes of *ḥadd* punishment when he claimed the prophet Dawud had a sexual relationship with a woman.[12] As a result, the jurists differ over this question, e.g. over how to treat insulting and swearing at the Prophet's wives, mother and children. Some jurists believe swearing at Fatima Zahra, the Prophet's daughter, is considered *sabb al-nabī*, whereas others regard it as *qadhf*, unless the insult implies insulting the Prophet Muhammad.[13] Mohaghegh Heli believes that insult to the Prophet's family does not constitute *sabb al-nabī*.[14] Insult to the highly valued Imams has also been the subject of discussion. For example, there is a narrative from Ameri that Imam Sadegh believed someone who had insulted Imam ʿAli should be punished to death.[15]

The 2012 legislation has become stricter in that it imposes the death penalty for insulting the Imams, Fatima and the prophets.

The vagueness of the law makes it easy to accuse people of insulting the holy persons and other sanctities of Islam when they express their opinion on the religious conceptions of the state. This is particularly problematic in a system without an independent judiciary, because religious opinions can be abused to oppress critics and political rivals through unfair trials.

Apostasy in Iran's penal code

Though drafts for the new penal code included a whole section on apostasy, heresy and witchcraft,[16] the new penal code in the end has no article specifically about apostasy. One might think at first sight that this is a victory for human rights, that the hanging punishment for apostasy has been eradicated and that apostasy has been decriminalized, given that Article 2 of the new criminal code defines a crime as 'any act or omission for which punishment is provided by law'. Closer examination, however, shows that not only has the crime of apostasy not been eliminated from Iranian law, it has in fact been reinforced, by giving judges increased authority to order the death sentence.

The crime of apostasy enters through the back door of Article 220 in the penal code, which says: 'Regarding the *ḥadd* punishments that are not mentioned in this law Article [167] of the Islamic Republic of Iran's Constitution shall be applicable.'

Article 167 of the constitution, in turn, provides:

> The judge is bound to endeavor to judge each case on the basis of the codified law. In case of the absence of any such law, he has to deliver his judgment on the basis

> of authoritative Islamic sources and authentic fatawa. He, on the pretext of the silence of or deficiency of law in the matter, or its brevity or contradictory nature, cannot refrain from admitting and examining cases and delivering his judgment.

If traditional religious law, then, provides a *ḥadd* punishment for a crime on which the penal code is silent, the penal code now invokes a constitutional principle that requires a judge to judge a case according to traditional, uncodified religious law. The new article in the criminal code enabling the judge to apply Article 167 to criminal matters is a significant novelty. Lawyers and judges in Iran have previously understood Article 167 to be concerned with civil law, because its application to criminal cases would conflict with basic principles of law. Both the penal code and the constitution otherwise hold that a judge can only impose punishments that are based in law.

Blasphemy and apostasy in the press law

In Iranian society, this crime is being prosecuted under the press law as well as the penal code. Many daily newspapers and magazines have been closed down, and their chief editors punished, for insulting the sacred. The press law of 1986 states in Article 6:

> The print media are permitted to publish news items except in cases when they violate Islamic principles and codes and public rights as outlined in this chapter:
> [...]
> [item] 7. Insulting Islam and its sanctities, or, offending the Leader of the Revolution and recognized religious authorities (senior Islamic jurisprudents); [...][17]

Article 26 of the press law states that whoever insults Islam and its sanctities shall be sentenced for apostasy if the guilt amounts to apostasy; otherwise, he or she shall be subject to the penal code. The press law does not further define the crime of apostasy or the punishment for it.

Grounds for defence

Both *fiqh* and codified law not only provide punishments, but also standards of evidence and valid grounds for defence of the accused. In case of doubt and uncertainty, if intent cannot be proved, or if the accused has repented, the death penalty should not be applied.

Intent

The *mens rea* or mental element is central to the crime of insulting the sacred. In the absence of *mens rea*, the accused is not held criminally responsible. However, the views of the jurists vary. Article 263 of the new Islamic criminal code provides that:

> When the accused of a *sabb-e nabi* (swearing at the Prophet) claims that his/her statements have been under coercion or mistake, or in a state of drunkenness, or anger or slip of the tongue, or without paying attention to the meaning of the words, or quoting someone else, then s/he shall not be considered as *Sāb ul-nabi* [a person who swears at the Prophet]. *Note:* When a *sabb-e nabi* (swearing at the Prophet) is committed in the state of drunkenness, or anger or quoting someone else, if it is considered to be an insult, the offender shall be sentenced to a ta'zir punishment of up to seventy-four lashes.

This can be used to defend the accused, as in the case of Ruhollah Tavana, who declared that he did not mean to insult any of the great prophets, and affirmed his strong belief in Islam and its religious values.

Repentance

Article 114 of the criminal code of Iran provides:

> In the case of offenses punishable by *hadd*, with the exception of *qazf* and *moharebeh*, if the accused repents any time before the commission of the offense is proved, and his/her regret and correction is certain in the eyes of the judge, the *hadd* punishment shall not be given. In addition, if the abovementioned offenses, except for *qazf*, are proved by confession, if the offender repents, even after the commission of the offense is proved, the court, through the Head of Judiciary, can apply for pardon of the offender by the Leader.

The law can be interpreted in favour of the accused, but judges' views on the matter vary. It is possible for a judge not to accept a person's repentance and impose the death sentence anyway, as in the case of Ruhollah.

Uncertainty and doubt

The *fiqh* rule that lets the accused go free in case of uncertainty and doubt, which previously was not codified as such in Iranian law, is now reflected in Articles 120 and 121 of the new penal code.

> If there is any doubt or hesitation about commission of a crime or any of its elements or any of the requirements for criminal liability and no evidence is found to remove that, the offense or the requirement in question, whichever is applicable, shall not be proved.
>
> Art. 120

> In the case of crimes punishable by *hadd*, with the exception of *moharebeh*, *efsad-e-fel-arz*, theft, and *qazf*, with a mere doubt or hesitation and without any need for further evidence, the offense or the requirement in question, whichever is applicable, shall not be proved.
>
> Art. 121

The evidence required to prove a crime is specifically set out in the new Iranian penal code as confession, testimony, oath/*qasama*, or the discernment of the judge (Art. 160); oaths are not relevant to the *ḥadd* and *ta ʿzīr* punishments under which apostasy and blasphemy fall (cf. Art. 208).

It is important to note that one of the grounds on which a judge can reach a decision is his 'discernment' or 'knowledge'. The foundation of this discernment is evidence such as expert opinion, examination of the crime scene, local investigations, interviews with informants, and police reports, among other things. If the judge's discernment conflicts with other legal evidence, the judge should investigate. He may decide to place his own reasoning above the legal evidence and rule according to his discernment. However, if the judge does not conclude which is correct, his reasoning or the other legal evidence, the legal evidence should prevail and he should rule accordingly.

As an Iranian lawyer, I know that I can mount a defence for a client on these grounds. However, I also know that my client's fate may be decided based on political realities rather than the merits of the case.

Application of the law to the mentioned cases

In the case of Ruhollah, the accused has repeatedly declared his remorse, at every level of the judicial proceedings. He has written an official letter of repentance, authorized by the head of the prison's cultural centre. Therefore, he should not suffer the death penalty. The penal code stresses repentance, which should be considered in this case, and Article 114 of Islamic criminal code states that the accused may be acquitted of crimes punishable by *ḥadd* (except *qadhf* and *muḥāraba*) if the accused has declared his repentance before the offence is proved. There is no doubt about Ruhollah's repentance.

There are, however, doubts about several other issues, not least his mental state at the time, and as set out in Article 120 of the penal code, a conviction cannot be made if the offence is not fully proved or if there is even a slight doubt about it. Furthermore, Article 121 provides specifically that crimes punishable by *ḥadd* punishments, except for *muḥāraba*, *ifsād fī al-arḍ*, theft and *qadhf*, are not proven in case of doubt.

Ruhollah writes in his repentance letter that he comes from a very religious family. His mother is a *maddah*, i.e. a singer at commemorations of the Prophet's family, and he himself served as a Qur'an reciter for several years, but his drinking problem, depression and stress twice led him to attempt suicide. According to the Iranian penal code, a person who has committed crimes while suffering mental problems cannot be sentenced to capital punishment (Art. 263).

Multiple facts of Ruhollah's case show that he made insults in a state of intoxication, and he has stated several times since his arrest that he did not mean to insult the Prophet and only made the insults as a result of drinking. This confession of the accused about his unconscious behaviour has been ignored.

Conversely, in the case of the Imam Naghi campaign, the judges took account of the requirements in Articles 120 and 121 of the new code, and the accused were sentenced to prison, not to death.

In the case of Shahin Najafi, some religious zealots sought to get him convicted by fatwa, as Iran's legal system could not touch him in Germany. The fatwa has serious consequences. At risk of violence from some Muslims, he cannot enjoy a normal life in security.

Conclusion

As we know, the laws have to be clear and complete, criminal law in particular. Iranian criminal law is not clear on the crimes of blasphemy and apostasy. For example, there are no provisions defining insult or limiting the definition of insult. Apostasy is being treated as a crime, even though there are no provisions for punishing apostasy as a crime either in the Islamic penal code or in the constitution.

Instead, apostasy cases are referred through a constitutional back door to uncodified, traditional religious law, which is also not clear and foreseeable, as Islamic legal scholars hold different views.

Even in the case of insult to sanctities, where certain standards of evidence and safeguards for the accused are set out in the penal code, judges are allowed wide discretion to follow their own discernment. Valid defences, such as the repentance of the accused, his mental state and elements of doubt, can be ignored in practice, as shown by Ruhollah's case. The system thus fails to satisfy basic requirements of justice, both when it comes to legal certainty and foreseeability and to procedural safeguards.

The criminal punishment of apostasy and blasphemy is a violation of human rights Iran has committed itself to respect by becoming a party to international conventions. The death penalty, if it is to be used at all, should only be imposed for the most serious crimes, as prescribed by law and with due process; and certainly not for exercising one's freedom of religion or belief or one's freedom of expression.[18]

Before the Islamic Revolution, such grave punishments did not exist in the law, though people held strong religious beliefs. After Islamic laws replaced the pre-revolutionary laws, insults to religious sanctities have only increased, which shows that Iran's religious rulers have failed in their approach to advocating Islam. The use of force and harsh punishments can only frighten people away from religion and will surely plant the seeds of hatred.

Notes

1 https://www.facebook.com/Emam.Naghi
2 Akhbar Rooz news agency, 20 May 2012; cf. DW news agency, 10 May 2012.
3 See e.g. Center for Human Rights in Iran, 'In Iran, from prison to exile for posting jokes on Facebook', 6 February 2017, https://www.iranhumanrights.org/2017/02/soheil-babadi-exile/, accessed 12 June 2019 (on the case of Soheil Babadi).
4 BBC interview with Shahin Najafi, 18 June 2010.
5 https://www.youtube.com/watch?v=4rDXhjIN030
6 http://www.bbc.co.uk/persian/iran/2012/05/120513_l44_shahin_najafi_fatwa_makarem.shtml.

7 '"Blasphemous" rapper Shahin Najafi goes into hiding after Iran's hardline clerics put a $100,000 bounty on his head', *Independent*, 17 May 2012, online at http://www.independent.co.uk/arts-entertainment/music/news/blasphemous-rapper-shahin-najafi-goes-into-hiding-after-irans-hardline-clerics-put-a-100000-bounty-7758076.html
8 Ebrahim Pad, *Hoquq-e Keyfari-ye Ekhtesasi: Jarayem Nesbat beh Ashkhas (Sademat-e Badani va Sademat-e Ma'navi)* (Tehran: Daneshvar, 2006 CE / 1385 SH), p. 286.
9 ʿAbbas Zeraʿat, *Sharh-e Mokhtasar-e Qanun-e Mojazat-e Eslami* (Tehran: Qaqnus, 2012 CE / 1391 SH), p. 498.
10 All quotations from the penal code are taken from the English translation provided by the IHRDC (Iranian Human Rights Documentation Center, http://www.iranhrdc.org), with transliteration, italics, and bracketed explanations preserved.
11 Al-Shaykh al-Hurr al-ʿAmili (d. 1693), *Wasāʾil al-Shīʿa (Tafṣīl Wasāʾil al-Shīʿa ilā Taḥṣīl Masāʾil al-Sharīʿa)*, Book 18.
12 Abu al-Salah al-Halabi, *al-Kāfī fī al-Fiqh*, collected in ʿAli Asghar Morvarid (ed.), *Silsila al-Yanābīʿ al-Faqihīyya* (Muʿassassat Fiqh al-Shariʿa – al-Dar al-Islamiyya, 1990), p. 74.
13 Mohammad Hasan al-Najafi, *Jawāhir al-Kalām fī Sharḥ Sharāʾīʿ al-Islām* (Tehran: Dar al-Kitab al-Islamiyya, 1984 [1363 SH]), p. 438.
14 Al-Shahid al-Thani Zayn al-Din al-Jubaʿi al-ʿAmili (d. 1559), *al-Rawḍa al-Bahīyya fī Sharḥ al-Lūmʿa al-Dīmashqīyya*, Book 9, p. 194.
15 ʿAbbas Zeraʿat, 'Barrasi-ye jorm-e ehanat beh moqaddasat islam', *Majalle-ye Daneshkade-ye Huquq va ʿUlum-e Siyasi-ye Daneshgah-e Tehran* 56/510 (2002–2003).
16 Translation of 2008 draft, in Paul Marshall and Nina Shea, *Silenced: How Apostasy & Blasphemy Codes are Choking Freedom Worldwide* (Oxford: Oxford University Press, 2011), pp. 39–40.
17 'Iran (Islamic Republic of), Press Law (as amended on April 18, 2000)', English translation hosted at WIPO, https://wipolex.wipo.int/en/text/248969, accessed 20 June 2019.
18 See also: Human Rights Watch, *Codifying Repression: An Assessment of Iran's New Penal Code* (August 2012); Shahin Milani, *Apostasy in the Islamic Republic of Iran* (New Haven, CT: Iran Human Rights Documentation Center, 2014).

6

Guarding the Mainstream: Blasphemy and Apostasy in Egypt

Moataz El Fegiery

Introduction

In December 2008, dozens of prominent Egyptian and Arab intellectuals and human rights defenders called upon Arab and Muslim governments in a public petition to refrain from using religion as a pretext to infringe on academic freedom, freedom of artistic creativity and religious freedom. They maintained that state censorship on religious ideas undermines the development of religious thought. This initiative was an outcome of a conference organized in Paris on 21 November 2008 by the Cairo Institute for Human Rights Studies (CIHRS) on religion and freedom of expression in the Arab world.[1] The conference was held three years after the political upheaval caused by the publication of the Danish cartoons considered offensive to the Prophet of Islam by many Muslims all over the world. As a response to this crisis and other similar incidents, many Muslim states under the umbrella of the Organization of Islamic Cooperation (OIC) consolidated their international efforts to defend blasphemy laws.[2]

The rise of Islamophobia and stereotypes against Muslims in the West over the last decades has been a source of legitimate concerns for Muslims all over the world. However, putting limitations on freedom of expression and religious freedom is not the adequate response, according to Arab intellectuals and human rights defenders who met in Paris and signed the petition. They are well aware of the consequences of taking beliefs and thoughts to courts in the name of protecting religion or religious sensibilities. Freedom of creativity, freedom of religion, the rights of religious minorities and academic freedom have been long jeopardized by the Egyptian state for the alleged purpose of protecting fundamental religious values and public morality.

Egypt provides us with a stark example of the tension that could arise between religion and freedom of expression and religious freedom. This chapter argues that Egypt's law and judiciary narrows the scope of religious freedom and freedom of expression when it comes to conversion from Islam and the expression of critical views about recognized religions. The opening section explores the evolution of anti-blasphemy laws and the position of Egypt's law towards apostasy. The following sections go on to analyse the jurisprudence of blasphemy and apostasy in Egypt's courts. The final section examines the socio-political context of the debates on blasphemy and apostasy and explores the positions of key supporters and antagonists on expanding the interpretation of religious freedom and freedom of expression in Egypt.

Overview of blasphemy and apostasy laws in Egypt

Blasphemy has been criminalized since the beginning of the codification of modern criminal laws in Egypt. Under Article 161 of the National Penal Law of 1883, 'any contempt for the sanctity of the recognized religions is punishable by up to one year in prison'.[3] Article 139 of the Penal Code of 1904 provided for up to one year's imprisonment for any offence against religions practised publicly in Egypt, including the printing or disseminating of distorted religious texts or the mocking or ridicule of religious ceremonies in public.[4] The famous prosecution of the Egyptian writer Taha Hussein (1889–1973) in 1926–7 was based on that article. After pressure from Al-Azhar, Hussein was charged with blasphemy for the publication of his book on pre-Islamic poetry,[5] but the prosecutor closed the case, finding that Hussein had conducted academic research and did not intend contempt for Islam.[6] The example of this prosecutor has rarely been followed in blasphemy cases examined before Egyptian courts over the last three decades.

Article 161 of the Penal Law No.58/1937 copied the text of Article 139, but the amendments adopted by Law No.29/1982 increased the penalty to up to three years in prison.[7] These amendments also added Article 98bis, whose declared purpose was to target extremist Islamists,[8] imposing up to five years' imprisonment 'on whoever makes use of religion in propagating (…) extreme ideas for the purpose of inciting strife, ridiculing or insulting a heavenly religion or a sect following it, or damaging national unity'. However, in Egyptian courts this article has largely been used against liberal intellectuals, atheists and religious minorities. Additionally, Article 160 of the Penal Law provides up to three years' imprisonment for the destruction, vandalization or desecration of religious buildings, sites, symbols, cemeteries and graves, as well as the obstruction of religious ceremonies.[9] In some cases, Egyptian authorities applied this article to punish Shiʿi Muslims if they practised their prayer rituals in mosques. The prohibition of blasphemy was incorporated in the 2012 Constitution written under the rule of the Muslim Brotherhood (MB), Article 44 of which stated that 'any insult or abuse of all religious messengers and prophets shall be prohibited'.[10] This article was removed under the Amended Constitution of 2014.[11]

Muslims in Egypt are not allowed to convert to any other religion, or to give up religion completely. Neither the law nor the successive Egyptian constitutions explicitly prohibit conversion, but this is a rule developed by Egypt's courts, as shown below. Apostasy is not a crime under Egyptian law, but it has civil implications. The civil consequences of apostasy often arise in civil courts as a result of disputes between citizens over marriage, inheritance or children's custody. In 1975, the Court of Cassation held that the traditional Islamic rules on the consequences and the prohibition of apostasy are core elements of Egypt's public order. In 1996, the Court held that the legal consequences of apostasy were derived from Article 2 of the Constitution of 1971.[12] Berger has argued that Egypt's case law in this area is consistent: 'apostasy is perceived as a legal impediment to almost all personal status rights by virtue of the apostate having incurred civil death';[13] thus 'it renders the marriage of the apostate null and void, prevents him from entering into a new marriage even with a non-Muslim and excludes him from inheritance'.[14]

Blasphemy in Egyptian courts

Egypt's anti-blasphemy laws were repeatedly applied under the rule of former President Mubarak to prosecute writers, novelists and bloggers accused of offending Islamic doctrines. For instance, in 1991 'Ala' Hamid, an Egyptian novelist, was sentenced to eight years in prison for the publication of his novel *Distance in a Man's Mind*. In 2001, the Egyptian writer Salah al-Din Muhsin was sentenced to three years in prison for writing critical books about Islam and divinity that the court considered blasphemous.[15] In 2007, the Egyptian blogger Karim Amer was sentenced to three years in prison for publishing articles on his blog that an Egyptian court considered blasphemous against Islam and al-Azhar.[16] The publication of the satirical cartoons of the Prophet Muhammad in the Danish newspaper *Jyllandsposten* in September 2005 rekindled the domestic and international debate on religion and freedom of expression. The Egyptian government was amongst the Muslim states that contributed to the transformation of this incident into an international upheaval. However, this act appears to have been politically motivated, as some have argued that Mubarak wanted to boost his domestic popular legitimacy and co-opt his influential Islamist political competitors by appearing as the guardian of Islam.[17]

In the post-Mubarak era, blasphemy cases reached a peak. The Egyptian Initiative for Personal Rights (EIPR) documented 36 blasphemy cases from March 2011 to December 2012. The defendants in 19 cases were members of religious minorities such as Christians, Shiʿa and Ahmadis, and the remaining cases involved Sunni Muslims.[18] The high number of cases continued under President Morsi.[19] A new trend in the post-Mubarak era was for laypersons to be increasingly charged with blasphemy for making statements or actions in their normal daily lives deemed offensive to Islam. One can argue that the political influence of Islamists in the post-Mubarak era stimulated the use of the blasphemy law. The MB had defended the criminalization of blasphemy since the crisis of the Danish cartoons. Salafists and the MB were keen to prohibit blasphemy in the 2012 Constitution for the first time in Egypt's constitutional history. In some blasphemy cases, members of the MB and Salafists incited the public against the accused persons.[20] The highest number of blasphemy cases occurred in Upper Egypt, a region where Islamists have enjoyed a significant presence.[21] The EIPR observed the interference of Islamists in some of these cases. For instance, in October 2011 in Minya Governorate in Upper Egypt, members of the MB and Salafists pressured the government to forcibly evict a Christian family from its housing area in reaction to an allegation of blasphemy against a member of the family. Other similar cases were also documented in Asyut in late 2011 and early 2012.[22]

In September 2012, the issue of blasphemy came to the fore after the crisis of the *Innocence of Muslims* film.[23] A group of Egyptian-American Christians had released on the internet a low-budget film accusing the Prophet Muhammad of fabricating the Qur'an and portraying him and some of his companions as power-hungry, bloodthirsty and sex-crazed. This film sparked fierce popular anger in Egypt and other Arab and Muslim states. A massive demonstration of Islamists was organized in front of the US embassy. The state tolerated the demonstrations on the first day of the crisis, letting some Islamists climb the walls of the embassy and replace the American flag with a black flag with the Islamic declaration of faith (*shahāda*). The US protested the lack of protection for its embassy, and the police started to disperse protesters the following day.[24]

In power, the MB was most likely keen to build confidence with the West, and particularly the US, which may explain why its reaction to this film was much softer than its reaction to the Danish cartoons had been when it was in opposition. After the release of the film, the MB urged the international community to adopt legal measures against the defamation of religion.[25] It supported the trial of the movie's producers but tried to avoid any political turbulence with the US. The Salafists led the popular mobilization against the movie. Under political pressure from Salafists, Morsi was reluctant to disperse protesters who attacked the American embassy, but he had to intervene later when Egypt's relations with the US were endangered.[26] A criminal court convicted the producers of the movie in absentia: Seven Egyptian-American Christians were sentenced to death for blasphemy and treason, and an American priest was sentenced to five years in prison for blasphemy. The charge of treason was based on other statements made by the Egyptian producers of the film where they called for a separate state for Egyptian Christians and invited the international community to intervene to protect Christians from persecution. The judges who examined the case urged the lawmakers to institute the death penalty for blasphemy.[27]

This crisis was an opportunity for Islamists to restate their restricted version of freedom of expression. In a public statement, the MB's Freedom and Justice Party (FJP) stated that blasphemous speech was not protected by international human rights law, since freedom of expression was limited by public order and morals. The statement accused Christian Egyptians abroad of conspiring against Egypt by producing this movie.[28] This general accusation came at a time when Egyptian Christians had been strongly critical of President Morsi and Islamists. The MB scolded Western states for tolerating the contempt of Islam and Muslims but prohibiting the denial of the Holocaust.[29]

The *Innocence of Muslims* crisis was followed by a large number of blasphemy charges and trials. The facts of these cases have indicated an increasing climate of intolerance to religious pluralism among a wide sector of Egyptians, particularly in rural areas and poor urban areas where the potential for sectarian tensions is high.[30] In many cases, Muslims involved in the cases complained that the accused bore a grudge against Egypt's Islamic identity. In this light, any critical statement made by non-Muslims about Islamic figures or history could be misinterpreted as blasphemy. For example, in some cases, Christian teachers were convicted of blasphemy because of their comments about Islam or Islamic history in class.[31] In other cases, everyday discussions ended with blasphemy trials.[32] Selectivity is an inherent problem in blasphemy laws in many states, where they often protect the dominant religions.[33] All blasphemy cases in Egypt from 2011 to June 2013 targeted persons who commented on Islam; however, Islamists who systematically attacked Christianity and other religions were left without punishment. Exceptionally, a Muslim preacher was convicted of committing blasphemy against Christianity after he tore up the Bible in a public demonstration against the *Innocence of Muslims* film.[34]

The application of blasphemy legislation has continued to increase in the post-Muslim Brotherhood era. Blasphemy charges have repeatedly targeted Muslim liberal intellectuals, young bloggers and Christians.[35] In 2015, authorities investigated or prosecuted at least 20 blasphemy cases.[36] The situation led some parliamentarians and prominent writers to call upon the government to either abolish or amend the law.[37] However, leading such a legal reform did not seem a priority for President Abdel Fattah el-Sisi, who strongly needed the political support of the conservative religious establishment to enhance his legitimacy and counterbalance Islamist forces following the overthrow of President Morsi and the massive repression of the Muslim Brotherhood. In this political climate, the abolishment of anti-blasphemy laws and the improvement of rights such as religious freedom have not been possible.[38]

The charge of blasphemy has been a long-standing threat to intellectuals who critically engage with Islamic theological and legal traditions or scrutinize the conservative stances taken by religious institutions. For example, in December 2015, researcher and TV host Islam Behery was sentenced to one year in prison in connection with the content of his TV programme, where he was critical of traditional Islamic law methods and treatises. Moreover, the criminalization of blasphemy limits the freedom of atheists to question religion. The case of Alber Saber, a young Egyptian atheist of Christian origin convicted for blasphemy, is a striking example. The case started with a petition submitted to the police by Saber's neighbours, accusing him of disseminating the *Innocence of Muslims* movie on Facebook and Twitter and posting other materials considered by the complainant to be blasphemous. In the interrogation, Saber denied any intention of insulting religion and affirmed that all of his postings on the internet were related to his study of comparative religions and Islamic philosophy and that he had started to post these materials on Facebook and YouTube in 2010. In his trial, Al-Marj Primary Court of Misdemeanour considered this statement by Saber a confession to blasphemy and sentenced him to three years in prison.[39]

Unrecognized religious minorities can also be prosecuted under the blasphemy law.[40] In Egypt, the state recognizes only Abrahamic religions (Islam, Christianity and Judaism). Members of these religions can publicly practise their rituals and, with certain restrictions, build their places of worship; they also apply their own religious family laws. The 1923 and 1971 Constitutions did not explicitly limit the practice of religious freedom to Abrahamic religions, but this principle has been well-established in Egyptian courts.[41] This principle was entrenched in the 2012 Constitution and the Amended Constitution of 2014 which said that 'the state shall guarantee the freedom of religious rites to established places of worship for the divine religions'.[42] Certain Islamic and Christian sects such as the Shiʿa and Jehovah's Witnesses have not been treated as recognized religious communities.[43] Article 98bis of the Penal Code protects only

Abrahamic religions from defamation.[44] This is evidence that the use of the blasphemy law is selective and discriminatory. The religious doctrines of the Shiʿa, the Bahaʾiyya and the Ahmadiyya are often considered blasphemous to Islam by Egypt's courts. Blasphemy cases against Egyptian Shiʿa have persisted in the post-Mubarak era.[45]

In most blasphemy cases, Egyptian courts opted for a broad and ambiguous definition of blasphemy that largely restricts freedom of expression and religious freedom. The courts hold in the cases under review that blasphemy law protects the fundamental doctrines of Abrahamic religions and safeguards society from temptation and turbulence. The courts do not censor certain provocative views with a view to protecting public order and social harmony, but rather protect specific understandings of religion and dismiss others even if there are no grounds for believing that the expression of these views would disturb public order. The problem here is how the courts identify certain views as blasphemous or not. The case law shows that new interpretations of the Qurʾan or Sunna can be considered blasphemous and that those expressing opinions against the idea of divinity and religions are liable to prosecution as well. Accordingly, the criminalization of blasphemy intimidates atheists and converts from publicly declaring their religious affiliation and views. This conflicts with the statement of the UN Human Rights Committee (HRC) that 'blasphemy laws should not be used to prevent or punish criticism of religious leaders or commentary on religious doctrine and tenets of faith'.[46]

In the case of Adel Imam, an Egyptian court has followed a different reasoning on blasphemy with the objective of widening the scope of freedom of expression. The Court has held that Egypt's law on blasphemy does not protect religions or religious feelings and that the crime of blasphemy had to be accompanied by a special intent to harm national unity, public order and societal peace. The Court has maintained that if the legal provision on blasphemy is meant to protect religions, it becomes incompatible with Article 19 of the ICCPR. It held that its understanding of blasphemy is in line with the legitimate limitations on freedom of expression in Article 19(3). Moreover, the Court has argued that the protection of religious doctrines blocks critical thinking and undermines the development of religious thought. It has also added that the mere invocation of the protection of religious feelings or sensibilities of others does not stand as a justification to restrict freedom of expression unless there is an imminent threat to public order caused by the expression of opinions.[47] The Court was right to emphasize this point, as the argument of the protection of religious feelings of individuals often pays more attention to the feelings of the majority of the population than to the feelings of non-believers or the beliefs of the few.

The reasoning of the Court in this case is exceptional in the case law and indicates that some Egyptian judges consider developments in international human rights law in their judgements. However, the criteria set by the Court in this case still present a justification for censoring the public manifestation of provocative or shocking views. Egypt's case law on religious freedom and freedom of expression indicates that concepts such as public order, public morals and national security are often used to violate the essence of rights. According to the HRC, limitations of rights must meet a strict test of justification, necessity and proportionality.[48] The proponents of the prohibition of blasphemy argue that states find themselves under pressure to censor and repress blasphemous expressions for the sake of maintaining public order, since in many situations blasphemy has led to massive protests and violent reactions. Arguably, this rationale poses a threat not just to freedom of expression but also to any other human rights norms disapproved of by any group of persons who are willing to use coercion and intimidation to silence other views in society. As noted by Langer, this approach risks 'provid[ing] an incentive to rampage and cause havoc in order to vindicate future suppression of offensive speeches'.[49] Even though the ban on certain provocative blasphemous or provocative speeches might be justified in certain circumstances for the purpose of public order, morals and national security, the general criminalization of blasphemy is not a proportionate response. Therefore, the HRC holds that prohibition of 'displays of lack of respect for a religion or other belief systems, including blasphemy laws, are incompatible with the [ICCPR]' as long as the expression of views do not amount to incitement to discrimination and violence as stipulated in Article 20 of the ICCPR.[50]

Apostasy in Egyptian courts

In traditional Islamic law, a Muslim can be declared an apostate after the commission of certain deeds or the utterance of words of unbelief. For instance, the perpetration of blasphemy and heresy can amount to apostasy.[51] Under this category, apostasy can be established even though the accused person denies his/her conversion from Islam. As noted by Johansen, 'apostasy thus becomes a depersonalized objective fact without any relation to the intentions of the individuals concerned'.[52] The first and only time a court declared an Egyptian citizen to be an apostate was in the famous case of the Egyptian academic, Nasr Hamid Abu Zayd. In this case the defendant did not intentionally convert from Islam, but the Court of Cassation held that Abu Zayd's published views on the development of the Qur'an and jurisprudence proved his apostasy. It consequently ordered the dissolution of his marriage to his Muslim wife.[53] The legal action against Abu Zayd had been filed by a group of Islamist lawyers. Until 1996, any citizen could file a *ḥisba* case at family courts, challenging the violation of family law or the doctrines of Islamic law. According to Article 6 of Law No.462/1955 Abolishing the Shari'a and *Milli* Courts, judges were to apply the dominant opinion of the Hanafi school of law to such cases, if they did not find a resolution for any legal matter in the Personal Status Law. Accordingly, the conversion of one of the spouses from Islam could make the marriage void.[54] In an attempt to calm the international and domestic outrage caused by this case, the government then moved to restrict the use of *ḥisba* in Egyptian courts, making the General Prosecutor the only entity that could file *ḥisba* cases in family matters.[55]

Another ground for the establishment of apostasy is that a Muslim intentionally converts from Islam to any other religion or to non-religious beliefs. The question here is 'the speaker's explicit self-perception of his[/her] religious identity'.[56] Cases related to this subjective type of apostasy are the most common ones in Egyptian courts. Egyptian converts have filed dozens of cases before the State Council to challenge the refusal of the Ministry of Interior to record their new religious status in their identity documents.

According to Article 47 of Law No. 143/1994 on Civil Affairs, 'the change or correction of official data on the nationality, professional or religious affiliation of citizens should be based on official documents or decisions made by the concerned organs'.[57] This article explicitly allows individuals to change their religious affiliation in their official documents of identification without any exceptions, but in practice Egypt's Ministry of Interior and most judges have restricted the scope of this article by prohibiting Muslims from changing their religious affiliation.

The case law in this area can be classified into three categories. The first category involves cases filed by citizens who were Christians but converted to Islam, then converted back to Christianity. They are known in the Egyptian media as returners to Christianity. A considerable number of these petitioners converted from Christianity to Islam in order to apply the Muslim Personal Status Law to divorce, since the Orthodox and Catholic Churches in Egypt take a strict position on divorce.

The second category includes cases filed by citizens who were born and brought up as Christians, but whose fathers converted to Islam before they reached 16 years of age and could hold their own identity cards. In this situation, the religious status of those citizens was changed in their birth certificates, sometimes without their knowledge. Many of these people later filed cases in an attempt to register their original affiliation to Christianity in their identity cards. Around 89 cases were documented under this category from 2005 to 2007. But the Court of Cassation held that according to the dominant opinion of the Hanafi school of law 'a child follows the best religion of his/her parents'.[58]

Most pre-modern Muslim jurists agreed that a child of Muslim parents is a Muslim and when a Muslim man marries a Christian or Jewish woman, children follow the religion of their father. If a Christian father or mother converted to Islam, his/her children become Muslim. This view is based on a saying of the Prophet which states that 'every newborn is born in the natural condition (*fiṭra)*; his parents transform him into a Jew, a Christian or Zoroastrian'.[59] Muslim jurists have commonly understood the term *fiṭra* in this hadith as a reference to Islam. According to the Hanafi jurist Ibn ʿAbidin: 'This innate nature is kept when a child is born to Muslim spouses but when parents adopt different religions, a child should follow what it is in line with this *fiṭra*, so he/she becomes a Muslim if one of his parents is Muslim'.[60]

To avoid possible sectarian tensions between Muslims and Christians in Egypt, the former General Prosecutor, ʿAbd al-Majid Mahmoud, attempted to challenge this principle before the Court of Cassation in March 2009 in the case of Andrew and Mario. He proposed that when one of the parents changes religion, a child should freely choose his/her religious belief at the age of seven. In June 2009, the Court of Cassation dismissed this view and adhered to its previous precedents that children follow the religion of their Muslim parents.[61] The Court of Administrative Justice invoked the same principle two weeks later.[62]

Based on Article 18(4) of the ICCPR and Article 14 of the CRC, the right of parents to provide religious guidance for their children should be guaranteed by the state. When the intellectual capacity of children evolves, they have the right to freely express their own religious choice without coercion.[63] The UN Special Rapporteur on Freedom of Religion and Belief Heiner Bielefeldt has noted that: 'It is important for the state to ensure that conflicts possibly arising from parents having different convictions are settled in an unbiased and non-discriminatory manner'.[64] The proposal presented by the General Prosecutor could have been a possible solution for such a legal dispute. There are a number of arguments adduced in support of the proposal of the Prosecutor. The verse of the Qur'an (2:256) that says 'no compulsion in religion' can support this view. This verse was revealed when a Christian man converted to Islam and asked the Prophet to forcibly convert his two sons but the Prophet refused.[65] However, some Muslim scholars might not consider this verse sufficient evidence that children are allowed to choose their religion freely, because in this account the two sons were adults, and in Islamic law, non-Muslim adults do not necessarily follow their father if he converted to Islam. Nevertheless, Muslim jurists today can develop their jurisprudence based on the views of some Maliki jurists in the eleventh century and Shi'i jurists who hold that every Muslim from the age of maturity can choose his/her own religious beliefs.[66]

Another rule also in support of this view was established by Abu Hanifa, al-Shafi'i and many other jurists who held that 'the forcible conversions ... are not valid and a person so converted who reverts to his former faith is not deemed as apostate'.[67] This rule could be applied to children since they do not have the required intellectual capacity to decide their religious beliefs and should, therefore, be given the opportunity to state their religious preferences at the age of maturity. However, Egyptian judges are bound by the law to implement the dominant opinion of the Hanafi school of law on legal issues that are not treated in the personal status law and they cannot select from other schools of law unless this view is codified in the law. No government in Egypt has been willing to use its legislative powers to amend the law on this matter.

The third category of cases involves cases filed by Muslims who converted to Christianity but who were not able to have their new religious status registered in their identity cards. A prominent Egyptian human rights defender has pointed out that there is no accurate figure for the number of Muslims who have converted to Christianity, since most of them are afraid of societal revenge if they announce their conversion publicly.[68]

The jurisprudence of the State Council has exhibited three trends in its handling of the issue of conversion from Islam; the hard-line, the liberal and the pragmatic approaches. Judges using the hard-line approach have rejected the complaints of Muslim citizens who want to register their new religious status in their identity cards, basing it on the traditional prohibition of apostasy in Islamic law and the protection of public order in a Muslim-majority country.[69] This approach has long represented the mainstream. However, it was modified in cases in 2008 and 2011 by a pragmatic reasoning, which maintained the same traditional understanding of apostasy, but favoured registering the new religious status of converts who were Christians, converted to Islam and then reverted to Christianity. This reasoning was based on the protection of public order and the requirements of the modern nation state, but without invoking support for the principle of freedom of religion.[70]

This reasoning has not, however, been applied to converts who were born and brought up as Muslims and decided to convert from Islam, or converts from Islam one of whose non-Muslim parents converted to Islam during their childhood. Moreover, some judges in the State Council opposed this reasoning, arguing that it was inconsistent with the constitutional provision on the principles of Islamic law as the main source of legislation. Therefore, these judges have challenged the judgments of the Supreme Administrative Court and referred many conversion cases to the SCC to examine the constitutionality of Article 47 of Law No. 143/1994 on Civil Affairs, arguing that this article is not compatible with the constitutional provision on Islamic law since it does not explicitly prohibit Muslims from converting from Islam.[71] The SCC has not delivered a judgement yet on this constitutional review case, but the referral has prompted some judges in the Court of Administrative Justice to suspend the examination of some conversion cases until the SCC accomplishes its review.

There have been a few cases where judges followed a liberal approach towards religious freedom and Islamic law, but they were limited to petitions filed by converts of Christian origin. For instance, in the case of Mohammad Mahdi ʿAbdullah, the claimant was a Christian who was born to Christian parents. He converted to Islam but later reverted to Christianity. Consequently, he requested the Ministry of Interior to change the religious affiliation in his identity card to Christianity, but his request was rejected. In this case the Court accepted the claim and ordered the Ministry of Interior to register the new religious affiliation of the claimant.[72] This case is among other 22 cases decided positively by the Court from April 2004 until September 2006. At the time, the Court of Administrative Justice was headed by judge Faruq ʿAbd al-Qadir, who adopted a liberal reasoning.

In these cases, the Court considered the refusal of the Ministry of Interior to register the new religious affiliation of the claimant to be an unjustifiable interference with his personal choice. The Court also argued that the official registration of the new religious affiliation of the claimant is just an administrative procedure which reflects reality. This registration is necessary to establish rights and duties based on the correct religious status. In its response to the argument that a Muslim who changes his religion violates public order, the Court affirmed that Article 40 of the Egyptian constitution provides for equality between citizens in all rights and duties without discrimination, based on religion, language, origin and sex. The Court also referred to Article 46, which protects the rights of individuals not only to freely believe in a religion but to manifest religious faith. The Court cited the UDHR and the Arab Charter of Human Rights. It has also argued that many centuries ago, Islam recognized freedom of religion, and in doing so, it cited several Qurʾanic verses that highlight the principle of freedom and non-compulsion in religious conviction.[73]

However, the Court's understanding of freedom of religion in Islam does not seem to apply to citizens who are born and brought up as Muslims and decide to convert to another religion. In explaining this position, the Court ambiguously maintained that according to Islamic jurisprudence, a Muslim cannot be considered an apostate unless he/she is wholeheartedly comfortable with his/her apostasy.[74] This argument implies that the Court would only guarantee the right of persons who converted to Islam for a while and then decided to apostatize from Islam. By this reasoning, the Court avoided engaging in a thorough discussion of the issue of religious freedom and apostasy in Islam. In fact, the cases, which were only examined before this Court, were filed by converts of Christian origin, and the Court did not try cases which were filed by converts of Muslim origin.

In conversion cases, judges have faced a subject matter that is not treated in the traditional Islamic law on apostasy. This law was concerned with the punishment of apostates and the legal consequences of apostasy for marriage, divorce, child custody, property rights and inheritance. The registration of religious affiliation in official documents of identification is a new legal matter that has emerged in the modern nation state. The protection of public order has become the focus of legal reasoning, with many judges holding that if they tolerate conversion, the public order of the Muslim state – whose official religion is Islam and whose main source of legislation is Islamic law – would be undermined. In their rulings, judges have also been influenced by the view that apostasy is not allowed under Islamic law. For converts of Christian origin, judges are aware that most of them became Muslims for temporary reasons, and therefore, the Supreme Administrative Court has exempted them from the main rule that apostasy is not allowed in Islam, since they did not join Islam out of deep conviction. Moreover, the rise of cases involving converts of Christian origin has also been a source of tensions in the relationship between Muslims and Christians in Egypt. This may explain why the Supreme Administrative Court has opted for a more flexible approach in treating their cases. However, as I have shown, not all judges are comfortable with this solution because they blame those converts for playing with religion for personal interests, and hold that a decision to convert to Islam should be done in good faith.

Prospects for reform

The development of religious knowledge inevitably results in pluralism of theological and jurisprudential views. Using force and coercion to protect certain views was a source of hatred, war and violence in the worlds of Islam and Christianity. In Europe, from the seventeenth century onwards, proponents of religious tolerance and freedom of religion and expression were reacting in large part to the divisive and bloody consequences of persecution and exclusion practised by different religious sects. The 'conclusion that religious differences could not be definitely resolved' was 'conducive to toleration'.[75] Today in the Muslim region, the monopoly of religious truth by state institutions or religious groups has fuelled sectarian violence and religious polarization. While the prohibition or criminalization of blasphemy is found in many legal jurisdictions, including in some Western countries, it is in the Muslim world today that the number of victims of these laws is high, the type of punishment is harsh and the scope of the prohibition and criminalization is vast.[76]

While religious freedom, especially the right to change one's religion, is still not widely accepted among Egyptians,[77] Egyptian converts have been searching for legal recognition since 1980. The number of conversion cases in Egyptian courts has significantly increased over the last two decades, and the issue has also come on the agenda of many Egyptian human-rights NGOs. Through litigation and domestic and international advocacy, the issue of the right of Egyptians to freely choose their religion and beliefs has come to the fore.[78] The intense litigation on conversion has led to the partial recognition of some rights for converts, as explained above. In 2006, a group of lawyers and activists established Egyptians against Religious Discrimination, a social coalition supportive of freedom of religion and the rights of religious minorities. A handful of politicians and media figures defend the expansion of the scope of freedom of religion in Egypt and use arguments from Islamic law to support their positions.[79]

The significant rise of the culture of protest and of claiming rights after the 2011 Revolution has encouraged many Egyptian atheists and converts to be outspoken in the media and internet about their rights and their views on religion. They wanted to make their voices heard by the drafters of the post-revolutionary constitution. The rise of Islamists and their intense discourse on the Islamization of Egypt has also led to the increasing emergence of young secularists and atheists who vocally advocate the removal of Islam and Islamic law from the constitution as the most viable way to preserve religious and political pluralism and international human rights.[80] The flow of ideas through the internet has allowed many Egyptian atheists to network with their counterparts in other regions in the world.[81]

Books by atheist and secular thinkers like Richard Dawkins, Christopher Hitchens and Stephen Hawking have become easily accessible in Arabic to young people in Egypt. For the first time in the history of Egyptian cinema, an Egyptian film entitled 'The Atheist' openly discusses the issue of atheism among young people,[82] and also for the first time, a debate was convened in February 2013 (during the rule of the MB) at an Egyptian mosque in the heart of old Cairo between atheists of Muslim origin and Muslims.[83] The fact that a debate like that was held in Egypt at that time does not mean that the MB was tolerating religious expression; rather, it is an indicator of the courage of those young people who took the risk of engaging in this debate. During this period, blasphemy cases increased remarkably and the Islamist-led government undertook repressive measures against religious minorities and the secularist opposition.

Egypt's politicians do not deny that there are atheists in Egypt. For instance, *al-Wafd* newspaper, the mouthpiece of the *al-Wafd* Party, published an investigative report in April 2013 on 'the secret world of atheists in Egypt' which reported that the number of atheists had significantly increased in Egypt since 2011.[84] Some Islamist and non-Islamist parliamentarians urged the government to study the reason behind the spread of atheism in Egypt.[85] The superstar satirist and columnist Bassem Youssef has held that 'the spread of [atheism] may carry unperceived benefits, such as modernizing and altering religious rhetoric in order to confront new challenges, instead of burying our heads in the sand'.[86] These indicators suggest that the demand for religious freedom is developing from within Egyptian society. But tensions continue because Egyptian law has failed so far to satisfy the needs of this sector in the society. At the same time, the most powerful political forces and institutions like al-Azhar and the judiciary have been reluctant to hold that Islam does not block individuals from freely choosing their religious conviction.

Since the first half of the twentieth century, Al-Azhar has been embracing a restricted version of freedom of expression and religious freedom. Its scholars, who consider themselves the most authoritative voices of Islam and Islamic law, have instigated many blasphemy and censorship cases. The ruling elite has consolidated the political role of Al-Azhar since the 1970s to counterbalance the rise of political Islam. Al-Azhar has been also subjected to the influence of Islamists. While the leadership of

Al-Azhar has been controlled by the state, Islamists succeeded in recruiting supporters in the different agencies of the establishment. During the 1970s, Al-Azhar pushed for the Islamization of Egypt's law. In 1972, the Islamic Research Academy at Al-Azhar proposed three codified versions of Islamic law based on the Hanafi, Hanbali and Maliki schools of law. It also adopted in 1977 a model Islamic constitution whose articles were strongly influenced by traditional rulings of Islamic law. This draft constitution vaguely tied religious freedom and freedom of expression to the rulings of Islamic law. Over the following three decades, Al-Azhar was less assertive on the Islamization of Egyptian law, but the institution was very active in restricting the freedom of expression of intellectuals and artists. Al-Azhar and Dar al-Iftaʾ disallowed conversion from Islam and deprived the members of non-Abrahamic religions of the right to publicly manifest their religions.

In the Morsi period, Al-Azhar stood to contain the increasing political influence of Islamist parties. Defending its status as the authoritative source of religious knowledge, Al-Azhar aimed at dominating the debate on the future of Islamic law in Egypt. It introduced itself as an enlightened and moderate voice of Islam in Egypt. The military and non-Islamist forces supported this role in order to curtail the power of the Muslim Brotherhood and Salafists. The current Grand Shaykh of al-Azhar, Ahmed al-Tayyib, sponsored a series of dialogues with the different political forces in Egypt and proposed a set of guiding principles for constitutional and legal reform. These principles were manifested in two documents.[87] In these documents, Al-Azhar emphasized its moderate and centrist approach to Shariʿa and the necessity of *ijtihād* that is guided by the general objectives of Shariʿa and the doctrine of public interest. The documents were critical of any hard-line turn from this moderate understanding of Islam. They affirmed that the new constitution should refer to the general principles of Islamic law as the main sources of law in Egypt and that non-Muslims who adhered to the other two divine religions (Christianity and Judaism) should apply their religious laws in family matters. Moreover, the documents stressed the centrality of human rights and democracy in the new political regime of Egypt. However, the documents were vague with respect to religious freedom and freedom of expression, leaving the door open for the use of Islamic principles to limit their scope. It was no surprise that Al-Azhar supported the efforts of the Islamist-led Constituent Assembly to prohibit blasphemy in the constitution. The influence of Al-Azhar on the religious discourse has increased after the fall of the Muslim Brotherhood. Despite some calls for separation between religion and the state, the reference to Islamic law was maintained in the new constitution.

The Muslim Brotherhood and Salafists adhere to a limited interpretation of freedom of expression and religious freedom. Acting as social and political movements, the impact of Islamists on Egypt's society and institutions has been far-reaching. The mainstream opinion among Islamists is that conversion from Islam is prohibited and can be punished with the death penalty.[88] Converts from Islam are also deprived of their rights in marriage, inheritance and children's custody. Some Egyptian jurists such as al-Qaradawi and al-ʿAwa have argued that the punishment of apostasy is a discretionary punishment and that it is not part of the fixed punishments in Islam.[89] Yet according to many Islamists, apostasy is still a serious crime that should be punished in an Islamic state. The MB and the Salafists contend that Islam is the system of belief in the Islamic state and apostasy represents a rebellion against this system.[90]

To be sure, many non-Islamist parties have also adhered to a conservative interpretation of religious freedom and freedom of expression. For them, certain unpopular human rights can be overlooked to maintain their social constituency. New liberal and leftist parties established in the post-Mubarak era were keen to become consistent in their human rights policies, as many of the leaders of these parties came from a human rights background and kept close ties with the human rights movement.

The steady rise of authoritarianism and repression under President el-Sisi, however, has massively embattled these forces, whose agenda has been now become focused on the struggle for basic political and civil rights.[91]

Conclusions

This chapter has analysed the development of Egypt's law and jurisprudence on apostasy and blasphemy. It argued that the scope of religious freedom and freedom of expression is restricted when it comes to conversion from Islam and the expression of critical views about recognized religions. Conversion from Islam is not allowed, and apostasy has serious consequences for the apostate's civil rights. The state protects religions and religious orthodoxy through censorship and criminal liability. Islam and Shariʿa are used in Egyptian courts as a pretext for limiting the scope of religious freedom and freedom of expression. The central role of Islam and Shariʿa in the state influences the conception of public order in Egypt's courts.

Apostasy and blasphemy laws do not only hinder the development of theological and religious thought in Egypt, they also undermine the struggle against the ideological foundations of extremist religious groups. Since courts and the religious establishment stand to protect what they consider orthodoxy, critical thought has usually been muzzled and delegitimized. The criminalization of blasphemy intimidates religious dissidents and atheists, who should have the right to express publicly shocking views on certain religions or religious doctrines and propagate their doctrines.

The legal debate on blasphemy and apostasy needs to be located within the on-going political and social struggle over the definition of rights in Egypt. The political influence of political Islam and the increasing role of religious establishments have long obstructed the expansion of religious freedom and freedom of expression. Many liberals and human rights defenders have represented a driving force for the advocacy for religious freedom and freedom of expression over the last two decades. However, their social constituency to promote such sensitive issues is still limited.

Notes

1 Cairo Institute for Human Rights Studies, 'A petition by Arab intellectuals and human rights NGOs on religion and freedom of expression in the Arab world' (Arab Network

for Human Rights Information, 2008), available at www.anhri.net/egypt/cihrs/2008/pr1204-2.shtml (last accessed 1 June 2019).

2 Leonard A. Leo, Felice D. Gaer and Elizabeth K. Cassidy, 'Protecting religions from "defamation": a threat to universal human rights standards', *Harvard Journal of Law and Public Policy* 34/2 (2011), pp. 769–84.

3 Article 161 of the National Penal Code, 13 November 1883.

4 Article 139 of the Penal Law of 1904.

5 In this book, Hussein challenged the authenticity of pre-Islamic Arabic poetry and questioned the occurrence of some incidents mentioned in the Qur'an.

6 The full text of the decision of the General Prosecutor in W. Silawi, *Fiqh al-Muḥākamat al-Adabiyya wa al-Fikriyya* (Cairo: Cairo Institute for Human Rights Studies, 2006), pp. 267–82.

7 Article 161 of the Penal Law No.58/1937 Amended by Law No.29/1982, Egyptian Gazette no.16, 22 April 1982.

8 Article 98bis of the Penal Law No.58/1937 amended by Law No.29/1982, Egyptian Gazette no.16, 22 April 1982.

9 Article 160 of the Penal Law No.58/1937 amended by Law No.29/1982, Egyptian Gazette no.16, 22 April 1982.

10 Article 44 of Constitution of the Arab Republic of Egypt, 25 December 2012, Official Gazette no.51 bis, 25 December 2012.

11 Amended Constitution of the Arab Republic of Egypt, 18 January 2014, Official Gazette no.3bis, 18 January 2014.

12 Maurits Berger, 'Conflicts law and public policy in Egyptian family law: Islamic law through the backdoor', *American Journal of Comparative Law* 50/3 (2002), pp. 555–94, at p. 584, citing Court of Cassation, Case no. 9/44, 14/12/1975 and Case No. 475, 478,481/65, 5/8/1996.

13 Maurits Berger, 'Apostasy and public policy in contemporary Egypt: an evaluation of recent cases from Egypt's highest courts', *Human Rights Quarterly* 25/3 (2003), pp. 720–40, at p. 723.

14 Maurits Berger, 'Conflicts', p. 584.

15 See Declan O'Sullivan, 'Egyptian cases of blasphemy and apostasy against Islam: *takfir al-muslim* (prohibition against attacking those accused)', *International Journal of Human Rights* 7/2 (2003), pp. 97–137.

16 See General Prosecutor v. Karim Amer, Eastern Alexandria Misdemeanor Court of Appeals, Case No.8240/2007, 12 March 2007.

17 Jytte Klausen, *The Cartoons That Shook the World* (New Haven, CT: Yale University Press, 2009), pp. 167–79.

18 EIPR, 'Ḥiṣār al-tafkīr' (Cairo: The Egyptian Initiative for Personal Rights, 2013), available at http://www.eipr.org/pressrelease/2013/09/11/1817 (last accessed 1 June 2019).

19 Kristen Chick, 'In Brotherhood's Egypt, blasphemy charges against Christians surge ahead', *Christian Science Monitor,* 22 May 2013, available at http://www.csmonitor.com/World/Middle-East/2013/0522/In-Brotherhood-s-Egypt-blasphemy-charges-against-Christians-surge-ahead (accessed 20 September 2013).

20 Ben Hubbard and Mayy El Sheikh, 'Islamists press blasphemy cases in a new Egypt', *New York Times,* 19 June 2013, available at http://www.nytimes.com/2013/06/19/world/middleeast/islamists-press-blasphemy-cases-in-a-new-egypt.html?pagewanted=1&_r=0 (accessed 1 October 2013)

21 According to research on voting patterns in the post-Mubarak era published by Rand Corporation, Islamists ran strongest in the governorates of Upper Egypt. Jeffrey Martini and Stephen M. Worman, *Voting Patterns in Post-Mubarak Egypt* (Santa Monica, CA: RAND Corporation, 2013), https://www.rand.org/pubs/research_reports/RR223.html (last accessed 1 June 2019).
22 EIPR, 'Ḥiṣār al-tafkīr'.
23 *Innocence of Muslims* (USA, 2012), directed by N. Basseley.
24 Christoph Sydow, 'Violent protests in Egypt and Libya', *Spiegel Online International,* 12 September 2012, available at: http://www.spiegel.de/international/world/muhammad-film-triggers-violent-protests-in-cairo-and-benghazi-a-855484.html (accessed 1 October 2013).
25 Muslim Brotherhood, 'Ila rasūl Allāh', *Ikhwan Online*, 12 September 2012, available at http://www.ikhwanonline.com/new/print.aspx?ArtID=120718&SecID=212 (accessed 20 September 2013).
26 Heba Afify, 'Egypt, US struggle to maintain relations while appeasing public anger', *Egypt Independent,* 14 September 2012, available at http://www.egyptindependent.com/news/egypt-us-struggle-maintain-relations-while-appeasing-public-anger (accessed 1 June 2019).
27 *General Prosecutor v. Morris Sadiq*, Murqus ʿAziz, Nabil Adib and others, South Cairo Felonies Court, Case No.636/2012, 29 January 2013.
28 Freedom and Justice Party, 'Al-Film al-Mussi', 12 September 2012, available at http://www.masress.com/egypress/16807 (last accessed 1 June 2019).
29 Muslim Brotherhood, 'Ila rasūl Allāh'.
30 Mariz Tadros, *Copts at the Crossroads: The Challenges of Building Inclusive Democracy in Egypt* (New York: American University Press, 2013), pp. 46–7.
31 *General Prosecutor v. Dimyana Obeid al-Nour*, Luxor Primary Court of Misdemeanor, Case No.1647/2013, 11 June 2013. EIPR, 'Ḥiṣār al-tafkīr' documented other blasphemy cases which involved teachers and professors.
32 *General Prosecutor v. Romani Murad*, Asyut Primary Court of Misdemeanor, Case No.2939/2013, 1 June 2013.
33 See 'Interim report of the Special Rapporteur on Freedom of Religion or Belief Asma Jahangir', 20 August 2007, UN doc. A/62/280, para. 70.
34 Basil El-Dabh, 'Abu Islam sentenced to 11 years hard labour', *Daily News Egypt*, 16 June 2013, available at http://www.dailynewsegypt.com/2013/06/16/abu-islam-sentenced-to-11-years-hard-labour/ (accessed 20 September 2013).
35 See Doug Bandow, 'Egypt's Copts likely to find persecution ahead from increasingly repressive military regime', 14 May 2016, available at http://www.huffingtonpost.com/doug-bandow/egypts-copts-likely-to-fi_b_9972810.html (last accessed 1 June 2019).
36 Kristen Chick, 'Egypt: why blasphemy cases are rising under President Sisi', *Christian Science Monitor*, 18 February 2016, available at http://www.csmonitor.com/World/Middle-East/2016/0218/Egypt-Why-blasphemy-cases-are-rising-under-President-Sisi (last accessed 1 June 2019).
37 Areej Hassan, 'Egyptian parliament attempts to repeal blasphemy law', 12 May 2016, available at http://arcoftheuniverse.info/egyptian-parliament-attempts-to-repeal-blasphemy-law.
38 Thomas Williams, 'Egyptian government rebuffs campaign to soften blasphemy laws', 15 June 2016, available at http://www.breitbart.com/national-security/2016/06/15/egyptian-government-rebuffs-campaign-soften-blasphemy-laws/ (last accessed 1 June 2019).

39 *General Prosecutor v. Alber Saber*, Al-Marj Primary Court of Misdemeanour, Case No.18377/2012, 12 December 2012.
40 See Misdemeanour Court of Appeals of South Cairo, No.21078/2015.
41 See Court of Administrative Justice, Case No.19/4,26 May 1952, Supreme Court, Case No. 7/2, 1 March 1975 and Court of Administrative Justice, Case No.183/58, 29 January 2008.
42 Article 43 of the 2012 Constitution and Article 64 of the 2014 Amended Constitution.
43 Johanna Pink, 'The concept of freedom of belief and its boundaries in Egypt: The Jehovah's Witnesses and the Baha'i faith between established religions and an authoritarian State', *Culture and Religion* 6/1 (2005), pp. 135–60.
44 Law No.29/1982 Amending Penal Code No.58/1937.
45 See for example, *General Prosecutor v. Mohammad Fahmi ʿAsfou*, Kafr al-Zayat Primary Court of Misdemeanour, Case No. 13044/2011, 24 April 2012; Misdemeanour Court of Appeals of Kafr al-Zayat, Case No. 1095/2012, 26 July 2012; Disciplinary Court of Qina, State Council, Case No. 115/20, 24 December 2012.
46 UN Human Rights Committee (HRC), General Comment No. 34, para. 50.
47 *ʿAsran Mansur v. Adel Imam and others*, 26 April 2012.
48 HRC, General Comment No. 34, para. 28–9.
49 Lorenz Langer, *Religious Offence and Human Rights: The Implication of Defamation of Religions* (Cambridge: Cambridge University Press, 2014), p. 107.
50 HRC, General Comment No. 34, para. 47.
51 Abdullah Saeed and Hassan Saeed, *Freedom of Religion, Apostasy and Islam* (Aldershot: Ashgate, 2004), pp. 36–40.
52 Baber Johansen, 'Apostasy as objective and depersonalised fact: two recent Egyptian court judgments', *Social Research* 70/3 (2003), p. 688.
53 See Court of Cassation, Cases Nos. 475,481 and 478/65, 5 August 1996. See also Tamir Moustafa, 'The Islamist trend in Egyptian law', *Politics and Religion* 3/3 (2010), pp. 610–30 and Fauzi M. Najjar, 'Islamic fundamentalism and the intellectuals: the case of Nasr Hamid Abu Zayd', *British Journal of Middle Eastern Studies* 27/2 (2000), pp. 177–200.
54 Killian Bälz, 'Submitting faith to judicial scrutiny through the family trial: the Abu Zayd case', *Die Welt des Islams* 37/2 (1997), pp. 135–55.
55 Law No. 3/1996 on the Regulation of *ḥisba* Cases in Family Matters, *Official Gazette* no. 4 bis, 29 January 1996.
56 Johansen, 'Apostasy as objective and depersonalised fact', p. 691.
57 Article 47 of Law No. 143/1994 Concerning the Civil Affairs, *Official Gazette* no. 23 bis, 9 June 1994.
58 Court of Cassation, Case No. 44/40, 29 January 1975.
59 Quoted in Yochanan Friedmann, *Tolerance and Coercion in Islam: Interfaith Relations in the Muslim Tradition* (New York: Cambridge University Press, 2003), p. 109.
60 Ibn ʿAbidin, *Radd al-Muḥtār ʿalā al-Durr al-Mukhtār Sharḥ Tanwīr al-Abṣār*, vol. 4 (Riyadh: Dar ʿAlam al-Kutub, 2003), pp. 370–1.
61 Court of Cassation, Case No.15277/78, 15 June 2009.
62 See Court of Administrative Justice 4475/58, 30 June 2009.
63 See Article 14 of the CRC.
64 'Report of the Special Rapporteur on Freedom of Religion or Belief, Heiner Bielefeldt', 13 August 2012, UN doc. A/67/303, para. 33.
65 Saʿīd Ḥawwa, *al-Asās fī al-Tafsīr*, Vol. 1, 3rd edn. (Cairo: Dar al-Salam, 1991). On the interpretation of this verse, see also Omaima Abou Bakr's chapter in this volume.

66 See Friedmann, *Tolerance and Coercion in Islam*, pp. 114–15; Kamran Hashemi, 'Religious legal traditions, Muslim States and the Convention on the Rights of the Child: an essay on the relevant UN documentation', *Human Rights Quarterly* 29/1 (2007), pp. 184–227, at p. 215.
67 Friedmann, *Tolerance and Coercion in Islam*, p. 144.
68 Hossam Bahgat, 'Khānat al-diyyāna' (Egyptian Initiative for Personal Rights, 2007), available at http://www.eipr.org/report/2007/09/10/620 (accessed 22 February 2019).
69 See Court of Administrative Justice, Cases No. 20/29, 8 April 1980; 35647/61, 29 January 2008.
70 See Supreme Administrative Court, Cases No. 13496/53, 9 February 2008; 19082/60, 12 February 2011; 33472/60, 3 July 2011.
71 See Court of Administrative Justice, Cases No. 444/61, 4 March 2008 and 38719/63, 29 December 2009.
72 Court of Administrative Justice, Case No. 26103/85, 26 April 2005.
73 Ibid.
74 Ibid.
75 Perez Zagorin, *How the Idea of Religious Toleration Came to the West* (Princeton: Princeton University Press, 2013), p. 260. See also Greg Forster, *John Locke's Politics of Moral Consensus* (Cambridge: Cambridge University Press, 2005).
76 See Angelina E. Theodorou, 'Which countries still outlaw apostasy and blasphemy?', Pew Research Centre, 2016, http://www.pewresearch.org/fact-tank/2016/07/29/which-countries-still-outlaw-apostasy-and-blasphemy/ (accessed 22 February 2019).
77 A study by the Pew Research Center on a sample of 2000 Egyptians shows that although more than 75 per cent of the sample supported religious freedom, 64 per cent of the respondents held the view that apostasy from Islam should be punished. Pew Research Center, *The World's Muslims: Religion, Politics and Society* (Washington: Pew Research Center, 2013).
78 Human Rights Watch and Egyptian Initiative for Personal Rights, *Prohibited Identities: State Interference with Religious Freedom* (Washington: Human Rights Watch, 2007).
79 See Bassen Youssef, 'Islamic debates on apostasy in Egypt', *Al-Arabiya News*, 7 June 2013, http://english.alarabiya.net/en/views/news/middle-east/2013/06/07/Islamic-debates-on-apostasy-in-Egypt-.html; Amr al-Shubaki, 'Mafhūm al-rida fī muwājahat ḥurriyyat al-ʿaqida', *Al-Masri Al-Yum*, 23 August 2007, 1116, http://today.almasryalyoum.com/article2.aspx?ArticleID=73362 (accessed 22 February 2019).
80 See Khaled Diab, 'A Christopher Hitchens dream: atheism on the rise in Egypt', *Salon*, 27 October 2013, http://www.salon.com/2013/10/27/a_christopher_hitchens_dream_atheism_on_the_rise_in_egypt/; Tamer Fouad, 'The Arab Spring and the coming crisis of faith', Open Democracy, 26 May 2012, http://www.opendemocracy.net/tamer-fouad/arab-spring-and-coming-crisis-of-faith (accessed 20 February 2014).
81 Brian Whitaker, *Arabs without Gods: Atheism and Freedom of Belief in the Middle East* (CreateSpace Independent Publishing Platform, 2014).
82 O. Gawad, 'Controversial Egyptian film "The Atheist" gets go ahead by censors', 14 March 2012, https://web.archive.org/web/20121230161031/http://english.alarabiya.net/articles/2012/03/14/200689.html.
83 Kristin Deasy, 'Debating atheism in the heart of Cairo', *World Affairs*, 21 February 2013, http://www.worldaffairsjournal.org/blog/kristin-deasy/debating-atheism-heart-cairo (accessed 22 February 2019).
84 M. Salama, 'al-ʿĀlam al-sirrī li al-mulḥidīn', *al-Wafd*, 11 April 2013, http://goo.gl/oOO7Fe (last accessed 1 June 2019).

85 W. Allah, 'Talabat Munaqasha Hawl Intishar al-Ilhad', *al-Watan*, 20 May 2013, http://www.elwatannews.com/news/details/184630 (last accessed 1 June 2019).
86 Youssef, 'Islamic debates on apostasy in Egypt'.
87 Al-Azhar Document for Basic Freedoms (2012), *OnIslam*, https://web.archive.org/web/20150714173534/http://www.onislam.net/english/shariah/contemporary-issues/islamic-themes/455396-al-azhar-basic-freedoms-document.html.
88 Legal opinions (fatwas) published on the official web site of the Department of Da'wa of the Muslim Brotherhood http://www.manaratweb.com/, on 23 June 2011 and 7 March 2012). See also the opinion of the leading Salafist scholar Yasser al-Borhami on apostasy in Islam, 12 May 2012, http://www.youtube.com/watch?v=lL3AhugZ_5E (accessed 22 February 2019).
89 Moataz El Fegiery, *Islamic Law and Human Rights: The Muslim Brotherhood in Egypt* (New Castle upon Tyne, UK: Cambridge Scholars Publishing, 2016), pp. 177–9.
90 Ibid.
91 See Moataz El Fegiery, 'Egypt: the return to authoritarianism and the crisis of citizenship rights', *Arab Citizenship Review* 6 (October 2014), http://aei.pitt.edu/56776/1/egypt_arab_citizenship_review_oct2014.pdf (last accessed 1 June 2019); Amr Hamzawy, 'Legislating authoritarianism: Egypt's new era of repression' (Carnegie Endowment for International Peace, 2017), http://carnegieendowment.org/files/CP_302_Hamzawy_Authoritarianism_Final_Web.pdf (last accessed 1 June 2019).

7

Plurality, Dissent and Hegemony: The Story Behind Pakistan's Blasphemy Law

Arafat Mazhar and Syed Zainuddin Moulvi

Introduction

This study is a critique of the narrative surrounding Section 295-C of the Pakistan Penal Code[1] (hereinafter referred to as '295-C' or 'the blasphemy law'), which deals with the offence of 'blasphemy' against the Prophet Muhammad. The law prescribes a fixed and unpardonable death penalty for the crime without distinction between Muslims and non-Muslims. Its status as 'God's law' makes the blasphemy law a highly potent weapon for pursuing enmities and persecuting minorities[2] and an effective tool of domination, threat and retaliation. Moreover, given the particular nature of Pakistan's criminal legal system, where lower courts tend to convict under 295-C, but every sentence of death imposed by a lower court has to be confirmed by the High Court, imprisonment for an inordinate length of time is all but guaranteed even in the case of innocence and eventual acquittal. The unpardonable capital punishment also breeds an ethos of vigilantism, since the dominant Islamic narrative renders an offender subject to certain execution and therefore deprived of the state's protection.[3]

The genesis of 295-C has received little in-depth scholarly attention for such a divisive piece of legislation. There has been no serious attempt to interrogate the law and the narrative justifying it with a historical-legal approach or from the perspective of Islamic jurisprudence, within the local context. The role of various Islamic legal narratives in the trajectory and contemporary development of 295-C has been largely ignored by the secular academia. This neglect is baffling given that local, public and legal discourse is dominated by references to the religious tradition. The evidence also suggests that a reliance on 'secular' critiques of the law has only served to deepen the 'secular'/'religious' divides in Pakistani society, rather than pave the way for any meaningful reform. In this context, an examination of the claims of the dominant legal narrative from the perspective of traditional *fiqh* (Islamic jurisprudence) is urgently needed. Equally necessary is a historical and sociological account of how competing Islamic narratives came to influence the law and its current judicial interpretation.

This chapter is the first formal attempt at undertaking this task. It examines the role of certain Islamic legal narratives in the historical trajectory and contemporary development of the blasphemy law.

A primary focus of this research is on testing the most significant claims of the prevailing narrative around 295-C. These claims are:

(a) that the crime of blasphemy is a *ḥadd* offence, punishable by death, with no possibility of pardon or mitigation of the sentence, to be applied indiscriminately to both Muslims and non-Muslims; and (b) that this ruling enjoys the absolute *ijmāʿ* (consensus) of all four schools in the Islamic legal tradition, and specifically that the law as currently interpreted is an accurate representation of the traditional Hanafi position on the issue of blasphemy.

Jointly, these claims have greatly influenced the judicial and legal discourse on blasphemy, playing a decisive role in the making of the law. The claim of a complete scholarly consensus, for instance, was vociferously espoused by parliamentarians who pushed to amend the law[4] in 1986, in order to include the death penalty as a punishment for insulting the Prophet Muhammad. In fact, the parliamentarian concerned invoked the authority of *ijmāʿ* more than thirty times during the proceedings.[5] Similarly, both Ismail Qureshi in his 1987 petition calling for blasphemy to be made a *ḥadd* offence and the Federal Shariat Court (FSC) in its subsequent 1991 judgment declaring the alternate penalty of life imprisonment null and void, also employed the twin tropes of *ḥadd* and *ijmāʿ*. In the social sphere, popular religious scholars have also made similar proclamations in order to garner the support of the masses against any endeavour to reform the law. Prior to the assassination of Salman Taseer, for instance, Mufti Haneef Qureshi and Mufti Ashraf-ul-Qadri issued fatwas declaring that the only punishment for insulting the Prophet Muhammad was death. Mufti Ashraf-ul-Qadri supported this claim by arguing that not a single jurist in the entire history of the Islamic legal tradition, including Abu Hanifa, dissented on the issue. It was on the authority of this assertion that he called – successfully – for the killing of Salman Taseer.

These claims powerfully influence public discourse in two important ways.

First, the claim of *ḥadd* carries immense weight because it signifies a divinely decreed fixed punishment for a particular crime and therefore places any such law in an unassailable position. Further, by claiming an *ijmāʿ* across all four schools of thought that blasphemy is a *ḥadd*, it essentially becomes an iron-clad law, leaving no space for debate or alternative positions.

Second, the claim that the law in its present form represents the authentic Hanafi position also contributes to the untouchable status it currently enjoys. The Hanafi school of law, which was the official school of the Ottoman and Mughal empires, predominates in the Indian subcontinent.[6] An overwhelming majority of the Pakistani population are Hanafis (Deobandis and Barelvis), and the Hanafi position on any legal matter carries an almost irrefutable authority. The claim that the current judicial interpretation is an accurate representation of the Hanafi position, lends it credibility in the courts, in parliament and among the public.

This study contends that these claims are wholly untenable, given the overwhelming historical evidence for a differing authentic Hanafi stance and for its subsequent misrepresentation and marginalization in the local context. We investigate the genesis of this misrepresented position and study the reasons for its transmission through a series of texts and its dominance in the contemporary local narrative around 295-C. Furthermore, we present recommendations for framing the discourse in a manner that allows for the identification of progressive solutions through the rich resources present within the religious tradition, rather than relying on secular frameworks. In effect, this means practising a form of immanent critique, i.e. critique from within, rather than positing an inevitable conflict between the demands of modern society and religious tradition. In fact, we contend that such an engagement might be the most effective means to create room for much-needed dialogue and debate, a fact borne out by the final aspect of our research, which addresses the 'us versus them' ideology that results in an impasse between socio-religious and secular actors' discussions of the law.

Background and overview of the crisis

Pakistan's blasphemy law has suffered a perpetual crisis of legitimacy since its earliest days. Its alarming record of abuse, injustice and violence has attracted extensive coverage in the global media and academia over the years. The damning evidence of its costs, both human and social, is now well documented in several academic studies[7] and numerous reports.[8] Quite apart from the international outrage at what many deem state-sanctioned persecution of citizens in general, and minorities in particular, the 'draconian' law has also mobilized minority communities and the more progressive sections of Pakistan's civil society into pushing for legal reforms.[9] These calls for reform have generally sought a repeal of the law inter alia on the grounds that it is discriminatory legislation,[10] riddled with design flaws,[11] has a legal form uniquely prone to abuse, and substantive content that blatantly contravenes settled principles of natural justice. In addition, it is severely criticized for being unrepresentative legislation imposed by praetorian diktat.[12] Others deplore what they consider its barbaric death penalty, which is deemed woefully inconsistent with international humanitarian standards.[13] Local resistance has also voiced the concern that Islamic discourse needs to evolve beyond the confines of archaic medieval tradition and has called for abandoning classical 'Shariʿa laws' in favour of a fresh *ijtihād*. Elsewhere vague references are made to the blasphemy law being 'man-made' and having 'no basis in Qurʾan and Sunna'.[14] The most consistent critiques of the law either rest on the theoretical foundations of human rights law,[15] democratic theory and international law, or at the very least employ them as analytic frameworks for assessing its validity and legitimacy.[16]

On the other hand, the law enjoys the passionate support of the vast majority of the populace.[17] The religious right vehemently asserts that Section 295-C is in fact very much derived from the Qurʾan and Sunna and that the law in its current form has enjoyed absolute consensus throughout the history of the Islamic legal tradition.[18] The crisis reached its climax in 2010 when Punjab governor Salman Taseer filed a mercy petition requesting executive pardon for Asia Bibi, who had been sentenced to death by a session court under 295-C.[19] His criticism of the law was met with outrage, public demands for his assassination and fatwas declaring it mandatory for him to be killed. In December 2010, he was assassinated by his own bodyguard, Malik Mumtaz Hussain

Qadri,[20] who was hailed as a hero by many religio-political parties and received a passionate welcome on his arrival in court.[21]

The most contentious and sensitive issue with the blasphemy law, however, has always been the question of its application to non-Muslims. As stated, the law as it currently stands applies indiscriminately to both Muslims and non-Muslims. Pakistan, however, has faced the greatest international and domestic criticism for its atrocious record of legally sanctioned persecution of minorities – especially its religious minorities. Not only do the law and its current judicial interpretation subject all non-Muslims to the *ḥadd* penalty, they also provide no guidelines whatsoever on the question of what constitutes blasphemy for those non-Muslims[22] whose religious doctrines necessitate a belief that may amount to blasphemy. In the long run, there is a danger that the blasphemy law may become a state-sanctioned tool for a slow-drip Holocaust one reported offence at a time.[23]

The religious right contends that any attempt at revising its form or content is tantamount to altering sacred law, which is fixed and immutable by divine commandment. The fact that a majority of the law's critics draw on 'western'/'secular' philosophies for evaluating the law only heightens the suspicion towards them. As a result, most attempts at reform through legislative amendments have met with abject failure.

We will now delve into the development of the dominant narrative surrounding 295-C in Pakistan.

Development of 295-C and the surrounding narrative in Pakistan

Section 295-C of Pakistan's Penal Code[24] reads as follows:

> Use of derogatory remarks, etc., in respect of the Holy Prophet.
> Whoever by words, either spoken or written, or by visible representation, or by any imputation, innuendo, or insinuation, directly or indirectly, defiles the sacred name of the Holy Prophet Mohammed (peace be upon him) shall be punished with death, or imprisonment for life, and shall also be liable to fine.

In order to gain an appreciation of the current status of the law, it is necessary to review the major players involved in its development. The key state and non-state actors examined in this section include the legislature (Parliament), the judiciary (Federal Shariat Court, FSC), Hanafi institutions (Deobandi and Barelvi scholars/groups) and modern Islamist groups (Ahl-e-Hadith, Jamaat-e-Islami, etc.).

A bare reading of the law suggests that any person convicted under the section could receive either the penalty of death or life imprisonment, with the decision being a matter of judicial discretion. In 1991, however, the FSC declared the alternate penalty of life imprisonment 'repugnant to the injunctions of Islam' and consequently a nullity in law.[25] The FSC judgment is both the controlling legal precedent as well as the state's foremost authority on Islamic interpretations of the blasphemy law.[26] It thus serves as the 'official' state narrative on 295-C. A detailed analysis of the FSC ruling as a legal narrative merits a separate study in its own right. Here we will only summarize the relevant findings, discuss those features of the judgment that pertain to the penalty for blasphemy, and consider the *fiqh* position at play.

Legislative: Parliament

When the bill was put up for debate in the National Assembly in 1986, repeated calls were made for its amendment so that the death penalty could be made mandatory.[27] The Assembly was near unanimous in its support for a fixed death penalty for blasphemy, which was presented as the single agreed-upon position across the Islamic legal tradition. Indeed, countless references were made to portray an absolute agreement and consensus (*ijmāʿ*) within the *umma* (entire Muslim community)[28] regarding the issue. The six main parliamentarians involved in the debate cited numerous authoritative texts including *al-Ṣārim al-Maslūl* by Ibn Taymiyya (d. 1328), *al-Sayf al-Maslūl* by Taqi al-Din Subki (d. 1355), *Fatāwā Shāmī* by Ibn ʿAbidin (d. 1842) and the *Fatāwā ʿālamgīriyya* or *Fatawa-e-Alamgiri* (seventeenth century) to support their position. A close reading of these primary texts, however, reveals that most texts cited by the parliamentarians regarding a consensus on fixed capital punishment for blasphemy included the caveat that non-Muslims would not be killed for insulting the Prophet. However, none of the parliamentarians, barring one dissenting voice, raised any concerns during the parliamentary proceeding, or called for a consultation with religious experts. Apart from relying on spurious claims, the parliamentarians also used emotional appeals in order to speed up the process. Parliamentarian Turab-ul-Haq Qadri, for instance, argued that 'if we reject this bill, let's keep in mind that 250,000 people can surround the parliament'.[29] Similarly, Nisar Fatima also claimed that 'if this bill is not passed, the government will need to provide us with sanctuary, though there is no sanctuary from God'.[30] Consequently, in a country where it takes months and years to pass the most mundane of laws, it took only a few hours to include the death penalty as a punishment for insulting the Prophet.

Judiciary: the Federal Shariat Court judgment

In 1991, the FSC was presented with the question of whether 'any disrespect or use of derogatory remarks etc. in respect of the Holy Prophet comes within the purview of Hadd and [whether] the punishment of death provided in the Holy Qurʾan and Sunna could be altered'.[31] The FSC was essentially called upon to decide whether the crime of blasphemy was a *ḥadd* offence. In the *fiqh* literature, the technical term *ḥadd* refers to a particular class of offences for which fixed penalties are provided in the Qurʾan and Sunna. As such, these offences carry unchangeable punishments sanctioned by divine commandment. The Muslim community cannot make any alterations or amendments to these offences by legislative, judicial, or any other means.[32] There are certain evidentiary standards for proving a *ḥadd* offence occurred, and its derivation from the scripture (Qurʾan and Sunna) is also subject to stringent conditions of certainty in the textual warrant(s).[33] In this case, the FSC ruled that the crime of blasphemy does indeed fall into the category of *ḥadd* crimes and therefore carries a fixed penalty of death. Although the judgment generally lacks precision and clarity, this particular finding is clearly articulated.[34] In addition to ruling that blasphemy constitutes a *ḥadd* offence, the FSC also holds that there is no possibility of reprieve, pardon or mitigation of the sentence.[35] Indeed, the Court expressly rules out any allowance for repentance, apology, or renewal of faith. Its verdict rests on the premise that only the Prophet possessed the right to pardon those who insulted him.[36] Presumably this right lapsed with his passing, and the *umma* cannot claim any authority or right to waive the *ḥadd* sentence. Despite a few jurisconsults stating that the sentence could be waived in case of repentance,[37] this position does not receive the attention of the Bench beyond a perfunctory listing in the summary of the various opinions of the scholars invited to assist the Court. As it stands, the legal interpretation of the blasphemy law is very clear on this matter and the ruling purports that the *ḥadd* punishment for blasphemy can neither be waived nor can the sentence be mitigated in any way. This position has also (arguably) been implicitly confirmed by the Supreme Court.[38]

In establishing this interpretation of the law, the Court repeatedly cites various noted authorities of the Islamic legal tradition to prove that there is a consensus on the matter. Qadi ʿIyad (d. 1149)[39] and Ibn Taymiyya are quoted as having endorsed the view that this position enjoys an absolute consensus (the word *ijmāʿ* is used) without a single known difference of opinion. The Court then proceeds to conclude that the tradition is unanimous on the question of the fixed penalty of death with no possibility of pardon or waiving/lowering of the sentence. It is important to note that in reaching this conclusion, the Court makes absolutely no distinction between Muslims and non-Muslims, men and women, or any other categories of legally distinct persons. Neither is there any attempt to discuss the context of the various discussions in the *fiqh* literature used, or the legal reasoning of the authorities cited. Similarly, no attempt is made to inquire into the nuances and differences of the various *fiqh* traditions that appear to have been subsumed under one blanket consensus. From the judgment it appears as if all schools of the Islamic legal tradition are identical in their legal ruling, reasoning and position on the crime of blasphemy, its penalty and the jurisprudential operations involved in the narrative.

Hanafi institutions and scholars (Deobandi and Barelvi)

Alongside these legal and political developments, Pakistani Hanafi scholars from both Deobandi and Barelvi circles were also responding to this issue as a reaction to the publication of Salman Rushdie's book *Satanic Verses* in the late 1980s, which was widely regarded by the Muslim public as highly offensive and blasphemous. The primary mode of these engagements was books clarifying the religious positions on the question of blasphemy. These texts also claimed an *ijmāʿ* on blasphemy being a *ḥadd* offence with no provision for *tawba* (repentance).[40] Despite being advocated by Hanafi *muqallids* (jurists following the teachings of earlier authorities), most of these texts relied primarily on the work of the non-Hanafi scholars Ibn Taymiyya and Qadi ʿIyad as well as individual direct reasoning through Qurʾan and Hadith, both of which methods fall outside of the purview of acceptable Hanafi scholarship.

The second wave of religious discourse on this issue in recent times came as a response to Salman Taseer's mercy petition for Asia Bibi in 2010. This engagement took place in books, television appearances, sermons and speeches.[41] There is a marked continuity in the narrative about blasphemy between this discourse and the earlier wave. As stated earlier, it included a public declaration by mufti Ashraf-ul-Qadri that it was mandatory to kill Salman Taseer unless he apologized to the general public, the Prophet and God.[42] Following the assassination of Taseer, representatives of the Hanafi legal tradition fiercely defended the law, claiming a complete consensus on its validity in the tradition and declaring that there could be no amendment to the law.[43]

Modern Islamist groups: unusual alliances

A greater convergence of religio-political leaders, Ahl-e-Hadith scholarship and traditional Hanafi legal scholarship on the issue can be noted around the time of Salman Taseer's assassination. This alliance was unusual since parties that had been ideologically opposite joined hands with a united position. This is especially strange for the Hanafi representatives from the Deobandi and Barelvi schools, since they are sceptical towards and vocal critics of modernist parties/ideologies such as the Ahl-e-Hadith, Jamaat-e-Islami and Tanzeem-e-Islami etc., and usually distance themselves from their positions. This alliance, which included parties such as Ahl-e-Sunnat wa Jamaat, Sunni Ittehad Council, Sunni Tehreek, Jamaat-e-Islami and JUI, culminated in the movement *Tehreek e Tahaffuz Namoos e Risalat* (Movement for Protection of the Prophet's Honour). The movement vowed to defend the law against any amendment and led numerous rallies across various cities.[44] Regarding blasphemy rulings, they claimed that it was God's law and a *ḥadd* offence; that no pardon was acceptable for any perpetrator whether Muslim or non-Muslim; and that there was an *ijmāʿ* on the matter.

Investigating the authentic Hanafi position

Most of the arguments used to validate the dominant legal interpretation rest on the claim that there is complete consensus in the tradition regarding the issue, and more significantly, on the claim that current law represents the authentic position of Hanafi *fiqh* throughout history. By presenting itself as the authoritative ruling of Hanafi *fiqh*, the dominant narrative garners much legitimacy and widespread acceptance amongst the masses and the clerical class.[45] However, careful sifting of the historical record reveals that this is not the case, and that in reality the traditional authoritative Hanafi position has taken a far more nuanced view of the matter and maintained a radically different position. This section summarizes the traditional Hanafi position on both Muslim and non-Muslim blasphemers. It further brings to light certain definitive moments of misrepresentation of the Hanafi position on blasphemy and traces the subsequent proliferation of the erroneous view into the dominant discourse on the blasphemy law as the authentic Hanafi position. Specifically, it will highlight how this error features in the case for the applicability of the death penalty, the status of blasphemy as a *ḥadd* offence and the question of pardon.

The traditional Hanafi position on Muslim and non-Muslim blasphemers

One of the major sources that challenges the basis for the current blasphemy law is the work of Muhammad Amin Ibn ʿAbidin (d. 1842). His status as the foremost *muḥaqqiq* (investigator) is significant; some have even called him the last important traditional Hanafi author.[46] He investigated the issue of blasphemy in his treatise *Kitāb Tanbīh al-Wulāt wa al-Ḥukkām ʿalā Aḥkām Shātim Khayr al-Anām aw Aḥad Aṣḥābihi al-Kirām* and also in *al-Radd al-Muḥtār ʿalā Durr al-Mukhtār*, which is widely considered an authoritative tome for deriving Hanafi rulings on a variety of issues, especially in South Asia.[47]

Ibn ʿAbidin traces the original Hanafi position on blasphemy all the way back to the founder of the school, Abu Hanifa (d. 767). Briefly, this position holds that blasphemy is to be considered as a form of apostasy for which a Muslim blasphemer is to receive the death penalty, but there exists a provision for pardoning the blasphemer and waiving the death penalty (whether the state offers pardon or the offender seeks it, and subject to his repentance).[48] If the perpetrator is a *dhimmī*/non-Muslim, he will not be sentenced to death, as this crime does not void his covenant of protection with the State.[49] The act of blasphemy is merely a continuation (and increase) of the disbelief of a non-Muslim. Since his life/wealth is protected by the State while he maintains his (dis)belief, it will stay protected in the case of an increase in his (dis)belief.[50] Tahawi (d. 933) in his elaboration suggests a verbal warning for a first-time offender and any punishment other than death for repeated offence.[51] However, if the perpetrator makes a habit of the offence, he may receive the death penalty at the exclusive discretion (*taʿzīr*) of the head of state, if it is deemed necessary for preserving peace and order in the society (*siyāsa*).[52]

Is this the authentic Hanafi position?

This study relies on the Hanafi position as presented by Ibn ʿAbidin. While Ibn ʿAbidin has been widely documented as the foremost authority on identifying authentic Hanafi positions, we find that two factors in particular make a compelling argument for the reliability of his claims in this case.

First, Ibn ʿAbidin relies on earlier texts such as Abu Yusuf's *Kitāb al-Kharāj*, Tahawi's *Mukhtaṣar al-Ṭaḥawī* and works such as Abu Bakr ʿAlaʾ al-Din al-Kasani's (d. 1191) *Badāʾiʿ al-Ṣanāʾiʿ*, which is based on *ẓāhir al-riwāya* (the most authentic records of the Hanafi position).[53] Ibn ʿAbidin therefore avoids pitfalls associated with research based on secondary or indirect resources.

Second, and most significantly, his stance finds confirmation in the highest possible Hanafi authorities. To verify the authenticity of a purported Hanafi stance it is sufficient to corroborate it in the rulings of the three highest ranks of jurists. A position may be deemed authentic if it is confirmed in the rulings of the *mujtahid fī al-sharʿ* (the founder of the school, Abu Hanifa); if not, then if it is corroborated by rulings found in the second rank of jurists, the *mujtahidīn fī al-madhhab* (his students who use his principles to derive rulings); and failing that, by consulting the works of the *mujtahidīn fī al-masāʾil* (jurists of the third rank, who determine answers to cases not settled by jurists of the first two ranks).[54] The legitimacy of Ibn ʿAbidin's report of the authentic Hanafi position, then, can be gauged by the fact that it is not only confirmed by Abu Hanifa himself, but also reiterated by jurists of the second and third ranks, respectively, Abu Yusuf (d. 798) (*mujtahid fī al-madhhab*) and Imam Tahawi (*mujtahidin fī al-masāʾil*).[55] In fact, as per Hanafi *uṣūl*, since there is a consensus of the jurists of these three ranks, it is not *permissible* for a jurist to diverge from it.[56]

Understanding how far the representation of Hanafi rulings today deviates from the authentic Hanafi stance allows us to examine this disparity and dissect its origin in detail.

Dissecting the divergent position on Muslim blasphemers

How Pakistan's legal interpretation of blasphemy law came to rest on a position so grossly divergent from the established Hanafi *madhhab* makes for a compelling research question. The possible genesis of this divergence can be traced through Ibn ʿAbidin's research. He claims that the jurist Muhammad bin Shahab al-Bazzazi al-Kardari (d. 1414) was the first person to expound these views in *al-Fatāwā al-Bazzāziyya*.[57] Al-Bazzazi claims that as per Hanafi consensus, blasphemy is punishable by death as a *ḥadd* offense for both Muslims and non-Muslims with no possibility of pardon. This, he incorrectly states, is the position of Abu Hanifa, Sufyan al-Thawri and the people of Kufa. He cites Qadi ʿIyad and Ibn Taymiyya as his sources. Ibn ʿAbidin theorizes that al-Bazzazi's position is a misreading of these sources.

Ibn ʿAbidin highlights al-Bazzazi's misreading of one of his primary sources, *al-Ṣārim al-Maslūl* by Ibn Taymiyya. In this book Ibn Taymiyya states:

> According to Abu Hanifa, if the blasphemer is a believing Muslim, he will be asked to repent. If he does repent, he will be spared. If he refuses to repent, then he will be killed like an apostate. If, however, the blasphemer is a dhimmi (non-Muslim), then the view of Abu Hanifa is that the dhimmi will not be killed, because the blasphemer does not legally break the covenant [under which he enjoys protection] by committing blasphemy.

In spite of Ibn Taymiyya's scholarly accuracy in presenting the Hanafi position in the book, al-Bazzazi in his reading of Ibn Taymiyya maintains that blasphemy under the Hanafi ruling is a *ḥadd* offense for Muslims, with no possibility of avoiding the death penalty. He further claims that this is the only established position on the matter.

While further investigating the roots of al-Bazzazi's claims, Ibn ʿAbidin reproduces two extracts from Qadi ʿIyad's *al-Shifāʾ* which were misunderstood by al-Bazzazi. The first extract in question indicates consensus amongst the majority of scholars, including Abu Hanifa, on the capital punishment of Muslim blasphemers. However, al-Bazzazi erroneously extends the consensus to intricacies regarding issues such as the status and acceptance of pleas for clemency and discerning punishments for Muslims and non-Muslims. For example, Qadi ʿIyad states that Abu Hanifa and his students, as well as the founders of two other schools, Malik (d.795) and Shafiʿi (d. 820), agree that a believing blasphemer should be given the death penalty. However, he distinguishes the Hanafi understanding of the crime as apostasy, in which case the death penalty may be avoided if the blasphemer repents and reverts. Ibn ʿAbidin claims that al-Bazzazi misses this distinction and consequently grossly misinterprets the nuanced position on the acceptability of repentance for Muslim blasphemers.

The second misreading of *al-Shifāʾ* by al-Bazzazi concerns the statement: 'one cannot imagine a difference of opinion in this matter'.[58] Al-Bazzazi interprets this statement as a claim that there exists, in reality, no difference of opinion in this matter. Ibn ʿAbidin however points out that Qadi ʿIyad, later in the same book, explicitly states the acceptability of repentance in the Hanafi *madhhab*. It is therefore safe to conclude that al-Bazzazi made serious mistakes in his reading and interpretation of the book.

Lastly, Ibn ʿAbidin addresses another problematic statement by al-Bazzazi: that if anyone doubts the mandatory death punishment for one who commits blasphemy, he/she also becomes an apostate. This doctrine is mirrored in the fatwas against Salman Taseer. Ibn ʿAbidin however expresses his frustration at this extremely flawed position, asking whether Abu Hanifa himself, who allowed for the waiver of the death penalty, should have also been killed.[59]

It is important to reiterate, however, that unlike Section 295-C which imposes a fixed capital punishment on both Muslims and non-Muslims, al-Bazzazi's incorrect reading of Abu Hanifa was still only limited to a discussion of the death penalty with respect to Muslim blasphemers. Therefore, even if al-Bazzazi's position was mistakenly employed to support the bill, it still could not justify capital punishment for non-Muslim blasphemers. Section 295-C cannot be viewed as a mere consequence and perpetuation of al-Bazzazi's initial misrepresentation.

Whilst analysing Ismail Qureshi's book *Namoos-e-Rasool Aur Qanoon Tauheen-e-Risalat*, however, we chanced upon a misquotation that does in fact point towards a likely explanation for the current framing of the law with respect to non-Muslims. Qureshi was not only the author and petitioner for the law, but it was in fact due to his relentless efforts in the courts that the law was passed in the first place. Later on, the declaration of the law as *ḥadd* and the elimination of any other punishment for blasphemy was also a direct result of his efforts/petition. In his book, Qureshi quoted Ibn ʿAbidin to support his view on blasphemy. He cited Ibn ʿAbidin as saying: 'A *kāfir* blasphemer of the Prophet (p.b.u.h.) will be killed under *ḥadd* and his pardon won't be acceptable.'[60] This statement was shocking since Ibn ʿAbidin had posited the completely opposite position. A reference to the original text however revealed that Qureshi had quoted that part of the text in which Ibn ʿAbidin actually quoted al-Bazzazi in order to refute the latter's position at length over the following pages, labelling al-Bazzazi's error a matter of extreme negligence and warning against the consequences of this mistake. Qureshi therefore misquoted Ibn ʿAbidin completely.

However, what was even more striking in Qureshi's citation was the substitution of the term *kāfir* (unbeliever) for 'Muslim'. The original quote of al-Bazzazi, as cited by Ibn ʿAbidin, referred to a *Muslim* blasphemer.[61]

Qureshi had therefore not only not relied upon al-Bazzazi's flawed reading, but had further, by replacing the word 'Muslim' with 'Kafir', extended the punishment to non-Muslims. In this way, Qureshi committed a double error in his reading of the primary sources. He not only misattributed al-Bazzazi's statement to Ibn ʿAbidin, but even whilst quoting al-Bazzazi, he made a further error by applying the death penalty to non-Muslims. It was on the basis of this layered misrepresentation that he framed Pakistan's blasphemy laws – applying the punishment without discrimination to both Muslims and non-Muslims.

Even a cursory analysis of the classical literature clearly reveals the flaws in Qureshi's claims. As stated, Abu Hanifa himself holds that if a dhimmi (non-Muslim) insults the Prophet, he will not be killed as punishment because this merely implies an increase in his disbelief, and does not break his covenant with the state. This position is corroborated by Abu Yusuf and Al-Tahawi in *Ikhtilāf al-fuqahā* and *Mukhtaṣar al-Ṭaḥāwī* respectively. These two jurists fall into the second and third highest ranks, with Tahawi noting that a 'non-Muslim blasphemer [. . .] will be asked to not do it again.' This position is also maintained by the last major jurist of the era, Abu Bakr al-Jassas al-Razi (d. 1191), in *Sharḥ Mukhtaṣar al-Ṭaḥāwī*.[62]

It is also important to note that the context in which blasphemy is treated reflects the jurist's conception of the relationship between the state and its non-Muslim inhabitants and how blasphemy affects that relationship. This relationship (known as *dhimma*) is a covenant of protection for non-Muslims' life and property afforded by the state upon certain terms. The offence of blasphemy does not violate these terms according to these authoritative Hanafi rulings.

In fact, capital punishment is conceivable only as a *siyāsa* (political) punishment, as opposed to a Shariʿa (religious) one,[63] in the case of a habitual offence that amounts to the spread of *fasād* (mischief) intended to undermine the authority of the State in what might be said to approximate treason. This means that for non-habitual offenders, the matter of blasphemy may be resolved with a simple verbal warning.

Even though a consensus among the early scholars would have been sufficient to establish that a death penalty is not prescribed for non-Muslims, we find further proof that this is the definitive Hanafi ruling on the subject through its transmission and endorsement by influential scholars from later periods as well. The highly influential and respected jurist Abu Bakr ibn Masʿud al-Kasani (d. 1191) from the classical era endorses the position recorded by Tahawi and Abu Hanifa in his work *Badāʾiʿ al-Ṣanāʾiʿ*,[64] an authoritative tome hailed by Meron as 'the flowering of legal thought in [the Hanafi *madhhab* at its] pinnacle'.[65] Another scholarly giant, Ahmad ibn Muhammad al-Quduri (d. 1037), writes in *al-Tajrīd*:

> Non-Muslims blaspheme against Allah saying He has a son, and the Zoroastrians by saying He has an 'opposite'. These are realities of their beliefs which do not break their contract [of security]. Similarly, the insult of the Prophet does not break their contract of security because it is just another representation of their disbelief.[66]

Furthermore, from the classical and post-classical period (1200 onwards) four critical Hanafi texts – *Mukhtaṣar al-Qudūrī*, *al-Hidāyā*, *Kanz al-Daqāʾiq* and *Multaqā al-Abḥur*, written by al-Quduri (d. 1037), al-Marghinani (d. 1197), al-Nasafi (d. 1310) and al-Halabi (d. 1517)[67] – share a consensus that the contract of protection for the life and property of non-Muslims is not invalidated in the event that a non-Muslim insults the Prophet. This cements what may be called the predominant authoritative

Hanafi position on the treatment of non-Muslim blasphemers because of the stature and influence of these particular texts. Collectively they have been the subject of over 170 different commentaries, whose influence transcended geographical boundaries: from Anatolia, Iraq and Egypt to Greater Syria, Central Asia, Yemen, modern Saudi Arabia, Macedonia and South Asia. For centuries these texts have also served as a reliable source for deriving fatwas, and they are educational staples for training Hanafi jurists today, from Al-Azhar University in Egypt to the Dar-ul-Uloom in Pakistan.[68] Thus these texts as well as the established rulings of the earlier Hanafi scholars present a concrete perspective on non-Muslim blasphemy that rules out capital punishment, and even allows for verbal warnings, which is in sharp contrast to the current conceptualization and treatment of non-Muslim offenders in countries like Pakistan.

In short, the authentic Hanafi position as identified in the previous sections is drastically different from its current representation in the narrative surrounding 295-C. In the current representation, blasphemy is a *ḥadd* offense on its own and applies to both Muslims and non-Muslims, and there is no provision for pardon. In the authentic position, blasphemy is an offence of *ridda* (apostasy) amongst Muslims, whereas Abu Hanifa classifies the capital punishment of a habitual non-Muslim offender as *siyāsa*; there is a provision for pardon both for Muslim and non-Muslim blasphemers. In the current representation, a single instance of blasphemy is enough to apply capital punishment to non-Muslims. The authentic position, to the contrary, is that in the case of non-Muslims, capital punishment will not be imposed. Imam Tahawi states that only a verbal warning suffices. In exceptional cases, capital punishment can be imposed on a habitual offender at the discretion of the head of state.

Misrepresentation of the authentic Islamic legal rulings on blasphemy

In his book, Ibn ʿAbidin writes: 'It so happens that sometimes one claims a position in a *madhhab* that is not true and it gets transmitted by others (who trust it) and hence creates an alternative, inauthentic position.'[69] In fact, this is precisely what happened as a result of al-Bazzazi's misrepresentation of the Hanafi position. According to Ibn ʿAbidin, Bazzazi's skewed position was copied by jurists such as Ibn al-Kamal al-Humam (d. 1457) in *Fatḥ al-Qadīr*. It was cited by Zayn al-Din Ibrahim Ibn Nujaym (d. 1563) in *al-Ashbāh wa al-Naẓāʾir*. His student Abd Allah al-Khatib al-Tumartashi (d. 1596) further transmitted the same position in his books. It was further echoed by later jurists such as Shaykh Muhammad bin Abdullah Alghazi, Allama Khayruddin Ramali, Sahib al-Nahr and Shurunbalali,[70] and of course in the discourse surrounding 295-C.[71] Ibn ʿAbidin holds al-Bazzazi responsible for the chain of scholars over time who have adhered to his ill-founded claims. He says: 'Al-Bazzazi's negligence has put the later scholars in error for they relied on his report and blindly followed him. None of them reported the issue from any of the books of the Hanafis.'[72] Ibn ʿAbidin is not a lone critic of al-Bazzazi's claims. Several other notable scholars in their investigations have concluded that this line of discourse is directly attributable to al-Bazzazi's erroneous foundations.[73] One such scholar, Allama Al Asr Sheikh Mustafa Al Reemati Ayyubi, warns future scholars that they must show wisdom in this issue and not believe in every statement brought to them lest they are fooled by it and stray from the right path.[74]

Further, Ibn ʿAbidin contends that even if al-Bazzazi's work did not suffer from methodological flaws, his stance could not have merited a footing against those of *mujtahidīn*, let alone take precedence over historically established Hanafi tradition, according to Hanafi *uṣūl*, since he is one of the *mutaʾakhkhirīn* (from later generations who relied on earlier *mujtahidīn*) and *muḥaqqiqīn* (investigators).[75] It is not permissible to follow the position of the *mutaʾakhkhirīn* over the *mujtahidīn* since they do not have authority to legislate. For Ibn ʿAbidin, this is not merely a matter of preferring a strong opinion over a weaker one: Abu Hanifa's position on *tawba* (repentance) and dhimmis (non-Muslims) is the only position. The opinion of al-Bazzazi and those who followed him should be treated as abrogated and non-existent.[76] It is interesting to note that Ammar Nasir, a Deobandi scholar, holds that there is a trend in Hanafi scholars in Pakistan who try to 'hide the authentic Hanafi position of *mujtahidīn* behind those of *mutaʾakhkhirīn*'.[77]

In the nineteenth century, the Hanafi scholars of the subcontinent faced criticism from the Ahl-e-Hadith movement over their various legal positions and *uṣūl*.[78] Particularly under fire was the Hanafi position prescribing the death penalty for a non-Muslim only if he/she was a habitual offender. Maulana Mansoor Ali wrote a series of legal opinions clarifying the Hanafi positions, using hadiths for support. These opinions were validated by 450 Hanafi scholars. Specifically, he writes in his book *Fath al-Mubin* that the use of the past continuous tense for the acts of offenders who were punished in hadiths, is proof that only habitual non-Muslim offenders may be killed at the discretion of the head of state. There isn't a single case in the hadiths where a one-time offence resulted in a punishment. Even though the alternative line of skewed Hanafi positions had already begun, the dominating narrative of the Hanafis in nineteenth-century South Asia regarding blasphemy was thus in line with the authentic position. We can make two observations from the above: first, that al-Bazzazi's misrepresentation became the dominant narrative on blasphemy law between the nineteenth century and the 1980s and, second, that Ahl-e-Hadith and reformist groups made attempts to influence the Hanafi position on blasphemy.

Transmission of false positions – three causes

Al-Bazzazi is criticized for presenting a Hanafi position by relying mainly on texts outside of the Hanafi tradition. Ibn ʿAbidin also warns that some jurists depend on books of later jurists that are not trustworthy. He contends that books such as al-Haskafi's *al-Durr al-Mukhtār* (which includes al-Bazzazi's position) have included rejected opinions or opinions that belong to other schools. Ibn ʿAbidin states: 'The transmission of an opinion may occur in about 20 books of the later jurists, and still the opinion may be incorrect, as the first jurist has erred and those coming after him have transmitted the opinion from him.' Ibn ʿAbidin is pointing towards the pressing need for a *faqīh* to trace a position to the earliest books rather than later ones. This, he believes is the essence of the methodology of *takhrīj*, which is the function of a *faqīh*.[79] As a principle, Ibn ʿAbidin also argues that in order to read and understand books of *fiqh*, the reader must be well trained in all categories of *uṣūl* and read it under guidance, otherwise grave mistakes are likely. Ibn ʿAbidin points towards three reasons why such a disparity may exist and sometimes even takes the apparent form of a dominant narrative. These three causes are relevant to the current representation of Hanafi *fiqh*.

1. When a jurist consults texts outside of his own *madhhab*. This is exemplified by al-Bazzazi's consultation of Ibn Taymiyya and Qadi ʿIyad (both non-Hanafis) to understand the Hanafi position. As pointed out above, the majority of the Hanafi texts on the subject of blasphemy in Pakistan today rely on the same two sources to represent their position.[80]
2. When a jurist does not trace a position that he comes across to the earlier books, hence not doing justice to the process of *takhrīj*. Opinions on blasphemy illustrate how the *faqīh* is relying on later books (such as *Fatāwā al-Bazzāziyya* and Ibn al-Kamal al-Humam's *Fatḥ al-Qadīr*) rather than the original texts (such as *Kitāb al-Kharāj*, *Mukhtaṣar al-Ṭaḥāwī*, etc.) to understand the original position. In Pakistan the mistake was echoed in the legislative process and in the FSC, e.g. in the representation of the Hanafi *madhhab* by Ismail Qureshi (who was not a *faqīh*, but was functioning as one).
3. When those transmitting these positions are not trained jurists. Without naming anyone, Ibn ʿAbidin pointed out that the erroneous transmission points to a lack of comprehensive training in *fiqh*. This has proved to be a prophetic warning. Today, religio-political figures such as Jamaat-e-Islami's Fareed Paracha position themselves as authorities on traditional schools and promote an oppressive narrative based on dubious methods and training. This is further discussed below.

The influence of non-Hanafis on the Hanafi narrative can be seen in all three mistakes in both time periods, whether it is in the form of relying on non-Hanafi texts or allowing modernist religious figures to represent the traditional *madhhab*.

Institutionalized misrepresentation of Islamic legal rulings

Apart from the causes highlighted by Ibn ʿAbidin, a close examination of the institutionalized and deliberate representation of the Islamic legal tradition in the social, judicial, legal and political spheres in Pakistan reveals another set of common mistakes and practices that allow the perpetuation of faulty legal assertions, often in complete opposition to the actual position espoused within the tradition. The four most common causes for the distortion of Islamic legal rulings regarding blasphemy are misapplication of apostasy rulings to non-Muslims, misquotation, strategic omission of counter-claims, and cherry-picking of hadiths and rulings.

First, apostasy rulings (which are only applicable to Muslims) are misapplied to non-Muslim blasphemers. Indeed, this is precisely what happened in the 1991 Federal Shariat Court judgment, when scholars quoted a number of verses that, either directly or indirectly, related to the punishment for apostasy (*ridda*). These scholars illustrated how, in each case, the mandatory punishment for leaving the religion is death. However, in the final judgment they failed to make any distinction between Muslims and non-Muslims with regard to the applicability of such rulings. In consequence, they implicitly justified a mandatory death penalty for non-Muslim blasphemers, at least in part, on the basis of apostasy rulings not applicable to them in the first place.

Second, authoritative legal rulings are repeatedly misquoted so as to apply a mandatory death penalty to non-Muslim blasphemers. This deeply troubling inclination is found at all levels, e.g. in Ismael Qureshi's double error when quoting Ibn ʿAbidin's position on blasphemy and in the 1986 parliamentary proceedings on the inclusion of the death penalty as a punishment for insulting the Prophet Muhammad. For instance, parliamentarian Turab-ul-Haq also completely misquoted Ibn ʿAbidin during the proceedings. As was mentioned previously, Ibn ʿAbidin had explicitly argued that non-Muslims would not be killed for insulting the Prophet Muhammad. Turab-ul-Haq however attributed the opposite position to Ibn ʿAbidin, in an effort to perpetuate the claim that there was a complete scholarly agreement on the mandatory death penalty for committing blasphemy.[81] His claim was uncritically accepted, without any fact check, by the parliamentarians who were already in a rush to pass the bill.

Third, there is deliberate omission of rulings in canonical legal texts that are contrary to Section 295-C. The strategic omission of counter-claims occurs not only in fiery speeches by popular religious scholars but also in fatwas by respected religious institutions. For instance, in a fatwa on the treatment of blasphemers (both Muslims and non-Muslims) published by Jamia Uloom-e-Islamia, Binori Town (one of the largest Hanafi seminaries in Pakistan), the scholars claimed a consensus regarding the mandatory death penalty for anyone who insults the Prophet. In support of this claim, the Binori Town scholars quoted Ibn Taymiyya's reference to Ibn Hazm, who had cited the opinions of all four schools of thought on the matter. Whilst quoting Ibn Taymiyya, however, the Binori Town scholars strategically employed ellipses to omit a reference made to Abu Hanifa's differing stance.

It is interesting to note that that the very same quote by Ibn Taymiyya was also distorted by Ashraf-ul-Qadri, in one of his speeches. Since Ashraf-ul-Qadri was making a speech, he couldn't employ ellipses to outright omit Abu Hanifa's position. In an ingenious move, Qadri instead literally concocted Arabic verses, and stated that Abu Hanifa had a similar opinion. In this way, he was able to effectively dodge questions relating to Abu Hanifa's position on the matter.[82] In short, unlike the Binori Town scholars who completely concealed Imam Abu Hanifa's position to make the claim of a universal *ijmāʿ*, Ashraf-ul-Qadri literally changed Imam Abu Hanifa's position on the matter by including the above statement in his speech, and consequently fulfilled the same objective. In a country where the majority of Muslims do not understand the Arabic language, it is no surprise that such play of language remains unnoticed.

Last but not least, scholars and legislators alike also cherry-pick hadith reports and legal positions that support their own position on blasphemy whilst negating various other differing, yet equally valid, legal positions. Furthermore, they also tend to quote unrelated Qurʾanic verses to justify their position. In the FSC judgment, for instance, scholars made reference to Qurʾanic verses dealing with divorce, fasting, morality, war in sacred months, distortion of the Old Testament, and similar topics. These verses were indirectly connected to the issue of blasphemy and were used as evidence for the justification of the law. The arbitrary and careless reference to such verses has become a commonplace occurrence, and completely ignores the complexity of Islamic legal reasoning.

Primary research: open-ended interviews

A thorough discussion of the socio-economic, political and religious factors that ultimately led to al-Bazzazi's erroneous views eclipsing and replacing the authentic Hanafi position, is beyond the scope of this chapter. However, we carried out informal interviews to understand why this position continues to be dominant today. If the traditional authoritative position differs so radically from what is claimed today, how is it that the local traditional Hanafis have joined hands with modern religious figures to declare the current law divine with no room for debate? Are they deliberately allowing al-Bazzazi's erroneous view to eclipse and replace the authentic Hanafi position? How do religious actors (modern and traditional) respond when presented with the factual inaccuracies of their position? In order to address these questions, we took all of our findings to the author/petitioner of 295-C, modern religious groups and local Hanafi scholarship and confronted them with the disparity we had found.

Ismail Qureshi (the author/petitioner of the blasphemy law)

The most significant of these interviews is that with Ismail Qureshi[83] who, as mentioned earlier, was the author of and petitioner for the law. The law was passed in the first place due to his relentless efforts in the courts. Later on, the declaration of the law as *ḥadd* and the elimination of any other punishment for blasphemy was also a direct result of his efforts/petition. When presented with the original source, Qureshi acknowledged that he had used a secondary source and cited the primary one in his book without actually referring to it. He said that there might be some problems with the law, but held to the opinion that with regards to *maṣlaḥa* (public good), bringing these issues to light would only serve to destroy the movement to protect the honour of the Prophet of Islam.

Modern religious groups

Fareed Paracha, the deputy general secretary of Jamaat-e-Islami,[84] was a regular fixture on TV and in public gatherings, and was vociferous in his support for 295-C. As such, he is an example of modern religio-political leaders. Fareed Paracha has consistently claimed a consensus on the death penalty for both Muslims and non-Muslims without provision of pardon. His feedback on our findings seemed to be grounded on the loosely interpreted principle of *maṣlaḥa*, a term he used to signify the greater wisdom in withholding certain information for the time being, as it might otherwise help the secular voices advance their own agenda.[85]

We also presented our findings to the leader of Tanzeem-e-Islami, Hafiz Akif Saeed.[86] Akif Saeed professed ignorance on the specifics, but like Ismail Qureshi and Fareed Paracha, he advocated the current position as a necessary *maṣlaḥa*.

Hanafi scholarship

We carried out interviews during visits to two Deobandi madrasas, Jamia Ashrifa[87] and Jamia Madnia.[88] In the departments for legal rulings (Dar-ul-Ifta), some muftis were surprised to see the criticisms that Ibn ʿAbidin had made against the position which does not provide for repentance of the offender and waiving of sentence. The Head Mufti in one of them was already aware of this contradiction, but deemed it unwise to make such a disturbance in the narrative right now.

We were able to download a fatwa from Jamia Binoria on 23 November 2010. This fatwa, using Ibn ʿAbidin's *Radd al-Muḥtār* as its source, stated that rulers could punish an alleged perpetrator of blasphemy in any way they liked at their discretion, irrespective of gender and religion. However, after Salmaan Taseer's murder the head of Binoria, mufti Naeem, appeared on television endorsing the dominant narrative of 295-C, hence contradicting the fatwa of his own Dar-ul-Ifta.[89] After a few weeks, the fatwa was removed from the website and replaced with a different fatwa which was stricter and closer to 295-C.

Maṣlaḥa – a license to hide the truth?

The findings of our interviews point towards a problematic misappropriation of the concept of *maṣlaḥa*, whether or not that term is explicitly used. This seems indicative of a deep-seated sense of insecurity and a need for preservation of identity. Due, perhaps, to socio-political factors that are too extensive to summarize here, adopting a hard-line approach to the blasphemy issue seems to be an effective rallying point for many parallel religious ideologies against a perceived global threat to Islam. There is, at the very least, a palpable fear that a more tolerant narrative can be hijacked by a secular agenda, even if it is true to tradition. The fact that such fears are entertained and acted upon, even at the cost of intellectual integrity, points to a widening chasm between the religious and secular sections of society, an 'us vs. them' guardedness that effectively places a bar on dialogue.

This lends support to our original assertion that the best and perhaps the only way to engage with the dominant narrative is to speak from within the tradition rather than criticizing the law from a secular framework. We now look at implications of this research and recommendations that can go a long way in resolving this crisis.

Corrective reform: implications of this research

The traditional Hanafi position on blasphemy has potentially far-reaching consequences for Pakistan's current crisis over its blasphemy law, both at the level of underlying legal theory and in terms of practical impact.

The contentious features of the blasphemy law

While the current design issues, procedural concerns and everyday operation of the blasphemy law involve a complex combination of several legal and cultural factors that cut across various academic disciplines and require separate study, there are certain contentious features of the law that emerge directly out of the *fiqh* narrative that informs its interpretation and sets the terms of legal discourse. Here we have focused on those features of the law that regularly invite, encourage and/or cause miscarriages of justice, but are subject to dissent and alternative approaches in the Islamic tradition: (1) the fixed and unpardonable punishment of death and (2) the lack of distinction between Muslim and non-Muslim offenders as separate legal categories.

The most daunting challenge facing the policy makers and the legal and academic community is developing a solution to curb the disastrous effects of the blasphemy law while retaining its identity as a religiously inspired law rooted in the Islamic legal tradition. Attempts at legislative reform have always lacked legitimacy in the eyes of the public for whom the law occupies the status of a divinely ordained commandment.

Recommendations for corrective reform

The practical effect of the difference between the Hanafi position and the dominant ruling is that under the Hanafi interpretation of the crime of blasphemy, if the accused is a Muslim, a conviction will not result in an immediate death sentence, but an invitation to repent and revert. Even in the absence of such invitation, the accused repenting on his/her own initiative and of free volition would be sufficient to prevent the sentence of death from being applied. In addition, the result is a complete waiver of penalty and immediate release of the accused. In this sense, some of the most serious miscarriages of justice, i.e. the death sentence and continued imprisonment, may be circumvented on a very practical level. Additionally, a swift confession and immediate repentance may even lead to trial being avoided altogether. These effects may significantly reduce the potential for abuse and injustice in the legal system. Naturally these measures are not sufficient for preventing the menace of vigilantism, but there is nonetheless some potential for reform, at least at the level of legal procedure.

If the accused is a non-Muslim, it is entirely conceivable under this framework that no charge be made out at all. An adoption of the Hanafi position may make it harder to abuse the legal system to persecute non-Muslim minorities. In addition, since under the Hanafi position their covenant with the state remains intact, under the legal framework there is no justification for considering them *mubāḥ al-damm* (unprotected by the state and thus liable to be killed). Their status as protected citizens, in spite of their guilt, may prove empowering. It may significantly blunt what the HRCP referred to as the 'killing edge to Muslim fanaticism'.[90] The punishment can be drastically reduced from a death penalty to a mere verbal warning. That this is an established position in *fiqh* literature allows for framing the discourse without compromising rootedness in tradition and religious legitimacy in the quest for a progressive solution to the crisis of the blasphemy law. An adoption of the Hanafi ruling may not even require a legislative amendment. A judicial recognition of this position at the apex court or in a review judgment at the FSC would be sufficient. Therefore, the radical changes mentioned above can be achieved without even changing the letter of section 295-C.

Even an apparently minor step can have significant consequences. Moreover, proving the fallibility of what was presented as a divine decree opens up possibilities for further reform and even contemporary re-interpretations. There is hope for drastically reducing the human-rights costs of the law one pragmatic step at a time.

Implications in the bigger picture – refuting 'God's law'

In few matters has consensus been as repeatedly declared by socio-religious and political actors as in the case of blasphemy. The term 'God's law' is constantly employed. We have witnessed the far-reaching social impacts on tolerance, free speech and human rights when such terms are loosely used. It is necessary to refute these claims in legal, social and political forums. If this refutation is successfully propagated, people might view the use of the term 'God's law' and *ijmāʿ* as a device more sceptically, finally ushering in the possibility of dissent and debate. This can lead to the creation of a space for alternative opinions and positions, which at present appears impossible. When 'God's law' is stripped of its irresponsibly attributed divine status, becoming merely a fallible opinion, true dialogue can take place between reformists, modern religious scholars and the rich religious tradition. Most importantly, the exploitation of religion as a tool for violence by religio-political actors can be discouraged.

Areas of further research

Many compelling research questions emerge from this chapter. Firstly, the concept of *maṣlaḥa* emerged to be of particular interest. Our interviewees consistently cite concern for the 'good of the public (the Muslim *umma*)' as the driving force behind their advocacy of an admittedly flawed system. An exploration of why such motives are becoming particularly relevant to these institutions right now could elucidate key crises in Pakistani religious scholarship. In addition, ulterior motives masquerading as *maṣlaḥa* are equally important to uncover. Further, there is a need for comparative analysis of how the term *maṣlaḥa* is employed by the traditional scholars as contrasted with its use by modern Islamist groups such as Ahl-e-Hadith. As is evident from the study, local traditional scholars may instrumentalize the concept of *maṣlaḥa* under influence from these modern religious actors in a quest for a united front. It follows that the influence of Ahl-e-Hadith and Ibn Taymiyya on the Hanafis of the subcontinent in general and on the issue of blasphemy in particular needs to be studied in depth. This includes an investigation of the unusual alliances of religio-political parties, Deobandis and Barelvis after Salman Taseer's assassination.

Our research also reveals that *qiyās*, or analogical reasoning, a legal tool from within the Islamic tradition, can be employed to address problems pertaining to the applicability of blasphemy rulings to non-Muslims in Pakistan. The concept of *qiyās*, and its constituent, the *ratio legis* (*ʿilla*), are especially relevant with respect to the applicability of blasphemy rulings to non-Muslims in Pakistan because religious scholars, parliamentarians and the judiciary alike have made an implicit analogy between dhimmis and Pakistani non-Muslims without ever explicitly articulating this interpretive move. As a result, they applied legal rulings that dealt with dhimmis without explicitly delving into whether such rulings actually applied to citizens in the modern state. However, unlike the prototypical analogy of the date-wine and grape-wine, dhimmis and Pakistani non-Muslims are in fact separate categories, and the unqualified transposition of rulings from the former to the latter category is not justified.

The relationship known as *dhimma* was a covenant of protection afforded by the state to non-Muslims' life and property contingent upon certain terms. This covenant of protection assumed the Muslim invasion of non-Muslim territories, which relegated non-Muslims in the occupied region to a subordinated position. In short, it indicated a paternalistic relationship between the conqueror and the conquered, in which the latter was subject to certain restrictions in return for sanctuary. In the Pact of ʿUmar, for instance, these restrictions included, but were not limited to, building of churches, beating of Muslims, resembling Muslims in dress and appearance, displaying idolatry or inviting towards it, etc.[91] As A.S. Tritton highlights, these restrictions represented the price that the subjugated dhimmis paid for living under a Muslim government.[92]

Moreover, Tritton highlights that, although theoretically speaking the dhimmi had to satisfy all of the conditions underlined in the peace agreement, the ground reality was quite different. Indeed, according to him, 'in practice a few actions only put him [the dhimmi] outside the protection of Muslim law [and] lawyers did not entirely agree what these actions were'.[93] This ambiguity is precisely the reason behind the diversity in Islamic legal rulings regarding the punishment for non-Muslim blasphemers – whereas some scholars held that blasphemy nullified the covenant between the non-Muslim and the Muslim State, others, such as Abu Hanifa, adopted the opposite position.

In any case, unlike the *dhimma* relationship, citizenship implies a social contract between the state and individual. In this case, the authority of the state does not stem from conquest; rather, it is based on a give-and-take relationship in which the state is responsible for protecting the inviolable rights of the citizen, and the citizen in turn must refrain from activities that undermine the sovereignty and integrity of the State. Moreover, the social contract doesn't merely outline a relationship between the state and the individual citizen; it also establishes equality between all citizens. In other words, non-Muslims in the modern state are equal citizens; like dhimmis, they are protected by the State, but that protection is not accompanied by a subjugated subject position.

It is also worth highlighting that contrary to the status of the dhimmi, non-Muslim minorities have actually played a pivotal role in the very creation of Pakistan. Moreover, many non-Muslim Pakistanis have joined the Pakistani army, the police and various other governmental departments, in order to serve the country. These non-Muslims, by actively participating in the running of the state, afford protection to Muslims, rather than the other way around. This reversal again underscores the radically different status of the dhimmi and the non-Muslim citizen in Pakistan. In short, non-Muslim citizens in Pakistan cannot be treated as the conquered 'other' permitted to live in Pakistani territory, and therefore scholars cannot apply rulings on the latter to the former without clearly and explicitly justifying this analogical leap.

The *ʿilla* or the *ratio legis* behind the prohibition of blasphemy was that it broke the covenant between the non-Muslim subject and the Muslim State. Those scholars who believed that blasphemy made the *dhimma* relationship null and void, consequently ruled that non-Muslims would be killed for blasphemy. However, since such a covenant no longer even exists in the first place, blasphemy rulings cannot be directly applied to non-Muslims in the modern state.

This does not, however, mean that these rulings serve no purpose in the modern world, and are not relevant to issues pertaining to the treatment of non-Muslims in the Islamic Republic of Pakistan. Rather, these rulings perhaps require a more nuanced and cautious approach, cognizant of the contextual changes. For instance, as was mentioned earlier, dhimmis and non-Muslim citizens are similar in that they are afforded protection by the State. In this case, since the quality of protection is found in both categories, rulings stemming from this first condition are equally applicable to non-Muslims in the present State. However, since subordination no longer exists, rulings embedded in the latter prerequisite are no longer applicable to non-Muslims in the modern State.

Conclusion

To conclude, Pakistan's blasphemy law and its social imagination outside of the Penal Code rests its authority on being connected to, and being an extension of, the Islamic legal tradition. Examining its historical trajectory however unveils a series of distorting discontinuities, both in premodern and modern times, which have created narrative disrupters regarding authentic rulings of blasphemy. Indeed, by the time we reach Pakistan's blasphemy law, the tradition has been completely transformed through misrepresentations and misquotations giving it a meaning completely contrary to the original intent.

Notes

1 The Pakistan Penal Code, usually called PPC, is a penal code for all offences in Pakistan.
2 David F. Forte, 'Apostasy and blasphemy in Pakistan', *Connecticut Journal of International Law* 10 (1994–5), pp. 27–68; Osama Siddique and Zahra Hayat, 'Unholy speech and holy laws: blasphemy laws in Pakistan – controversial origins, design defects, and free speech implications', *Minnesota Journal of International Law* 17/2 (2008), pp. 303–85.
3 Forte, 'Apostasy and blasphemy in Pakistan'.
4 Prior to 1986, the punishment for insulting the Prophet Muhammad was only payment of a fine or life imprisonment.
5 See the complete proceeding in National Assembly of Pakistan, *Debates: Official Report*, 9 July 1986, pp. 3209–38, photocopy of the record, available at http://www.na.gov.pk/uploads/documents/1455604277_115.pdf.
6 John L. Esposito, 'Perspectives in Islamic law reform: the case of Pakistan', *NYU Journal of International Law and Politics* 13/2 (1980), pp. 217–45.
7 See for instance Forte, 'Apostasy and blasphemy in Pakistan'; Siddique and Hayat, 'Unholy speech and holy laws'.
8 See for instance the Asian Human Rights Commission (AHRC) report available at http://www.humanrights.asia/news/ahrc-news/AHRC-STM-090-2013.

9 Most notable was the then Punjab Governor Salman Taseer's call for amendments. Former Information Minister Sherry Rehman, former Member of the National Assembly Jamila Gilani, and Supreme Court Bar Association President Asma Jahangir have repeatedly pushed for repeal or at the very least procedural reform.
10 This argument is consistently made by most human rights organizations. See for instance an interview with Ali Dayan Hasan of Human Rights Watch, 'Minorities are collateral damage in battle for Pakistan's soul', 25 April 2011, http://www.hrw.org/news/2011/04/25/minorities-are-collateral-damage-battle-pakistan-s-soul. Some of the demands actually ask for a complete disbanding of the state 'Islamic' institutes such as the Federal Shariat Court and Council of Islamic Ideology. See for instance Marvi Sirmed, 'Release Aasiya Bibi, repeal blasphemy laws, abolish Shariat Court', 30 December 2010, http://marvisirmed.com/2010/12/30/release-aasiya-bibi-repeal-blasphemy-laws-abolish-shariat-court/.
11 Siddique and Hayat, 'Unholy speech and holy laws'.
12 Ibid.
13 Ibid.
14 See for instance Asma Jahangir, 'The animal within', *Express Tribune*, 24 August 2012, http://tribune.com.pk/story/425700/the-animal-within/; Javed Ahmed Ghamidi, 'Punishment for blasphemy against the Prophet (sws)', n.d., https://javedahmedghamidi.org/#!/renaissance/5adb7248b7dd1138372d99aa. Salman Taseer famously used the words 'man-made' for the law just before he was killed.
15 Human Rights Watch, 'Minorities are collateral damage'.
16 Siddique and Hayat, 'Unholy speech and holy laws'.
17 E.g. AFP, 'Protestors warn of anarchy if blasphemy law is changed', *Express Tribune*, 24 December 2010,http://tribune.com.pk/story/94256/protestors-warn-of-anarchy-if-blasphemy-law-changed/. The results of one poll conducted on this can be found here: http://www.pewresearch.org/fact-tank/2013/09/10/in-pakistan-most-say-ahmadis-are-not-muslim/.
18 Muhammad Ismail Qureshi, *Law of Blasphemy in Islam and West* (Lahore: Nuqoosh, 2008). Qureshi was the petitioner in getting the law approved in the first place and then eliminating all other punishment but *ḥadd*. His relentless, decade-spanning efforts in the courts to get this ruling makes the law his brainchild.
19 Ayesha T. Haq, 'Interview: Salmaan Taseer, Governor of Punjab', NewsLine, 2010, http://www.newslinemagazine.com/2010/12/interview-salmaan-taseer-governor-of-punjab/.
20 'Punjab Governor Salman Taseer assassinated in Islamabad', BBC, 2011, http://www.bbc.co.uk/news/world-south-asia-12111831.
21 AP, 'Lawyers shower roses for governor's killer', DAWN, 2011, http://www.dawn.com/news/596300/lawyers-shower-roses-for-governors-killer.
22 Here taken to include Ahmadis for the purpose of drawing out the legal discussion on blasphemy as a result of the doctrinal belief of a religious minority community.
23 The alarming nature of potential abuse of law in this context is most evident in the case of the Ahmadi community. The precedent set by *Zaheeruddin v. State* (SCMR 1993 Supreme Court 1718) effectively reduces the very existence of the Ahmadi faith to one continuing act of blasphemy by an entire community.
24 Section 295-C was inserted into the Pakistan Penal Code through the 'Criminal Law (Amendment) Act', Act No. III of 1986, s. 2.
25 *Muhammad Ismail Qureshi v Pakistan* (PLD 1991 Federal Shariat Court 10).
26 The Federal Shariat Court enjoys a unique status in the structure of Pakistan's judicature. It is constitutionally empowered by Article 203 D of the Constitution of

Pakistan to declare laws – or provisions of laws – 'repugnant to the Injunctions of Islam'. Failure of the legislature to amend a law accordingly renders it inoperant. This peculiar nature of its jurisdiction confers a near-legislative authority on the FSC. In addition, under Article 203 GG of the Constitution of Pakistan, the decisions of the FSC are binding on High Courts and their subordinate courts.

27 National Assembly, *Debates*.

28 Maulana Gohar Rehman for instance uses the words 'This is a matter of consensus of community'. Similarly, Maulana Sayed Shah Turab-ul-Haq Qadri states at one point that 'There is absolutely no two opinions on this!'

29 National Assembly, *Debates*, 9 July 1986.

30 Ibid.

31 *Qureshi v. Pakistan*.

32 Fazlur Rahman, 'The concept of *ḥadd* in Islamic law', *Islamic Studies* 4/3 (September 1965), pp. 237–51.

33 Muhammad A. Nasir, *Baraheen* (Lahore: Dar ul Kitab, 2008). Nasir lays out a set of conditions that need to be met for a penalty to be classified as a *ḥadd* penalty: (a) It is considered as such by the scripture; (b) it is made mandatory; and (c) the language of the scripture used as proof for the ruling is free from any uncertainty or alternative interpretation.

34 For instance, the Court observes in para. 32 of the judgment that: 'The above discussion leaves no manner of doubt that according to Holy Qur'an as interpreted by the Holy Prophet (p.b.u.h.) and the practice ensuing thereafter in the Ummah, the penalty for the contempt of the Holy Prophet (p.b.u.h.) is death and nothing else.' In para. 49 the Court states: '...the wrongs of the first category [. . .] will attract the penalty of Hadd and it will apply to the contemner of the Holy Prophet (p.b.u.h).'

35 In para. 32 of the judgment the Court states: 'We have also noted that no one after the Holy Prophet (p.b.u.h.) exercized or was authorized the right of reprieve or pardon.'

36 In para. 26 of the judgment, the Court observes: 'Holy Prophet (p.b.u.h.) had pardoned some of his contemners but the Jurists concur that Prophet himself (p.b.u.h.) had the right to pardon his contemners but the Ummah has no right to pardon his contemners.'

37 Namely, Maulana Subhan Mahmood Sahib, Maulana Mufti Ghulam Sarwar Qadri Sahib and Maulana Hafiz Salahuddin Yousaf Sahib. *Qureshi v. Pakistan*.

38 Judgment on Criminal Petition No. 774 of 2002 (Unreported). This petition was filed by one Dr Muhammad Amin through Muhammad Ismail Qureshi. It challenged an earlier Lahore High Court judgment, *Muhammad Mahboob v The State* (PLD 2002 Lahore 587), in which the judge, Ali Nawaz Chohan, held that a person who commits blasphemy and then repents is like an apostate and may be exempted from punishment. The petitioner argued that in holding this, the judge went beyond his jurisdiction, as he was bound by the FSC judgment in the matter, which expressly denies the possibility of pardon or repentance mitigating the sentence. The Supreme Court reiterated that the High Courts were bound by the FSC declarations, but neglected to comment specifically on whether repentance could exempt the accused from the sentence. It is the author's opinion that this judgment remains too vague and evasive to constitute a binding ruling on the issue at the apex court level.

39 *Qureshi v. Pakistan*, para. 28 cites Qadi ʿIyad [as 'Qadi Ayaz']: 'Ummah is unanimous on the point that the punishment of a Muslim who abuses the Holy Prophet (p.b.u.h.) or degrades him is death. . . .' This particular extract is further clarified below.

40 Examples include: Maulana Muhammad Hassan, *Gustakh-e-Rasool ki Saza: Madrasa Tahaffuzul Qauran al Kareem*; Dr Maulana Mohsin Usmani Nadwi, *Ahanat-e-Rasool ki Saza*; Maulana Mufti Mahmood Ashraf Usmani, *Tauheen-e-Risalat aur uski Saza*; Ibn e Umar Farooqi, *Hurmat-e-Rasool*; Mufti Muhammad Taqi Usmani, *Namoos-e-Risalat ki Hifazat kijiye*.

41 Rana Tanveer and Naeem Ullah, 'Blasphemy law protests: Major markets shut but no violence', *The Express Tribune*, 1 January 2011, http://tribune.com.pk/story/97572/blasphemy-law-protests-major-markets-shut-but-no-violence/.

42 Statement given by a Hanafi Mufti in this sermon: http://youtube.com/watch?v=FJD8wVlSdU8.

43 A. Rashid, 'Blasphemy law: long march to counter any change', *The News*, 31 January 2011, http://www.thenews.com.pk/Todays-News-13-3662-Blasphemy-law-long-march-to-counter-any-changes.

44 Ibid.

45 During the course of this study, various ethnographic methods were employed to gather data on the conception of blasphemy amongst inter alia *madrasa* clerics, Islamic activists and civil society in general. A vast majority believe the current legal position on blasphemy to be the authoritative ruling of the Hanafi tradition. This includes muftis working within the Dar-ul-Iftas of notable religious institutes such as Jamia Ashrafia and Jamia Madaniyya Lahore.

46 Frank Vogel, *Islamic Law and Legal System: Studies of Saudi Arabia* (Leiden: Brill, 2000), p. 63.

47 Muhammad Khalid Masud, 'Apostasy and judicial separation in British India', in M. Khalid Masud, Brinkley Messick and David Powers (eds), *Islamic Legal Interpretation: Muftis and their Fatwas* (Cambridge, MA: Harvard University Press, 1996), pp. 193–203.

48 Ibn ʿAbidin (d. 1863), *Tanbīh al-Wulāt wa al-Ḥukkām ʿalā Aḥkām Shātim Khayr al-Anām aw Aḥad Aṣḥābihi al-Kirām* (Lahore: Suhayl Academy, 1976). According to Ibn ʿAbidin, this position has been corroborated as the *madhhab* of Abu Hanifa by: Abu Yusuf in *Kitāb al-Kharāj*, imam Tahawi in *Mukhtaṣar al-Ṭaḥawī*, imam Sufyan al-Thawri (d. 778), imam Abu Bakr ʿAla al-Din Kasani (d. 768) in *Badāʾiʿ al-Ṣanāʾiʿ* and Taqi al-Din al-Subki (d. 1355) in *al-Sayf al-Maslūl ʿalā man Sabba al-Rasūl*. Outside the works of Hanafi scholars, it has also been reported by Qadi ʿIyad in *al-Shifāʾ* and by Ibn Taymiyya in *al-Ṣārim al-Maslūl*.

49 Al-Tahawi (d. 933), *Mukhtaṣar al-Ṭaḥawī* (Pakistan: M. H. Saeed Publishers, 1990).

50 Abu Bakr ibn Masʿud al-Kasani (d. 1191), *Badāʾiʿ al-Ṣanāʾiʿ* (Beirut: Dar al-Kutub al-Ilmiyya, 1984).

51 Al-Tahawi, *Mukhtaṣar al-Ṭaḥāwī*.

52 Ibn ʿAbidin, *Tanbīh al-Wulāt*. According to Ibn ʿAbidin this position has been reported by Tahawi, Sufyan al-Thawri, Abu Bakr Ala al-Din Kasani in *Badāʾiʿ al-Ṣanāʾiʿ*, Abu Sulayman al-Khattabi (d. 998) in *Maʿālim al-Sunan Sharḥ Sanan Abī Dawud*, al-Qurtubi (d. 1273) in *al-Jāmiʿ li-Aḥkām al-Qurʾān*, Mulla ʿAli Qadri in the eleventh century and Shawkani in the thirteenth century.

53 Imran Ahsan Khan Nyazee, *Islamic Jurisprudence: Uṣūl al-Fiqh* (Islamabad: International Institute of Islamic Thought, 2000).

54 Upon conflicting positions, the higher ranks take precedence over the lower ones. Exception can be made in the case of Abu Yusuf / Muhammad al-Shaybani disagreeing with Abu Hanifa. This is explained in detail by Ibn ʿAbidin in the above treatise.

55 Ibid. and Abu Yusuf in *Kitāb al-Kharāj*, Imam Tahawi in *Mukhtaṣar al-Ṭaḥāwī*, Imam Sufyan al-Thawri, Taqi al-Din al-Subki in *al-Sayf al-Maslūl ʿalā man Sabba al-Rasūl*.
56 Ibid.
57 Ibn ʿAbidin, *Tanbīh al-Wulāt*; Muhammad Bazzazi, *al-Fatāwā al-Bazzāziyya* (Karachi: Qadimi Kutub Khana, 1414 H).
58 Ibn ʿAbidin, *Tanbīh al-Wulāt*.
59 Ibid.
60 Ismail Qureshi, *Namoos-e-Rasool Aur Qanoon Tauheen-e-Risala*t (Lahore: Al-Faisal Nashran-o-Tajran Qutab, 1994), pp. 115–21, citing the section on the apostate (*Kitāb al-Jihād/Bāb al-Murtadd*) in Ibn ʿAbidin, *al-Radd al-Muḥtār ʿalā Durr al-Mukhtār* (no edition given).
61 Ibn ʿAbidin, *al-Radd al-Muḥtār ʿalā Durr al-Mukhtār* (Riyadh: Dar ʿAlam al-Kutub, 2003), p. 373; cf. Ibn ʿAbidin, *Tanbīh al-Wulāt*.
62 Tahawi, *Mukhtaṣar al-Tahāwī* (Pakistan: M.H Saeed Publishers, 1990); Jassas, *Sharḥ Mukhtaṣar al- Tahāwī fī al-Fiqh al-Ḥanafī* (Beirut: Dar al-Kutub al-ʿIlmiyya, 1984).
63 *Siyāsa* and *sharīʿa* are mutually exclusive terms referring to non-religious and religious laws. *Siyāsa* means the ruler's discretion in the application of *fiqh*. Muhammad Khalid Masud, 'The doctrine of siyāsa in Islamic law', *Recht van de Islam* 18 (2001), pp. 1–29. On this point, see also the recent study by Muhammad Mushtaq Ahmad, 'Pakistani blasphemy law between *ḥadd* and *siyāsah*: a plea for reappraisal of the Ismail Qureshi case', *Islamic Studies* 52/1–2 (2018), pp. 9–43.
64 Abu Bakr ibn Masʿud al-Kasani, *Badāʾiʿ al-Ṣanāʾiʿ* (Beirut: Dar al-Kutub al-ʿIlmiyya, 1984).
65 Ya'akov Meron, 'The development of legal thought in Hanafi texts', *Studia Islamica* 30 (1969), pp. 73–118, at p. 82.
66 Ahmad ibn Muhammad al-Quduri, *al-Tajrīd* (Beirut: Dar al-Kutub al-ʿIlmiyya, 1983).
67 Quduri, *Mukhtaṣar al-Qudūrī* (Beirut: Dar al-Kutub al-ʿIlmiyya, 1997); Marghinani, *al-Hidāyā* (Lahore: Maktab al-Bushra, 2008); Nasafi, *Kanz al-Daqāʾiq* (Beirut: Dar al-Kutub al-ʿIlmiyya, 1983); Halabi, *Multaqā al-Abḥur* (Istanbul: al-Matbaʿa al-Uthmaniyya, 1891).
68 Meron, 'The development'; Guy Burak, *The Second Formation of Islamic Law: the Hanafi School in the Early Modern Ottoman Empire* (Cambridge: Cambridge University Press 2015); Şükrü Selim Has, 'A study of Ibrāhīm al-Ḥalabī with special reference to the *Multaqā*' (PhD thesis, University of Edinburgh, 1981).
69 Ibn ʿAbidin, *Tanbīh al-Wulāt*.
70 Ibid.
71 Nasir claims that even this skewed position was only limited to Muslims. This mistake was not extended to non-Muslims by Bazzazi and his followers. The contemporary Hanafi scholars in Pakistan have, however, extended this error to non-Muslims as well. Nasir, *Baradeen*.
72 Ibid.
73 Ibid.
74 Ibn ʿAbidin, *Tanbīh al-Wulāt*.
75 Ibid.
76 Ibid.
77 Ibid.
78 Ibid.
79 Ibn ʿAbidin, *Hāshiya* (Quetta, 1399 H), vol. 1, p. 57; *Rasāʾil* (Lahore: Suhayl Academy, 1976), p. 49. *Takhrīj* refers to the derivation of legal norms according to the principles

and methodology of the founding jurist; less than *ijtihād*, it is more than *taqlīd*. See Wael B. Hallaq, Authority, *Continuity and Change in Islamic Law* (Cambridge: Cambridge University Press, 2001), pp. 43–54.

80 One interesting example is a sermon by mufti Ashraf-ul-Qadri, a Hanafi scholar. In this sermon, the Mufti declares that Ibn Taymiyya died as a heretic, yet moves on to using Ibn Taymiyya's book for hours to defend and justify the law. He justifies this by saying that this particular text is very comprehensive and well researched. Part of the sermon can be seen here: http://youtube.com/watch?v=FJD8wVlSdU8.

81 National Assembly of Pakistan, *Debates*, pp. 3214–29.

82 A video clip of the speech is shown in Arafat Mazhar, 'Blasphemy: the untold story of Pakistan's law', YouTube, 21 April 2016, www.youtube.com/watch?v=y1W78EDIgIo, at about 53 minutes.

83 Arafat Mazhar and Zainuddin Moulvi, interview with Ismail Qureshi, August 2011.

84 Jamaat-e-Islami is one of the most influential religio-political parties in Pakistan and is similar to the Muslim Brotherhood in Egypt.

85 Arafat Mazhar, interview with Fareed Paracha, September 2011.

86 Arafat Mazhar and Zainuddin Moulvi, interview with Hafiz Saeed, September 2011.

87 Arafat Mazhar and Zainuddin Moulvi, visit to Jamia Ashrifa, August 2011.

88 Arafat Mazhar and Zainuddin Moulvi, visit to Jamia Madnia, August 2011.

89 Mufti Naeem's support for the law on national television can be seen at http://www.youtube.com/watch?v=XbJ0v5V2vzw and http://www.youtube.com/watch?v=_vpUhCzlpcs. The fatwa contradicting the law was buried in a huge pool of hundreds of fatwas on the website of Mufti Naeem's *madrasa* – www.binoria.org. The fatwa has now been removed. However, a copy is on file with the author.

90 Human Rights Commission of Pakistan, cited in Forte, 'Apostasy and Blasphemy in Pakistan'.

91 A.S. Tritton, *The Caliphs and Their Non-Muslim Subjects: A Critical Study of the Covenant of ʿUmar* (London/Bombay: Oxford University Press, 1930), pp. 5–8.

92 Tritton, *The Caliphs*, p. 5.

93 Tritton, *The Caliphs*, p. 16.

8

Politics of Fatwa, 'Deviant Groups' and *Takfīr* in the Context of Indonesian Pluralism: A Study of the Council of Indonesian Ulama

Syafiq Hasyim

The terms fatwa, deviant sects (Indonesian: *aliran sesat*) and blasphemy (*penodaan agama*) have come to prominence in the public discourse of Indonesian Muslims since the resignation of Suharto's authoritarian regime in Indonesia in 1998. Fatwas published by MUI (*Majelis Ulama Indonesia*, Council of Indonesian Ulama)[1] have declared that the beliefs of some groups of Muslims in Indonesia deviate from Islam, that is, from Sunni mainstream Islam. This chapter seeks to show how the instrument of the fatwa (Islamic legal opinion) is employed to exclude allegedly deviant Muslims from 'true' Islam and declare certain acts, whether committed by Muslims or non-Muslims, as blasphemy. It outlines the criteria, procedures and methods used by MUI to determine religious deviance. Further, it highlights how fatwas on deviant sects not only function as Islamic legal opinions, but also as political tools in what may be called the 'politics of fatwa'.

State, religion and the institutionalisation of fatwa

Policing the beliefs of Indonesians is not easy, since Indonesia is not an Islamic state, but has grappled with relations between the State and the religious communities as well as interreligious relations since its inception. At the same time, however, dominant Muslim groups such as Nahdlatul Ulama, Muhammadiyah, MUI and others have wanted Islam to play an influential role in public and legal discourse. This chapter, accordingly, emphasizes the interplay between fatwa-makers on one hand, and state actors on the other, focusing on the MUI for its particularly active role in responding to 'deviance' over the last decades. It discusses the role of fatwa-makers who seek to implement Islamic normativity, not by changing Indonesia from a '*Pancasila* state' (based on a national ideology of five principles) to an Islamic theocratic state, but by influencing the legal and political discourse in the Indonesian public sphere through the power of fatwas.

One crucial aspect of the sought-after Islamic normativity is the exclusion of 'deviant' streams of Islam from the group of Muslim communities in Indonesia. Borrowing the perspective of 'denomination theory' from the context of Western Christian countries,[2] one may say that the mainstream groups of any religious community, including Sunni Islam in Indonesia, often regard the other, smaller denominations with a different theological stance as a problem. Köstenberger and Kruger state that those who uphold orthodoxy often view deviant groups as parasites on their religion.[3] Talal Asad states that orthodoxy always creates power relations in which Muslims who follow an Islamic orthodoxy will 'condemn, exclude, undermine, and replace' Muslim practices considered heterodox and incorrect.[4]

After the fall of the Suharto regime in 1998, a dynamic has developed between the government's approach to maintaining stability through criminal law, the fatwas on deviancy and blasphemy issued by the MUI and majoritarian public pressure including mob violence. Although those who are defined as *aliran sesat* (deviant sect) are not deprived of their Indonesian citizenship, they face infringements of their political and civil rights and liberties, including difficulties in such matters as getting identity cards and registering marriages. Moreover, persons alleged to lead deviant sects or to have committed blasphemy have faced criminal prosecution, in which fatwas have been used as evidence. These legal, social and cultural consequences of issuing fatwas on deviant sects in Indonesia raise doubts whether the fatwa-making serves the public good, as it is supposed to. The chapter therefore concludes with a reflection about fatwas on deviant sects as a disintegrating factor for a pluralist society like Indonesia's *Pancasila* state.

Although the majority population of Indonesia (86 per cent) are Muslims, Indonesia was not conceived by its founding fathers as an Islamic state, but as a *Pancasila* state. That is, they based Indonesia on the ideological foundation of five principles set out by Sukarno (1901–1970, president 1945–1967): belief in one God, humanity, the unity of Indonesia, social justice and welfare, and democracy. The *Pancasila* state was a middle way or compromise between the states envisioned by the secular nationalists and the Islamist groups.[5] State and religions have thus never been entirely separate in Indonesia; the State is founded on the belief in one God and is involved in religious life through a Ministry of Religious Affairs and religious offices at district level, and religious courts have jurisdiction in family law matters concerning Muslims.[6]

Nevertheless, in this political and legal system, fatwas are like other social and religious discourses in that they are not legally binding on Indonesian citizens. However, this does not mean that the legislative process in Indonesia is free from the influence of fatwa. Like custom (*adat* law), fatwas can be used by Indonesian lawmakers as a source for making State law or any policy. In fact, several Indonesian laws and policies appear to have been influenced by fatwas, such as State Law No. 4/2008 on Pornography, State Law No. 33/2014 on Halal Product Assurance and many others. However, the incorporation of fatwas through State legislation is selective; for example, the government has not banned yoga (as a religious practice) and cigarettes, even though they were declared *ḥarām* by the MUI 2009 Annual Assembly – nor did MUI expect it to; rather, they underlined that their fatwa was legally non-binding.[7]

Besides influencing legislation, fatwas can also have direct effects if the State apparatus disregards the non-binding legal role of fatwa in Indonesia and acts as if a fatwa has legal force. When the National Police deal with Ahmadi and Shiʿi groups, for instance, as a basis for their decisions and actions they often refer to MUI fatwas that define these groups as deviant sects of Islam. The vehicle for incorporating fatwas in criminal proceedings is the controversial Law no. 01/PNPS/1965, often referred to as the 'blasphemy law'.

Prior to the establishment of MUI in 1975, fatwas were considered an ordinary religious discourse in the public sphere. Fatwas are a kind of knowledge which is freely circulated and chosen by Muslims without enforcement by the State or by the Islamic community in general: Someone raises a question on Islamic issues, and someone else gives an answer; the fatwa-seeker is not obliged to follow the answer of the fatwa-giver (*muftī*). It is true that, from the perspective of Islamic legal theory, the fatwa-seeker (*muṣtaftī*) is inferior to the fatwa-giver in terms of religious knowledge, but both are equal as citizens of Indonesia.

In term of their makers, fatwas in Indonesia can generally be divided into individual and institutional fatwas. The individual fatwa is issued by an individual mufti, and the institutional fatwa is issued by an organization of ulama. During the colonial era of Indonesia, especially under the Dutch, the individual fatwa was more prominent than the institutional one. In the post-colonial era, fatwas issued by institutional fatwa makers are considered more important than those by individual fatwa-makers. Nahdlatul Ulama (NU), the largest Islamic organization in Indonesia, has *Bahsul Masa'il* as their fatwa body, and Muhammadiyah, the second largest, has *Majlis Tarjih*. These two fatwa bodies dominated the issuance of fatwa until the establishment of MUI in 1975.

These Islamic organizations, NU and Muhammadiyah, were outside Suharto's control; they guarded their independence against intervention by the regime. Suharto therefore formed MUI to give the State a visible presence in religious issues that had previously been left to the community. Although its establishment was supported by the regime and it had a quasi-governmental function, MUI was not a state institution, but an organization of ulama from various Muslim organizations including NU and Muhammadiyah. The establishment of MUI was preceded by the establishment of ulama assemblies in all provinces in Indonesia, and the local MUIs are associated with the central MUI.

Since the establishment of MUI, there has been an increasing tendency among some groups in NU, Muhammadiyah and other Islamic organizations to seek to formalize fatwa either as part of State law or as the norm of society. In the Suharto era (1966–98), such demands were not implemented. On the one hand, this was due to the Suharto regime's opposition to including a religious aspect in the State and society. On the other hand, as a quasi-governmental fatwa-maker, MUI lacked the courage to challenge Suharto. MUI did issue fatwas, but the fatwas were not popularly used in the wider Muslim community. The post-Suharto situation is very different. Indonesia has become more open and democratic, and the government needs legitimacy and support from the Muslim majority population. MUI itself sees this circumstance as an opportunity for marketing its ideas to the public. MUI has been quite successful in this endeavour, as is evident in the increasing number of state laws, policies, and societal norms influenced by MUI.[8]

Fatwas on deviant sects and blasphemy in Indonesia

In the legal context of Indonesia, then, it is problematic to include or exclude a group as Islamic based on such fatwas. First, fatwas cannot be used as grounds for judging a person's religious status in a State that does not base its constitution and law on Islam. Second, in the literature of Islamic legal theory, a fatwa is different from a *qaḍā'* (judicial decision). A fatwa does not directly have any legally binding status after its issuance by the mufti, whereas the decision of an Islamic court does, because this institution is recognized in the legal system of Indonesia in matters of family law concerning Muslims (and in Aceh province, exceptionally, in certain criminal matters). In a non-theocratic country like Indonesia, a fatwa could be used as an inspiration for legislation, but a fatwa is not directly applicable as law; it can only be transformed into state law through the legislative process.

Note that MUI distinguishes between fatwa and *tawṣiya* (recommendation). In the legal policy of MUI, the former has a higher standing than the latter, though their content is similar; what differentiates them is that a fatwa is part of Islamic legal tradition, and a recommendation is not; a fatwa is issued by MUI in response to a question from a *mustaftī*, while *tawṣiya* is issued in the absence of such a question.

Fatwas on deviant sects: Method and procedure of *takfīr*

As the most authoritative fatwa body, MUI issues fatwas and legal advice on *ʿaqīda* (belief, creed, doctrine), one of the key foundations of Islam (Arabic: *uṣūl al-dīn*, principles of religion). These fatwas are intended by MUI to police the thoughts and beliefs expressed and adhered to by Indonesian Muslim society, that is, to ensure that all Indonesian Muslims adhere to Sunni Islam. The discourse on deviant groups (Indonesian: *kelompok sesat*) indicates that the MUI fatwas on belief (Arabic: *ʿaqīda*) hold a privileged place in the public sphere. MUI is keen to protect the authenticity and purity of *ʿaqīda*. Hence it holds that Ahmadiyah, Shiʿa and other groups it sees as being outside the Sunni belief system, have to be regulated, restricted and/or banned, as subjects of *al-amr bi al-maʿrūf wa al-nahy ʿan al-munkar* (commanding right and forbidding wrong).[9]

Before the MUI fatwas on belief-related issues are elaborated below, it is relevant to explain what is meant by *aliran sesat* and the MUI process (Arabic: *takfīr*) for declaring a person to be an unbeliever (*kāfir*). Thus the Indonesian term *aliran sesat* is used to condemn those viewed as *kāfir* by the MUI.[10] The term *kāfir* is used for those who, in the tradition of Western scholars, are referred to as heretics. MUI employs two terms to distinguish between the actions of such 'heretics': *kesalahan* (mistake) and *kesesatan* (deviance).[11] Those who have a mistaken understanding and practice related to an aspect of Islamic jurisprudence are deemed sinful, whilst those have a deviant understanding or practice related to the principle of *ʿaqīda* are described as adherents of a false belief. Those who practice the wrong *ʿaqīda* are seen by MUI to be committing apostasy.

To construct a robust conceptualization of *aliran sesat* for the State and the Indonesian Muslim community, MUI has firstly formulated criteria to be used as a point of reference by the State, Islamic organizations and lawmakers in defining such groups, and secondly, it has set up a transparent procedure by which such groups can be judged *sesat*. MUI has produced a set of ten criteria defining 'heresy'. The first is rejecting one of the six foundations of Islamic belief (Arabic: *arkān al-imān*) or one of the five foundations of Islam (*arkān al-islām*). The second is believing in or following a faith that is not in accordance with the teaching of the Qur'an and Sunna (the tradition and sayings of Muhammad). The third is believing that there exists divine revelation revealed after the Qur'an. The fourth is rejecting the authenticity of the content of the Qur'an. The fifth is interpreting the text of the Qur'an without referring to the principal foundations of the science of exegesis. The sixth is rejecting the sayings of Muhammad as one of the legitimate sources of Islam. The seventh is demeaning, belittling or denigrating Muhammad and other prophets. The eighth is rejecting the position of Muhammad as the last prophet of Islam. The ninth is changing, adding to or reducing any part of worship that is fundamental under Shariʿa, such as asserting that the pilgrimage is not to Mecca, or that the five daily prayers are not compulsory for Muslims. Lastly, the tenth is calling other Muslims unbelievers or *orang kafir* without a strong argument based on Shariʿa.[12] Any of these ten criteria, if present, could lead to accusation of a group following an *aliran sesat*.

MUI follows a certain procedure to determine the *ʿaqīda* status of a group, and whether or not it should be understood as *sesat*. The first step of the investigation is to collect data, information, evidence and witness interviews regarding the notions, thoughts and activities of the group under investigation. The MUI obtains more detailed information by conducting hearing sessions with the suspected heretical groups, intended to persuade the groups to abandon their perceived heretical beliefs. However, MUI's experience indicates that efforts to return such groups to adherence to the 'correct' Shariʿa through such hearings are generally unsuccessful, perhaps because the dialogue process is dominated by MUI. Although MUI calls the process dialogue, invited groups have no right to defend their faith.[13] This has drawn criticism from other Islamic actors; e.g., Masdar F. Mas'udi from the NU criticized MUI's posture as the 'representative of God' in judging the faith of other Muslim groups and declaring them heretical.

The second step of the investigation is an inquiry with experts who are knowledgeable in the thought and activities of the deviant groups, using a framework derived from Sunni thought. Experts whose beliefs differ from MUI's are not eligible to be witnesses. The investigation process is a means of Islamic proselytizing (Arabic: *daʿwa*) to convert unbelievers into believers, with a closer resemblance to indoctrination than to open philosophical debate with freedom of thought.

In the third step, leaders of the heretical group are invited to meet with experts for verification (Arabic: *taḥqīq*) and confirmation (Arabic: *tabāyun*) about the data, information and evidence related to the heretical group's thoughts and activities. If theological evidence of aberration is found in this third step, a recommendation will be made to the heretical group, aimed at bringing them back into the proper faith and forcing them to abandon their false convictions and activities.

The fourth step of the investigation is to submit the research findings to the MUI leadership or board members. The fifth and final step, if required, is for the leadership and board members to issue an instruction to the Fatwa Commission to undertake further discussion, and for the Commission to issue a fatwa, if needed.

The politics of fatwa

The issue of religious deviance in Indonesia has produced a discourse with multiple layers of meaning ranging from the theological to the political and from the local to the transnational. In the case of MUI fatwas, discourse on deviance from Islam always starts from the domain of theology. Usually, the Indonesian Sunni mainstream groups are distressed by groups with a belief system that is considered to be in conflict with their own. The other belief system is seen as having the potential to confuse and destroy the established, agreed-upon belief system of society, leading people into *kekafiran* (Indonesian expression for heretical behaviour). Hence, the desire to protect and promote the purity of Islamic belief has become the central leitmotif of MUI fatwa on deviant groups, as can be seen in the MUI statements banning Indonesian deviant groups such as Islam Jama'ah, Jama'ah Muslimin Hizbullah, Darul Arqam and Ahmadiyah.[14] The theological argument put forward by MUI is that all these groups adhere to theological notions that oppose the *ʿaqīda* of Sunnis. MUI argues that the belief system of *ahl al-sunna wa al-jamāʿa* (literally 'people of the Sunna and community', the Sunni group) is the only proper tenet in Islam.[15]

Islam Jama'ah[16] was banned by MUI for introducing a new concept of blind obedience to the *amīr al-muʾminīn* (leader of the believers),[17] which could lead to severance of relationships with family and relatives. The Ahmadis of Qadian were deemed *kāfir* due to their belief that Mirza Ghulam Ahmad continued a line of prophethood from the Prophet Muhammad.[18] This is different from the position of the Ahmadis of Lahore, who view Mirza Ghulam Ahmad as a *mujaddid* (renewer of the age), rather than a prophet.[19] In the MUI fatwa, however, both Ahmadi factions are considered sects that endanger the purity of Islamic belief. On 27 June 1994, the Inkar Sunnah[20] were denounced as heretical by MUI for their rejection of the Sunna as the second foundation of Islamic teaching. Some groups are deemed deviant by MUI for having mystical systems that differ from those of the majority Indonesian Sufi orders, such as Sufi orders that are associated with NU. In this regard, Muslim organizations such as MUI and NU distinguish Sufi orders into two groups as to whether they are based on credible sources (*ṭarīqa al-muʿtabar*) or not (*ghayr al-muʿtabara*). The former are acceptable, and the latter are rejected. According to MUI, the Darul Arqam group, a Malaysian group rejected by MUI in 1994, falls under the latter category. This group believes that *Aurad Muhammadiyah*[21] was revealed by God through the Prophet Muhammad to the group's founder Shaykh Suhaymi (b. 1925) at the Kaʿba when he was in a conscious state (which might be seen as a claim to prophethood).[22] MUI states that the teachings of Islam have been complete since the death of Muhammad, with no subsequent new teachings because no new prophet has been sent since Muhammad, and thus Darul Arqam's false teachings need correction. A similar case to Darul Arqam is the messianic Eden group, which was banned by MUI due to its claim that its leader Lia Aminuddin (b. 1947) was accompanied by and received revelation from the angel

Gabriel. This belief provoked various negative responses from Indonesian Muslims, who did not accept that anyone other than the Prophet Muhammad could meet Gabriel.

Deviant groups are considered by MUI not only as theological threats to Muslim beliefs but as potential political threats to the State because their presence potentially creates religious polarization and challenges to the integration of the nation state of Indonesia.[23] This was one of the reasons why MUI called for political and legal intervention against them, based on the belief that if the *aliran sesat* were allowed to exist in the public space, they would trigger a reaction from mainstream groups. On the basis of this argument, a division of power between the state authority and religious authority in handling the issue of deviant groups was established.

To raise the legal status of its fatwas on deviant groups, MUI has been attempting to persuade the State and lawmakers to consider incorporating its fatwas, or at least their ideas and spirit, into the legislation of Indonesia. In this way the fatwas would gain legal and political influence and could eventually be used to control and regulate deviant groups.[24]

MUI supports the implementation of State Law No. 01/PNPS/1965 on blasphemy, as its content is very close to the spirit and ideas of MUI's fatwa on deviant groups. Normally, blasphemy laws are employed to prosecute acts which insult religion, but in Indonesia, the blasphemy law is used to charge deviant groups who have strayed from mainstream religion. The law provides procedures for disbanding deviant groups and prosecuting individuals for defaming a religion adhered to in Indonesia or persuading others to commit apostasy. (The officially recognized religions are Islam, Protestant or Catholic Christianity, Hinduism, Buddhism, or Confucianism; though the law has been invoked to protect these other religions as well, here we are concerned with Islam.) MUI categorizes deviant groups as those who insult (Indonesian: *menghina*) and denigrate (Indonesian: *merendahkan*) Islam. When MUI declared its opposition to the Ahmadiyah, Shia and other deviant groups, it was on the grounds that their beliefs were blasphemous or defamed Islam. On many occasions, MUI has supported the prosecution of Ahmadis, Shiʿa and other so-called heretical groups under this law. Encouraging the implementation of this law is thus a fundamental method for MUI of maintaining the supremacy of the true faith as they see it.

The blasphemy law was passed in the Sukarno era, under the pressure of religious groups, particularly Islamic political groups, to protect mainstream religions from the challenge of *aliran kebatinan* (indigenous belief), which was perceived as an emergency situation. Niels Mulder argues that the passage of State Law No. 01/PNPS/1965 was related to the formulation of the official definition of religion in 1961, which excluded the indigenous beliefs that had challenged the mainstream religions of Indonesia since the 1950s. In 1953, the Ministry of Religious Affairs had listed 360 *aliran kebatinan* in Java alone.[25] Due to the influence of such groups, Islamic parties were defeated in the 1955 general elections. In order to control the increase of *aliran kebatinan*, the Ministry of Religious Affairs established an inter-departmental body for monitoring mystical beliefs in 1954 and placed it under the Attorney General in 1963.[26] In 1965 the blasphemy law was enacted.

During the Suharto era, then, government authority over the activities of deviant groups was in the hands of the Office of the Attorney General and its monitoring body – later to become the Coordinating Agency for Monitoring Mystical Beliefs in Society (BAKORPAKEM, *Badan Koordinasi Pengawas Aliran Kepercayaan Masyarakat*)[27] – while religious authority was split between such Islamic organizations as NU, Muhammadiyah and MUI.[28] During that era, many fatwas on deviant groups issued by Islamic authorities were triggered by requests from the state authorities, who also followed them up. Still, during the Suharto era, the use of blasphemy law was limited; the State did not always need the support of MUI to curb sects that the regime considered a security threat.

Since the fall of the regime and the start of the reform era in 1998, however, the law has been increasingly used. Donald L. Horowitz, for instance, reports that the blasphemy law was used much more sparingly in the Suharto era compared to the current era. In the first decade and a half after 1998, at least 120 people were convicted under the law, most of them Christians or members of Muslim deviant groups.[29] Tajul Muluk, the Shiʿa leader of Sampang, was for instance sentenced to two years' imprisonment under this law. It seems that the Horowitz report confirms the influence of MUI fatwas on the escalated punishment of the deviant groups.

The other main change brought by the post-1998 reform era is the increasingly dominant role of MUI as a fatwa body for *ʿaqīda*-related issues. Prominent figures from both NU and Muhammadiyah revealed in interviews that MUI's authority to regulate beliefs has significantly increased since NU and Muhammadiyah allowed MUI to take the lead in this area. Muhammadiyah and NU decided to take a smaller role to promote unity of belief in the *umma*. The late Ahmad Fatah Wibisono, chairman of Muhammadiyah's Majlis Tarjih, clarified that the unity of the *umma* would be ensured through the centralization of fatwas on *ʿaqīda* in the one body. Wibisono argued that Islamic organizations could have different stances on *fiqh*-related issues, but not on the issue of *ʿaqīda.*[30] Several important NU figures also chose not to issue belief-related fatwas. Although members of the NU community demanded their own fatwa on the Ahmadiyah and Shiʿa, after long discussion among the NU elite the organization failed to reach an independent position on the issue. When I asked NU chairman Said Aqil Siradj and deputy chairman Asad Ali about this issue, both simply answered that the matter of *ʿaqīda* was an MUI matter.[31]

The increasing use of the blasphemy law as a legal provision for charging deviant groups shows that MUI fatwas on deviant groups have a significant impact on the Indonesian public sphere in the post-reform era. In 2008, a joint decree on the limitation of Ahmadiyah activities was signed by the Minister of Home Affairs, the Minister of Religious Affairs and the Attorney General; it was obviously influenced by the MUI fatwa on Ahmadiyah in 2005. The same year (2005), Lia Aminuddin was arrested and subsequently convicted of blasphemy in court; an MUI fatwa against her had been issued already in 1997. As discussed below, the Constitutional Court also rejected a judicial review of State Law 01/PNPS/1965 on blasphemy due to the prevalent public opinions of mainstream groups opposed to this judicial process. All these cases demonstrate the influence of MUI fatwas on legal discourse and practice in Indonesia.

Rights groups have reacted to this use of the blasphemy law against religious minorities. On 1 December 2009, some religious groups and NGOs joined together to apply for a judicial review of this law by the Constitutional Court (Mahkamah

Konstitusi, MK).[32] One argument used to support the review was that the law had been misused by mainstream religious groups, both Muslim and non-Muslim, as a source of legitimacy for banning other groups. The application for judicial review was rejected by the Constitutional Court, and thus the blasphemy law remains on the books in Indonesia. The Court based its decision on the grounds that the law was needed to sustain religious harmony.[33] Suryadharma Ali, the Minister of Religious Affairs, argued that if the law were eliminated, it could trigger religion-based conflicts that might endanger the State. MUI's opposition to the judicial review was evident in statements by Ma'ruf Amin, now General Chairman of MUI. Amin stated that the judicial review would lead to freedom without limits in Indonesia. If the Constitutional Court accepted the judicial review, the ban on religious heresy and blasphemy would have no legal support. Amin insisted that the judicial review must be rejected and that the status of the law had to be strengthened. He further argued that Indonesia needed stricter regulations to overcome the problems of heretical groups; otherwise, the failure to restrict these groups would create misunderstandings about Islam among Muslims and 'erosion' of believers.[34] Although the Constitutional Court claimed its decision was a middle path between two contesting groups, from the legal material considered it would appear that the verdict relied more on evidence provided by mainstream groups, represented by MUI and leading figures from Muslim organizations such as Hasyim Muzadi (NU) and Din Syamsuddin (Muhammadiyah).[35] This indicates that MUI is influential in legal discourse and practice, and that the government and MUI have converging interests.

Ahmadiyah and Shiʿa as the main targets of victimization

In the post-reform era, the Ahmadiyah have been identified by MUI as a key blasphemous sect. The Ahmadiyah issue reappeared in 2005, with a new fatwa against Ahmadiyah (the first fatwa was issued in the 1980s), due inter alia to growing demands from mainstream Muslim groups for a stop to their spread in Indonesia. Whereas in the Suharto era the public discourse on Ahmadiyah was manageable, without violence or public hatred, in the reform era this has not been the case; on 6 February 2011, for example, three Ahmadiyah followers were killed by a militant Islamic group in mob violence in Cikeusik, Banten. Perhaps this is partly due to the fact that almost no Muslim groups – not even the so-called moderate Muslim organizations Nahdlatul Ulama, Muhammadiyah or Persatuan Islam – opposed the MUI fatwa denouncing Ahmadiyah as heretical.[36] For instance, Hasyim Muzadi (General Chairman of NU 2009–10) does not recognize Ahmadiyah as part of Islam and advises the sect's followers to create a new religion. A similar position was taken by Muhammadiyah, whose leader, Din Syamsuddin, rejected Ahmadiyah due to its heresy.[37] In a parliamentary hearing held in response to the Cikeusik tragedy, Suryadharma Ali, the minister of religious affairs (2009–14), supported the MUI fatwa banning Ahmadiyah.[38] These cases show that the influence of MUI on Muslim society and the State remains very significant. Although Nahdlatul Ulama and Muhammadiyah denounce Ahmadiyah belief as falsehood, however, both the two largest Islamic organizations were outraged by the violence against and killing of Ahmadis by radical Islamic groups such as FPI, FUI and other Islamic vigilante groups. It should be noted that 342 reported attacks on this group took place from the publication of the MUI fatwa on Ahmadiyah in 2005 until 2010.[39]

Besides Ahmadis, MUI has started to target Shiʿa. The Shiʿi community is the second largest Islamic denomination after the Sunnis. The Ikatan Jama'ah Ahlul Bayt Indonesia (IJABI, Association of Ahlul Bayt Congregation) claims there are 2.5 million Shiʿa in Indonesia.[40] In 1984, MUI published advice on the 'Shiʿi Ideology' (Indonesian: *Faham Syiah*). This advice was quite mild, because it only indicated some fundamental differences between Sunni and Shiʿa without declaring *takfīr*,[41] although the unwritten spirit of this advice was to denounce Shiʿa as heretics. The flagrant denouncement of Shiʿa communities as heretics by MUI and some NU groups in East Java began to escalate in 2011, with several attacks on the Islamic boarding school, Yayasan Pesantren Islam (YAPI), managed by the Shiʿi community in Bangil, East Java. Bangil is a district of East Java which has been home to many Shiʿa since the pre-independence period of Indonesia. It was reported that in February 2013, 200 protesters entered the YAPI premises, comprising a kindergarten, primary school, middle school and two high schools, and destroyed property and buildings.[42] In 2007, a Sunni cleric from Sunni al-Bayyinat Foundation, Surabaya, had engaged in hate speech, calling on Sunnis to 'sterilize' Bangil of Shiʿa.[43] Although human rights violations took place, none of the attackers have faced serious charges. In many cases, rather than act as the neutral protector of those who are attacked, the state apparatus warns the victims against reacting or retaliating against the attackers, because it could complicate the issue.

The rapid escalation of anti-Shiʿa attitudes was marked by the 'Peristiwa Sampang' (Sampang Incident), on Madura, a small island to the north of Surabaya, East Java, in December 2011. This tragic incident was sparked by the accusation that Madurese local Tajul Muluk, a Shiʿi cleric, was proselytizing in the predominately Sunni town of Sampang.[44] Protests soon escalated into physical attacks and violence against the group. The Sampang Sunnis evicted the tiny minority Shiʿi community (around 276 people), leading to the loss of their land and property; 47 houses were destroyed.[45]

Tensions flared between the central board of MUI in Jakarta and its provincial chapter in East Java in the public debate that followed the Sampang incident. Much of this debate, captured in the media, concentrated on the 1984 MUI recommendation on the legal status of this Islamic sect. The voice of the MUI central board was divided between those who did not view Shiʿa as heretical – such as senior MUI ulama Umar Shihab[46] and Din Syamsuddin,[47] deputy general chairman of MUI – and those who did, such as Cholil Ridwan[48] and his supporters.[49] Cholil Ridwan further claimed that MUI board member Khalid al-Walid, a graduate from Qum in Iran, was a Shiʿa adherent, and therefore his position at MUI should be reconsidered.[50] However, Sahal Mahfudh, MUI general chairman, remained silent on the Shiʿa controversy; according to information obtained from one correspondent, he rejected a group of Madurese ulama who sought him out for advice.[51] While the national MUI debates continued, the Sampang branch of MUI issued a fatwa on the heresy of the Shiʿa on 1 January 2012, without any consultation with the central board of MUI, and the East Java provincial chapter followed suit three weeks later.[52] According to MUI fatwa-making regulations, however, it is the central board of MUI that has the authority to publish a fatwa of national import, or at the very least, the central board should be consulted in such matters.[53]

As a result of the incident, around 200 families became internally displaced persons, living as refugees in the Sampang Sports Hall. On 20 June 2013, local authorities forced the Sampang Shiʿa community to relocate from their temporary camp in Sampang to Sidoarjo on the East Javanese mainland, 113 km from Sampang.[54] Reactions to this violation of the Shiʿa community's human rights varied, with NU and Muhammadiyah taking a different stance to MUI. NU general chairman Said Aqil Siradj viewed the relocation of the Sampang Shiʿa as a poor policy decision and not a permanent solution.[55] Muhammadiyah general chairman Din Syamsuddin tried to persuade the government of Indonesia to sponsor a reconciliation between the Sampang Shia community and its Sunni antagonists.[56] Yet, rather than seeking a solution to the conflict, the minister of religious affairs, Suryadharma Ali, sided with the fatwa of the MUI's East Java chapter, blaming the Shiʿa for the incident and declaring them deviant.[57] It should be noted, however, that to date (2018) no Joint Ministerial Decree pursuant to the blasphemy law has been issued against the Shiʿa.

Local and transnational deviant sects of Indonesian Islam

International agencies and NGOs have expressed concern at the oppression faced by Islam Jama'ah, Lia Eden, Inkar Sunnah and other groups, but the State and Islamic organizations such as MUI, Muhammadiyah, NU and many others have ignored such international pressures. Even when raised by multilateral and bilateral organizations such as the UN, European Commission and ASEAN, such concerns have failed to persuade the government of Indonesia to protect the local deviant groups.[58]

Indeed, MUI has continued to issue fatwas on *aliran sesat* and the authorities have continued to act on them – a recent example is the Gafatar religious movement, which bought land to settle in Kalimantan but was evicted by mobs in January 2016; in February that year, the MUI issued a fatwa that Gafatar is *aliran sesat*, and three leaders of the group have since been prosecuted and convicted for blasphemy.[59]

Moreover, whether or not a fatwa on *aliran sesat* has been issued, indigenous beliefs have been systematically marginalized by the State by implementing the logic of the blasphemy law in all aspects of public administration. Until recently, adherents of religions or beliefs not acknowledged by the State had to leave blank the 'religion' column on their national identity card. This either made it difficult to obtain a card at all or could lead to stigmatization and discrimination in accessing public services (such as birth and marriage certification, school enrolment and public health services) or applying for work. Fortunately, this discriminatory provision of the Law on Civic Administration was struck down by the Constitutional Court in 2017, though it remains to see how the decision is implemented.[60]

From interviews and media observations it would appear that MUI's rejection of the Ahmadiyah and Shiʿa has received stronger support from the broader Muslim public after the resignation of Suharto in 1998. MUI and their supporters have asked the government of Indonesia on several occasions to use the Pakistan model in handling the Ahmadiyah issue, i.e., declaring the Ahmadis to be non-Muslims.[61] MUI and its supporters have tried to force the Ahmadis to declare themselves publicly as non-Muslims, whilst the Ahmadis reject this pressure.[62] By referring to the policy of Saudi Arabia that prohibits Ahmadiyah adherents from entering Mecca and Medina, due to their status as non-Muslims, MUI has also pressured the Ministry of Religious Affairs to treat Ahmadis in the same way. General Chairman of MUI Ma'ruf Amin states 'the Ministry of Religious Affairs should forbid them [the Ahmadis] from undertaking the pilgrimage [hajj]'.[63] MUI's East Java chapter also declared that the Sampang Shiʿa have no right to live in Madura. In relation to the position of Shiʿa, it seems that MUI does not consider its position to contradict the Amman Message (2004)[64] that recognizes Shiʿa as part of mainstream Islam and has been signed by the Indonesian government[65] and representatives of mainstream Muslim groups in Indonesia.[66]

Fatwas have also come to target not only heresy in religious beliefs, but also *aliran pemikiran* (schools of thought). Clearly MUI perceives not only deviant beliefs, but also secular thought as a great threat. Liberal Islamic groups in Indonesia have used secular paradigms to argue that religions should not judge other religions. However, in 2005, MUI issued a fatwa banning secularism, liberalism and pluralism, stating that these ideas were against the doctrine of Islam, and therefore Indonesian Muslims were not allowed to embrace them.[67] Pluralism was assumed by MUI to be a form of religious relativism, and the fatwa reveals the MUI viewpoint that Muslims should be devoted to Islam and prohibited from mixing and combining their beliefs and rites with non-Islamic precepts. In the social and cultural domain Muslims should be open-minded, but not in the domain of belief. MUI framed this fatwa as a form of resistance to the *perang pemikiran* (Arabic: *ghazw al-fikr*, English: ideological battle) perceived to be led by the West. The general underlying argument was that Indonesian Islam was under attack from Westernization through secularism, liberalism and pluralism. MUI considered that the West had not only opened and maintained an information channel; the channel carried a liberal, secular and plural ideology that threatened Indonesian Islam, and if the Muslim community was not well prepared, Western ideology would eventually intrude and destroy their beliefs. MUI, it seemed, had fallen victim to conspiracy theories about globalization, perceiving all outside influences as a potential danger. The increasing reception of the three ideas among Indonesian Muslim communities and the possibility that secularism, pluralism and liberalism would result in conflict within Muslim societies were cited as other grounds for the fatwa.

However, a fundamental concern behind the fatwa was related to the concept of freedom, which MUI defines as something that will have a negative impact on religious life in Indonesia:[68] MUI sees 'freedom' and 'liberal' as Western concepts that function to destroy Islam, arguing that religious freedom as based on international human rights concepts paves the way for heretical groups to flourish. Ma'ruf Amin states that the implementation of religious freedom in Indonesia must refer to the concept of human rights enshrined in the Qur'an.[69]

The fatwa banning secularism, pluralism and liberalism (often shortened to the acronym *Sepilis*, playing on the Indonesian word for syphilis) has elicited various responses from progressive and moderate Muslim groups. Most of them believe that the fatwa opposes religious freedom and faith.[70] Debate centres on the use of the fatwa to object to those having different Islamic thought from MUI, and it seems that the edict is not based on serious scrutiny of recent thought on liberalism, secularism and pluralism,[71] which proponents may understand very differently from MUI. With regard to public criticism, including that of MUI figures Slamet Effendy Yusuf and Din Syamsuddin, who do not agree with the particular critique of pluralism,[72] MUI has provided a special appendix clarifying these three prohibited ideologies. In the fatwa appendix, MUI states that secularism, liberalism and pluralism that do not coincide with the MUI definitions are not the subject of the fatwa. The MUI definitions are based on the interpretation and reading of its own references, and are not intended as academic definitions, but rather as empirical definitions that refer to the living conditions of Muslim society. The pluralism banned by MUI is one understood as religious syncretism and relativism.[73] In this regard, MUI can accept the real diversity of Indonesian citizens who follow different religions and beliefs, which it does not call pluralism, but plurality (Indonesian: *pluralitas*).

However, the fatwa has been employed by radical Islamic groups to attack any ideologies they assume to be liberal and secular. Many progressive Muslim thinkers such as Abdurrahman Wahid (former General Chairman of NU and President of Indonesia), Nurcholish Madjid (Muslim scholar and founder of Paramadina Foundation), Munawwir Sadzali (former Minister of Religious Affairs in the Suharto era), Quraish Shihab (Muslim scholar and Qur'an expert), Syafi'i Ma'arif (former General Chairman of Muhammadiyah) and others were accused, by the coalition of radical and Salafi groups, of being *antek-antek liberal* (stooges of liberalism). Stigmatization of and public campaigns against liberalism, pluralism and secularism are now prevalent both in real and social media.[74]

Concluding remarks

The determination of *aliran sesat* is not merely a matter of Islamic legal theory: identity politics also plays an important role. In the Amman Message, it is clear that based on the consensus of the Muslim world, the Shiʿa are part of Islam, but on the practical level of Indonesian Islam, the Shiʿa remain regarded as a deviant sect by the mainstream Sunni Islamic organization of Indonesia. This Islamic schism is exacerbated by a tendency to make fatwas without considering the aspect of state unity and human rights, disregarding equal citizenship as a fundamental aspect of the modern state. Such fatwas contribute more to disintegration than integration, particularly when the lines between State and religion are blurred, and can challenge the nature of Indonesia as a *Pancasila* state.

Instead of purifying the faith of Indonesian Muslims, the fatwas have provoked horizontal conflict among Muslims and generated instability in the country. MUI's so-called ideological battle runs the risk of leading to stagnancy or even the death of knowledge and scientific development in Indonesia because all new and critical thought can be accused of 'liberalism, secularism and pluralism'. Therefore, it is not surprising that some social and political scholars predict that Indonesia could eventually become a more 'shariatized' country. The negative consequences of MUI's fatwas are never admitted by the organization, which instead shifts responsibility to the State.

Indonesia is now facing tension and conflict, not only between Islam and non-Islam, but between the followers of Islam, because whereas the rights of non-Muslims are clearly mentioned in both Islamic sources and the Constitution, those of Islamic 'deviant' groups are unclear due to their rejection by the dominant Islamic groups. Fatwa makers can contribute to resolving this conflict by producing fatwas that do not contradict, but rather support a *Pancasila* that promotes pluralism.

Notes

1 In this chapter, institutions with Arabic names retain their Indonesian spelling.

2 Mark Sedgwick, 'Establishments and Sects in the Islamic World', in Philip Charles Lucas and Thomas Robbins (eds), *New Religious Movements in the Twenty-First Century*, pp. 231–56 (New York: Routledge, 2004), at p. 239.

3 Andreas J. Köstenberger and Michael J. Kruger, *The Heresy of Orthodoxy: How Contemporary Culture's Fascination with Diversity Has Reshaped Our Understanding of Early Christianity* (Wheaton, IL: Crossway, 2010).

4 Talal Asad, *The Idea of an Anthropology of Islam* (Washington, DC: Center for Contemporary Arab Studies, Georgetown University, 1986), p. 15; Kambis Ghanea Bassiri, 'Religious Normativity and Praxis Among American Muslims', in *The Cambridge Companion to American Islam*, ed. Juliane Hammer and Omid Safi, pp. 208–27 (Cambridge: Cambridge University Press, 2013).

5 Eka Darmaputera, *Pancasila and the Search for Identity and Modernity in Indonesian Society: A Cultural and Ethical Analysis* (Leiden; Boston: Brill, 1988); Soekarno, *Filsafat Pancasila Menurut Bung Karno* (Yogyakarta: Media Pressindo, 2006); Seung-Won Song, *Back to Basics in Indonesia? Reassessing the Pancasila and Pancasila State and Society, 1945–2007*, PhD thesis (The College of Arts and Sciences of Ohio University, 2008); Robert E. Elson, 'Another look at the Jakarta Charter controversy of 1945', *Indonesia* 88 (2009), pp. 105–130.

6 Elson, 'Another look', p. 117.

7 'MUI: Merokok haram', BBC Indonesia, http://www.bbc.co.uk/indonesian/news/story/2009/01/090125_rokokharam.shtml (accessed 10 December 2018).

8 Discussing the expanded influence of the MUI, including new legal powers in the fields of Islamic finance, halal certification and the hajj, Lindsey noted that the then president Yudhoyono wanted the MUI to retain 'its semi-official, quasi-state, "central" role as a religious "watchdog"', but unlike Suharto, who saw the MUI as a means for the state to impose its policies on ulama, Yudhoyono instead saw it as a means 'by which ulama could influence and guide the state'. Tim Lindsey, 'Monopolising Islam: The Indonesian Ulama Council and state regulation of the "Islamic economy"', *Bulletin of Indonesian Economic Studies* 48/2 (2012), pp. 253–74, at p. 259.

9 Michael Cook, *Forbidding Wrong in Islam: An Introduction* (Cambridge: Cambridge University Press, 2003); Cook, *Commanding Right and Forbidding Wrong in Islamic Thought* (Cambridge: Cambridge University Press, 2001).

10 The Dutch anthropologist Martin van Bruinessen has written an Indonesian-language article on *gerakan sempalan* (split-away movements) in which he correctly defines *aliran sesat* or *gerakan sempalan* as a movement or religious stream which is regarded

as deviating from the belief, rites and position of the majority of the *umma*. Martin van Bruinessen, 'Gerakan sempalan di kalangan ummat Islam Indonesia: Latar belakang sosial-budaya', *Ulumul Qur'an* 3/1 (1992), pp. 16–27.

11 MUI, *Mengawal Aqidah Umat: Fatwa MUI Tentang Aliran-Aliran Sesat di Indonesia* (Jakarta: Sekretariat Majelis Ulama Indonesia, n.d.).

12 Syafiq Hasyim, *The Council of Indonesian Ulama (Majelis Ulama Indonesia, MUI) and Religious Freedom*, Irasec's Discussion Papers no. 12 (December 2011), http://www.irasec.com/ouvrage36 (accessed 5 July 2018), p. 10; MUI, *Mengawal Aqidah Umat*, pp. 7–8.

13 Hasyim, *The Council of Indonesian Ulama*.

14 MUI, *Himpunan Fatwa MUI Sejak 1975* (Jakarta: Erlangga, 2011).

15 This is a claim associated with the prediction of the Prophet Muhammad, as reported in various versions, that Islam will split into 73 sects (Arabic: *firāq*) and the only 'saved' sect will be the *ahl al-sunna wa al-jamā'a*. Ibn Taymiyya, *Sharḥ al-'Aqīda al-Wāsaṭiyya* (Riyadh: Dar al-Salam li al-Nashr, 1989), p. 219.

16 Islam Jama'ah has many other names, such as Darul Hadits, Lembaga Karyawan Islam (Lemkari, Islam's Working-Class Institution) and Lembaga Dakwah Islam Indonesia (LDII, Indonesian Islamic Propagation Institute). B. I. Hafiludin, D. M. Nasution and Z. A. Aly, *Bahaya Islam Jama'ah, Lemkari, LDII: Pengakuan Mantan Gembong-Gembong LDII, Ust. Bambang Irawan Hafiluddin, Ust. Debby Murti Nasution, Ust. Zaenal Arifin Aly, Ust. Hasyim Rifa'in, Fatwa-Fatwa Ulama dan Aneka Kasus LDII* (Jakarta: Gema Insani, 1988), pp. 1–2; Sutiyono and A. Dzulfikar, *Benturan Budaya Islam: Puritan & Sinkretis* (Jakarta: Penerbit Buku Kompas, 2010), p. 184.

17 MUI, *Himpunan Fatwa*, p. 38.

18 MUI, *Himpunan Fatwa*, p. 40.

19 Iqbal Singh Sevea, 'The Ahmadiyya print jihad in South and Southeast Asia', in R. Michael Feener and Terenjit Sevea (eds), *Islamic Connections: Muslim Societies in South and Southeast Asia*, pp. 134–48 (Singapore: Institute of Southeast Asian Studies, 2009), at p. 137.

20 This name refers to its rejection of the tradition of the Prophet Muhammad (*Sunna*), regarded as the second primary source of Islam after the Qur'an.

21 *Aurad Muhammadiyah* is a guidance for the followers of this group to do *dhikr* (silently recite the names of God in prayer).

22 Judith Nagata, 'Religious ideology and social change: The Islamic revival in Malaysia', *Pacific Affairs* 53/3 (1980), pp. 405–39, at p. 418.

23 https://www.republika.co.id/berita/nasional/umum/16/01/26/o1jhag377-mui-nilai-gafatar-berbahaya-bagi-nkri (accessed on 26 December 2018).

24 John Olle, 'The Majelis Ulama Indonesia versus "heresy": The resurgence of authoritarian Islam', in Gerry van Klinken and Joshua Barker (eds), *State of Authority: The State in Society in Indonesia*, pp. 95–116 (Ithaca, NY: Cornell Southeast Asia Program, 2009).

25 Niels Mulder, *Mysticism in Java: Ideology in Indonesia* (Yogyakarta: Kanisius, 2005); I. Ali-Fauzi, S. R. Panggabean and T. S. Sutanto, 'Membela kekebasan beragama: catatan pengantar', in *Membela Kebebasan Beragama: Percakapan Tentang Sekularisme, Liberalisme, dan Pluralisme*, (Jakarta: Lembaga Studi Agama dan Filsafat, 2010), p. xviii; S. Weinata (ed), *Himpunan Peraturan di Bidang Keagamaan* (Jakarta: BPK Gunung Mulia, 1994).

26 Melissa Crouch, 'Law and religion in Indonesia: The Constitutional Court and the blasphemy law', *Asian Journal of Comparative Law* 7/1 (2012), pp. 1–46, at p. 6.

27 Crouch, 'Law and religion', p. 7; Human Rights Watch, *In Religion's Name: Abuses against Religious Minorities in Indonesia* (2013), p. 42; U. P. Sihombing, *Menggugat Bakor Pakem: Kajian Hukum Terhadap Pengawasan Agama dan Kepercayaan di Indonesia* (Jakarta: Indonesian Legal Resource Center, 2008).

28 Hasyim, *The Council of Indonesian Ulama*; van Bruinessen, 'Gerakan Sempalan'.

29 Donald L. Horowitz, *Constitutional Change and Democracy in Indonesia* (Cambridge: Cambridge University Press, 2013), p. 250.

30 The author's interviews with Ahmad Fatah Wibisono and Din Syamsuddin, both in 2011.

31 The author's interviews with Said Aqil Siradj (2010) and Asad Ali (2011).

32 Abdurrahman Wahid (Former Indonesian President and General Chairman of Nahdlatul Ulama), Dawam Rahardjo (prominent progressive Muslim thinker from Muhammadiyah and director of Lembaga Studi Agama dan Filsafat (Institute for the Study of Religion and Philosophy), Musdah Mulia (prominent Muslim feminist), Maman Imanul Haq (young ulama from Nahdlatul Ulama, director of the traditional Islamic Boarding School al-Mizan in West Java, and later parliament member of Partai Kebangkitan Bangsa (PKB, National Awakening Party)) and some NGOs were among those who lodged the application for judicial review of State Law No. 1/PNPS/1965 at the Constitutional Court (Mahkamah Konstitusi, 2009, pp. 1–3).

33 The council of Protestant churches (PGI: Persekutuan Gereja Indonesia) is now also facing a rise in deviant sects.

34 'Pemerintah keberatan pencabutan UU Penodaan Agama', http://www.tempointeraktif.com/hg/hukum/2010/02/04/brk,20100204-223522, id.html (accessed 8 March 2011).

35 Mahkamah Konstitusi, *PUTUSAN Nomor 140/PUU-VII/2009* (2009).

36 Hasyim, *The Council of Indonesian Ulama*, p. 13.

37 Interview with the author (2011), http://www.tribunnews.com/2011/03/05/din-Ahmadiyah-anggap-pemeluk-islam-orang-kafir (accessed 4 March 2013).

38 'Menag: Ahmadiyah Qadiyan yang sesat', http://us.detiknews.com/read/2011/02/10/012328/1568162/10/menag-Ahmadiyah-qadiyan-yang-sesat (accessed 4 March 2013).

39 See the report which was prepared by Komnas Perempuan on this issue at http://news.okezone.com/read/2011/02/07/337/422265/redirect (accessed 11 July 2013).

40 Human Rights Watch, *In Religion's Name*, p. 21.

41 The following are differences between Sunni and Shiʿa as outlined by MUI. Firstly, the Shiʿa reject the use of hadith that were not reported by *ahl al-bayt* (the Prophet's relatives from the line of Fatima and ʿAli), whereas Sunnis does not make a distinction between what was narrated by *ahl al-bayt* and others as long as the scrutiny of hadith follows the science of hadith terminology (Arabic, *muṣṭalaḥ al-ḥadīth*). Secondly, the Shiʿa assume that all their spiritual leaders (imams) are protected by God against committing wrongful actions, whereas Sunnis argue that as human beings, all imams are capable of making mistakes. Thirdly, the Shiʿa do not admit the legality of Islamic consensus without the presence of their spiritual leaders, while the mainstream Sunni understanding is that an agreement among ulama, even in the absence of the highest-ranked spiritual leaders, is legal. Fourthly, the Shiʿa believe that *imāma* (Islamic leadership) is part of the principles (*uṣūl*) of Islam, while Sunnis see it as part of Islamic interpretation (*furūʿ*) to ensure the implementation of Islamic proselytizing and the interests of Muslim society. Fifthly, the Shiʿa do not recognize the leadership of Abu Bakr, ʿUmar and ʿUthman, whereas Sunnis acknowledge all of these as well as ʿAli as the Prophet's rightly guided companions. MUI, *Himpunan Fatwa*, p. 46.

42 Human Rights Watch, *In Religion's Name*, p. 21.
43 Ibid.
44 The population of this town is estimated to be 876,950; almost 100 per cent of them are Sunnis and members of the Nadhlatul Ulama community.
45 http://www.antarajatim.com/lihat/berita/94313/jumlah-rumah-syiah-di-sampang-yang-dirusak-bertambah (accessed 11 July 2013).
46 Umar Shihab was one of the MUI chairpersons. He had a traditional Islamic educational background in Islamic studies.
47 Din Syamsuddin was the vice chairman of MUI and the former general chairman of Muhammadiyah, the second largest Muslim organization.
48 Cholil Ridwan was one of the MUI's chairpersons who propagated anti-Shiʿa attitudes. He was delegated to MUI by his organization, called Dewan Dakwah Islamiyyah (DDI, Islamic Propagation Council). This organization has a close connection with Saudi Arabia.
49 http://www.hidayatullah.com/read/26320/12/12/2012/mui-pusat-sulit-keluarkan-fatwa-syiah-sesat-karena-ada-penyusupan.html (accessed 6 July 2013).
50 http://news.fimadani.com/read/2012/12/12/ada-penganut-syiah-dalam-kepengurusan-mui-pusat/ (accessed 6 July 2013).
51 I obtained this information from Masykuri Abdillah, a Muslim scholar who is also active in MUI, when he visited Berlin on 19 June 2013.
52 For Sampang, see A-035/MUI/Spg/1/2012, signed by Mahmud Huzaini (head of the fatwa commission), Mahrus Zamroni (secretary of the fatwa commission and Moh. Sjuaib (secretary general); cf. Human Rights Watch, *In Religion's Name*, p. 60. For East Java, see Keputusan Fatwa Majelis Ulama Indonesia (MUI), Prop. Jawa Timur No. Kep-01/SKF-MUI/JTM/2012.
53 MUI, *Himpunan Fatwa*, p. 939.
54 http://www.tempo.co/read/news/2013/06/21/173490090/Relokasi-Warga-Syiah-Sampang-Dinilai-Pelanggaran (accessed 1 July 2013).
55 http://www.antaranews.com/berita/381240/pbnu-menilai-relokasi-warga-syiah-bukan-langkah-tepat (accessed 1 July 2013).
56 http://www.antaranews.com/berita/381724/muhammadiyah-minta-pemerintah-rekonsiliasi-konflik-syiah (accessed 1 July 2013).
57 http://www.republika.co.id/berita/dunia-islam/islam-nusantara/12/01/27/lyfnwj-sebut-syiah-sesat-ikatan-jamaah-ahlul-bait-sesalkan-komentar-menteri-agama (accessed 11 July 2013).
58 http://www.islamtimes.org/vdceev8wnjh8pfi.rabj.txt (accessed 6 July 2013).
59 Human Rights Watch, 'Indonesia's anti-Gafatar campaign ends in blasphemy convictions', 9 March 2017, https://www.hrw.org/news/2017/03/07/indonesias-anti-gafatar-campaign-ends-blasphemy-convictions (accessed 10 December 2018); BBC News Indonesia, 'Fatwa MUI Nyatakan Gafatar Sesat', 3 February 2016 (accessed 12 August 2018); Anadolu Agency, 'Indonesia: Leaders of "deviant" religious group jailed', https://www.aa.com.tr/en/asia-pacific/indonesia-leaders-of-deviant-religious-group-jailed/765891 (accessed 10 December 2018).
60 Law No. 23 (2006) on Civic Administration, amended by Law No. 25 (2013); article 61 regulates the Household Registry Card (*Kartu Keluarga*) and article 64 the electronic Population Identity Card (*Kartu Tanda Penduduk*), the individual card that serves as the basis for all public service provision in the country; see for example the testimony of Hj. RA Tumbu Saraswati in Constitutional Court Petition No. 97/PUU-XIV/2016, pp. 52–53, or the testimony of Sardy in Petition No. 140/

PUU-VII/2009, p. 88, relating to the Law on Civic Administration and the 'blasphemy law' respectively.
61 Ishtiaq Ahmed, 'Religious nationalism and minorities in Pakistan', in Ishtiaq Ahmed (ed.), *The Politics of Religion in South and Southeast Asia*, pp. 81–101 (New York: Routledge, 2011), at p. 88.
62 http://www.tempo.co/read/news/2010/10/10/078283752/Ahmadiyah-Menolak-Usulan-PBNU-Keluar-dari-Islam (accessed 9 October 2013).
63 http://www.sasak.org/kabar-lombok/agama/depag-ntb-perbolehkan-ahmadiyah-naik-haji/08-09-2009 (accessed 1 July 2013).
64 The Amman Message clarified three points: it recognized eight legal schools of thought (*madhāhib*), including the Shiʿa; it forbade excommunicating or denouncing as disbelievers (*takfīr*) others recognized as Muslims; and it clarified the issuing of fatwas. See http://rissc.jo/the-amman-message/.
65 Alwi Shihab (Minister of Foreign Affairs) and Maftuh Basyuni (Minister of Religious Affairs), Rabhan Abd al-Wahhab (Ambassador of the Republic of Indonesia to the Hashemite Kingdom of Jordan.
66 Hasyim Muzadi, Rozy Munir, Masyhuri Naim, Muhammad Iqbal Sullam (NU), Tutty Alawiyyah (Islamic women's organization), Din Syamsuddin (Muhmmadiyah).
67 MUI. (2011). *Himpunan Fatwa MUI Sejak 1975*. Jakarta: Erlangga, see translation and commentary in Piers Gillespie, 'Current issues in Indonesian Islam: Analysing the 2005 Council of Indonesian Ulama Fatwa No. 7 opposing pluralism, liberalism and secularism', *Journal of Islamic Studies* 18/2 (2007), pp. 202–40.
68 MUI, *Mengawal Aqidah Umat*, p. i.
69 Interview with Ma'ruf Amin in 2010.
70 Interview with Johan Effendi in 2011.
71 Hasyim, *Council of Indonesian Ulama*.
72 Interviews with Slamet Effendy Yusuf (2010) and Din Syamsuddin (2011).
73 MUI, *Fatwa Munas VII Majelis Ulama Indonesia* (Jakarta: Majelis Ulama Indonesia, 2005), pp. 130–31; MUI, *Himpunan Fatwa*, pp. 93–95.
74 I. Hasani and B. T. Naipospos, *Wajah Para Pembela Islam* (Jakarta: Pustaka Masyarakat Setara, 2011), p. 138.

Part Three

New Directions

9

Transgressing All Bounds? Gendering Authority and Engendering Orthodoxy[1]

Kecia Ali

Among Muslims worldwide, Islamic law functions today predominantly as an identity marker rather than a comprehensive system of jurisprudence. The particulars vary dramatically. Sometimes religious law marks a boundary between Muslims and another religious group: Hindus in India, Christians in Nigeria. Sometimes it signals a ruler or interest group's determination to prove its own religious credentials to other Muslims. In the twentieth century, both in countries with Muslim majorities and in places with Muslim minorities, Islamic laws regulating women and the family became a 'preferential symbol of Islamic identity'.[2] In the late twentieth and early twenty-first centuries, various actors have sought to legislate or enforce fixed or 'boundary' punishments, *ḥudūd* (sing. *ḥadd*) for sexual offences as well as religious crimes such as blasphemy and apostasy.[3]

Laws targeting those who transgress religious and sexual boundaries may accord with 'traditional' Islamic jurisprudence (though typically without its stringent evidentiary standards), but the zeal for prosecution is new.[4] Historically, Ahmad Atif Ahmad argues, 'the majority of Muslim jurists saw apostasy as a rare problem and apostates as largely inconsequential'. Echoing Judith Tucker's arguments regarding *zinā'*, Ahmad attributes the increased salience of apostasy in Muslim thought today to 'modern anxieties [which] have contributed to fishing for intolerant and unusually harsh voices of the past to condemn adversaries in the name of religion'.[5] The same is true for advocacy of *ḥadd* punishments for illicit sex.[6] Premodern states seldom seem to have executed people for illicit sex (*zinā'*) or apostasy, however strongly authorities upheld such punishments in theory.[7] In contrast, contemporary governments eager to assert their religious credentials seem determined to enforce *ḥadd* sentences. This is not the first time such punishments have come to the fore; Selim Deringil finds that in the nineteenth-century Ottoman empire, because of the potential threat to national identity, 'apostates from Islam were considered particularly dangerous because they could infect others by their example'.[8] The boundaries shored up by *ḥudūd*, then and now, are as much communal as doctrinal.

This chapter explores the gendered conjunction of the doctrinal and the sexual in ideas about orthodoxy and order. I briefly discuss the Sudanese case of Meriam Ibrahim

(2014), then turn to a discussion of the interrelationships among orthodoxy, patriarchy and power in classical Sunni Muslim thought. Two case studies follow. The first discusses the potentially transgressive nature of maternal grief. The second considers apostasy, divorce and the right of exit. I conclude with reflections on the feminist critic as a threat to the status quo, and women's autonomy as a theological threat.

Gender influences prosecution and punishment for sexual and doctrinal offenses. Women tend to be punished disproportionately for illicit sex under government ordinances, partly because of the role of pregnancy as evidence for transgressions.[9] In contrast, it seems that more men than women are targeted under blasphemy statutes, in the process becoming feminized by their association with unbelief.[10] Women are also vulnerable; high profile cases like that of Ibrahim in the Sudan and Asia Bibi in Pakistan have made the news. 'Gendered Islamophobia', as Juliane Hammer notes, means that Muslim women's victimization plays an outsized role in criticism of Islam.[11] The portrayal of women as vital to communal boundaries – and women's defection or misbehaviour as dangerous to community – points to interconnections between the sexual and the theological.

In May 2014, a Sudanese court sentenced Ibrahim to death for apostasy and lashes for illicit sex. Over the last few decades, the Sudan has adopted putatively Islamic laws in a number of areas, including those regulating personal status – religious affiliation, marriage and family. The charge of apostasy was based on the claim that Ibrahim was born Muslim, her religion following that of her (Muslim) father, who left her (Christian) mother when Ibrahim was young, after which she was apparently raised as a Christian. Islamic jurisprudence traditionally allows interreligious marriage between a Muslim man and a Christian woman, but not the reverse, and presumes that the child's religion follows that of its father.[12] This presumption is part of the rationale for forbidding marriage by Muslim women to non-Muslim men, in line with broader hierarchical presumptions about the superiority of Islam to other religions and the appropriateness of male dominance in marriage. These views are enshrined in Sudanese law. The court deemed her marriage to a Christian man void, charging her with illicit sex and sentencing her to fifty lashes. Since she is considered Muslim (because of her father's religion), and since, unlike the situation in her parents' marriage, marriage between a Muslim woman and a Christian man cannot be valid, the court determined that she had had sex outside of marriage. Her children – a toddler as well as a baby born while she was imprisoned – proved her offense. According to news reports, Ibrahim's case was brought to the attention of the authorities by a Muslim relative who objected to her marriage to a Christian. After an international outcry, as well as diplomatic efforts (her husband, also a Christian of Sudanese origin, is an American citizen), she was released in late June 2014. Briefly rearrested when trying to leave the country, she was released shortly thereafter and reunited with her family in the United States.[13]

Ibrahim's case reveals the connections between sexual and theological offenses and their mutual dependence on a hierarchical and patriarchal legal system and, underpinning it, cosmology. Ibrahim's case highlights not just the patriarchal nature of Sudanese law but more broadly the patriarchal nature of Muslim marital jurisprudence. Her case links community belonging and marital legitimacy very clearly, but there are precedents. A case from ninth-century Iberia parallels Ibrahim's story: 'Born to a

Muslim man and a Christian woman, Flora was secretly raised Christian by her mother after her father's death. Eventually, Flora declared her Christianity publicly, for which she was arrested and decapitated on November 21, 851.'[14] As I discuss below, the rash of apostasy cases in British-ruled India in the early twentieth century, in which women left Islam as a roundabout means of leaving their marriages, illustrates the connection between the right of exit from marriage and the right of exit from a religious community; these cases illustrate instead the ways that entrance into a marriage becomes entrance into one religious community—and exit from another.[15]

Apostasy – or choosing to identify with one's (subordinate) mother's (subordinate) religion rather than the religion of one's father – is a threatening act. It puts one outside the pale of community or beyond the reach of a husband's authority. Other forms of transgression can also threaten. This is the case, potentially, with post-bereavement expressions of maternal grief. Unlike entering a marriage forbidden by religious rules (Ibrahim in the Sudan), or exiting a marriage when rules say one may not (apostate wives in British India), mothers who lose children may not consciously choose to depart from orthopraxy, but nonetheless transgress the boundaries of the permitted.

Orthodoxy, patriarchy, power

Theological error, like sexual transgression, challenges norms. Orthodoxy depends on and helps reinforce certain patriarchal structures, including marriage; challenges to orthodox doctrine may be intertwined with or presage dissent from community norms. I am interested in connections in (male) Muslim scholars' thought between female theological error, including a grieving woman's questionable conduct and married women's apostasy, on the one hand, and gendered models of social and cosmic order, on the other. Apostasy, blasphemy and heresy are deeply gendered in that they subvert an authoritarian, hierarchical cosmology and its social manifestations; in consequence, Muslim thinkers have gendered theological error, feminizing apostates, blasphemers and heretics.

Apostasy, blasphemy and heresy, as well as unbelief generally, are all forms of boundary violation. Muslim thinkers have never agreed entirely on firm definitions or lines between and among these forms of error despite sophisticated arguments over demarcations.[16] Theological error concerns boundaries. Creeds can become litmus tests for communal boundaries – who is in and who is out. 'Boundary' punishments may apply to those who transgress. Of course, despite its theological significance, private disbelief not publicly expressed has no effect on communal belonging and occasions no worldly punishment.

Punishment involves the state, the ruler and power. Power is always gendered. Gender signifies relationships of power.[17] Classical Muslim cosmologies consisted of nested hierarchies in which subordinate figures were feminine or feminized and dominant partners masculine or masculinized. (Gender need not correspond to 'actual' biological sex.) As Ayesha Chaudhry has shown, masculinity was associated with dominance, control and protection.[18] Although God has both majestic (masculine) as well as beautiful (feminine) attributes, the masculine tends to dominate the juristic and theological imaginary.[19] Despite the oneness and uniqueness of God, in certain crucial ways the ruler is *like* God in relation to the populace.[20] A husband is *like* a ruler in relation to his wife, a father *like* a ruler in relation to his child, a slaveowner *like* a ruler in relation to his enslaved servant. Or, as the jurists' and exegetes' metaphors and analogies reveal, a husband is *like* a slaveowner in relation to his wife, and a slaveowner *like* a father in relation to his enslaved servant.[21] It may also be that the (male) ruler is like a father to his subjects.[22] (God is *not* like a father, but this has to do with maintaining a different boundary: that between Islam and Christianity.[23]) Other metaphors also describe these relationships, but hierarchical and patriarchal imagery is crucial. Notably, one list of things that constitute apostasy includes 'to conceive of Allah as a woman or child' alongside denying God's divinity or attributing partners to God. Conceiving of God as a man, while obviously inaccurate, does not appear in this list of egregious errors.[24] Metaphors linking human authority and divine authority are especially productive with regard to authority and punishment, as Christian Lange has observed: 'the private spheres of the family and the [royal] court were constituted as largely autonomous and extrajudicial provinces of punitive authority'.[25]

Thirty years ago, Fatna Sabbah argued in *Woman in the Muslim Unconscious* that man was to woman as God was to man.[26] In doing so, she conflated scripture and its interpretation, canonical tradition and popular proverbs. Since then, scholars including amina wadud and Asma Barlas have illustrated that hers is not the only or most convincing way of seeing the scriptural texts. Nonetheless, Sabbah was correct that this cosmological presumption pervades much of the Muslim tradition.[27] The proposition that a husband is like a God to his wife is theologically deeply problematic and subject to ongoing contestations; it nonetheless lurks at the edges of some discourses: No one would even think to disclaim the metaphor if it were unthinkable.[28]

Scholars acknowledged a woman's independent relationship to God and affirmed, repeatedly, that a woman's duty of obedience to God overrides any obligation to obey her husband.[29] Yet these same thinkers carved out rather a large sphere for wifely deference. So long as his whims did not contravene God's commands to pray and fast, a wife was to obey. These views about female autonomy and male/masculinized authority – God's and husbands' – are fraught with tension. In the Muslim legal tradition females are – with the same sorts of exceptions as males for insanity, minority, enslavement and so forth – legal persons, accountable for their own beliefs and actions.[30] They are responsible before God for their sins. They are liable before human authorities for relevant acts or omissions, whether business transactions or punishable religious transgressions. And yet, female or at least wifely freedom to act is curtailed in ways that have repercussions for women's religious personhood. The classical legal tradition allows a husband to bar his wife from performing supererogatory acts of worship, just as a slaveowner can forbid an enslaved servant (though the legal tradition says little about this latter issue). He cannot forbid her from offering her required daily prayers or from fasting in Ramadan but may forbid her from engaging in voluntary fasts or extra prayers.[31]

The case of wifely restriction is unique in several respects, but it has implications for a broader understanding of how gender and hierarchy tie in with restrictions on religious expression. It presumes that one party by virtue of a particular authority granted by God and secured by human power structures has the right to assert how others must believe and practice (or may not believe or practice). A more obvious example from the political realm is the *miḥna*, or inquisition, in which the ninth-century ʿAbbasid State sought to enforce acquiescence to the doctrine of the createdness of the Qurʾan. It focused on a narrow theological position, insisted on a declaration of belief and upheld what became a heretical doctrine, in one view tantamount to apostasy, before fading into obscurity.[32] The fact that it created a major backlash against the Muʿtazila may account for the fact that Muslim-ruled states have seen few attempts to enforce creedal views; instead, governments have typically tolerated a variety of them.[33]

Issues of orthodoxy and its enforcement are gendered insofar as notions of individual and community, as well as the power dynamics between them, depend on gendered notions of hierarchy and agency. The inextricable linkage of power and gender also connects to sexuality, raising – in a different context – the relationship between individual and community. In some respects, Islamic law seeks to maximize community harmony, sometimes at the expense of individual 'rights'.[34] The larger collective whose welfare is sought may be the family unit, the local community, the nation, or the *umma*, the worldwide collectivity of Muslims. Tensions remain between the ideal by which the kinship of belief supplants blood kinship. In either case, emphasis on a collective good exists in tension with potent notions about individual rights and accountability.

The salience of group interests over individual rights has positive and negative aspects. Consider sexual morality. Questions about sexual conduct as well as religious belief and practice are among those things that 'moderns' consider vital elements of self-formation and definition.[35] Just as there is widespread agreement in Western democracies today that people are free to believe (or not believe) anything they wish, the idea that premarital sex between two consenting adults could be a problem is largely foreign to contemporary Western mores. The ideals about freedom of belief and worship go back a few centuries; the no-judgment views of non-marital sex only a few decades.[36] Both differ from classical Muslim understandings: just as one must observe certain religious rituals and adhere, at least publicly, to certain beliefs, one must behave – or more to the point, not behave – in certain ways sexually. Sex involves the 'rights of God' as well as the rest of society. Sexual misconduct, real or perceived, threatens social stability and communal order, partly by casting doubt on the attribution of paternity. So-called honour killings, extrajudicial executions in which relatives slay a woman or girl presumed or suspected of violating chastity norms without formal adjudication, are an extreme manifestation of the communal principle over the individual. In similar fashion, Selim Deringil writes that 'acts of conversion or apostasy could be seen as something *shameful*, something one does not like to talk about, like having a rape in the family or someone convicted of murder'.[37] In both sorts of cases, social practice may depart from religious law; both also raise the question of whose interests are defined (and enforced) as the collective good.[38]

In his discussion of freedom of religion and apostasy, Abdullah Saeed juxtaposes killing apostates and honour killing, centring communal interests:

> If faith is, strictly speaking, a matter between the individual and God, why does apostasy cause such anxiety among Muslims and why is it seen as the ultimate betrayal of the Muslim community? The answer, in part, lies in the fear of desertion

> of one's 'tribe' [...] By converting [from Islam], a Muslim is seen as not only deserting a religion but also their tribe. Such a conversion is seen as bringing dishonour upon the community of Muslims, including one's immediate and extended family. Like the 'honour killings' related to cases of rape or of women involved in sexual relationships outside marriage, seen in communities such as Lebanon or Pakistan, apostasy-related killing is also considered by some as a form of 'honour killing'.[39]

In this circumscribed analytical circle, both women who transgress sexual boundaries and apostates who transgress religious boundaries merit death. Punishments reinforce boundaries. Saeed's juxtaposition feminizes apostates. A person – a man – who commits theological error is like a woman who transgresses sexual boundaries. A male apostate is, like a woman, subject to discipline to maintain order. It is not incidental that *fitna* can refer to both political upheaval and sexual disorder. Both are threatening to the established state of things. The notion that the blood of an apostate may be licitly spilt has taken on a new edge in recent decades; there has been not only pressure to legislate punishment for apostasy but also, in the absence of government-enforced punishments, declarations from some actors 'that the killing of an apostate has become a duty of individual[s]' rather than state authorities.[40]

In a fashion that partly parallels the role family law came to play in the transition to modern nation states, apostasy served a communal function in late Ottoman times. Deringil argues that 'Religion does not fade away with the advance of nationalism, but rather becomes yoked to it through the process of conversion and apostasy.' By the nineteenth century, and after the ruling out of the punishment of death for apostasy from Islam in 1844,

> potential conversion from Islam to Christianity [was] seen as a loss of identity, a harbinger of greater catastrophe ... not as an individually reprehensible act, but as an affront to the whole (more or less amorphously imagined) community, a deadly threat and an insult to the self-conscious group.[41]

Apostates 'establish a *precedent*; they are potential *unravellers*.'[42] They threaten the status quo.

Case 1: Unravelled: Maternal grief

The status quo, of course, is always fragile. Orthodoxy involves the power to legitimate or invalidate certain perceptions or understandings of human experience. This power tends to deny female or feminized experience.[43] That experience is, in crucial ways, the feeling of powerlessness. No one feels more powerless or rages more against the status quo than a mother whose child has died.

Maternal grief resonates in different ways at different places and times and in different genres. The Qur'an, hadith and prophetic biography say more about paternal than maternal grief. The Prophet reportedly buried all his children save Fatima, including, in his later years, his infant son Ibrahim.[44] His sadness is recorded and reported; sources say little or nothing about Khadija or Mary the Copt's mourning for the sons they bore him and lost. Despite these foregrounded paternal losses, it is maternal grief that more often preoccupies the scholars.

Sunni scholars present two opposed models of maternal loss. One is cautionary; the other, exemplary. A bereaved mother who, in her grief-stricken state, rants at God for depriving her of her offspring must be contained, her comportment curtailed. Stoic acceptance is praised, weeping tolerated, wailing lambasted. More troubling than any disruption caused by wailing is the theological error underlying her transgression: to bewail the death of one's child is to contest God's decree. To object to God's decree is an act of disbelief. It is to commit the error of believing that one knows better than God. To actively protest, or to curse God, or to voice one's objections is blasphemy.

The praiseworthy bereaved mother acts in the opposite fashion. A story goes that a boy died while his father was away. The mother 'prepared the corpse for burial and put it aside in a corner of the house'. The father returned and inquired about his son; the mother 'responded with measured ambiguity' that she 'expect[ed] he has found rest'. She waited until the next morning to tell her husband of their son's death; he too responded with acceptance.[45] According to Leor Halevi, this 'exemplary composure and equanimity' were noteworthy not only because they were desirable but also because they confounded widespread expectations about parental, particularly maternal, grief: 'Muslims expected that bereft mothers would actually display loudly various signs of personal distress and tragic bereavement, not bear the calamity in silence.'[46] This story and its reverberations must be understood within broader debates over appropriate mourning practices. The bereaved mother adorned herself for her husband and bedded him before telling him of their son's death, supporting the view that wifely obligations supersede maternal ones.[47] A widow's lengthy mourning period contrasts with the rule that a woman mourns only three days for children, parents or siblings. Children and brothers seem to have been particularly problematic.[48] Muslim thinkers tried to transform many elements of pre-Islamic practice. Some they fitted with new justifications and meaning; others they attempted, more or less successfully, to eradicate. Widows were permitted or required, depending on how one reads the texts, to mourn for four months and ten days – reportedly, a lightening of the pre-Islamic mourning period, which lasted a year. One obvious rationale for the lengthier mourning period for husbands than for kin is the detection of pregnancy; indeed, some jurists held that a pregnant woman who delivered her child after her husband's death and before his burial, while his corpse remained on his deathbed, would be immediately free to remarry. Others disagreed, insisting that while delivery of a child ended the waiting period of a divorcee, the widow was bound to observe the entire period.

In any case, parental – especially maternal – grief is widely acknowledged though its expression is tightly circumscribed. The exemplary bereaved mother behaved laudably, reflecting appropriate theology and modelling correct actions. For others whose inner disposition might not conform, patterning one's conduct on hers moulds sentiments appropriately. Avner Gilʿadi explores medieval consolation treatises aimed at bereaved parents. Such works aim 'to channel the strong emotional re-actions of bereaved parents into legitimate religious modes of mourning'.[49] Although these works implicitly reinforce the theological point that one should not bemoan God's decisions, 'The focus of these treatises was not on abstract theological questions concerning the death of tender innocent creatures, but rather on practical ways of coping with the loss of one's offspring.'[50] Contemporary Muslim thinker Aliah Schleifer emphasizes inner disposition when discussing maternal loss: *accepting* the death of one's children is the key to receiving reward. Schleifer quotes two hadith saying that women who lose three or even two children will enter Paradise. Only the second hadith indicates that acceptance of the loss is necessary, but Schleifer's discussion emphasizes this point, as well as maternal feeling: 'Because of the strong bond of affection that accompanies the great effort of the mother, the loss of children is a heavy burden, but if she accepts it as Allah's will, her reward is Paradise[.]'[51]

Without positing a universal, transhistorical model of maternal grief, I would note that sources from various milieux, Muslim and non-Muslim, persistently associate disruptive, excessive mourning with women and especially mothers. Anthropologist Nancy Scheper-Hughes caused a tempest with her study of child mortality in poverty- and drought-stricken northeastern Brazil. *Death Without Weeping* is powerful – and courted controversy – precisely because it contested widespread assumptions about how women would react to their children's deaths. Although Scheper-Hughes' work illustrates that there is nothing essential about the expression of female grief at the loss of a child, the reaction to it proves how deeply notions about the universality of mothers' mourning permeate many spaces.[52]

Early Muslims expected women's loud lamentations. Professional mourners were female. The phrase *al-nā'iḥa al-thaklā*, which Halevi translates as 'a wailer burdened by grief', 'usually designat[es] a bereft mother'.[53] But expected is not the same as accepted. Pious Sunni scholars and rulers deemed women's wailing a threat to order, particularly in times of widespread death such as that caused by the plague. Gil'adi notes that the plague's disproportionate toll on children led to an increase in 'consolation treatises for bereaved parents [which] were rather popular and circulated widely'.[54] While these treatises addressed private grieving, other texts addressed public comportment. Sadr al-Din ibn al-'Ajami was Cairo's market supervisor (*muḥtasib*) during an early fifteenth century plague. He focused on destroying wine, prohibiting the display of hashish, keeping prostitutes from soliciting customers, and prohibiting women's wailing for the dead.[55] Similar manuals by Muhammad ibn Ahmad ibn Bassam (d. before 1440) and 'Abd al-Rahman ibn Nasr al-Shayzari (d. 1193) say that the *muḥtasib* should police graveyards/cemeteries and use his discretionary authority to punish wailing women.[56] These manuals treat wailing like illicit sex and intoxication, symbolizing and causing disorder.

As Halevi notes, 'Early Muslim laws on mourning concentrate on repression of violent emotions of bereavement.'[57] Again, the attempt to suppress and regulate female emotion was not merely a concern with decorum. Women's wailing was 'offensive' because, for 'early Islamic pietists . . . wailing was an act of complaining against the judgment of God, a manner of rebelling with exasperation "against His decree"'.[58] It was also said, at times, to torment the deceased, causing suffering. Wailing came to be understood as a persistent remnant of Jahili practices.[59]

Moreover, by the 'Abbasid era, excessive mourning came to be associated with Shi'ism, where passionate mourning for the mistreated, dispossessed and (unjustly) slain members of the Prophet's family was characteristic.[60] Women's excessive mourning had originally made them dangerous because of the practice's intractable association with the pre-Islamic age of ignorance.[61] Later, Shiʿi excesses in expressed grief could be denigrated as feminine. Both women and sectarian rivals were dangerously excessive mourners. Both could be associated with the 'ignorant' past rather than the triumphal (Sunni) Muslim order.

Case 2: Divorce and apostasy

There are connections and parallels between marital hierarchy and political hierarchy. A husband's power of repudiation was both meaningful and dangerous, but not nearly so much as the wife's potential power to unravel the marriage from below, destabilizing the family and by extension society.[62] No school of law was more resistant to a women's right to dissolve a marriage without her husband's consent than the Hanafi *madhhab*.[63] Hanafi doctrine on the married female apostate links religious-communal boundaries with spousal relations. Hanafi jurists consider women's apostasy qualitatively different from men's.[64] One reason a woman should not be executed for apostasy is that 'a woman's submissiveness to her husband was considered to exclude a fully independent judgment on her part, and to render her thus not fully responsible.'[65] Having a husband profoundly modifies a woman's freedom of action.

Muhammad Qasim Zaman summarizes the doctrine that female apostates should not be executed but detained indefinitely:

> The dominant view among the medieval Hanafi jurists had been that the apostate wife ought to be forced to reconvert to Islam and be remarried to her (former) husband. A second, less prevalent view had been that apostasy had no effect on the status of the marriage; and a third, and most extreme, view was that the wife's apostasy turned her into her husband's slave-girl.

Two main factors induced a number of Muslim women in North India in the early decades of the twentieth century to leave Islam in order to dissolve their marriages: the absence of Muslim judges to preside at dissolutions when men had gone missing or were otherwise unwilling to dissolve their marriages; and British colonial courts which, 'recogni[sing] Islamic legal norms in matters of personal status [. . .] accepted [women's apostasy] as a valid termination of the marriage *without*, however, requiring the apostate wife to either reconvert to Islam or to remarry her former husband'.[66] The two-pronged religio-legal solution to the crisis was predominantly formulated by renowned Deobandi scholar Ashraf ʿAli Thanawi. He argued (contrary to his own previously expressed positions) for adopting the minority Hanafi view that a wife's apostasy had no effect on her marriage and advocated less restrictive rules for granting a divorce to a woman whose husband had disappeared.[67] These provisions made it into the 1939 Dissolution of Muslim Marriages Act.

The connection between marital connection and communal belonging long predates colonial India. Eric Dusteler's study of renegade women in the early modern

Mediterranean finds parallels between Christian women's conversion to Islam and Muslim women's apostasy. Women's exit from or entry into either religion was often linked to avoidance of or escape from an undesired marriage. Thus, not only are there important parallels between women's allegiances/ties to a husband and those to a religious community or a state, there are also tangible linkages between the two. That is, a woman's entry into or especially exit from a marital relationship may be connected to or contingent on her belonging to a religious community. Both Christian and Muslim women changed religions to leave husbands (or occasionally avoid potential husbands) to whom they were otherwise bound: 'throughout the Ottoman Mediterranean women's conversion to escape marriage was widespread'.[68] These early modern women were 'renegades' not just in the sense that they changed religions (the usual meaning of the term in the early modern Mediterranean) but in that they defied a variety of social and sexual conventions of the era. These forms of deviance or defiance were connected. Some contemporary scholars discuss a 'right of exit' – to leave one's religious community – but the same issue might also appear with regard to marriage, or rather divorce.[69] A woman who cannot leave her husband and a woman who cannot leave her religious identification (whatever her individual belief) are constrained by masculine structures of dominance that they may perceive not only as inimical to their interests but also as unjust and unfair.

Orthodoxy and critique

Orthodoxy holds that things are, generally, how they are supposed to be. Theological error tends to consist in challenge to the power structure. Those who commit apostasy, heresy or blasphemy challenge the status quo. The grieving mother, the unhappy wife and the feminist critic all declare, at least implicitly, that the current state of affairs is unjust. Things should be different than they are. The child should live. The marriage should end. The patriarchy should fall.

What, though, is the status of such desires for change? Desires to challenge the injustice of the status quo are laudable. But in their self-centred, sometimes misperceiving and self-deceiving states, human beings are liable to forget things and distort reality. Collectively vetted wisdom can guide people, serving as a check on egocentric deviance. It makes sense that such guides help believers to remember the transitory nature of human experience, the fragility of life and the implacability of death and judgment. Yet to offer guidance in matters of spiritual discipline, thinkers must draw and distil wisdom from a pool of experiences. It matters, very much, whose experiences serve as the basis for guidance.

We can here set to the side the issue of divorce, and modern insistence on treating women as 'too emotional' to make rational decisions about remaining in marriage. Let us remain with grief: Attempts to smother, police, regulate, or control a woman's grief or the expression of that grief or objection or dissent to the established order is a way of controlling female rebellion or protest. As Nadia El Cheikh points out in discussing early Islamic history, non-Muslim women's passionate grief was conjoined with rage and irrationality.[70] Nicole Loraux observes, in the context of Greek tragedy, an 'affinity that exists between grief and anger'.[71] 'Women's mourning' in 'the archaic city' may threaten 'civic order'.[72] This fear of disorder places women's wailing on the list of things the market supervisor must monitor and suppress. Public order, meanwhile, remains deeply connected to private order: the orderly household, under the control of a husband who controls his wife's marital fate as well as, according to these jurists, her mobility.

Authoritarianism and patriarchy are not the only possible foundations for order and stability. Yet, treating female experience, particularly experiences of vulnerability and powerlessness, as a source of norms challenges dominant traditional claims about God, humanity and the relationship between them. Premodern Muslim thinkers' attempts to regulate or suppress believers' expressions of suffering help to construct and maintain orthodoxy. Dominant authorities legitimize or delegitimize certain articulations of human experience. Those whose experiences are delegitimized are typically women and (other) socially marginal people. Rethinking whose experience is authoritative challenges traditional accounts of morality.[73]

Although apostasy and its less threatening counterparts have not been a major preoccupation for Muslim jurists, and few scholars devoted much attention to questions of who is in and who is out of the community, those who did, including al-Ghazali (d. 1111) and Ibn Taymiyya (d. 1328), are among the luminaries of the Sunni tradition. And even if Muslim jurists and authorities were not particularly focused on meting out punishment to those who strayed, and allowed substantial dissent, in fact ideas about orthodoxy and correct belief have been, and remain, central. The articulation and defence of ideas about authority – who has it, and how may it be exercised – helps determine who may articulate dangerous ideas, or critique dominant ideas, and under what circumstances. Al-Ghazali's treatise *On the Boundaries of Theological Tolerance in Islam* expresses a minimalist view of the theological essentials.[74] Apart from a handful of unquestionable assumptions, believers were theoretically free to quarrel with or dissent from established doctrines.

Qualified independent scholars (*mujtahid*s) were granted substantially more leeway than ordinary believers or junior scholars in terms of what they could do to express dissent. Yet few women fell into this category of independent thinker.[75] Even today, one of the most effective ways of claiming that women are violating tradition is to refuse to grant them the status of insider to that tradition. Those who master the tradition may question its longstanding premises. Of course, by then they have been quite thoroughly indoctrinated into its assumptions and procedures. As Ahmad notes, writing of Damascene Hanafi Ibn ʿAbidin (d. 1836), 'Ibn ʿAbidin has nothing but reprimand for those untrained volunteer spokespersons in the name of Islamic law who accuse people whom they disagree with of being apostates.'[76] At one level, this is a cosmopolitan depiction of tradition; Ahmad retrieves its core principle of intellectual capaciousness in the service of a more expansive contemporary Islam. Yet at the same time Ibn ʿAbidin invokes, and Ahmad implicitly endorses, a strictly delimited authority: *only* those in the know can judge who is in and who is out. It also reinforces their right to do so: those in the know *are* qualified to judge. This pronouncement about the inclusiveness of the tradition at the same time undercuts the ability of *unauthorized* speakers, into whose ranks many men and nearly all women fall, to make claims on its behalf.[77] Although Ibn ʿAbidin castigates those who draw the boundaries of tradition too narrowly, the same rules forbidding 'untrained volunteer spokespersons' would apply to those who sought to expand the bounds of what counts as acceptable. For those who wish to contest the boundaries as drawn thus far, this presents a formidable challenge; women's passionate grief and legitimate anger, channelled constructively rather than suppressed, can serve as a valuable resource.

Notes

1 I am grateful to participants in the January 2013 and September 2013 Oslo Coalition workshops, as well as the editors of this volume, for their comments on previous versions of this chapter.
2 Marie Aimée Hélie-Lucas, 'The preferential symbol of Islamic identity: women in Muslim personal laws', in Valentine Moghadam (ed.), *Identity Politics and Women: Cultural Reassertions and Feminisms in International Perspective* (Boulder, CO: Westview Press 1994), pp. 391–407.
3 On definitions of *ḥudūd*, see Christian Lange, *Justice, Punishment and the Medieval Muslim Imagination* (Cambridge: Cambridge University Press, 2008), p. 185. Lange quotes Rudolph Peters' definition of *ḥudūd* as 'fixed, mandatory punishments' (n. 25) but prefers the phrase 'divinely ordained punishments' (n. 27).
4 Judith E. Tucker, *Women, Family, and Gender in Islamic Law* (Cambridge: Cambridge University Press, 2008).
5 Ahmad Atif Ahmad, *Islam, Modernity, Violence, and Everyday Life* (New York: Palgrave Macmillan, 2009), p. 149, more generally pp. 147–68. Ahmad argues that Western scholarship has been too quick to posit a central place for apostasy and its punishment in Muslim legal thought and in Muslim social history.
6 Kecia Ali, *Sexual Ethics and Islam: Feminist Reflections on Qur'an, Hadith, and Jurisprudence* (rev. and expanded ed., Oxford: Oneworld Publications, 2016), p. 75.
7 For one recent study that grapples with these topics, see Sarah Eltantawi, *Sharī'ah on Trial: Northern Nigeria's Islamic Revolution* (Oakland, CA: University of California Press, 2017). For the emphasis on averting *ḥudūd* in Hanafi jurisprudence, see Norman Calder, *Islamic Jurisprudence in the Classical Era* (Cambridge: Cambridge University Press, 2010), chapter 1. Calder also explores the key literary and religious functions of stable doctrine and the general irrelevance of social practice to the activity of author-jurists. For an overview of apostasy rules, consult Rudolph Peters and Gert J. J. De Vries, 'Apostasy in Islam,' *Die Welt des Islams* 17/1 (1976–7), pp. 1–25. For changing Ottoman Hanafi rules on punishment for apostasy, see Selim Deringil, *Conversion and Apostasy in the Late Ottoman Empire* (Cambridge: Cambridge University Press, 2012). Deringil recounts an eighteenth-century case in which an apostate turned monk 'actively sought martyrdom' but had to resort to repeated public provocations before he was sentenced to death (p. 11). On the upholding of the doctrine of death for apostasy even when the penalty was seldom applied, see pp. 20–1. On applied *ḥudūd*, see cases cited in Lange, *Justice*, pp. 10 n. 32 (*zinā'*), 45 (apostasy), 46, 66–8 (*zinā'*, apostasy); Deringil, *Conversion and Apostasy*, pp. 11, 21 (apostasy). Lange also briefly discusses detention for apostasy (p. 90); he discusses blasphemy and heresy (p. 82) and heterodoxy (p. 78). See below for further discussion of women's apostasy.
8 Deringil, *Conversion and Apostasy*, p. 22.

9 For a comparison of Maliki and Hanafi doctrine on sexual violence and illicit sex, with references to contemporary legal systems in Nigeria and Pakistan, see Hina Azam, *Sexual Violation in Islamic Law: Substance, Evidence, and Procedure* (New York: Cambridge University Press, 2015).

10 While no firm statistics are available, Joelle Fiss's policy paper for the conservative Brookings Institute lists scores of incidents of persecution and prosecution in several countries; the vast majority target men. Joelle Fiss, 'Anti-blasphemy initiatives in the digital age: When hardliners take over', (The Brookings Project on U.S. Relations with the Islamic World, Analysis Paper No. 25, September 2016, especially pp. 10-16. https://www.brookings.edu/wp-content/uploads/2016/09/brookings-analysis-paper_joelle-fiss_web.pdf. For a survey of apostasy laws, consult the Library of Congress report on 'Laws Criminalizing Apostasy in Selected Jurisdictions' (May 2014, https://www.loc.gov/law/help/apostasy/apostasy.pdf); a summary appears at https://www.loc.gov/law/help/apostasy/.

11 Juliane Hammer, 'Center stage: gendered Islamophobia and Muslim women', in Carl W. Ernst (ed.), *Islamophobia in America: The Anatomy of Intolerance* (New York: Palgrave Macmillan, 2013), pp. 107–44.

12 Yohanan Friedmann, *Tolerance and Coercion in Islam: Interfaith Relations in the Muslim Tradition* (Cambridge: Cambridge University Press, 2003); Kecia Ali, *Sexual Ethics and Islam*, pp. 14–22. A conflicting principle holds that in a mixed marriage, 'the child follows the "best of his parents"' which led, in an Egyptian inheritance case from 1943, to the ruling that the son of a Coptic father and Muslim mother was born Muslim, but since 'he lived as a Copt, he could only be an apostate', leaving his estate liable to seizure by the Ministry of Finance. Peters and DeVries, 'Apostasy in Islam', p. 20.

13 Portions of this paragraph are adapted from Ali, *Sexual Ethics and Islam*, pp. 94–5.

14 This summary is by Ibtissam Bouachrine, *Women and Islam: Myths, Apologies, and the Limits of Feminist Critique* (Lanham, MD: Lexington Books, 2014), p. 10. Bouachrine juxtaposes and thereby links cases from disparate times and places, portraying a transhistorical Islamic repression of women. My linkage of Ibrahim and Flora's cases should be understood as suggestive rather than probative: an indicator that there is something to explore, not a broad brushstroke condemnation of violent Muslim gendered repression.

15 Eltantawi discusses colonial law and the legacy of the British in Nigeria. Eltantawi, *Shari'ah on Trial.*

16 Ahmad points out the 'elasticity' of the concept of apostasy for Sunni jurists and a lack of agreement among them as to its essential features. Ahmad, *Islam, Modernity*, p. 150.

17 For a classic formulation of this position, consult Joan Wallach Scott, *Gender and the Politics of History* (rev. ed., New York: Columbia University Press, 1999).

18 Ayesha Chaudhry, *Domestic Violence in the Islamic Tradition* (Oxford: Oxford University Press, 2013).

19 See Sachiko Murata, *The Tao of Islam: A Sourcebook on Gender Relationships in Islamic Thought* (Albany, NY: State University of New York Press, 1992).

20 Lange, *Justice*, p. 32. Historical chronicles report people's punishment 'in front of the ruler' as Lange translates '*bayna yadayhi*.' This phrase echoes the widely known and frequently quoted 'throne verse' of the Qur'an (2:255), which describes God's omniscience and omnipotence. This overlap suggests vital parallels between earthly and divine sovereignty.

21 Kecia Ali, *Marriage and Slavery in Early Islam* (Cambridge, MA: Harvard University Press, 2010), pp. 37–8, 52–3.
22 Lange, *Justice*, p. 32.
23 On the desacralization of fatherhood in the Qur'an, see Asma Barlas, *Believing Women in Islam: Unreading Patriarchal Interpretations of the Qur'an* (Austin: University of Texas Press, 2002).
24 Peters and De Vries, 'Apostasy in Islam,' p. 3.
25 Lange, *Justice*, p. 32.
26 Fatna A. Sabbah, *Woman in the Muslim Unconscious* (New York: Pergamon Press, 1984). On Fatna Sabbah, and Fatima Mernissi, see Raja Rhouni, *Secular and Islamic Feminist Critiques in the Work of Fatima Mernissi* (Leiden: Brill, 2010).
27 Amina Wadud, *Qur'an and Woman: Rereading the Sacred Text from a Woman's Perspective* (New York: Oxford University Press, 1992) and *Inside the Gender Jihad: Women's Reform in Islam* (Oxford: Oneworld, 2006); Barlas, '*Believing Women' in Islam*. In keeping with her preferred style, we do not capitalize amina wadud's name. Citations reflect usage at the time of publication.
28 See, for instance, the discussion of 'spiritual abuse' and the use of the Urdu phrase 'Majazee Khuda' ('Temporary God') in Zahira Latif, 'The silencing of women from the Pakistani Muslim Mirpuri community in violent relationships', in Mohammad Mazher Idriss and Tahir Abba (eds), *Honour, Violence, Women and Islam* (Oxon; New York: Routledge 2011), pp. 29–41, at p. 32.
29 Kecia Ali, 'Obedience and disobedience in Islamic discourses', in Suad Joseph (ed.), *Encyclopedia of Women in Islamic Cultures* (Leiden: Brill, 2007), Vol. 5, pp. 309–13; Karen Bauer, *Gender Hierarchy in the Qur'ān: Medieval Interpretations, Modern Responses* (Cambridge: Cambridge University Press, 2015); Chaudhry, *Domestic Violence*.
30 On female personhood in Hanafi law and legal theory, see Fatima Seedat, *Sex and the Legal Subject: Woman and Legal Capacity in Hanafi Law* (PhD thesis, McGill University 2013).
31 Ali, *Marriage and Slavery in Early Islam*, pp. 73, 193–5.
32 Peters and De Vries, 'Apostasy in Islam', p. 4.
33 Tim Winter, 'Introduction' in Tim Winter (ed.), *Cambridge Companion to Classical Muslim Theology* (Cambridge: Cambridge University Press, 2008), pp. 1–16, at p. 7.
34 See, for instance, Wael Hallaq, *An Introduction to Islamic Law* (Cambridge: Cambridge University Press, 2009). David Jacobson (*Of Virgins and Martyrs: Women and Sexuality in Global Conflict*, Baltimore: Johns Hopkins University Press, 2013) argues that the individual versus communal sensibility is the key dividing line between societies where 'tribal patriarchy' structures thinking, particularly about control over female bodies, and those of the West where individual interests are respected. This oversimplification fails to account for Western patriarchal norms that persistently disregard women's claims of harm. See Kate Manne, *Down Girl: The Logic of Misogyny* (New York: Oxford University Press, 2017).
35 Dwight F. Reynolds (ed.), *Interpreting the Self: Autobiography in the Arabic Literary Tradition* (Berkeley: University of California Press, 2001), pp. 79–80.
36 Ali, *Sexual Ethics and Islam*, pp. 72–5, 86–9.
37 Deringil, *Conversion and Apostasy*, p. 256.
38 On the problematic category of honour killings, consult Lila Abu-Lughod, *Do Muslim Women Need Saving?* (Cambridge, MA: Harvard University Press, 2013).
39 Abdullah Saeed and Hassan Saeed, *Freedom of Religion, Apostasy, and Islam* (Aldershot, UK: Ashgate, 2004), p. 119.

40 Peters and De Vries, 'Apostasy,' p. 18.
41 Deringil, *Conversion and Apostasy*, p. 4.
42 Ibid., p. 3. Also, p. 253: 'The apostates evoked hatred and fear when they became the living, walking *symbols* of the potential *unravelling* of the community.' Emphasis in original.
43 See Miranda Fricker, *Epistemic Injustice: Power and the Ethics of Knowing* (Oxford: Oxford University Press, 2007) for a philosophical investigation; for a specific case study of the contemporary American context, consult Leigh Gilmore, *Tainted Witness: Why We Doubt What Women Say about Their Lives* (New York: Columbia University Press, 2017).
44 Prophetic biographies often say more about this loss and the grief it occasions than the losses of his daughters. The whole subject deserves a full study.
45 Leor Halevi, *Muhammad's Grave: Death Rites and the Making of Islamic Society* (New York: Columbia University Press, 2007), p. 114. For a longer discussion of this story, see Avner Gil'adi, '*Ṣabr* (steadfastness) of bereaved parents: a motif in medieval Muslim consolation treatises and some parallels in Jewish writings', *The Jewish Quarterly Review* (New Series) 80/1–2 (July–October 1989), pp. 35–48.
46 Halevi, *Muhammad's Grave*, p. 114.
47 Nadia Maria El Cheikh, *Women, Islam, and Abbasid Identity* (Cambridge, MA: Harvard University Press, 2015), p. 42 mentions a different version of the story in which the wife conceives another child.
48 Halevi, *Muhammad's Grave*, p. 122.
49 Avner Gil'adi, '"The child was small . . . not so the grief for him": sources, structure, and content of Al-Sakhawi's consolation treatise for bereaved parents', *Poetics Today* 14/2 (Summer, 1993), *Cultural Processes in Muslim and Arab Societies: Medieval and Early Modern Periods*, pp. 367–86.
50 Gil'adi, 'The child was small', p. 370. See also Avner Gil'adi, 'Islamic consolation treatises for bereaved parents: some bibliographical notes', *Studia Islamica* 81 (1995), pp. 197–202.
51 Aliah Schleifer, *Motherhood in Islam* (Louisville, KY: Fons Vitae, 1996 [1986]), pp. 53–54. Schleifer quotes two hadith saying that women who lose three or even two children will enter Paradise. Only the second hadith indicates that acceptance of the loss is necessary, but Schleifer's discussion emphasizes this point, as well as maternal feeling: 'Because of the strong bond of affection that accompanies the great effort of the mother, the loss of children is a heavy burden, but if she accepts it as Allah's will, her reward is Paradise' (p. 53).
52 Nancy Scheper-Hughes, *Death Without Weeping: The Violence of Everyday Life in Brazil* (Berkeley, CA: University of California Press, 1992).
53 Halevi, *Muhammad's Grave*, p. 294 n. 41.
54 Gil'adi, 'The child was small,' p. 369.
55 Kristen Stilt, *Islamic Law in Action: Authority, Discretion, and Everyday Experiences in Mamluk Egypt* (Oxford; New York: Oxford University Press, 2011), pp. 92–100.
56 Stilt, *Islamic Law in Action*, p. 99.
57 Halevi, *Muhammad's Grave*, p. 122. Although many Sunni pietists merely tolerated (moderate) weeping, other groups, including some figures associated with the Shi'a and with Sufism, cultivated weeping as a form of devotion.
58 Halevi, *Muhammad's Grave*, p. 120.
59 'Muslim tradition came to represent the rite of wailing not as a custom transformed or eradicated by Islam but as a pre-Islamic institution that had persisted stubbornly despite Islam.' Halevi, *Muhammad's Grave*, p. 136.

60 Matthew Pierce, *Twelve Infallible Men: The Imams and the Making of Shi'ism* (Cambridge, MA: Harvard University Press, 2016), pp. 55–65, 151.

61 El Cheikh, *Women, Islam, and Abbasid Identity*.

62 Frank Vogel, 'The complementarity of *iftā'* and *qaḍā'*: three Saudi fatwas on divorce,' in Muhammad Khalid Masud, Brinkley Messick, and David Powers (eds), *Islamic Legal Interpretation: Muftis and Their Fatwas* (Massachusetts: Harvard University Press, 1996), pp. 262–9; Yossef Rapoport, *Money, Marriage, and Divorce in Medieval Islamic Society* (Cambridge: Cambridge University Press, 2005), pp. 104–5, 108–10. Divorce might be a real threat to women's well-being, or a tool for self-determination, depending on context.

63 On Hanafi divorce, see Ali, *Marriage and Slavery*, chapter 4 and literature cited there.

64 On women's apostasy, and the clear distinctions Hanafi jurists make between male and female apostates, see Baber Johansen, 'Apostasy as objective and depersonalized fact: two recent Egyptian court judgments,' *Social Research* 70/2 (2003), pp. 687–710. On apostasy of either spouse as grounds for marital dissolution, see Colin Imber, *Ebu's-Su'ud: The Islamic Legal Tradition* (Stanford, CA: Stanford University Press, 1997), pp. 195–7. There are important distinctions between the husband's apostasy or blasphemy, even inadvertent, and the wife's; according to Imber, who bases himself on Ottoman sources, women's attempts to end their marriages by blaspheming result only in eventual forcible remarriage to their original husbands. According to Muhammad Khalid Masud (personal communication, July 2016), despite muftis' proclamations that this should be the result, in India such women 'married other Muslim men'. On the Indian case, see Muhammad Khalid Masud, 'Apostasy and judicial separation in British India,' in Muhammad Khalid Masud, Brinkley Messick, and David S. Powers (eds), *Islamic Legal Interpretation: Muftis and Their* Fatwas (Cambridge, MA: Harvard University Press, 1996), pp. 193–203; Rohit De, 'The two husbands of Vera Tiscenko: apostasy, conversion, and divorce in late colonial India,' *Law and History Review* 28/4 (November 2010), pp. 1011–41; Muhammad Qasim Zaman, 'Evolving conceptions of ijtihad in modern South Asia,' *Islamic Studies* 49/1 (Spring 2010), pp. 5–36, at pp. 16–17. The penalty for *zinā'* is gender neutral, with the exception of the Maliki view on pregnancy as evidence and, possibly, gender-differentiation in the use of banishment as a punishment. See Ali, *Sexual Ethics and Islam*, Chapter 4.

65 Peters and De Vries, 'Apostasy in Islam', p. 5.

66 Zaman, 'Evolving Conceptions', p. 17. Zaman indicates the absence of qualified Muslim judges to dissolve the marriages of missing husbands rather than women's unhappiness with their husbands as the motivation behind the perceived crisis. 'Evolving conceptions,' pp. 16–17. The shift from a pluralistic system which allowed flexibility to draw on judges from other legal schools to codified and rigidly Hanafi Anglo-Muhammadan law removed leeway for women from the system.

67 Masud, 'Apostasy and Judicial Separation'.

68 Eric Dursteler, *Renegade Women: Gender, Identity, and Boundaries in the Early Modern Mediterranean* (Baltimore, MD: Johns Hopkins University Press, 2011), p. 115. Dursteler writes of *conversion*, yet from the perspective of the Muslim authorities, the Muslim women's adoption of Christianity constituted apostasy. On a related issue, the 'conversion' and potential reconversion (or apostasy) of abducted women, forced into sex and marriage, see Deringil, *Conversion and Apostasy*, pp. 241, 248; on the use of conversion to make possible otherwise forbidden marriages, see *ibid*, p. 248; to get otherwise impermissible divorces, see p. 257. Hindu and other women in India also

used conversion as part of forum-shopping in matters of divorce. See De, 'The two husbands of Vera Tiscenko'.

69 Consult, for example, Dagmar Borchers and Annamari Vitikainen (eds), *On Exit: Interdisciplinary Perspectives on the Right of Exit in Liberal Multicultural Societies* (Berlin; Boston: Walter de Gruyter, 2012).

70 El Cheikh, *Women, Islam, and Abbasid Identity*, pp. 46–50.

71 Gregory Nagy, foreword to Nicole Loraux, *Mothers in Mourning* (Ithaca, NY: Cornell University Press, 1998), p. xi.

72 Loraux, *Mothers in Mourning*, p. 11. She goes on to observe that this is '[a] threat to be contained, but also to be fantasized about.' We can perhaps see in Muslim texts on the topic too that however insistent they are on the value of calm acceptance of the death of a child, and however praise-filled they are at the possibility of women containing their emotions in such an event, they also return repeatedly to the irrepressible, insuppressible rage and grief of mothers, the uncontrollable which must in some way attract attention, amazement, wonder or respect.

73 Sa'diyya Shaikh, 'Feminism, epistemology, and experience: Critically (en)gendering the study of Islam', *Journal for Islamic Studies* 33 (2013), pp. 14–47.

74 Sherman Jackson (ed. and trans.), Al-Ghazali, *On the Boundaries of Theological Tolerance in Islam* (Oxford; New York: Oxford University Press, 2002). Ibn Taymiyya's popularity and reputation may owe something to modern attempts to promote his ideas. See Shahab Ahmed and Yossef Rapoport, *Ibn Taymiyya and His Times* (Karachi: Oxford University Press, 2010), as well as Muhammad Khalid Masud's chapter in this volume.

75 On who has the right or legitimate social capital to engage in *ijtihād*, see Muhammad Qasim Zaman on modern debates in the Indian subcontinent. Zaman, 'Evolving conceptions'. Women's widespread use of the term *ijtihād* post-dates the period covered in the article by several decades; nonetheless, it is noteworthy that it mentions no female reformers or thinkers. On the failure to recognize female writers, scholars, and activists as 'thinkers,' consult Kecia Ali, 'The omnipresent male scholar', *Critical Muslim* 8 (September 2013), pp. 61–73, at pp. 67–70.

76 Ahmad, *Islam, Modernity*, p. 61.

77 I briefly address the challenges to women's 'traditional' Islamic learning in Ali, *Sexual Ethics and Islam*, pp. 197–8, 203–4, 207.

10

Re-framing Reform: Lessons from the Apostasy Trials of Hassan Yousefi Eshkevari and Hashem Aghajari

Mahmoud Sadri

Introduction: The 'Islamic dilemma' is an 'American dilemma'

Islam is neither a monolithic entity nor an arena in which two distinct opponents contend for the upper hand. Indeed, it is more accurate (and honest) to speak about one conflicted Islam rather than two contending Islams. Therefore, dichotomies such as moderate/radical,[1] secular/absolutist,[2] discourse/practice[3] or moderate/puritan,[4] while heuristically useful, tend to conceal the complex coexistence of the opposites within the same global community and the subtle gradations along the spectrum.

The reality is that the people of the Islamic world believe in human dignity, autonomy and internationally recognized rights. Paradoxically, they also frequently tolerate (and occasionally justify) retributive justice sanctioned by literal interpretations of Shariʿa law. The question is: how can a community that respects freedom of conscience, humane justice and religious parity condone a legal system that violates all three? This is certainly a dilemma, but not a unique or new one. Many other cultures and religions harbour such divergent beliefs and practices, but one will suffice to represent all.

Seventy-five years ago, the Swedish social scientist Gunnar Myrdal published a seminal study entitled *American Dilemma: The Negro Problem and Modern Democracy*.[5] The book dealt with a bewildering blend of high ideals and poor practices. Myrdal noticed that two sets of beliefs coincided in the American psyche: on the one hand, democratic and humane ideals enshrined in the American Constitution and the tenets of Christianity; on the other, racist fear and hatred of 'Negroes'. Americans, Myrdal astutely observed, were oblivious to this inconsistency in their cultural milieu. Later, the civil rights movement incorporated Myrdal's insights into its rhetoric of racial justice and equality. It exposed the hidden cultural tension and demanded consistency.

Normative dissonance

I believe a comparison between the American culture in the early twentieth century and the Islamic world in the early twenty-first century would be illuminating: there is a 'normative dissonance' comparable to the 'American Dilemma' that pervades the Islamic world. I propose 'normative dissonance' as a cognate of the concept Leon Festinger and Solomon Ash first introduced as 'cognitive dissonance'.[6] The phenomenon I am reporting concerns conflicting belief systems held at the cultural level and, as such, filtered down to the individual believer. Since these conflicts emanate from the society, the individual has limited latitude to resolve them.

How can such incompatible precepts and beliefs evolve and coexist in the same mindset? There are two possibilities: (1) 'creedal ambiguity' that allows a grey area of insufficiently articulated assumptions to operate as a buffer zone between the two divergent beliefs, so that ambiguity obscures inconsistency; (2) 'ideational lag' that signifies a normative delay allowing a portion of indigenous beliefs, not yet exposed to modern critical and moral faculties, to be sequestered from the culture's current sensibilities. Consequently, the believers harbour unexamined and uncritical vestiges of religious beliefs in the recesses of their consciousness.

Whatever the cause of this normative dissonance, conflicted cultures – Islamic and otherwise – are reluctant to either abandon or to countenance their idealistic or taken-for-granted convictions. They prefer explaining away their cultural contradictions to confronting and resolving them. This is reliably documented by two international surveys during the last ten years by Pew Research Center and the Gallup Company.[7] A solid majority of Muslims, for example, reported that they agreed with the punishments specified by Shariʿa law, but a significant majority of Muslims also favoured democracy over tyranny, detested imposition of Islamic rules on non-Muslims and believed in human rights. Similarly, people's ideas of Shariʿa law vary from place to place. The Pew survey found that only about half of the Muslims in Southeast Asia think of Shariʿa law in terms of severe physical penalties. Many believers have vague and idealistic visions of swift justice and sure results under Shariʿa law. But when they actually experience the brutal enforcement of *ḥudūd* (floggings, amputations and executions) meted out in places like Eastern Pakistan and Northern Iraq, they encounter the incompatibility of the modern humanistic ethos with these practices. In Pakistan, where there is a reliable measure of popular approval of such Shariʿa law enforcements, we know that only 6 per cent of the Muslim population support parties that advocate them in periodic elections.

Needless to say, the right wing in the Western media took advantage of these findings, focusing only on the parts of the findings that reinforced its prejudices. In an article entitled 'Sharia uber alles',[8] Andrew Bostom used the above studies to paint a grim portrait of the Islamic ethos and waxed poetic about Islam's hostility toward modernity and humanity. However, Bostom and his colleagues evidently overlooked the other aspect of the Pew and Gallup findings: Muslims' egalitarian and democratic beliefs and aspirations.

In what follows I will examine this duality of mind under the rubric of 'the Islamic dilemma'.[9] I will depict it as a fissure within the Muslim consciousness rather than two discrete states of mind. I will use the apostasy trials of two dissident intellectuals in

Iran as a prism through which this 'double consciousness'[10] of contemporary Islam can be viewed. Concentrating on the harsh penalties of Shari'a law concerning apostasy and blasphemy provides an opportunity to lay bare the incompatibility between the ideals and the practices of traditional Islam. As such, they are ideal loci for launching a reform program aiming at this and other brutal interpretations and implementations of Shari'a law. The following cases illustrate the efficacy of this approach.

Tacit triumph of humanistic values: Iran's apostasy trials

Nowhere is the 'Islamic Dilemma' more starkly on display than in Iran's apostasy trials. Although there are precedents for such trials in the Islamic Republic of Iran, they have, contrary to the general impression, been exceedingly rare and inconclusive in that country. Indeed, there have been only two public trials conducted on these grounds. Remarkably, the inconsistency of ideals and practices is evident in the written laws of the land. The legal code under which prosecutors have pursued alleged perpetrators of apostasy and blasphemy is article 513 of the Penal Code.[11] However, Article 23 of the Constitution of the Islamic Republic strictly prohibits interrogation and persecution of individuals because of their religious beliefs. This article of the Constitution is popularly known as the '(Anti-)Inquisition Article'.[12] In other words, the ideals of the Islamic Republic, prominently showcased in its Constitution, contradict the provisions of its penal code. Since the Constitution takes precedence over the penal code, prosecutors in apostasy cases have had a difficult time establishing that the accused are being tried for reasons other than their beliefs and opinions. A review of the apostasy trials of two prominent Iranian intellectuals reveals these dynamics.

The trial of Hasan Yousefi Eshkevari

On September 13, 2000, Mohammad Ibrahim Nekoonam, Tehran prosecutor for the Special Court for the Clergy, read several counts of indictment against Mr Hassan Yousefi Eshkevari, a reform-minded Iranian cleric, who had evinced various opinions concerning the time-bound nature of Islamic jurisprudence.[13] One such comment has been made in a famous conference in Berlin shortly before the court's proceedings. The first count was: 'insulting the sacred beliefs of Islam, and rejecting the essentials of Islam and gainsaying the eternal decrees of the Qur'an, through delivering speeches against Islamic Hijab and the penal laws of Islam and the Qur'an and, also, giving interviews to foreign radio programs and denial of the eternal nature of Islamic and Qur'anic laws' (the subject of the first ruling on 'apostasy' in Imam Khomeini's *Taḥrīr al-Wasīla*[14] and article 513 of the penal code). The second count was: 'waging war and propagating corruption on earth and action against national security through participation and leadership of a group that operated under the banner of toppling the religious regime'. Mr Eshkevari and his lawyer mounted a vigorous defence.[15] They argued that Islam's penal and civil laws, even the ones specified in the Qur'an, are not eternal components of the religion, and that their criticisms do not constitute instances of insult to the Prophet (*sabb al-nabī*) or apostasy (*irtidād*).[16]

For a glimpse into these proceedings, let me add a passage from my interview with Eshkevari. It has to do with an exchange with the judge of the appeal court, Ali Razini, in which Eshkevari defended his assertion that the penal regulations of Islam were time-bound. He asserted that the inability of the Islamic Republic of Iran to implement the 'minorities tax' (*jizya*) demonstrated that such regulations were impossible to operationalize in the modern world. The judge responded that there was a difference between the position of the regime and the position of Eshkevari: 'You say these are impracticable and that makes you an apostate; we say these are temporarily impracticable, which makes us believers.' Eshkevari replied: 'Be honest, you think the social and global reality is going in the direction of making such practices more plausible?' He then added: 'Whether one says these are temporarily impracticable or impracticable in principle, the pragmatic results are the same. They are not practiced and for good reason!'

Having dismissed the defendant's arguments, the court sentenced him to two years of imprisonment for the lesser charge of propaganda against the regime and insulting Ayatollah Khomeini, and to the death sentence for one count of apostasy or, possibly, a rejoinder to the charge of apostasy: 'corruption on earth'. To this day, it remains unclear which of the two above charges led the judge to decree the death sentence.

After Eshkevari was sent to prison to serve his sentence and to await execution, there was an outcry against the verdict. Ayatollah Montazeri (1922–2009), the foremost dissident jurist and the chief architect of the principle of clerical supremacy in the Islamic Republic, condemned the death sentence and relentlessly championed his cause. Subsequently, an influential association of progressive clerics announced that the judge and the prosecutor of the trial must themselves stand trial for their unjust verdict.[17] The case drew so much attention that even the Prosecutor General of the Special Court for the Clergy, Golamhossein Mohseni Eje'i, was forced to announce that he disagreed with the death sentence and publicly encouraged Eshkevari and his lawyer to appeal the judgment.[18] According to Eshkevari, the general prosecutor, before declaring his disagreement with the initial court's verdict, had appealed to renowned and established clerical jurists including Mohammadi Gilani, Mohammad Yazdi, Mahdavi Kani and Ali Khamenei (the supreme leader), in order to obtain a decree of apostasy for the condemned, but they all had refused. This, according to Eshkevari and his court-appointed lawyer, was the main reason for the general prosecutor's eventual public declaration of dissatisfaction with the initial court's verdict. Further, grand ayatollah Makarem Shirazi (according to Eshkevari) wrote a letter to the head of Iran's judiciary at the time, Hashemi Shahroudi, in which he ruled that none of the arguments evinced by Eshkevari concerning the 'time-bound' nature of Islamic laws constituted 'apostasy'. Upon the entreaties of Eshkevari's brother, two other grand ayatollahs, Yousef Saneʿi and Abdulkarim Mousavi Ardebili, also lent support to Mr Eshkevari's position. Among political leaders, Mehdi Karroubi (speaker of the parliament) and Mohammad Khatami (president) explicitly disputed the sentence.

Hassan Yousefi Eshkevari endured two years in Evin prison under the Damocles sword of impending execution. During this time his prison nickname was 'person under the verdict' (*zir-e hokm*), an equivalent of the phrase 'dead man walking' in American prisons. Two years later, the appellate court, under the gavel of Ali Razini, overturned Eshkevari's death sentence but sentenced him to an additional five years on other charges.[19] Eshkevari collaborated with his brother in compiling a 700-page tome detailing his trials and travails entitled *From Berlin to Evin*. The book never received official permission for publication in Iran and remains in manuscript form.

The trial of Hashem Aghajari

Hashem Aghajari was the only other Iranian intellectual to be tried and convicted for apostasy in the history of the Islamic Republic. The case against Aghajari was brought two years and two months after the trial of Eshkevari. A veteran of the Iraq war, a reform-minded Muslim intellectual, and a university professor, Aghajari had delivered a speech in November of 2002 in the city of Hamedan, on the occasion of the anniversary of the death of Dr Ali Shariati. In that speech he had quoted Shariati (an iconic intellectual in pre-revolutionary Iran), who himself was quoting another cleric, concerning the trivial and lascivious details of a 300 year old religious text (*Ḥilyat al-Muttaqīn*).[20] Subsequently, a provincial court in Hamadan indicted, tried and summarily condemned Mr Aghajari to death.[21] The charge of apostasy and insult to the Prophet on such insubstantial grounds invoked universal opprobrium from civil and clerical critics. Ayatollah Montazeri again issued a declaration condemning the charges. Liberal representatives of the Majlis, jurists, journalists and opposition leaders expressed 'dismay', 'bewilderment' and 'anger' over the charges of apostasy against Aghajari. There were also widespread street protests against the court sentence.[22] Aghajari's defence team was so confident of its moral advantage that it declared the accused would not seek an appeal from the ruling of the initial court, in effect daring the court to carry out the death sentence. In an unprecedented move, attorney Saleh Nikbakht, on behalf of his client, requested an apology from the court. Iran's Supreme Court, in an attempt to dispense with this case, returned the Aghajari dossier to the Hamadan court on a technicality. The court, however, refused to reconsider or rescind the verdict. Citing legal irregularities, the Supreme Court then reassigned the case to the Tehran court, which unceremoniously threw out the conviction.[23]

In the meantime, President Khatami, Ayatollah Hashemi Shahroudi, and the Supreme Leader Ali Khamenei all opined that the offenses cited by the court did not reach the threshold of 'apostasy'. Nevertheless, like Yousefi Eshkevari, Aghajari was sentenced on lesser charges and condemned to prison for three years, internal exile for two years and suspension from university instruction for five years.[24]

Lessons learned from the trials of Eshkevari and Aghajari

The common denominators of Eshkevari's and Aghajari's cases could be enumerated as follows: (1) They both argued that whatever their opinions and quotations concerning Islamic texts, they did not rise to the level of 'apostasy'. (2) They both cited Article 23 of the Iranian Constitution (the 'Inquisition Article') concerning the protected status of people's personal beliefs and opinions, challenging the provisions of the clause 513 of the criminal code.[25] (3) Their respective courts dismissed their arguments and condemned them to death. (4) The courts' initial verdicts were subsequently reversed or dismissed. In the case of Eshkevari, the appellate court performed this task. In the case of Aghajari, the Ministry of Justice was instrumental. (5) Most importantly, in both cases, there were multiple authoritative written rejections of the verdict by high-ranking clerics and jurisprudents as well as widespread lay protest and media attention. The combined effect of the above challenges made it all but impossible for the prosecutors to carry the day. These outcomes show that the judicial zeal for prosecution in such cases has not withstood the pressure of society's belief in individual autonomy and human rights. In other words, once the issue gains publicity, the society's high moral and normative standards short-circuit provisions for punishing 'apostates' and 'blasphemers'.

The long-term solutions, of course, lie in opening the jurisprudential foundations of the law to sustained critique and reform. Eshkevari believes that, due to the nature of Shiʿi jurisprudence and the relative autonomy of Shiʿi jurists, this will be a more feasible project in Shiʿi Islam.[26] The groundwork for this undertaking has already been laid. Ayatollah Gharavi Isfahani (1879–1942), Ayatollah Montazeri, and the contemporary jurists Mohsen Kadivar and Ahmad Ghabel (1954–2012) have challenged the very legal basis of the apostasy laws. However, for as long as the 'Islamic dilemma' persists, the battle is joined in the public arena. A case in point is the assassination of the Azeri journalist, Rafiq Tagi, in 2011. The murderer was a Shiʿi extremist armed with a knife and an apostasy fatwa issued by Ayatollah Fazel Lankarani (1931–2007), who had in the meantime passed away. In this case, the dissident jurist, Mohsen Kadivar, engaged in a heated moral and legal debate over the legitimacy of the fatwa with the son of the recently deceased Ayatollah.[27] He argued that the fatwa and its extra-territorial enforcement was inhumane, sacrilegious and unconstitutional.[28] More recently, other religious scholars have entered the fray. Taha Jabir al-ʿAlwani's critical study on the historical and legal precedents of the law of apostasy,[29] and Soroush Dabbagh's strident essay entitled 'Apostasy on the scale of justice' represent this trend.[30]

The fact that the two apostasy trials in Iran concluded in favour of the accused is a hopeful sign. It shows that the Islamic ethos, at least in this contemporary Iranian context, opposes the prosecution – much less execution – of religious dissidents. Thus, Islamic jurisprudence has moved to reconsider the execution of the apostates just as Hindu religiosity renounced pious self-immolation (*sati*), and Jewish juristic tradition turned away from the stoning of transgressors.[31]

Reform reframed

Reform is not about inventing humanitarian versions of religion; it is about recovering those values from the traditional – even dogmatic – practices of religion. We can learn from cases such as the apostasy trials of Iran in which humanitarian values of freedom of conscience, once invoked, drowned out calls for the execution of the alleged blasphemers or apostates.

Appealing to cultural ideals in order to challenge cultural atrocities is a holistic approach to social change akin to Antonio Gramsci's 'counter-hegemonic' struggle, in which activists dare their conflicted culture to practice what it preaches.[32] The aforementioned civil rights movement in the United States adapted this strategy. Martin Luther King Jr. exclusively appealed to the twin sources of the American constitution and the Judeo-Christian Bible in his advocacy for racial equality and called on Americans to live up to the high standards of the constitution and the scripture. This approach is known to have reduced cultural and political resistance to social change.[33]

Thus, far from constructing a humanistic interpretation of Islam, the Islamic reformers simply rediscover humanistic precepts of divine compassion, moral universalism, legal universalism, tolerance and respect for human agency in Islam,[34] and highlight the incompatibility of these values with harsh retributive justice prescribed by a narrow and literalist interpretation of Shariʿa law. This is a project well under way in academia, but it still remains to be fully articulated in the public discourse within the Islamic world.[35]

The reform movement has several strategies available to it: reformers can appeal to intricate and indigenous interpretations devised by Islamic jurists (muftis, *mujtahid*s and qadis) who have successfully mitigated unequal or inhumane treatment of the litigants and the accused. Judith Tucker has convincingly argued that contrary to the common belief, the traditional juridical interpretations of the sacred tradition have been far from uniformly severe and punitive, even in matters concerning women, family and sexuality. Brutal community practices such as virginity testing, bride bartering and bride abduction have been censured or otherwise modified within the context of Islamic jurisprudence, without outside influences. [36] Unearthing such historical evidence that authoritative texts are open to interpretation bolsters the reform position against a puritan Islamism that blatantly dismisses historical and juridical precedents.[37] Islamic reformers describe puritan Islam as 'authoritarian' and distinguish it from the historically 'authoritative' Islam of the jurisconsults.[38] Khaled Abou El Fadl provides a lucid account of the rise of intolerant authoritarian Islam in the eighteenth century.[39] Concurrently, Moaddel and Krabenick recount the legacy of the 'Islamic modernism' of Egyptian, Iranian and Iraqi clerics and theologians who succeeded in introducing democracy and constitutionalism to the Islamic world in the late eighteenth and early twentieth centuries.[40] Iran's Constitutional Revolution (1905–9), led by prominent clergy (Khorasani, Behbahani, Tabataba'i), provides concrete evidence for the historical efficacy of Islamic modernism. Islamic reform thus challenges Islamic extremism on sound legal, historical, and doctrinal grounds.

Conclusion

People of conscience, lay and cleric alike, are joining in the struggle to usher in a humane interpretation of Islam. The campaign goes beyond legal interpretation of concepts such as blasphemy and apostasy. This will be a great undertaking and may require a full-fledged intra-civilizational confrontation: a momentous internal clash within a conflicted Islamic civilization. This idea was proposed by the prominent political scientist Dieter Senghaas, who rejected Samuel Huntington's 'clash of civiliations' thesis in favour of what he called 'clash within civilizations'. Senghaas contends that the Hindu, Islamic, and Confucian worlds were far too complex to be lumped together as monolithic entities. He considers the question of coming to terms with pluralism as essential to arriving at modernity in each civilization. While the West has largely resolved this problem, the post-colonial world has its own unique challenges with coming to terms with it.[41]

Islam is, as a legal scholar has stated, 'at the current time passing through a transformative moment no less dramatic than the Reformation movements that swept through Europe at one time'.[42] The struggle over the soul of Islam is under way; it will be waged with increasing vigour within Islamic civilization, by Muslims, and for Muslims.

Notes

1 Ahmad Moussalli, *Moderate and Radical Islamic Fundamentalism: The Quest for Modernity, Legitimacy, and the Islamic State* (Gainesville: University of Florida Press, 1999).
2 Akeel Bilgrami, 'The clash within civilizations', *Daedalus* 132/3 (Summer 2003), p. 90.
3 Mansoor Moaddel and Stuart A. Karabenick, *Religious Fundamentalism in the Middle East: A Cross-National, Inter-Faith, and Inter-Ethnic Analysis* (Leiden: Brill, 2013).
4 Khaled Abou El Fadl, *The Great Theft: Wrestling Islam from the Extremists* (New York: Harper Collins, 2005).
5 Gunnar Myrdal, *American Dilemma: The Negro Problem and Modern Democracy* (New Brunswick, NJ: Transaction Publishers, 1995).
6 On the notion of 'cognitive dissonance', see Leon Festinger, 'A theory of social comparison processes', *Human Relations* 7/2 (1954), pp. 117–40; Festinger, *A Theory of Cognitive Dissonance* (Stanford, CA: Stanford University Press, 1957); Solomon Asch, 'Studies of independence and conformity', *Psychological Monographs: General and Applied* 70/9 (1956), pp. 1–70.
7 Pew Research Center's survey of opinions (2007–13) included 39,000 face-to-face interviews in 80 locations throughout the Islamic world. The findings illustrate this duality of mind: a 'solid majority' of Muslims reported that they agreed with the retributions specified by Shariʿa laws. Pew Research Center: 'The world's Muslims: unity and diversity', 9 April 2012, http://www.pewforum.org/2012/08/09/the-worlds-muslims-unity-and-diversity-executive-summary/; Pew Research Center, 'Muslim publics share concerns about extremist groups', 10 September 2013, http://www.pewglobal.org/2013/09/10/muslim-publics-share-concerns-about-extremist-groups/. The Gallup study (2001–7) too was based on interviews with a population representative of 90 per cent of the world's 1.3 billion Muslims (with a three-point margin of error). The results were reported in John Esposito and Dalia Mogahed, *Who Speaks for Islam? What a Billion Muslims Really Think* (New York: Gallup Press, 2007).
8 Andrew G. Bostom, 'Sharia uber alles', *American Thinker* (May 2013).
9 In a previous publication of the Oslo Coalition, this phenomenon has been approached and conceptualized as an 'epistemological crisis' in the Islamic world. Ziba Mir-Hosseini, Kari Vogt, Lena Larsen and Christian Moe (eds), *Gender and Equality in Muslim Family Law: Justice and Ethics in the Islamic Legal Tradition* (London: I. B. Tauris, 2012), pp. 26, 146.
10 The expression was first coined by W.E.B. Dubois in the context of black Americans who, at once, feel American and not American. W.E.B. Dubois, *The Souls of Black Folk* (New York: Dover, 1994).

11 The clause states: 'Whoever insults the sacred principles of Islam, or any of the great prophets or any of the (12) pure Imams or her holiness Fatimah (the prophet's daughter), if he or she falls under the category of "offender against the Prophet", he or she will be executed. Otherwise, the offender will be sentenced to one to five years of imprisonment.' Source: http://www.dadkhahi.net/law/Ghavanin/Ghavanin_Jazaee/gh_mojazat_eslami2.htm.

12 Article 23 of the Constitution of the Islamic Republic of Iran: 'The investigation [inquisition] of individuals' beliefs is forbidden, and no one may be molested or taken to task simply for holding a certain belief.' The term 'inquisition' (*taftish*) is the Persian equivalent for the Spanish Inquisition in Christianity and, as such, carries a cultural baggage pertaining to religious persecution of dissidents. http://www.iranchamber.com/government/laws/constitution_ch03.php#sthash.VJzRrdxE.dpuf (accessed 23 January 2017).

13 Ziba Mir-Hosseini, *Islam and Democracy in Iran: Eshkevari and the Quest for Reform* (London: I.B.Tauris, 2005).

14 Ruhollah Khomeini, *Taḥrīr al-Wasīla* (Qum, n.p., 2001).

15 Quoted from the indictment of the Special Court for the Clergy, Mohammad Ibrahim Nekoonam, clerical prosecutor of Tehran, 23 Shahrivar 1379 (13 September 2000). Unpublished court document. The court refused to release the text of Eshkevari's lawyer's defense, but the author has copies of the indictment, the accused's defense, his objection to the verdict of the judge Mohammad Salimi, and his last statement in the court, courtesy of Mr Hassan Yousefi Eshkevari.

16 From the author's interview with Mr Yousefi Eshkevari, 2 September 2013.

17 *Majma'-i Roohanioon-i Mobarez* which translates to: 'The association of the militant clergy'.

18 Interview with Yousefi Eshkevari, 2 September 2013.

19 It was during this period, in 2004, that I met Mr Eshkevari for the first time, in his apartment in Tehran.

20 This text, written in 1670 by Mohammad Baghir Majlisi, a renowned Safavid cleric and scholar, elaborates on ritual performance of routine actions, from clipping toenails to foreplay. It has long been a favorite of both the meticulously observant and the mischievously critical.

21 A translation of the full text of Aghajari's speech is available in Ayelet Savyon, 'The call for Islamic protestantism: Dr Hashem Aghajari's speech and subsequent death sentence', *MEMRI Special Dispatch* 445 (2 December 2002), http://www.memri.org/report/en/0/0/0/0/0/0/770.htm, accessed on 23 January 2017.

22 According to the New York Times (30 November 2002), four students who had taken part in these demonstrations were detained and charged for disorderly conduct.

23 It is noteworthy that Aghajari's caustic language may have played a role in angering local clerics. It is reputed that a wisecrack during the speech was the real reason for his arrest: 'why should we emulate (imitate) a Shiʿi source of Imitation (*marjaʿ taqlīd*)? Imitation is fit for monkeys.' More specifically, he criticized the transformation of the clergy into a ruling class immune to critique and democratic responsibility. For an example of pertinent opinions and declarations, see: http://www.asre-nou.net/1381/aban/18/m-akhbar.html, accessed on 23 January 23, 2017; http://www.asre-nou.net/1381/aban/23/m-nikbakht.html, accessed on 23 January 2017.

24 The news of this sentence was reported by various international agencies. BBC on its Persian website (20 January 2004) published an interview with Saleh Nikbakht in which the sentence was explained. Also, New York Times published an article entitled:

'Iran drops death penalty for professor guilty of blasphemy' (24 January 2004) that included interviews with Zahra Behnoodi, the defendant's wife.

25 The Iranian human rights lawyer, Mohammad Mostafaei, argues that the granting of greater recognition to the 'knowledge of the judge' in the face of such inconsistencies in the new legal code signifies an attempt to bypass such dilemmas. Thus, the Iranian legal system takes another step back toward the 'qadi justice' system of the medieval Islam. See Mohammad Mostafaei's chapter in this book.

26 In my interview, Mr Eshkevari quoted Nasr Hamid Abu Zayd, the Egyptian thinker who was tried and convicted of apostasy in Egypt. In a conversation with Eshkevari, Abu Zayd had admitted that the Shiʿi Muslims were more flexible with respect to such provisions of apostasy, not only because they were more philosophical (Muʿtazilite) in temperament, but because they had already tasted the 'forbidden fruit' of Islamic government for three decades and were, thus, more savvy with respect to what a religious rule entails.

27 Mohsen Kadivar, 'Mohammad Javad Lankarani's response to the criticisms about apostasy', http://kadivar.com/?p=8979, accessed 27 January 2017. Also see Mohsen Kadivar's chapter in this volume.

28 From the interview with the author, cited above.

29 Taha Jabir Alalwani, *Apostasy in Islam: A Historical and Scriptural Analysis*, transl. Nancy Roberts (London; Washington: International Institute of Islamic Thought, 2011).

30 Soroush Dabbagh, 'Irtidād dar tarazoo ye akhlagh', *Jaras* (August 2013).

31 On 23 September 2014, the grim news of the execution of Mohsen Amiraslani Zanjani, a 28-year-old self-styled religious counselor and soothsayer, arrived. The charges are multiple, murky and inconsistent. One of the accounts (presented by the accused's wife) has it that in one of his trials, he had questioned the literal account of the prophet Yunus's (Jonah's) survival in the belly of a whale, thus opening himself to the charge of 'insulting the Prophet'. The bizarre story of his initial death sentence, struck down three times by appellate courts and finally – and incomprehensibly – enforced, however, does not include apostasy charges and trials, as such, but the nebulous charge of 'corruption on earth'. Whatever the truth of the story, it is remarkable that the authorities have consistently denied that the death sentence was occasioned by heresy or apostasy, which is understandable, given the judiciary's reluctance to punish presumed apostates in the public eye. The tragedy of Mr Amiraslani is reminiscent of Kafka's surreal novels *The Trial* and *The Castle*: deprived of the notoriety that might have saved his life (as it did in the Eshkevari and Aghajari cases) he wandered the deadly maze until he ran out of luck. For further information, see http://persian.iranhumanrights.org/1393/07/ami-aslani/; http://www.rahesabz.net/story/86367/; http://iranwire.com/features/6645/; accessed 10 October 2014. Attorney Mohammad Mostafaei's account in this volume of Ruhollah Tavana's continuing ordeal with the charges of apostasy has much in common with the late Amiraslani's case. The precedent shows that greater publicity in such cases will help the victims avoid harsher punishments.

32 Antonio Gramsci, *Selections from the Prison Notebooks of Antonio Gramsci* (New York: International Publishers, 1971).

33 Martin Luther King Jr., *The Autobiography of Martin Luther King Jr.*, ed. Claiborne Carson (New York, Warner Brothers, 1998). In a similar maneuver, the Estonian independence movement incorporated Soviet slogans (including quotations from Lenin) in its nationalistic songs, thus minimizing governmental interference. See

Guntis Smidchens, *The Power of Song: Nonviolent National Culture in the Baltic Singing Revolution* (Seattle: University of Washington Press, 2014).

34 Marcel A. Boisard, the prominent French legal historian, expands on the notion *Humanism in Islam* (Plainfield, IN: Indianapolis American Trust Publications, 1961, 1979). He expands on four aspects of universalism in Islam: 'metaphysical, religious, sociological, and political', pp. 118–123. Also, Lenn E. Goodman in his *Islamic Humanism* (Oxford: Oxford University Press, 2003, 1987) calls attention to various manifestations of 'humanism' in the works of Islamic scholars such as Ghazali, Ibn Khaldun and Ibn Sina. In a much more colloquial vein, Omar Imady uses stories and folklore as indications of 'Islamic humanism' in his *When You're Shoved from the Right, Look to Your Left: Metaphors of Islamic Humanism* (Salinas, CA: MSI Press, 2005). Also see: George Makdisi, *The Rise of Humanism in Classical Islam and the Christian West* (Edinburgh: Edinburgh University Press, 1990).

35 Charles Kurzman has provided two invaluable collections of Islamic reform thought in his *Liberal Islam* (Oxford University Press, 1998) and *Modernist Islam 1840–1940* (Oxford: Oxford University Press, 2002). These read as a Who's Who of Islamic reform thinkers in our age.

36 Judith Tucker, *In the House of the Law: Gender and Islamic Law in Ottoman Syria and Palestine* (Berkeley, CA: University of California, 2000).

37 In an inspired article Ziauddin Sardar summarizes the Puritan Islamist orientation toward history: 'In modern Wahhabism, there is only the constant present. There is no real past and there is no real notion of an alternative, different future. Their perpetual present exists in the ontological shadow of the past – or rather, a specific, constructed period of early Islamic history, the days of the Prophet Muhammad. The history/culture of Muslim civilization, in all its greatness, complexity and plurality, is totally irrelevant; indeed, it is rejected as deviancy and degeneration.' See: Ziauddin Sardar, 'Is Muslim civilization set on a fixed course to decline?' *New Statesman,* 14 June 2004.

38 Khaled Abou El Fadl, *And God Knows the Soldiers: The Authoritative and Authoritarian in Islamic Discourse* (Lanham, MD: University Press of America, 2001)

39 Khaled Abou El Fadl, *The Great Theft: Wrestling Islam from the Extremists* (New York: Harper One, 2005).

40 Moaddel and Karabenick, *Religious Fundamentalism.*

41 Akeel Bilgrami characterizes this clash within the Islamic world as one between 'secularists' and 'absolutists'. Bilgrami believes, as I do, that a 'practicing Muslim can be secular'. This is possible if we, along with Daniel Bell and Robert Bellah, distinguish between 'objective secularism' (differentiation of religion and politics) and 'subjective secularism' (purging of religion from culture and mind). Practicing Muslims can be objective secularists. This will distinguish them both from indifferent geographic Muslims and exclusivist fundamentalist Muslims. Bilgrami sees two layers of 'internal clash' in the world of Islam: between the moderate and absolutist Muslims and within 'the minds and hearts' of moderate Muslims themselves, rendering them meek in the face of the challenge of fundamentalist Muslims. Bilgrami laments the effects of this psychological retreat that has led to quiescence among the numerous moderates in the face of the vocal radical minorities. He believes the ubiquitous moderates need to be convinced that criticizing their own people is not betraying the unity of Muslims.' Bilgrami calls this psychological skirmish a 'more subtle clash'. This timidity has helped engender an environment in which the fundamentalists are allowed to hijack the soul and the brand of Islam. Tariq Ramadan distinguishes between 'adaptation reform' and 'transformation reform'. He advocates the latter, for which he calls for 'confidence' and

'contestation' of the fundamentalist creed. See Samuel Huntington, 'The clash of civilizations', *Foreign Affairs* 72/3 (Summer 1993), pp. 22–49; Dieter Senghaas, *The Clash Within Civilizations: Coming to Terms with Cultural Conflict* (Oxon: Routledge, 2002); Akeel Bilgrami, 'The clash within civilizations'; Edward Said, 'The clash of ignorance', *The Nation*, 4 October 2001; Mahmood Mamdani, *Good Muslim Bad Muslim* (New York: Three Leaves Press, 2005); Tariq Ramadan, *What I Believe* (Oxford; New York: Oxford University Press, 2010).

42 Abou El Fadl, *The Great Theft*, p. 6.

11

Toward Removing the Punishment of Apostasy in Islam

Mohsen Kadivar

How can we solve the fundamental contradiction between the Qur'an and Prophetic deed, on the one hand, and hadiths and consensus, on the other? This chapter is designed to answer these questions, or at least to provide guidelines for clarifying the problems of this major issue. These problems include the following: What was the subject and context of apostasy in the Qur'an and Sunna, and what is the subject and context of apostasy in the modern time? Is there any temporal punishment for apostasy in the Qur'an? Did the Prophet sentence anyone to the death penalty solely because of apostasy? When did the first killing of apostates happen in the history of Islam? Where did the first events take place: on the battlefield or in the courtroom? What are the injunctions on apostasy in the hadith? Is there any disagreement among the jurists of the Islamic legal schools concerning the major punishments for apostasy, or is there consensus over this issue? Is there any juridical way to restrict the punishment for apostasy? Is it possible to decriminalize apostasy, and abolish the punishments for it, by using *ijtihād* methodology?

This chapter[1] has four sections – punishments for apostasy, punishments for apostasy in the major sources, restricting the punishments for apostasy, and removing the punishments for apostasy – divided into twelve subsections, and a conclusion. It concludes by arguing for the complete abolition of the punishment for apostasy and of shedding the blood of an apostate, using constructional *ijtihād*.

Punishments for apostasy

What is the Muslim mainstream perspective on apostasy and the punishments for it? I seek to answer this key question in this section in two subsections: apostasy in fatwas and apostasy in hadiths, as the major sources of these fatwas.

Fatwas

There is agreement and even consensus among all Islamic legal schools on severe punishments for apostasy: apostates are to be executed, their marriages annulled and their property liquidated. The Hanafi and Ja'fari schools exempt females from capital punishment. Regarding the requirement of offering the apostate a chance to repent in the first three days of apostasy, the Hanafi and Ja'fari schools have different fatwas compared with the Maliki, Shafi'i and Hanbali schools. The Ja'fari school is unique in dividing apostasy into two types, *fiṭrī* and *millī*. There is a small difference between these schools concerning the liquidation of property and the requirement of a waiting period. Although I first consider the agreements of all legal schools, I restrict myself to only one of these schools (the Ja'fari school) for deeper discussion. In this section, I first briefly mention the fatwas of the four Sunni legal schools, and then the fatwas of Ayatollah Khomeini as typical of contemporary Ja'fari juridical opinion.

Sunni decrees

The decree on apostasy is more serious and complex than that on unbelief (*kufr*), because the former is to return to *kufr* by manifesting it in one's intention (*niyya*), action (*fi'l*) or statement (*qawl*). The latter could include mocking Islam, expressing animosity or rejecting its doctrines. Apostasy is defined as denying God's existence, rejecting or denying even one of the prophets, considering an item unlawful (*ḥarām*) when consensus (*ijmā'*) has been reached that it is allowed (*ḥalāl*) and vice versa, rejecting an obligation that is supported by consensus, belief that something is mandatory when the consensus says that it is not so, and remaining steadfast in disbelief (*kufr*) or showing hesitation. A *zindīq* is one who outwardly represents himself as a Muslim but inwardly is an unbeliever. If he does not repent (*istitāba*), such a person is also decreed to be killed.

There is consensus among the four Sunni legal schools that a Muslim man who insults a prophet or one of the angels is to be executed. The Maliki school, based upon a widespread opinion, says that repentance is not a possible option. The Sunni jurists are united that a male apostate must be executed. The Hanafi school has ruled that a female apostate be imprisoned indefinitely and only released if she returns to Islam or dies. Every three days she should receive a corporal punishment. If one were to kill her, the offender would not be held liable for anything.

The Hanafi school also considers it recommended (*mustaḥabb*) to present Islam to the male apostate for each of the three days so that he might repent and return to the fold. If he does not, he is to be executed on the fourth day. Sunni jurists from the other schools consider it mandatory (*wājib*) for Islam to be presented to the male or female apostate three times prior to execution to clear up any ambiguity or confusion in their mind and lead them toward repentance.

Only the ruler or his deputy can carry out the punishment. Thus, if one kills an apostate without his permission, the culprit will be subjected to a discretionary punishment (*ta'zīr*); however, he is not held accountable (*ḍāmin*). Male or female apostates who do not recant, forfeit their entire estate. According to Abu Hanifa, Abu Yusuf and Malik, if either spouse apostatizes, the marriage is automatically annulled (*faskh*) and there is no need to utter the divorce formula. The Shafi'i and Hanbali schools suspend the annulment until the wife's waiting period (*'idda*) ends. If the apostate repents before that time, the marriage remains valid.[2]

Jaʿfari decrees

An apostate is defined as a Muslim who departs from Islam and chooses unbelief or another religion in its place. There are two types of apostates: *fiṭrī* and *millī*. A *fiṭrī* apostate is one who had one Muslim parent at the time of his conception, and expressed his belief in Islam after having attained maturity or puberty (*bulūgh*), but subsequently renounced Islam. A *millī* apostate is one whose parents were unbelievers at the time of his conception and who expressed his unbelief (*kufr*) after having attained maturity (*kāfir aṣlī*). Thereafter, he became a Muslim and later on reverted to unbelief.

A male *fiṭrī* apostate will be sentenced to three punishments: He is executed; his marriage is annulled without any need to recite the divorce formula, and his wife must complete the regular term of *ʿidda* prescribed after the death of one's husband (four months and ten days); and his property is liquidated while he is still alive. After paying off his debts, the rest of his estate should be divided among his heirs. Apparently, even if he repents and professes Islam with conviction, he cannot escape these three punishments.

A male *millī* apostate should be given an opportunity to repent; if he refuses to do so, he may be killed. But before that event, based on caution (*iḥtiyāt*), he should be given three days of grace and encouraged to repent and recant. If he persists, then he should be killed on the fourth day. His marriage is automatically annulled if he fails to repent during his wife's *ʿidda*, provided that the couple's marriage has been consummated and she is not going through menopause. His property is distributed to his heirs after his death.

A female *fiṭrī* or *millī* apostate receives life imprisonment; she should be whipped during the five daily prayers and given only modest amounts of food and water, as well as insufficient clothes, in order to induce her to repent and recant; if she does so, she will be freed. If she has never consummated her marriage, it is dissolved immediately without any need to wait for the *ʿidda*. However, if she has had conjugal relations, her marriage remains valid if she repents during the regular *ʿidda* (three months and ten days). She retains ownership of her property and it is not distributed until after her death.

A *fiṭrī* or *millī* apostate's prepubescent children are considered to be Muslim; however, if they choose unbelief after maturity, they are given an opportunity to repent. If they refuse to do so, they should be killed. This also applies to the children of a Muslim if they reject Islam after having attained maturity but prior to having professed Islam.[3]

Hadiths

There are many hadiths attributed to the Prophet, his companions and the Shiʿi Imams on severe punishment for the apostate. In addition, these severe punishments in general, and execution in particular, are accepted as consensus in all Islamic legal schools. The main sources for the punishment of the apostate, then, are hadiths and consensus. As the consensus is not an independent source, but was made based on these hadiths, we can say that the real main evidence for any punishment of apostasy is hadith.

The most famous hadith on capital punishment of the apostate is the following: ʿAbdallah b. ʿAbbas narrated that the Prophet said: 'Whosoever changes his religion, kill him.'[4] In Shiʿa hadith sources, this hadith has been mentioned in al-Nuri's *Mustadrak al-Wasāʾil* from al-Nuʿman's *Daʿāʾim al-Islām* with no chain of transmission to the Prophet (*mursala*)![5]

The second famous hadith: ʿAbdallah b. Masʿud narrated from the Prophet that he said: 'It is unlawful to shed the blood of a Muslim except in one of these three instances: unbelief after belief, adultery after chastity, and murder.'[6]

Sunni fiqh based on these authentic hadiths issued the fatwa on severe punishment of the apostate from the beginning. This ruling entered Shiʿi jurisprudence from Sunni sources. Some of the earlier jurisprudential works, such as Saduq's *al-Hidāya*, al-Murtada's *al-Intiṣār*, and Sallar Daylami's *al-Marāsim*, regarded this as an insignificant issue not worth dealing with. Others dealt with it in the chapter of *Jihād*, which supports the view that the subject of apostasy was formulated with reference to the contextual indicant that I discuss below (i.e., apostasy comprised both leaving Islam and actively working with the Muslims' enemies). Many scholars have taken this approach.[7] In some of the Shiʿi jurisprudential works that condemn the apostate to death,[8] most of the supporting evidence consists of prophetic statements from Sunni sources. Later, the Shiʿi hadith compilations attributed the severe punishments for the apostate to the Imams. Neither Tusi, who narrated the two aforementioned prophetic hadiths in his legal work *al-Mabsūṭ*, nor any other Shiʿi hadith compilations attributed such hadiths to the Prophet!

I have examined the Shiʿi sources on apostasy in greater detail. There are in total 21 hadiths on the death penalty that are invoked in the jurisprudential discussion of apostasy, all of which have been gathered in *Wasāʾil al-Shīʿa* and *Mustadrak al-Wasāʾil*.[9] At best, there are no more than eight authentic hadiths in total.[10] Of the other thirteen narrations on the death penalty for apostasy, eight are *mursal* (without a complete chain of transmitters) and five are *ḍaʿīf* (weak). That is, fewer than one-third of the narrations on this subject are *ṣaḥīḥ* (authentic). The major arguments on the three punishments are cited here according to Ayatollah Abu al-Qasim al-Khuʾi, the longest-serving leading Jaʿfari *faqīh* in the twentieth century.

The division of apostates into two types is based on a couple of hadiths. There is agreement on the three punishments for the male *millī* apostate. A couple of hadiths indicate these punishments, such as the authentic hadith of ʿAmmar al-Sabati:

> I heard Imam Jaʿfar al-Sadiq say, '[For] every Muslim who apostatizes and repudiates and rejects Muhammad's prophethood, it is lawful for the one who hears him say these things to kill him. His wife will be irrevocably divorced upon his apostasy, his estate should be distributed among his heirs, his wife should observe the waiting period (*ʿidda*) for a deceased husband, and the leader (*al-Imam*) must kill him and reject his repentance.'[11]

The authentic hadith of Muhammad b. Muslim from Imam Muhammad Baqir indicates the same ruling on three punishments.[12] The authentic hadiths of ʿAli b. Jaʿfar from his brother Imam Musa al-Kazim and of al-Hussayn b. Saʿid from Imam ʿAli b. Musa al-Ridha[13] indicate only the first punishment (execution).

The aforementioned authentic hadith of ʿAli b. Jaʿfar indicates that a male *millī* apostate should not be killed immediately, but should be given an opportunity to repent. The evidence supporting three days for repentance is the authentic hadith of Sakuni from Imam Jaʿfar al-Sadiq: 'The apostate from Islam, his wife is separated automatically. It is unlawful to eat his slaughtered animal (*dhabīḥa*); he should be given three days for repentance; he will be executed on the fourth day, if he persists'[14] His property is distributed to his heirs after his death, not when he is alive.[15]

Anyway, are these hadith at the level of *mutawātir*? No. This would require the report to be transmitted by a number of independent chains of transmission – not a particular number, but so many that it could not possibly have been fabricated through collusion.[16] The jurists have examined the validity of the chain of transmission as regards apostasy, and it is clear that none of them ever claimed that it has reached the *mutawātir* level.

Punishments for apostasy in the major sources

What was the precise meaning of apostasy in the first half-century of Islam? After learning the consensus of all Islamic legal schools on the severe punishments for apostasy, according to a couple of hadiths that have manifested themselves in a few fatwas, there are three key questions on apostasy that I try to answer in this section. The muftis did not refer to any verses of the Qurʾan. Is there any verse in the Qurʾan in support of these punishments for apostasy? Although the biography of the Prophet (*sīra*) does say something about punishments for apostates in his time, the muftis and hadiths cited did not refer to any Prophetic deeds (*fiʿl al-Rasūl*) on this subject. Did the Prophet sentence anyone to any of these three punishments, especially execution, solely on the grounds of apostasy? Who were the first apostates in the history of Islam? What were their stories? Which of these punishments were imposed on them? When were the three punishments comprehensively implemented? These are the major questions of this section.

A Qurʾanic Doctrine?

Although jurists and the scholars of the interpretation of the injunction verses (*tafsīr āyāt al-aḥkām*) discussed only verses that contain the term apostasy (*irtidād*) and the other words derived from the same root (*r-d-d*), it is only one type of verses on this subject. There are at least three other types of verses directly related to apostasy! I describe these four types of verses briefly in this section and go on to make a few concluding remarks. The key question of this section is: 'Which of these two doctrines are supported by the Qurʾan: severe punishment for apostasy, or freedom of religion?'

Negation of force and coercion in the matter of religion and belief

'There is no compulsion in religion; true guidance has become distinct from error, so whoever rejects false gods and believes in God has grasped the firmest hand-hold, one that will never break. God is all-hearing and all-knowing' (2:256, cf. also 10:99 and 11:28). It contains a negation (i.e., God has not based religion on compulsion) and a prohibition (i.e., do not force anyone to believe, forced belief has no validity). Rejecting force is equivalent to accepting freedom of religion in two aspects: freedom both to enter and to leave a religion. Providing a choice between following a particular religion and death is equivalent to compulsion. If people are free to enter but not to leave, then they stay only due to compulsion and fear of punishment. At the same time, God has clearly distinguished truth from falsehood in the Qur'an instead of using force.

The occasion of this verse's revelation has to do with apostasy.[17] Contrary to the opinion of some Sunni exegetes, it was not abrogated by the 'sword verse' (9:73)[18] and will remain forever an emblem of Islam's allowance of freedom of religion. Punishments ranging from permanent exile to death for an apostate, or telling an unbeliever to choose between Islam and death, are examples of blatant coercion and therefore negate and contradict the verse under consideration.

Freedom to choose guidance or go astray

'Say, "Now the truth has come from your Lord: let those who wish to believe in it do so, and let those who wish to reject it do so." We have prepared a Fire for the wrongdoers that will envelop them from all sides' (18:29).

Verses of this type corroborate that the basis of religious freedom and belief is freedom to choose between guidance and misguidance (cf. 10:108, 39:41, 27:91–3). Imposing any form of temporal punishment for leaving Islam contradicts the Qur'an, which proclaims 'let those who wish to reject it, do so', 'whoever strays does so to his own loss', 'I am not your guardian' and 'I am only here to warn'. If the negation of any temporal punishment were not connected with an unbeliever going astray, then this verse would be redundant regardless of whether it was meant for original (*aṣlī*) unbelievers or non-original unbelievers. If people are given a choice between death or permanent exile in servitude, then how can the Qur'an proclaim 'let those who wish to reject it do so'? If no temporal punishment is to be instituted for an apostate, then it would be possible to say 'and whoever strays does so to his own loss: I am not your guardian'. Admonition would have meaning and purpose if there were no punishment in this world, but only a painful chastisement awaiting them in the Hereafter. If such people were executed, the Prophet's admonition and lack of guardianship over the believers would make no sense.

Mandate of the Prophet: to convey the truth, but not to force people to accept it

'So [O Prophet] warn them: your only task is to give warning, you are not there to control them' (88:21–22, cf. also 50:43, 25:56–8, 13:40, 5:99).

Given that the content of both the Meccan and the Medinan suras, even the last revealed one, makes it clear that the Prophet was sent only to guide and admonish, how can others have a greater mandate? If only God can evaluate and take account of people's faith, and the Prophet is only entrusted with conveying the message via specific methods, then negating religious freedom and implementing the punishments and rewards in this temporal life would be, in a sense, arrogating God's mantle to oneself. In order to preserve the Prophet's mission and to take account of God's prerogative, people must have the choice of freely entering and leaving Islam. If only execution awaits the apostate, the Prophet's mandate to be only a reminder, admonisher, and conveyor of glad tidings would be meaningless.

No temporal punishment for apostasy

There are at least eight verses on apostasy in the Qur'an (2:217, 3:86–90, 4:137, 5:5, 5:54, 9:74, 16:106, 47:25–8). The most famous one is 2:217:

> They will not stop fighting you [believers] until they make you revoke your faith, if they can. If any of you revoke your faith and die as unbelievers, your deeds will come to nothing in this world and the Hereafter, and you will be inhabitants of the Fire, there to remain.

The verse points to an apostate's natural death, as opposed to his/her execution or killing. If this individual were meant to be condemned to death, then the verse would have used verbs like 'to kill' or 'to crucify' instead. The phrase 'die as disbelievers' shows that the apostate may feel penitent, return to Islam, and die as a believer. Thus, apostasy in itself is not reason enough to prescribe the mentioned punishment; rather, he must stay in this state until death.

To tie up some loose ends on the apostasy verses:

(a) *Effects in this world:* the nullification of deeds (2:217); being eternally cursed by God, the angels, and the people (3:87); deprivation of divine guidance (3:86, 4:137); God's anger (16:106); exclusion from being among His beloved (5:54); and subjection to Satan's machinations and trickery (47:25).

(b) *Effects in the hereafter:* nullification of deeds (2:217, 5:4); grievous punishment (16:106); eternal punishment in the hellfire (2:217); deprivation of any concessions in the punishment or delay of its implementation (3:88); deprivation of God's forgiveness (4:137); and loss in the hereafter (5:4).

(c) In most verses, apostasy refers to a group and thus the plural pronoun is employed. (2:218, 3:86, 4:137, 9:74, 16:106, 47:25). This is true for all but two of the verses (5:4, 5:54).

(d) The apostasy discussed in these verses is due to apostates' animosity and hostility after the Truth was made clear to them (3:86, 9:74, 47:25).

(e) The repentance of an apostate should be accepted (3:89, 9:74). If his/her disbelief grows stronger, then he/she will lose the capacity to repent (3:90).

No temporal punishments (e.g., imprisonment, flogging, execution, exile or ban from participation in socio-political affairs) are mentioned. All of the temporal punishments for apostasy cited above are of a non-physical nature and completely unrelated to the *ḥudūd* punishments. An apostate who dies in a state of disbelief will, like an unbeliever, find his/her good deeds nullified and unable to help him attain prosperity.

Reflecting upon all of the verses dealing with apostasy, one comes to the following conclusions:

First, replacing Islam with unbelief is a repugnant, repulsive and despicable act. This change can take two forms: (1) 'deliberative and knowledge-based apostasy' (*al-irtidād al-naẓarī wa al-ʿilmī*), when one comes through study and research to deny the existence of God and the Hereafter or to doubt Islam's veracity; and (2) 'political and action-based apostasy' (*al-irtidād al-siyāsī wa al-ʿamalī*), when one renounces faith and rejects the truth, despite knowing them to be true, in order to gain worldly benefits and pleasures or for political and other satanic temptations.

Second, the Qur'an prescribes no punishment for the former (i.e. deliberative and knowledge-based apostasy) in either world. However, such a person will clearly be deprived of the blessings connected with having attained an understanding of the Truth and implementing its values.

Third, as for the latter (i.e., 'Those who turn on their heels after being shown guidance'), their prescribed punishment in the afterlife takes the form of eternal punishment in the hellfire. This is the type of apostasy with which the Qur'an is concerned.

Fourth, the Qur'an neither mentions nor prescribes any temporal punishment for apostasy.

The Prophet's deed?

Was anyone killed during the Prophet's time solely for apostasy? I hereby summarize the findings of two comprehensive pieces of research on this subject. The first was done under the supervision of my mentor Ayatollah H.A. Montazeri.

> When certain people who were sentenced to death and subsequently killed on the Prophet's order – according to some historical reports – it was not due to their disbelief or apostasy, but to their involvement in killing [the Muslims], or actively fighting them, persecuting them, or inflicting harm [upon them] via espionage or other violations [. . .].[19]

He scrutinizes the historical reports in which the Prophet sentenced people to death and categorizes them into five groups. This is his finding for the first group: Even if we accept the veracity of the report that the Prophet sentenced a number of people to death, he did not do so solely because of apostasy. Rather, there were additional facts to consider: murder, espionage or actively fighting the Prophet and the Muslims. Moreover, in those days apostasy was not confined to changing one's religion or belief system. According to ancient Arab tribal custom, every person and tribe had to affiliate and bond with other tribes for self-preservation. Therefore, anyone who left Islam or killed a Muslim immediately became regarded as a belligerent and an enemy of Islam who would offer his support to the enemy.[20]

I quote here the result of his study and research for the third group, as it is of great relevance and importance: The third group deals with the claim that the Prophet ordered the death penalty solely because of apostasy. Montazeri cogently proved the absolute weakness and clear fabrication of all narratives of this claim.[21]

The second piece of research was done under the supervision of my other teacher, Ayatollah A. Musawi Ardabili. This is the conclusion of his survey:

> Some books of narrations, exegesis, and history have recorded the incidents in which some individuals during the time of the Prophet left Islam. Most of these reports do not possess a sound chain of transmission. I did not find in them any person who embraced Islam with conviction and subsequently decided to leave it solely for finding faults in its dogma or rulings. The reason for leaving Islam was associated with some crimes, like murder and spying for the enemy. As a result, the criminals would flee to the lands of the unbelievers and polytheists and stay there until they died, fearing the implementation of the Islamic ruling. Upon closer examination and reflection, it becomes clear that those identified as apostates were, in all cases, guilty of economic and political crimes or other criminal activity. In no single decisive case did the Prophet ever order someone's death for leaving Islam solely due to doubts about the belief system, without the person being involved in one of the other forbidden acts. Thus, their so-called act of apostasy was linked with crimes. In fact, some of them had never embraced Islam, which means that their supposed apostasy could not have been the cause of their death.[22]

According to this research and examining all of the historical evidence, I can make the clear and strong statement that no one during the time of the Prophet was killed solely on grounds of apostasy (i.e. change of religion). Rather, it was for some other transgression. Apostasy, at his time, was not confined to changing one's religion or belief system. It had several inseparable political correlations, such as becoming a belligerent and an enemy of Islam.

Ridda: The first implementations of the punishment for apostasy

Is there any reliable evidence that the first four caliphs after the Prophet actually sentenced anyone to capital punishment solely for apostasy or blasphemy? A group of Muslims refused to pay the *zakāt* tax to the central government in the time of Abu Bakr. However, this does not constitute apostasy, for in no way does it sever their attachment to Islam. Rather, their non-compliance was due to their misgivings about handing it over to the caliph.[23]

Al-Tusi elaborated on the case:

> Those who were categorized as 'people of *ridda*' were of two kinds: (1) those who had reverted to unbelief, like Musaylamah, Tulayha, ʿUnsa, and their supporters – without a doubt or dissent, by leaving Islam they became apostates – and (2) those who refused to remit the *zakāt* while remaining faithful to Islam. [Some of the Sunni scholars] have grouped both of them under 'people of *ridda*', even though the second group, in the estimation of the Shiʿa [and most Sunnis], were not apostates. *Ridda* means to abandon a truth one has been committed to and has espoused. By this action, the person becomes a *murtadd* (apostate). Thus, *irtidād* (apostasy) is of two types: (1) abandoning Islam for disbelief and (2) neglecting

> something (e.g., not remitting the *zakāt*) while remaining faithful to Islam. Clearly, the latter cannot be labelled a *murtadd* [in the technical sense] because not fulfilling or refusing to fulfil a financial obligation does not turn one into a *murtadd*. Some have argued that such people should still be labelled a *murtadd* because they consider it permissible to withhold the *zakāt*, and that one who believes in such a 'right' should be labelled an unbeliever. This is incorrect in light of the clarification just provided: They did not consider its non-payment permissible, but rather had [certain] misgivings and apprehensions [about handing it over to the caliph].[24]

People of *ridda* were killed on the battlefield in 632–3. They were not executed after a trial. Nothing was mentioned at the time about separation from their spouses or cancelling their property ownership.[25] A precise historical survey clarifies that the hadiths about temporal punishments for apostasy represent the conduct of the post-Prophetic time (i.e. 632 onward).[26]

> During the period of ʿAli's caliphate, one encounters many narrations in Sunni and Shiʿi sources containing stories about some Muslims embracing a false belief and doctrine. Not only are the chains of transmission of some of these narrations weak, but they also give off the stench of fabrication by the enemies of Islam and political opportunists, among them such people as Muʿawiya b. Abi Sufyan and the Umayyads, who sought to disparage Imam ʿAli, inspire the people to hate him, dishonour him, and lower his status.[27]

There is no doubt that some Muslims were killed after the time of the Prophet. However, no reliable evidence indicates that Imam ʿAli, during his caliphate, executed anyone for apostasy. I have examined all hadiths to the contrary, and have not found even one authentic reliable hadith in Shiʿi sources. He never viewed his armed opponents in three battles as apostates.[28] However, political killings under the guise of 'apostasy' were rampant under the Umayyad and ʿAbbasid dynasties.

In conclusion, my research indicates that historically there is no reliable argument that the Prophet sentenced anyone to the death penalty or other punishments solely for apostasy. According to Shiʿi sources no reliable evidence proves that Imam ʿAli or the other Imams sentenced people to execution solely for apostasy. There is a paradox here. On one hand, the Qurʾan and the Prophet's deeds (and for the Shiʿa, the deeds of Imam ʿAli and other Imams) do not support the punishment for apostasy. On the other hand, the sayings of the Prophet (and the sayings of the Imams for the Shiʿa) that are considered authentic, together with the consensus, are used as arguments for severe punishments for apostasy. If the former are correct, the latter are wrong and vice versa. The mainstream took the hadiths and the consensus as truth, and neglected the former arguments. I seek to give a critical analysis of this traditional perspective.

Restricting the punishments for apostasy

Although the punishments for apostasy were not explicitly rejected, in practice many Shiʿi jurists felt something wrong in them. They tried to restrict these severe punishments, especially executions. I describe three approaches in Ja'fari *fiqh* for restricting the punishments for apostasy. One of them goes back some ten centuries, but the other two have developed in recent decades.

Suspension of the *ḥudūd* in the Time of Occultation

Many past jurists have held that implementing the *ḥudūd* and calling for jihad are the exclusive prerogative of the Prophet and the Imams.[29] In contrast, a good number of jurists hold that they have been entrusted with implementing the *ḥudūd* punishments, to the extent possible, during the Occultation of the Imam.[30] In brief, jurists who are absolutely opposed to implementing the *ḥudūd* during the Occultation comprise three groups: (1) those who have issued an explicit fatwa that the jurists have absolutely no mandate to implement the *ḥudūd* punishments; (2) jurists who believe that they have a limited mandate in the area of *ḥudūd* so long as the punishment does not lead to death or cause injury; and (3) jurists who believe that implementing the *ḥudūd* has been suspended during the Imam's Occultation. In practice, the first and third groups are the same.

Full suspension of the ḥudūd *during the Occultation*

Eight eminent jurists believed that only the Imam or his specially appointed deputy could implement the *ḥudūd* punishments.[31] In this regard, I would like to quote only one of them, Ibn Idris al-Hilli:

> Only the [divinely] designated ruler of the time or the one he has appointed to carry this out can implement the *ḥudūd* [. . .] A consensus has been attained among the Shi'i jurists and Muslims in general that only the infallible Imams, as well as the judges appointed by them for this task, can implement the *ḥudūd* or deliberate upon it. No one has the right to contest and challenge [his decision]. This consensus cannot be overridden by *al-khabar al-wāḥid*, but would require another consensus of the same calibre or categorical evidence from the Qur'an or a *mutawātir* hadith.[32]

Discontinuation of the ḥudūd *in cases leading to death or injury during the Occultation*

Three jurists were from this group: the authors of *Jāmi'-i 'Abbāsī*, *Kashf al-Lithām* and *Jāmi' al-Madārik*.[33]

Suspension of the ḥudūd *during the Occultation*

Four distinguished jurists supported this stance – al-Muhaqqiq al-Hilli, al-'Allama al-Hilli, al-Muhaqqiq al-Ardabili, and Mirza al-Qummi.[34] Al-Muhaqqiq al-Hilli, who undoubtedly excels as one of the leading three Shi'i jurists, writes in both of his books (which still feature in contemporary jurisprudential discussions) that if 'enjoining good and forbidding evil' led to death or injury, then just like the *ḥudūd* punishments, it would be restricted to the infallible Imam or his specially designated deputy. He alludes to the dissenters' point of view as 'frail and weak opinion.'[35]

All punishments for apostasy, including capital punishment, would be suspended according to the first and third approach; the second approach would suspend the capital punishment, but not the other two punishments for apostates. The suspension of punishments or capital punishment is not valid for the jurists who have a different fatwa on this issue and their followers. This formula is acceptable in the framework of traditional *ijtihād*, but if its main argument is that the implementation of *ḥudūd* punishment requires infallibility, it is problematic in the framework of constructional *ijtihād*. There is no difference between the Occultation and the presence of the Prophet and Imams, because the judiciary and political activity of the Prophet and Imams was human, not divine. This point profoundly weakens the argument of this formula.

Suspension of the *ḥudūd* and 'impairing' Islam

'Weakening' or 'impairing' Islam (*wahn al-Islām*) means defacing its visage so that it becomes one of violence, repugnance, and brutality; one that is distant from mercy and compassion. A ruling that impairs Islam can be approached from two perspectives: as a primary injunction, and as a secondary injunction. I will discuss the former in the next section. Now I focus on the latter. 'Secondary injunction' means that the original ruling would remain untouched, although its implementation would be suspended as long as it impaired Islam; 'primary injunction' means that the original ruling would be abrogated due to its impairing Islam. Secondary injunction could be based on at least three specific situations: necessity (*ḍarūra*), expediency (*maṣlaḥa*), and governmental rule (*al-ḥukm al-ḥukūmī*). Each of them has this ability to suspend a primary injunction as long as there is necessity or expediency, or a governmental rule is active.

In light of the difficulties and problems faced by the Muslims after a video of a stoning (*rajm*) – a harsh punishment based on a couple of hadiths without any Qur'anic base – was distributed internationally in the late 1980s, many of the governmental clerics in Iran suspended that practice in order to protect Islam's honour and dignity. The late Ayatollah Khomeini supposedly also consented to this judgment orally. Thus, can we not do likewise for apostasy and blasphemy based upon the same principle? The answer is 'yes'. From the perspective of traditional jurists, stoning, apostasy and blasphemy are all legal rulings and part of the Shariʿa. However, implementation of these judgments today would impair Islam's visage. As such, preserving Islam's dignity in general, when compared to implementing one secondary judgment, is undoubtedly far more important.

Ayatollah Montazeri favoured suspending the implementation of those judgments that impair Islam's visage under the rubric of secondary injunction:

> It is possible that some of the punishments, due to the insufficient explanation of their objectives or incorrect implementation, cause people to be cynical of the Shariʿa's fundamentals and impair Islam's image. In such a situation, the judgement's philosophical underpinnings must be explained to, and accepted by, the public before it can be implemented. If this has not been done, then its implementation

> must be suspended [...] If implementing the *ḥudūd* in a particular time or place will negatively affect an individual or an Islamic society, then it must be suspended temporarily.[36]
>
> Even if, under normal circumstances, implementation of the *ḥudūd* provides numerous benefits to society, on the condition that the crime is proven through the method provided by the Shariʿa [...], the ruler can still suspend their implementation if, under special circumstances, the public welfare demands that they be abandoned [temporarily]. In a reliable *khabar al-wāḥid* of Ghiyath b. Ibrahim from Imam ʿAli, 'I do not implement the *ḥudūd* on a person until he has exited the enemy-ruled land, out of fear this would push him to seek the enemy's protection and forge an alliance with them.' If implementing the *hudūd* punishment in a particular locality or in all of the regions or during a particular time would engender revulsion against Islam and its rulings, resulting in weakening of Islam's foundations, then the ruler or his designated judiciary representative is allowed (rather, he is obligated) to suspend implementation of that *ḥadd* punishment until public opinion is convinced about the Islamic regulations and rulings and their aims.[37]

So Montazeri could be one of the supporters of the second formula.

Although this formula has the ability to suspend all punishments of apostasy and blasphemy, its clear function has been in contesting capital punishment. If the muftis or rulers could hide the implementation of these injunctions in any way, the formula does not work. This could be a major shortcoming. Human rights NGOs and activists, as well as social networks, media and journalists, therefore have an important role in activating this formula. This formula is acceptable in the framework of traditional *ijtihād*. Constructional *ijtihād* prefers applying 'impairing Islam' as a primary injunction, rather than as a secondary injunction.

Demarcating change of religion from apostasy: An encouraging step

Recent opinions of my mentor, the eminent Ayatollah Montazeri,[38] on apostasy and blasphemy form an encouraging step in the recent juridical literature on apostasy. In 2005, for the first time, he issued a legal ruling in which he clearly demarcates *changing one's religion* from *apostasy*.[39] He regards the freedom to change one's religion as one of the inherent rights of a human being. His recent position on apostasy and defaming the Prophet can be summarized in the following points.

Changing one's religion as a result of intellectual endeavour and without any hostility or enmity toward the Truth would not trigger any temporal punishment and, as such, bears no resemblance to the crime of apostasy. One cannot regard as an apostate any person who rejects the essentials of religion (*ḍarūriyyāt*), so long as it does not lead to the negation of prophethood. The rejection of Islam (i.e., apostasy) is dependent upon enmity and hostility as constituent components of the situational context (*mawḍūʿ*). To change one's religion because one has been convinced by research and rational arguments, has nothing to do with the crime of apostasy (*ridda*) as defined in the original context. The phenomenon of apostasy invoked at the dawn of Islam was associated with a political rebellion against the central government and thus was not confined to a change in religious belief. Judgments on apostates pertain to the political and administrative spheres bound by their own particular time and place. It is not obligatory for an apostate to convey his convictions to anyone. Moreover, such a person has an opportunity to repent and seek forgiveness from God, which would revoke the implementation of the three possible forms of punishment.

Montazeri stressed that it is the mandate of a proper judicial system to adjudicate on an alleged case of apostasy or blasphemy. If the person is found guilty, then it is for the court to implement the punishment, provided that negative consequences would not ensue from it. The judge has to reach a conclusion that the person in question intended to denigrate and defame the Prophet. The only possible way to attain this is for the accused to voluntarily confess to the validity of the charge laid against him/her. The judge is required to take into account the sect (*madhhab*), culture and social conventions of the region when determining the criterion of insult or offence. Even if blasphemy is established by way of personal confession in the court, the judge has the discretion to forgive the accused. All punishments for defamation and slander are to be carried out under the supervision of the judge. Under certain circumstances, the judge can rescind the punishment and forgive the accused. Scholarly objections and criticisms in an Islamic society should not be construed as defamatory, for it is permissible to offer them on any subject matter – even on the oneness of God. The public is free to ask questions and carry out research on any aspect of the belief system. With regard to implementing the punishment for certain offences mentioned in the Qurʾan (*ḥudūd*) and others (*taʿzīr* – discretionary punishment to chastise and deter), the slightest weakness in establishing these offences renders them void.[40]

Ayatollah Montazeri, by narrowing the situational context of the ruling on apostasy, has rendered the implementation of religiously sanctioned punishments extremely difficult and rare in theory. Moreover, the judge has the discretion to forgive any person found guilty of defaming the Prophet. The severe punishment for apostasy can only be administered via the judicial system after it has established that the accused intended to make a mockery of religion and incite a rebellion. Montazeri recognized that changing one's religion and rejecting the essentials of religion (*ḍarūriyyāt*), subject to some conditions, would not trigger any temporal punishment. Although it is an important innovation in jurisprudence, and offers a helpful practical formula for the judicial system to restrict the severe punishments for apostasy, distinguishing this situation from the intention of 'hostility or enmity' is in the hands of the judge, and open to dangerous justifications. Although Montazeri's innovations were good starting points, they did not completely remove the punishments for apostasy. However, I think what he did was the maximum of what one could do in the framework of traditional *ijtihād*.

Removing the punishment for apostasy

Constructional *ijtihād* or *ijtihād* in principles and foundations is the reformist competitor with traditional or classical *ijtihād*, which confines itself to *ijtihād* in Shariʿa rules (*al-furūʿ al-fiqhiyya*) without any reconstruction in the methodological foundations (*uṣūl al-fiqh*) and the epistemological, cosmological, anthropological, philosophical and theological principles of Shariʿa.[41] Constructional *ijtihād* abolishes all types of temporal punishments of apostasy, especially execution, and completely removes apostasy from the list of crimes. This important achievement could be achieved through at least four formulas. Applying one or more of these formulas is sufficient for our goal. It is obvious that these formulas are not on the same level or of the same strength. Some are more fundamental than others. In this section, I discuss each of them briefly, highlighting their domain and efficiency on the one hand, and their supporting arguments and proofs on the other.

Alteration of the subject

In the estimation of reasonable people (*sīrat al- ʿuqalāʾ*), is the subject matter of apostasy in the Qurʾan, Tradition, and past rulings identical to how we understand it in our time? In all likelihood, the answer is 'no', because the subject matter in the former is broader than changing one's religion or leaving Islam. In fact, it extends to aligning oneself with the enemies of Muslims (i.e., unbelievers and polytheists) and propagandizing against Muslims, which would constitute a form of political and cultural rebellion against the state's authority. But today, changing one's faith is understood to be merely a conversion without any ulterior motives. In other words, contemporary reasonable people (*al-ʿuqalāʾ*) consider the subject matter of apostasy to be connected with religious and cultural freedom, whereas traditional Islamic jurisprudence considers it to be a political crime: belligerency against the state. These two viewpoints are poles apart.

The Qurʾan uses 'apostasy' to indicate those hostile unbelievers who sought to demoralize the Muslims and cause them to abandon Islam by spreading negative propaganda, scheming and exploiting ex-Muslims to strike at Islam's stature.[42] The Qurʾan (5:33) explicitly and absolutely prescribes specific punishment for those guilty of belligerency (i.e. *muḥārib*, causing disorder and disturbing societal peace and security by using weapons).[43] By contrast, in the case of apostasy – with all its political conditions – the Qurʾan confined itself to stating that the apostate would have his good deeds effaced, both in this world and Hereafter, and suffer eternal punishment in the Hereafter, but said nothing about temporal punishment!

Gradually, the ruling on killing an apostate was de-linked from the initial political circumstances, which included joining the Muslims' enemies. From the tenth century onward, we come across hadith reports on this issue attributed to the Imams (without specifying any restrictions); however, most of them either have no chain of transmission, or the narrators are unknown or of deficient character. A large number of such hadith reports pertain to the exaggerators (*ghulāt*) and how ʿAli dealt with them. But all such reports must be treated with great caution, because there was rampant fabrication of hadith reports under the Umayyads.

Montazeri envisioned the change of subject matter as follows: In those days, apostasy was not confined to changing one's religion or belief system, for anyone who left Islam or killed a Muslim was immediately regarded as a belligerent and a person who would immediately offer his support to the Muslims' enemies. According to ancient Arab tribal custom, every person and tribe had to affiliate and bond with other tribes for self-preservation. As such, anyone who left Islam was viewed as a belligerent.[44]

The subject of apostasy during the time of the Prophet, and even that of the Imams, was broader than changing one's religion or announcing this decision.[45]

The benefits of discretionary punishments (*taʿzīr*) and *ḥudūd* are neither hidden nor incomprehensible, Montazeri argued, for they can be derived from the contextual indicants and many explanations found in the relevant narrations. As mentioned earlier, the Prophet's primary objective is to warn and admonish criminals and help them reform themselves. It is unlikely that there are other hidden benefits that are incomprehensible to us. On the other hand, progress in criminology, psychology and methods of reforming and rehabilitating criminals has shown that the previous methods may not produce the effect intended by the Legislator. Moreover, these new methods may be better and more able to attain the Legislator's primary goal than the punishments that were then in vogue. If a jurist is able to deduce from the proofs that, from the perspective of promoting human welfare and averting corruption, some of the aforementioned rulings that were part of a subject matter have changed, then the rulings would also change. However, Montazeri noted, this process must be totally reliant upon the Qurʾan, hadith, and the norms of *ijtihād*, as opposed to being under the pressure or influence of the environment and special circumstances.[46]

If this explanation fails to establish that the subject matter of apostasy has changed (which, in my estimation, has been well established), the situation at the least gives rise to a preponderance of doubt and ambiguity. As such, the principle of *darʾ* (the lapse of the *ḥudūd* punishment in the presence of any doubt or ambiguity) would negate the principle of *istiṣḥāb* (continuity) of the subject matter. This, in turn, would result in a change of ruling in accordance with the Prophet's instruction that the *ḥudūd* punishment lapses if any doubt is present. And what doubt is stronger than that which arises from a change of the subject matter? In clear words, the three punishments of execution, separation from the spouse and nulling the property ownership are the injunction concerning apostasy with belligerency against the state; but apostasy as individual conversion does not have any temporal punishment. These two apostasies are homonyms (*al-mushtarak al-lafẓī*). The profound difference of these two homonyms should be kept in mind.

The invalidity of *al-khabar al-wāḥid* in matters of critical importance

So far, we have attempted to establish and prove the following: The ruling on sentencing apostates and blasphemers to death has no Qurʾanic basis; there is no reliable evidence that the Prophet sentenced anyone to any punishment solely for apostasy; the cited hadiths are not *mutawātir*; the narrations supporting it are *akhbār al-āḥād* reported by a *thiqa* (trustworthy person); the claim of consensus has no support other than the narrations cited; permission to kill apostates or blasphemers has no stronger proof than *al-khabar al-wāḥid al-thiqa*. It is now time to examine the validity of employing *al-khabar al-wāḥid al-thiqa*[47] as proof for this issue.

The proof that *al-khabar al-wāḥid al-thiqa* is inadequate in critical matters goes as follows.

> Premise 1: The most important evidence – indeed the only proof – for the validity of *al-khabar al- wāḥid* is the conventions of 'reasonable people' (*sīrat al- ʿuqalāʾ*).

Premise 2: Reasonable people do not rely upon *akhbār al-āḥād*, which have a likelihood of being false; rather, they seek 'certainty' in vital and critical matters. In other words, *al-khabar al-wāḥid al-thiqa* cannot be adduced as proof in such matters.[48]

Premise 3: The life of a human being constitutes an important and critical matter. Thus, issuing a death sentence based on *al-khabar al-wāḥid al-thiqa* is unacceptable.[49] Al-Muhaqqiq al-Hilli writes, 'It is dangerous to rely on *al-khabar al-wāḥid* for important and critical matters like sentencing someone to death.'[50]

Conclusion: To pass such a ruling, a qualified judge requires either a decisive and unquestionable transmitted proof (i.e., an explicit Qur'anic text or an explicit *mutawātir* hadith, or an explicit *khabar al-wāḥid al-thiqa* that is conjoined with definitive contextual indicators), or a decisive rational proof. As such, such a decree of execution cannot be issued merely on the basis of *al-khabar al-wāḥid al-thiqa*, even if the narration is *ṣaḥīḥ* and all of the transmitters in all generations are considered trustworthy.

It should be clarified that for reasonable people, human life and the human being itself occupy the top tier of importance; honour and dignity would be on the second tier. Imam ʿAli's inspiring and stunning epistle to Malik al-Ashtar, 'Beware! Abstain from shedding blood'[51] confirms their view. The proof text on the prohibition of robbing people of their honour and dignity manifests the same truth. Scholars who refer to 'important matters in the estimation of the Legislator, like the death penalty and chastity'[52] officially recognize this 'importance' in the Shariʿa according to reasonable people.

Things that the Prophet is known to have prescribed, on the basis of reliable proofs, as lawful or prohibited in perpetuity, must remain effective until the Day of Judgment. However, what relation does this have with the derived rulings, which are only presumptive (*ẓannī*) and have proven to be unreliable? The legal rulings are nothing more than a means and a path, not the subject itself. The jurists' fatwas are meant to help one walk this path; however, they are neither sacrosanct nor infallible. It goes without saying that reasonable people hold the jurists responsible for investigating and analysing everything that is relevant to the penal provisions. God willing, their rulings agree with the will of the Wise Legislator. However, imitating past jurists and considering doing so to be *ijtihād* is definitely against precaution and *ijtihād*. Another way of phrasing the same principle is 'the necessity of exercising precaution in matters that lead to death'.

The invalidity of hadiths contrary to Qur'anic dictates

We have learned that *al-khabar al-wāḥid* is not authoritative in matters of critical importance, including the death penalty. But there is a very essential condition for the authoritativeness (*ḥujjiyya*) of any hadith, including *al-khabar al-wāḥid*: The hadith should not be contrary to the Qur'anic dictates.[53]

Argumentation

This part is devoted to demonstrating that the hadith reports on apostasy fail to meet the standard of evidence because they do not conform to the Qur'an. The argument proceeds as follows:

> Premise 1: The primary justifications that support executing an apostate are *al-akhbār al-āḥād*.
>
> Premise 2: These hadiths do not conform to the explicit Qur'anic verses (*al-nuṣūṣ al-muḥkamāt*).[54]
>
> Premise 3: Every hadith[55] that does not conform to the explicit Qur'anic verses must be rejected.
>
> Conclusion: Hadiths on killing an apostate are rejected because they do not conform to the Qur'anic standards.

The validity of the first premise has been established in the earlier sections: This ruling lacks any support from the Qur'an; the so-called consensus is an *ijmāʿ al-madrakī*, which relies exclusively upon hadiths; and it is primarily based upon *al-akhbār al-āḥād*, some of which contain sound chains of transmission and are considered reliable. The fundamental basis of those who assert the death penalty for an apostate are the hadith reports, which is the first premise. As for the other two premises, they will be established below in this subsection.

The Qur'an is the primary source, followed by the hadith reports of the Prophet[56] (and for the Shiʿa, the subsequent hadiths of the Imams).[57] The essential condition for the latter is that they must be in conformity with the Qur'an as the primary essential source of Islam. This principle relies upon two definitive arguments.

The first argument is a proof from independent rational evidence:

> Premise 1: Internal consistency and harmony is a rational condition justifiable in all doctrines.
>
> Premise 2: The Qur'an is the foundational and preeminent source of Islam.[58]
>
> Conclusion: Everything other than the Qur'an in the name of Islam, including the hadith reports of the Prophet and the Imams, the Companions, and the consensus, should not conflict with explicit Qur'anic verses (*al-nuṣūṣ al-muḥkamāt*).

The first premise, that two contradictory things cannot be united, is a self-evident rational truth confirmed by the Qur'an and the hadith reports. Premise 2 comprises *a priori* aspects of Islam and is based upon *mutawātir* hadiths and clear consensus. The conclusion of this reasoning is decisive and definitive. This independent argumentation is different from those based on the hadith reports to follow.[59]

The second argument is based on a narrative principle (*al-qāʿida al-naqliyya*) in Prophetic tradition (as well as the tradition of the Imams for Shiʿi Islam). The Prophet conveyed the following principle: 'Present every hadith report that you hear ascribed to me to the Book of God. If it conforms to it, then act upon it. If not, then it is not from me but has been falsely ascribed to me.'[60] The Sunni jurists did not accept this principle and challenged the authenticity of the related hadiths and described them as fabricated (*mawḍūʿ* or *majʿūl*).[61] It is not clear what should be done with hadiths that are explicitly contrary to the Qurʾanic doctrine.[62] Denying the existence of such hadiths[63] is not acceptable.

The Shiʿi sources narrated the prophetic tradition in four hadiths with different chains of transmitters (in seven sources)[64] as well as the tradition of the Imams. It is clear that in the Shiʿi school the authoritativeness of Prophetic hadiths is conditional on the absence of absolute conflict with the explicit Qurʾanic verses (*al-nuṣūṣ al-muḥkamāt*) and that the authoritativeness of the Shiʿa Imams' hadith reports is also conditional on their conformity with the definitive prophetic traditions (*al-nuṣūṣ al-mutāwatira*). They have commanded that a tradition ascribed to them must first be presented to the Qurʾan and, if found to be in conflict with it, rejected as false and absurd because it does not originate from them. I will cite here a sample of such traditions that were narrated from Imam Sadiq through authentic chains of transmitters. It is narrated on the authority of Jamil b. Darraj: 'Whatever conforms to the Book of God, hold fast to it, and abandon whatever conflicts with the Book of God.'[65]

This principle is based on at least thirty-four narrations in at least twenty separate hadiths. Fifteen of these hadiths are narrated by the three Shiʿi hadith masters (*al-mashāyikh al-thalātha*) in all of the four major Shiʿi hadith compilations. It means that these hadiths are *mutawātir al-maʿnawī*.[66] The *mutawātir* hadith produces certainty (*al-yaqīn*), not conjecture (*al-ẓann*).

The principle of 'the invalidity of hadith contrary to Qurʾanic dictates' has been mentioned as a definite principle of Islamic teachings and introduced and applied by the most prominent Shiʿi hadith compilers or jurists. It is clear that this principle was a definite principle of the validity of hadiths since the early time of Shiʿi Islam.

The non-conformity of the hadiths on killing an apostate with explicit Qurʾanic verses

Those hadith reports that sanction death for an apostate must be in harmony with the Qurʾan, or at least not conflict with explicit Qurʾanic verses, to be considered evidential proofs. It is now an opportune time to respond to a fundamental question: Are the hadith reports on executing an apostate in harmony or conflict with the Qurʾanic verses? The verses speak of a punishment waiting in the Hereafter and an existential non-physical punishment in this world, namely, stripping him/her of divine guidance and forgiveness, as well as nullifying all of his/her good deeds. Clearly, these hadith reports are not in accord with the verses. Are they contradictory, then? If we were to consider the verses to be general in nature and not restrict them to punishment for an apostate, then there would be no contradiction for, at most, we could say that these verses are talking about punishments in the Hereafter and that the hadith reports are talking about this world. But if the punishments pointed out in the Qurʾan are the maximum limits set specifically for apostates, then the verses and hadith reports would contradict each other, for the verses negate temporal punishment whereas the hadith reports confirm it.

Do the verses on apostasy specify these maximum limits of punishment for an apostate? They appear to do so, based on the following core contextual evidence: First, the Legislator in this case legislates for a sin that occurs frequently, which requires maximum limits (*ḥaṣr*) and scope. If something were supposed to be added to it later on, a notice would have been given in the form of an expression like 'God may perhaps bring about a new command' (65:1), but the Qur'an did not give any notice in this case. Second, the fact that other types of verses mention freedom of religion confirms that there are no temporal punishments for apostasy. This is a good pointer in favour of the limits placed on such punishments. Conclusion: Those hadith reports that condemn an apostate to death are in clear opposition to the Qur'anic verses.

Conclusions derived from the Qur'anic evidence

When the hadiths on execution of apostates are invalidated because they are contrary to the Qur'anic dictates, we should refer to the conclusion of our survey of the Qur'an above: Islam, the true religion, has introduced its creed and belief system to the people in the clearest and most unambiguous way, along with a reminder of the perversion and adverse effects caused by leaning toward falsehood. Islam proclaims that human beings can attain true prosperity by following it, and severely denounces any deviation from it. From Islam's perspective, people are free to choose their religion. Islam gives other religions an official status after inviting their adherents to choose it, in the sense that some will accept it and others will not. According to Islam, anyone who rejects it out of obstinacy and stubbornness and opts to follow the wrong path will be punished in the Hereafter. Islam prescribes no temporal punishment for following a wrong belief system. The logic of Islam, when it comes to inviting others to the faith, is to use a rational approach that is peaceful, compassionate and non-dogmatic. One cannot be forced not to convert. Apostasy carries no temporal punishment; however, if accompanied by animosity and stubbornness, then the person will be severely chastised in the Hereafter. Bearing all of these points in mind, it becomes clear that Islam has enshrined freedom of religion and, as such, all hadith reports on killing an apostate conflict with the Qur'anic verses. As this is one of the most important arguments of this chapter, I have discussed it in greater detail.

Abrogation of the punishments for apostasy and 'impairing' Islam

What constitutes *wahn,* 'impairing' Islam, is deduced from a totality of proofs, just like *ḍarūra* (necessity, exigency); it is not to be found in the Qur'an or transmitted narrations. To define the criteria, the conventional practice of reasonable people in each particular age must remain the yardstick of that time. In our own time, the majority of reasonable people, both believers and unbelievers, would regard the following acts as defacing the visage of Islam: Enslaving the women and children of those who fought against the Muslims in a war; stoning; executing apostates; burning a living person; hurling a person from a high altitude such as mountain; demolishing a house with the occupants inside; crucifying; amputating an alternate hand and foot, amputating fingers; flogging; carrying out retaliation (*qisās*) of the organs such as literal 'eye-for-an-eye' retribution and throwing acid in someone's face as reciprocity (*muqābala bi al-mithl*); and husbands striking their wives. Most of these actions, which can be found in criminal laws, can clearly be said to deface the visage of Islam by making it appear to be violent, repulsive, brutal and distant from mercy and compassion. And so instead of honouring and respecting the divine rulings, such rulings repulse people and make them fear Islam.

To be sure, the standard of what constitutes 'weakening and impairing Islam' has changed over time, due to changing customs and conventions. Thus, based on the mentality of the contemporary world, both believers and unbelievers, one can surmise that they would not accept such violent punishments. In general, the era of physical punishments is over and has been replaced by one of imprisonment, social boycott, fines, and rehabilitation. Undoubtedly, enslaving individuals is repugnant and indefensible. Although this was acceptable in the past, it is condemned by our own era's reasoning and moral standards. The criteria of reasonable people have changed over time, as the (formally) discontinued practices of slavery and physical punishments show.

An increase in incidents that one can consider as defacing and weakening Islam at any given time implies that the public reasoning of Islam has diminished. This gradually deepens the cleavage between religion and reasonableness. There are three possible causes: (1) the principles of reasonableness have diverged from the truth, (2) our definition and interpretation of Islam was wrong, or (3) neither of them was reliable. Undoubtedly, generalizing a ruling in every case is not correct, for in each domain one needs to take into account the premises of reasonable people and the principal tenets of Islam. After researching this subject from several perspectives, I concluded that all of the criteria that I have specified above are present in the domain of human rights. I have candidly written that the premises of reasonable people in the modern period are superior to the fatwas of pre-modern jurists.[67] This does not pertain to the divine rulings. This superiority relates to those *apparent* legal rulings (*al-hukm al-ẓāhirī*) that have incorrectly been attached to the *fiqh*, and therefore have no connection with the *actual* divine judgments (*al-ḥukm al-wāqiʿī*).

This is not a rebuke of the Qurʾan and Sunna as the source of such fatwas, for these fatwas were justifiable – but at a different time and in a different place. If any fault exists, it has to be attributed to those jurists who removed specific Qurʾanic verses and narrations from their contexts, de-historicized them and clamoured for the generalization (*taʿmīm*), absolutization (*iṭlāq*) and continuity (*dawām*) of those rulings, disregarding their historicity. If the fatwas of al-Mufid (948–1022), al-Tusi (995–1067), al-Muhaqqiq al-Hilli (1205–77), al-Shahid al-Awwal (1334–85), al-Muhaqqiq al-Karaki (1466–1534) and al-Shahid al-Thani (1506–57) were sufficient and appropriate in their own times for the objectives set out, one is not justified in imitating them and their rulings within the context of a very different time and place, one in which the standards of reasonable people have substantially changed. In the case of mere apostasy (i.e., not linked with any other crimes), Islam would be defaced by any form of temporal punishment – not to mention execution, life imprisonment with penal servitude and physical punishment (flogging). Based on the standards of contemporary reasonable people, punishing apostasy in any way violates the inherent right to freedom of religion. Hence, what is at issue here is the very notion of temporal punishment and, even more so, allowing anyone to kill a person who has been deemed guilty of apostasy under the label of 'one whose blood may be shed with impunity' (*mahdūr al-dam*).

Wahn as primary injunction (*al-ḥukm al-awwalī*) means taking account of the change of standards among reasonable people. *Wahn* targets the previous legal injunction itself, not its implementation in a particular time and place. A temporal punishment, in particular killing apostates and especially allowing anyone who has heard them apostatize to kill them, in and of itself leads to *wahn*. Such a ruling is founded on an erroneous deduction. Even if no error were made, the ruling was still limited to a specific time when it was conventional to render such punishments. Clearly this is not the case today. That is, such an injunction was temporary, ephemeral and subject to change.

The Legislator has prescribed no specific temporal punishment for changing one's religion, and absolutely no punishment (whether temporal or in the afterlife) for erring in one's research. But apostasy based on obstinacy or wickedness (*ʿinād, jaḥd*) will require severe punishment on the Day of Judgment. On this basis, being certain that *wahn* will be generated means that the time of validity of the previous ruling is over; i.e., it is abrogated. Even if the theory of confining the authenticity of *akhbār al-āḥād* to non-critical matters is not accepted, the indications of prohibition of *wahn* destroy the validity of narrations on the death penalty for the apostate as a primary injunction. In my estimation, invoking prohibition of *wahn* under the rubric of primary injunction is a contextual indicator of an error in the ruling's deduction from the proofs pertaining to killing apostates.

Conclusion

We found a paradox in Islamic literature concerning the criminalization of and severe punishments for apostasy. These severe punishments are the execution of the apostate, the annulment of his/her marriage, and liquidation of his/her property. These are generally the subject of consensus in all five legal schools. These fatwas are based on a couple of hadiths presented as *ṣaḥīḥ* (authentic) according to the criteria of *ʿilm al-rijāl* (the science of the qualification of the narrators of hadiths).

The above review of all relevant verses of the Qur'an, analysed into four types, demonstrated that the Qur'an prescribes no punishment for deliberative and knowledge-based apostasy in either world. However, such a person will clearly be deprived of the blessings connected with having attained an understanding of the Truth and implementing its values. As for 'political and action-based apostasy', the prescribed punishment in the afterlife takes the form of eternal punishment in the hellfire. The Qur'an neither mentions nor prescribes any temporal punishment for apostasy. The Qur'an strongly advocates the freedom of religion and is very clear in its negation of force and coercion in the matter of religion and belief. According to careful research and examination of all the historical evidence, it is clear that no one during the time of the Prophet was killed solely for apostasy (i.e. change of religion). Rather, when killings took place, it was for some other transgression. Apostasy, at his time, was not confined to changing one's religion or belief system. Killing was the consequence of several political issues that were inseparable at the time, such as becoming a belligerent or an enemy of the community.

The first killing related to apostasy happened in 632–3 after the death of the Prophet, in the events of *ridda*, the conflict with those who did not want to pay the *zakāt* (tax). They were not executed after a trial, but were killed in the battlefield. Nothing was said at that time about separation from their spouses, the liquidation of their property or killing them for changing their religion! All the hadiths on apostasy appeared later. One may think of them as seeking to preserve the Islamic identity through severe punishments for political apostasy. Anyway, I take the hadiths and consensuses as 'hypotheses' and do not challenge them. Instead, I have focused on two procedures in Jaʿfari *fiqh* for restricting and removing these severe punishments.

The first procedure runs in the framework of traditional *ijtihād*. I describe three approaches for restricting the punishments for apostasy. The first approach was the suspension of the *ḥudūd* in the time of Occultation in three ways: full suspension of the *ḥudūd*, discontinuation of the *ḥudūd* in cases leading to death or injury, and suspension of the *ḥudūd* in the present day. In practice, the first and third ways are the same. All punishments for apostasy, including capital punishment, would be suspended according to the first and third approach, whereas the second approach suspends the capital punishment, but not the other two punishments. Many outstanding Shiʿi jurists including al-Muhaqqiq al-Hilli, al-ʿAllama al-Hilli, al-Muhaqqiq al-Ardabili, and al-Muhaqqiq al-Khansari believed in this approach. It means stopping executions from the tenth century until close to the end of the world.

The second approach is the suspension of executions for apostasy on the grounds that they impair the visage of Islam, under the rubric of secondary injunction. A secondary injunction could be based on at least three specific situations: necessity (*ḍarūra*), expediency (*maṣlaḥa*), and governmental rule (*al-ḥukm al-ḥukumī*). This approach was followed as a check and balance by the governmental clerics in post-revolutionary Iran. The third approach was the innovation of Ayatollah Montazeri. By narrowing the situational context of the ruling on apostasy, his approach would render the implementation of religiously sanctioned punishments extremely difficult and rare. Moreover, the judge has the discretion to forgive any person found guilty of defaming the Prophet. The severe punishment for apostasy has to be administered via the judicial system after it has established that the accused intended to make a mockery of religion and incite a rebellion. Montazeri recognized that changing one's religion and rejecting the essentials of religion (*ḍarūriyyāt*), on some conditions, would not trigger any temporal punishment. Although his innovations were good starting points, they did not remove the punishments for apostasy absolutely.

According to constructional *ijtihād*, or *ijtihād* in principles and foundations, the end of abolishing all types of temporal punishments for apostasy, especially execution, and removing apostasy from the list of crimes can be achieved through at least four formulas. The first formula is acknowledgement of the alteration of the subject and context. The subject of apostasy in early Islam was not solely changing one's religion, it was changing one's religion in conjunction with carrying out public and political propaganda as a belligerent. This broader subject was the subject of those severe punishments. But in the modern time, apostasy as individual conversion is not a crime and there is no temporal punishment for it. These two apostasies are homonyms. The deep difference of these two homonyms should be kept in mind.

The second formula is focusing on the invalidity of *akhbār al-āḥād* in matters of critical importance. The only evidence for the validity of *akhbār al-āḥād* is the conventions of 'reasonable people'. Reasonable people do not rely upon *akhbār al-āḥād*, which have a likelihood of being false; rather, they seek 'certainty' on such vital and critical matters. In other words, *khabar al-wāḥid al-thiqa* cannot be adduced as proof in such matters. The life of a human being constitutes an important and critical matter. Thus, issuing a death sentence based on *khabar al-wāḥid al-thiqa* is unacceptable. According to this formula, then, all the hadiths on executing the apostate are invalidated. It is a very important achievement.

The third formula is highlighting the invalidity of hadiths that run counter to Qur'anic dictates. Every hadith that does not conform to the Qur'an must be rejected. Hadiths on killing an apostate are rejected because they do not conform to the Qur'an. I have proved through several arguments that those hadith reports which condemn an apostate to death are in opposition to the Qur'anic verses. In a conflict between hadith and clear Qur'anic principle, the hadiths lose their required conditions. So, this supports a strong statement: the hadiths on executing the apostate are invalid.

The fourth and last formula is the abrogation of the punishments for apostasy because of *wahn*, or 'impairing' Islam, as a primary injunction. If any fault exists, it has to be attributed to those jurists who removed specific Qur'anic verses and narrations from their contexts and de-historicized them. Based on the standards of contemporary reasonable people, punishing apostasy in any way violates the inherent right to freedom of religion.

If these four formulas fail to remove the punishment for apostasy, which, in my estimation, has been abolished completely, the situation at the least gives rise to a preponderance of doubt and ambiguity. As such, the helpful Prophetic principle of *dar'* (the lapse of the *ḥudūd* punishment in the presence of any doubt or ambiguity) would negate any punishment.

Notes

1 This chapter is the product of my reaction to two events discussed in the two presentations 'Apostasy/ insulting the Prophet: a sin, not a crime' and 'The rules of apostasy and blasphemy: rules of an old-fashioned paradigm, not rules of Islam' (Oslo Coalition on Freedom of Religion or Belief: New Directions in Islamic Thought Project, First international workshop: Oslo, January 2013, second international workshop: Istanbul, September 2013). Meanwhile, I have published a web-book in Persian on this issue: *Mujazat-e Ertedad wa Azadi-ye Mazhab: Naqd-e Mujazat-e Ertedad wa Sabb al-Nabi ba Mawazin-e Feqh-e Estedlali* (Apostasy, blasphemy and religious freedom in Islam: A critique based on demonstrative jurisprudence), Islam and Human Rights Series (No. 2), (July 2014, 406 pages). Hamid Mavani (Associate Professor of Islamic Studies at Bayan Claremont Islamic Graduate School / Claremont School of Theology in California) has translated the whole book into English. This

new edition will be published soon by Edinburgh University Press as *Blasphemy and Apostasy in Islam: Debates on Shi'a Jurisprudence*. This chapter is a succinct statement of the argument of the first edition with some additions (19 November 2018).

2 Wahba al-Zuhayli, *al-Fiqh al-Islāmī wa Adillatuhu* (Damascus: Dar al-Fikr, 1996), vol. 6, pp. 181–86; Vol. 7, p. 62.

3 Ruhollah Khomeini, *Taḥrīr al-Wasīla* (Damascus: Iranian Embassy in Syria, 1998), vol. 2, pp. 334, 450–51.

4 Al-Bukhari: 6922, Ahmad b. Hanbal: 1871, al-Tirmidhi: 1458, Abu Dawud: 4351, Ibn Maja: 2536, al-Nisa'i: 4059.

5 Husayn al-Nuri al-Tabrasi, *Mustadrak al-Wasā'il* (Qom: Mu'assasat al-Al al-Bayt, 1988), vol. 18, p. 163; Abu Hanifa al-Qadi al-Nu'man b. Muhammad al-Tamimi al-Maghribi, *Da'ā'im al-Islām wa Dhikr al-Ḥalāl wa al-Ḥarām*, ed. Asif b. 'Ali Asghar Faydi (Cairo: Dar al-Ma'arif, 1965), vol. 2, p. 480.

6 Al-Bukhari: 6878, al-Muslim: 1676.

7 Such as Abu al-Salah al-Halabi, *al-Kāfī fī al-Fiqh*, ed. Reza Ustadi (Isfahan: Maktabat al-Imam Amir al-Mu'minin al-'Ammah, 1983), p. 250; Qutb al-Din al-Bayhaqi al-Kaydari, *Iṣbāḥ al-Shī'a bi Maṣābiḥ al-Sharī'a*, ed. Ibrahim al-Bahadari (Qom: Mu'assasat al-Imam al-Sadiq, 1996), p. 191; Ali b. al-Hassan b. Abi al-Majd al-Ḥalabi, *Ishārat al-Sabq*, ed. Ibrahim al-Bahadari (Qom: Mu'assasat al-Nashr al-Islami, 1994), p. 144; Yahya b. Sa'id al-Hilli, *al-Jāmi' li al-Sharā'i'*, ed. Ja'far Sobhani (Qom: Mu'assasat Sayyid al-Shuhada', 1985), p. 240; Abu Ja'far Muhammad b. al-Hassan al-Tusi, *al-Khilāf* (Qom: Mu'assasat al-Nashr al-Islami, 1987), vol. 5, pp. 501–5; id., *al-Mabsūṭ*, ed. Muhammad Taqi al-Kashfi (Tehran: al-Maktabat al-Murtadawiyya li Ihya' al-Athar al-Ja'fariyya, 1999), vol. 8, pp. 71–4.

8 Such as al-Tusi, *al-Mabsūṭ*, vol. 7, p. 281; id., *al-Khilāf*, vol. 5, p. 351; and al-Shahid al-Awwal Muhammad b. al-Makki, *al-Durūs al-Shar'iyya* (Qom: Mu'assasat al-Nashr al-Islami, 1992), vol. 2, p. 5.

9 Muhammad b. Hasan al-Hurr al-'Amili, *Wasā'il al-Shī'a* (Qom: Mu'assasat Al al-Bayt li Ihya' al-Turath, 1993), vol. 28, pp. 323–56; al-Nuri, *Mustadrak al-Wasā'il*, vol. 18, pp. 163–88.

10 The narrations by 'Ali b. Ja'far from Imam Kazim, Muhammad b. Muslim from Imam Baqir, Hasan b. Mahbub from Imams Baqir and Sadiq, and 'Ammar Sabati from Imam Sadiq (all of them in *al-Kāfī*); Husayn b. Sa'id from Imam Rida (*Tahdhīb* and *Istibsār*); Muhammad b. Muslim from Imam Baqir (*Faqīh*); 'Ibad b. Suhayb from Imam Sadiq (*Tahdhīb* and *Istibsār*); and Sakuni from Imam Sadiq (*Faqīh*). al-Hurr al-'Amili, *Wasā'il al-Shī'a*, vol. 28, pp. 323–56.

11 Al-Hurr al-'Amili, *Wasā'il al-Shī'a*, vol. 28, p. 324 no. 3.

12 Ibid., pp. 323–4, no. 2.

13 Ibid., p. 325, no. 5–6.

14 Ibid., p. 328, no. 5.

15 Abu al-Qasim al-Musawi al-Khu'i, *Mabānī Takmilat al-Minhāj* (Najaf: Mata'a al-Adab, 1976), vol. 1, pp. 324–37.

16 Muhammad Baqir al-Sadr, *Buḥūth fī 'Ilm al-Uṣūl*, compiled by Mahmmud Hashimi (Najaf, 1976), vol. 4, p. 327, 332; al-Shahid al-Thani Zayn al-Din b. 'Ali, *al-Ri'āya fī 'Ilm al-Dirāya*, ed. 'Abd al-Husayn Muhammad 'Ali Baqqal (Qom: Maktabat Ayatollah al-'Uzma al-Mar'ashi al-Najafi, 1988), p. 62.

17 Al-Hassan al-Tabrasi, *Majma' al-Bayān fī Tafsīr al-Qur'ān* (Beirut: Mu'assasat al-A'lami li al-Matbu'at, 1994), vol. 3, pp. 363–64.

18 Abu al-Qasim al-Musawi al-Khu'i, *al-Bayān fī Tafsīr al-Qur'ān* (Beirut: Dar al-Zahra', 1975), pp. 307–9; Muhammad Husayn al-Tabataba'i, *al-Mīzān fī Tafsīr al-Qur'ān* (Qom: Jama'at al-Mudarrisin fi al-Hawzat al-'Ilmiyya, 1992), vol. 10, p. 207.

19 Hossein 'Ali Montazeri, *Ḥukūmat-e Dīnī va Ḥuqūq-e Insān* (Tehran: Sara'i, 2007), pp. 88–9.

20 Ibid., p. 91.

21 The *Sunan* of Dar al-Qutni states, 'It is said that during the Battle of Badr, a Muslim woman apostatized and that the Prophet ordered others to seek her repentance and to kill her if she refused.' 'Ali b. 'Amr al-Dar al-Qutni, *al-Sunan*, ed. Majdi b. Mansur b. Sayyid al-Shura (Beirut: Dar al-Kutub al-'Ilmiyya, 1996), vol. 3, p. 119, no. 121. This narration has been reported through a number of channels. In one of them, Muhammad b. 'Abd al-Malik Ansari is present. One can read in the margins: 'Ahmad and others have said that Muhammad b. 'Abd al-Malik used to fabricate narrations.' (Ibid.) The same text is related through another hadith by way of Jabir b. 'Abdullah; however, in the margins it says that 'Abdullah Udhaina is mentioned in the chain of transmission, about whom Ibn Huban writes: 'Under no circumstances can one rely upon hadiths related by him.' Dar al-Qutni says, 'His narrations should be abandoned' (ibid.) and Ibn 'Addi writes, '[Any] hadith related by 'Abdullah Udhaina has to be rejected . . .' (ibid., no. 125). Another narration, with Jabir b. 'Abdullah in the chain, says that Umm Marwan apostatized and that the Prophet ordered others to explain Islam to her. If she refused to repent after that, she should be killed. However, in the margins of the same book it says, 'Mu'ammar b. Bakkar is present in the chain of transmission. Al-'Uqili [Muhammad b. 'Amr] and al-Dhai'ali ['Abdullah b. Yusif] have determined that he composes hadith based upon conjecture and delusion. Muhammad b. 'Abd al-Malik is also present. Bayhaqi, who relates this hadith through two channels, says that both of them are *ḍa'īf* (ibid., no. 118 and 122). Apparently, these three hadiths deal with the same subject. As their respective chains of transmission are weak, they cannot be relied upon (ibid., no. 96 and 97).

22 'Abd al-Karim Musawi Ardabili, *Fiqh al-Ḥudūd wa al-Ta'zīrāt* (Qom: Intisharat Daneshghah Mufid, 2005), vol. 4, p. 4.

23 Ardabili, *Fiqh al-Ḥudūd*, vol. 4, p. 5.

24 Al-Tusi, *al-Mabsūṭ*, vol. 7, pp. 267–8.

25 See Muhammad b. Jarir al-Tabari, *Tārīkh al-Rusul wa al-Mulūk*, ed. Muhammad Abu al-Fadl (Egypt: Dar al-Ma'arif, 1983), vol. 3, pp. 225–42 for the details of the *ridda* struggle. English translation: al-Tabari, *The Conquest of Arabia: The Riddah Wars A.D. 632-633/A.H. 11,* transl. Fred McGraw Donner, SUNY Series in Near Eastern Studies: The History of al-Tabari (Albany: SUNY Press, 1993), vol. 10.

26 This is the subject of another comprehensive research beyond the scope of this chapter. I take the authenticity of the hadiths on punishment for apostasy (the claim of jurists and people of *'ilm al-rijāl*) as a 'hypothesis' and do not challenge it here.

27 Ardabili, *Fiqh al-Ḥudūd*, vol. 4, p. 17.

28 Mus'ada b. Ziyad relates an authentic report on the authority of Imam Ja'far Sadiq, who relates it from his father, Imam Muhammad Baqir: '(During his caliphate) Imam 'Ali never accused those who fought against him of polytheism or hypocrisy. Rather, he would say, "They are our brothers who have wronged us and caused oppression."' 'Abdullah b. Ja'far Himayri, *Qurb al-Asnād* (Qom: Mu'assasat Al al-Bayt li Ihya' al-Turath, 1993), p. 45; al-Hurr al-'Amili, *Wasā'il al-Shī'a*, vol. 15, p. 83.

29 'Ali b. Husayn al-Muhaqqiq al-Karaki, *Rasā'il*, ed. Muhammad al-Hassun (Qom: Maktaba al-Mar'ashi al-Najafi, 1988), vol. 1, pp. 142–3.

30 Muhammad b. Muhammad b. Nu'man al-Mufid, *al-Muqni'a* (Qom: Mu'assasat al-Nashr al-Islami, 1990), p. 810.

31 Abu Ja'far Muhammad b. al-Hassan Al-Tusi, *al-Tibyān*, ed. Ahmad Habib Qusayr al-Amili (Beirut: Dār Ihyā' al-Turath al-'Arabī, 1989), vol. 7, p. 407; al-Qadi 'Abd al-'Aziz Ibn al-Barraj, *al-Muhadhdhab* (Qom: Mu'assasat al-Nashr al-Islami, 1986), vol. 1, pp. 341–2; vol. 2, p. 518; al-Tabrasi, *Majma' al-bayān fī tafsīr al-Qur'ān* (Beirut: Mu'assasat al-A'lami li al-Matbu'at, 1994), vol. 7, p. 219; Qutb al-Din Sa'id b. Hibatullah al-Rawandi, *Fiqh al-Qur'ān*, ed. 'Abbas Bani Hashimi Bidguli (Qom: Manshurat Imamat Ahl al-Bayt, 2015), vol. 2, p. 422; Ibn Sa'id al-Hilli, *al-Jāmi' li al-Sharā'i'*, p. 548; Ibn Fahd al-Hilli, *al-Muhadhdhab al-Bāri' fī sharḥ al-Mukhtaṣar al-Nāfi'*, ed. Mujtaba al-'Araghi (Qom: Mu'assasat al-Nashr al-Islami, 1987), vol. 2, pp. 326–27.

32 Muhammad b. Ahmad al-Hilli ibn Idris, *al-Sarā'ir al-Ḥāwī li Taḥrīr al-Fatāwā* (Qom: Mu'assasat al-Nashr al-Islami, 1989), vol. 2, pp. 24–25.

33 Nizam al-Din Sawiji (d. 1037), the student of Shaykh Baha'i (d. 1030), in *Jāmi'-i 'Abbāsī* (Tehran: Farahan, n.d.), p. 162; al-Fadil al-Hindi Baha' al-Din Muhammad b. al-Hasan al-Isfahani (d. 1138) in *Kashf al-Lithām* (Qom: Mu'assasat al-Nashr al-Islami, 1995), vol. 10, p. 477; and Ahmad al-Musawi al-Khwansari, *Jāmi' al-Madārik*, ed. 'Ali Akbar Ghaffari (Tehran: Maktabat al-Saduq, 1976), vol. 5, pp. 411–13.

34 Hasan b. Yusuf al-'Allama al-Hilli, *Muntahā al-Maṭlab* (Mashad: Majma' Buhuth al-Islamiya, 2007), vol. 15, pp. 244–5; Ahmad b. Muhammad al-Ardabili, *Majma' al-Fā'ida wa al-Burhān fī Sharḥ Irshād al-Adhhān*, ed. Mujtaba al-'Iraqi, 'Ali Panah al-Ishtihardi and Husayn al-Yazdi (Qom: Mu'assasat al-Nashr al-Islami, 1983), vol. 7, p. 545; Mirza Abu al-Qasim al-Qummi, *Jāmi' al-Shitāt*, ed. Murtada Radavi (Tehran: Kayhan, 1992), vol. 1, pp. 394–5.

35 Ja'far b. Hasan al-Muhaqqiq al-Hilli, *Sharā'i' al-Islām*, ed. al-Sayyid Sadiq al-Shirazi (Tehran: Istiqlal, 1989), vol. 1, pp. 312–13; id., *al-Mukhtaṣar al-Nāfi'* (Tehran: Mu'assasat al-Bi'tha, 1990), p. 115.

36 Hussein 'Ali Montazeri, *Pāsokh beh Porsesh-hā-ye Peyrāmūn Mujāzāthā-ye Islāmī va Ḥuqūq-e Bashar* (Tehran: Sara'i, 2008), p. 35.

37 Ibid., pp. 102–3.

38 Ayatollah Hussein 'Ali Montazeri (1922–2009) was the most distinguished student of Ayatollah Borujerdi and Ayatollah Khomeini, and the second figure of the revolution of 1979 and the Islamic Republic of Iran. Montazeri was one of the Shi'i authorities (*marja'-i taqlīd*) in the Qom seminary from 1984. The Assembly of Experts designated Montazeri as the successor of Ayatollah Khomeini in 1986. After a deep conflict between Khomeini and Montazeri on the human rights and freedoms of the citizens, he resigned three months before the death of Ayatollah Khomeini. After criticizing the administration of Khamene'i, the second leader of Islamic Republic, and disqualifying him as a Shi'i authority (*marja'*), Montazeri was placed illegally under house arrest for more than five years and released in 2003. He was the leading critic of the Islamic Republic for two decades. Montazeri had certain innovative ideas in jurisprudence.

39 Hussein 'Ali Montazeri, *Islām: Dīn-e Feṭrat* (Tehran: Sayeh, 2006), pp. 692–98.

40 Montazeri, *Ḥukūmat-e Dīnī va Ḥuqūq-e Insān*, pp. 130–22.

41 Mohsen Kadivar, 'Ijtihad in usul al-fiqh: Reforming Islamic thought through structural ijtihad,' *Iran Nameh* 30/3 (2015), pp. xx–xxvii (published by University of Toronto, Canada).

42 For example: 'They ask you concerning fighting in the sacred month. Say, "Fighting therein is a grave (transgression), but graver is, in the sight of God, to prevent access to

the path of God, to deny Him, to prevent access to the sacred mosque, and drive out its members. Persecution and sedition (*fitna*) is worse than slaying . . ."' (2:217). 'And a party of the People of the Book say, "Believe in that which has been revealed to those who believe at the opening of the day, and disbelieve at the end thereof, in order that they may revert"' (3:72).

43 A *muḥārib* is an armed robber or gangster. There is no political or religious motive in *muḥāriba*. It is a crime primarily against citizens and society.

44 Montazeri, *Ḥukūmat-e Dīnī va Ḥuqūq-e Insān*, p. 91.

45 Ibid., p. 132.

46 Montazeri, *Pāsokh beh Porsesh-hā-ye Peyrāmūn*, pp. 86–87.

47 Note that *al-khabar al-wāḥid* does not mean a hadith that was narrated by a single person, or a hadith transmitted by a singular transmitter in each generation. Its meaning is a narration of hadith which is not regarded as *mutawātir*. In *mutawātir* the number of narrators in all generations of transmitters is sufficient to accept the authenticity of hadith with certainty, meaning that a common intentional agreement to lie is absolutely impossible. The number of narrators in all generations of transmitters or at least one generation is not enough to accept the authenticity of hadith with certainty. When all narrators of a non-*mutawātir* hadith in all generations are trustworthy persons (*thiqahāt*), this is *al-khabar al-wāḥid al-thiqa* or *al-ḥadīth al-ṣaḥīḥ*. This type of hadith is accounted as valid (*ḥujja*) in *uṣūl al-fiqh*. What I discuss here is the domain of this validity: Is it absolute or does it only include matters of non-critical importance? On the latter view, *al-khabar al-wāḥid al-thiqa* or *al-ḥadīth al-ṣaḥīḥ* is invalid in matters of critical importance.

48 al-Khansari, *Jāmiʿ al-Madārik*, vol. 7, p. 35.

49 Ibid.; see also al-Muhaqqiq al-Ardabili, *Majmaʿ al-Fā'ida*, vol. 13, p. 90.

50 al-Muhaqqiq al-Hilli, *Sharāʾiʿ al-Islām*, vol. 4, p. 114.

51 Al-Sharif al-Radhi, *Nahj al-Balāgha*, letter no. 53, ed. Subhi Salih (Cairo: Dar al-Kitab al-Misri, 2004), p. 443.

52 Murtada al-Ansari, *Farāʾid al-Uṣūl*, ed. Turath al-Shaykh al-ʿAzam (Qom: Majmaʿ al-Fikr al-Islami, 1998), vol. 2, p. 137; cf. Muhammad Kazim al-Khurasani, *Kifāyat al-Uṣūl* (Qom: Muʾassasat Al al-Bayt li Ihya al-Turath), p. 354.

53 Contrary means absolute conflict (*al- taʿāruḍ bi al-tabāyun*) without possibility of any reconciliation (*al-jamʿ al-ʿurfī*) or compromise. So, the possibility of *al-takhṣīṣ li al-ʿāmm*, *al-taqyīd li al-muṭlaq* and *al-tabyīn li al-mujmal* of the Qurʾanic verses by authentic hadiths falls outside our discussion.

54 So, Qurʾanic dictates in this discussion do not include Qurʾanic *ẓawāhir* and *mutashābihāt*. For more clarification, they are restricted first to *muḥkamāt* and second to *al-nuṣūṣ al-muḥkamāt*.

55 For further clarification, it covers the absolute conflict between so-called authentic hadiths (*ṣaḥīḥ al-isnād*) and *nuṣūṣ al-muḥkamāt* of the Qurʾan. This means that it is accepted that we can find some hadiths in authentic transmission contrary to the Qurʾan.

56 It is clear that Prophetic tradition is the second essential source of Islam, as its authoritativeness is explicitly confirmed by the Qurʾan, such as 'Accept whatever the Messenger gives you, and abstain from whatever he forbids you' (59:7) or 'The Prophet is more protective towards the believers than they are themselves' (33:6). The point concerns the domain of validity of this source, which is not absolute in the case of contradiction with the primary source of Islam.

57 The authoritativeness of the Shiʿi Imams' hadiths (as the third source of Islam for Shiʿi Muslims) is also conditional. Any hadith that is in absolute conflict with the explicit

Qur'anic verses (*al-nuṣūṣ al-muḥkamāt*) and explicit Prophetic tradition (*al- nuṣūṣ al-mutāwirāh)* is not authoritative regardless of its chain of transmission. This condition is prior to the condition of the authenticity of the chain of transmission.

58 But it is not the 'only' source of Islam. In contrast to 'scripturalism' (*ḥasbunā kitāb Allāh*), Prophetic tradition is the second essential source of Islam, and the Imams' tradition is the third source for Shi'i Islam.

59 In *uṣūl al-fiqh*, any discussion on the necessity (or not) of conformity to the Qur'an appears in one of three areas: preferring one of the contradictory reports, circumstances under which the condition incorporated into a binding contract is valid, and conditions for attesting to the proof-worthiness of hadiths. The first two issues have been adequately discussed under the section of *al-ta'ādul wa al-tarājiḥ* (balancing of evidence and preferring one over another); the third issue has been discussed in connection with the first issue, not separately. See for example Abu al-Qasim al-Khu'i, *Misbāh al-uṣūl*, written by Muhmmad Sarwar al-Wa'iz al-Husayni al-Bihsudi (Qom: Maktabat al-Dawari, 1996), vol. 3, pp. 407–8; Muhammad Baqir al-Sadr, *Buhūth fī 'ilm al-uṣūl*, written by Mahmud al-Hashimi [al-Shahrudi] (Qom: Da'irat-u Marif al-fiqh al-Islami tibqan li Madhhab-i Ahl al-Bayt, 2005), vol. 7, pp. 315–35.

60 Sunni source: 'Ali b. Abi Bakr al-Haythami al-Misri, *Majma' al-Zawā'id wa Manba' al-Fawā'id*, ed. Muhammad 'Abdul-Qadir Ahmad 'Ata (Beirut: Dar al-Kutub al-'Ilmiyya, 2001), Vol. 1, p. 230. Shi'i sources: Ahmad b. Muhammad b. Khalid al-Barqi, *al-Maḥāsin*, ed. Jalal al-Din al-Husayni (al-Muhaddith) (Tehran: Dar al-Kutub al-Islamiyya, 1952), vol. 1, p. 221; Muhammad b. Ya'qub al-Kulayni, *al-Kāfī*, ed. 'Ali Akbar Ghaffari (Tehran: Dar al-Kutub al-Islamiyya, 1968), vol. 1, p. 69, no. 5.

61 Muhammad b. Idris Al-Shafi'i, *al-Risāla*, ed. Ahmad Muhammad Shakir (Egypt, 1938), pp. 224–25; 'Ali b. Ahmad ibn Hazm, *al-Iḥkām fī Uṣūl al-Aḥkām*, ed. Ahmad Muhammad Shakir (Beirut: Dar al-Afaq al-Jadida, [1979]), vol. 2, pp. 76–82; Ahmad b. al-Hussain al-Bayhaqi, *Ma'rifat al-Sunan wa al-Athār*, ed. 'Abdul-Mu'ti Amin Qal'aji (Cairo: Dar al-Wafa', 1991), vol. 1, pp. 116–17.

62 Listing these so-called authentic hadiths in the major hadith books (such as *Ṣiḥāḥ al-sitta* and *al-Kutub al-arba'a*) of both Sunni and Shi'a is beyond the purpose of this chapter.

63 Ibn Hazm, *al-Iḥkām fī Uṣūl al-Aḥkām*, vol. 2, p. 81.

64 *Hadith of al-Sakuni:* al-Kulayni, *al-Kāfī*, vol. 1, p. 69, no. 1; Muhammad b. Muhammad al-Mufid, *Risālat fī al-Mahr*, ed. Mahdi Najaf (Qom: al-Mu'tamar al'Alami li alfiya al-Shaykh al-Mufid, 1992), p. 28 (the name of al-Sakuni is not mentioned, but the content is closely similar). *Hadith of Ayub:* al-Barqi, *al-Maḥāsin*, vol. 1, p. 221, no. 131. *Hadith of Hisham b. al-Hakam:* al-Kulayni, *al-Kāfī*, vol. 1, p. 69, no. 5; al-Barqi, *al-Maḥāsin*, vol. 1, p. 221, no. 130; Muhammad b. Mas'ud al-Samarqandi al-'Ayyashi, *Tafsīr al-'Ayyashī* (Qom: Mu'assasat al-Bi'tha, 2000), vol. 1, p. 82, no. 1. Muhammad b. al-Hassan al-Tusi, *Tahdhīb al-aḥkām*, ed. Hassan al-Musawi al-Kharsan (Tehran: Dar al-Kutub al-Islamiyya, 1985), vol. 7, p. 275. The content (*matn*) of the third hadith is the same as the content of the authentic hadith on the authority of Jamil b. Darraj (next footnote).

65 Sa'id b. Hibatullah al-Rawandi, *Treatise on the transmitters of aḥādith and proofs of their authenticity*, not yet published, reported by Al-Hurr al-'Amili, *Wasā'il al-Shī'a*, vol. 27, p. 119, no. 35. The content of this authentic hadith was narrated by different transmitters in five other books: al-Barqi, *al-Maḥāsin*, vol. 1, p. 225, no. 150; al-Kulayni, *al-Kāfī*, vol. 1, p. 69, no. 1; al-'Ayyashi, *Tafsīr al-'Ayyashī*, Vol. 1, p. 82, no. 1;

Muhammad b. ʿAli b. al-Husayn b. Musa b. Babawayh al-Saduq, *al-Āmālī* (Qom: Muʾassasat al-Biʿtha, 1996), vol. 1, p. 449, no. 18; al-Mufid, *Risālat fī al-Mahr*, p. 28.

66 *Al-ḥadīth* al-*mutawātir* is divided into at least two types: *al-mutawātir al-lafẓī* and *al-mutawātir al-maʿnawī*. The former means that the utterances of the hadith text could be attributed to the Prophet or Imam with certainty. The latter means that although we are not sure about the utterances of the hadith, a specific meaning as the common ground of a series of hadiths could be attributed to the Prophet or Imam with certainty. For more information see Hassan b. Zayn al-Din, *Maʿālim al-Dīn wa Malādh al-Mujtahidīn* (Qom: Muʾassasat al-Nashr al-Islami, n.d.), vol. 1, p. 187.

67 Mohsen Kadivar, 'Human rights and intellectual Islam', in Kari Vogt, Lena Larsen and Christian Moe (eds), *New Directions in Islamic Thought: Exploring Reform and Muslim Tradition* (London: I.B.Tauris, 2009), pp. 47–74.

Index

Aan, Alexander 25
al-ʿAbbas (d. 653) 58
ʿAbbasids 22–3, 54, 63, 76, 181, 184, 216
ʿAbd al-Muʾmin (r. 1147–63) 63
ʿAbd al-Qadir, Faruq 120
ʿAbd al-Rahman II (r. 822–52) 22, 27, 61
ʿAbduh, Muhammad (d. 1905) 41–3, 48
ʿAbdullah, Mohammad Mahdi 120
Abou El Fadl, Khaled 46, 201
abrogation 35–7, 39, 41, 44, 48, 86
    of punishment for apostasy 226, 230
    reversed 45
Abu ʿAbdallah (d. 903) 80
Abu Bakr al-Siddiq (d. 634) 6, 20, 59, 172 n.41, 215
Abu Hanifa (d. 767) 5, 139, 154 n.54
    included in consensus despite differences 90, 96 n.74, 132, 138–43, 145
    on breach of pact 87
    on death penalty for blasphemy 59, 84, 95 n.34, 138
    on *dhimmī* blasphemer 97 n.75, 138–9, 141
    on forced conversion 119
    on repentance 81, 139
Abu Sufyan 20
Abu Yusuf (d. 798) 81, 138–9, 141, 154 n.54
Abu Zayd, Nasr Hamid 1, 6, 117, 204 n.26
academic speech 112, 220
Aceh 160
Afghanistan 3, 12 n.6
al-Afzal (d. 975) 81
Aghajari, Hashem 199, 203 n.23
ahl al-kitāb see People of the Book
Ahl-e-Hadith 134, 137, 143, 149
Ahl-e-Sunnat wa Jamaat 137
Ahmad (d. 855) 59
Ahmad, Ahmad Atif 177
Ahmad, Mirza Ghulam 162
Ahmadiyah *see* Ahmadiyya, in Indonesia
Ahmadiyya
    banned from Hajj 168
    branches of 162
    in Egypt 113, 116
    in Indonesia (Ahmadiyah) 25, 159–60, 162–6
    in Pakistan 10, 152 n.22, 152 n.23, 167–8
    in Saudi Arabia 168
Ahok (Basuki Purnama) 25
ʿAʾisha bint Abi Bakr (d. 678) 60
Al Qaeda 65 n.1
Alavi, Armin 103
Albarrán Iruela, Javier 53
ʿAli b. Abi Talib (d. 661) 30 n.55, 58, 105, 172 n.41, 216, 221, 223, 232 n.28
Ali, Asad 164
Ali, Suryadharma 165, 167
aliran kebatinan (indigenous belief) 163
aliran pemikiran (schools of thought) 168
aliran sesat (deviant sects) 157–8, 160
al-ʿAllama al-Hilli (1250–1325) 217
Almohads 9, 53–5, 62–5
Almoravids 53–5, 64
al-Alusi, Shihab al-Din al-Sayyid Mahmud (1802–54) 41
al-ʿAlwani, Taha Jabir (1935–2016) 47, 200
Amer, Karim 113
American Dilemma 10, 195
Amin, Ma'ruf 165, 168
Aminuddin, Lia (b. 1947) 162, 164
Amman Message (2004) 168–9, 174 n.64
Amnesty International 24, 31 n.60
al-amr bi al-maʿrūf wa al-nahy ʿan al-munkar 160
Anas b. Malik (d. *c.* 712) 59
al-Andalus 54–5, 71 n.86
    blasphemy cases in 61
    see also Spain, Muslim
Andrew and Mario case 118

Andræ, Tor (d. 1947) 53, 66 n.3
Anglo-Muhammadan law 192 n.66
anthropomorphism 76
apologetics 41
apostasy 49, 188 n.7
  centrality of 26, 79, 177, 187, 188 n.5
  civil-law consequences of 1, 3, 9, 112–13, 118, 121, 123–4, 208, 228; *see also* divorce; property and inheritance rights
  court cases on 117, 196; *see also* Iran, apostasy trials in
  death penalty for *see* death penalty, for apostasy
  definition and scope of 87, 208, 221, 229
  discretionary punishment for 123; *see also ta'zīr*
  effects in this world/hereafter 213, 221
  fiṭrī and *millī* 208–11
  intellectually vs. politically motivated 214, 219, 228
  in Iranian penal code 105
  juristic disagreement on 189 n.16, 207–8
  of married women 179, 185–6, 192 n.64, 192 n.68
  public/private (*ẓāhir/bāṭin*) 89
  punishments for 207
  religious error as 160
  removing the punishment of 207–30
  as sin 214
  terms for 6
  as treason, rebellion or hostility 49, 91, 124, 210, 213–15, 219, 221, 228–9; *see also* waging war and spreading corruption
  various deeds seen as 82, 90, 180, 197
  'simple' 88, 90
  see also Prophet Muhammad, dealing with insulters or apostates
'aqīda 160, 162
'Aqil b. Abi Talib 58
'aql 6
Arab Charter of Human Rights 120
al-Ardabili, al-Muhaqqiq (d. 1585) 217, 223, 229
Ardabili, Ayatollah Abdulkarim Musawi 198, 215
arkān 161
Asad, Talal 4, 158
ASEAN 167
Ash, Solomon 196
Ash'ari school 56, 63, 76
Ashraf-ul-Qadri, Mufti 132, 137, 145, 156 n.80
al-Ashtar, Malik 223
'Assaf, Amir 77
  Christian secretary of 77–8, 92, 94 n.21, 94 n.22
The Atheist (film) 122
atheists 112, 115–16, 122
al-'Awa, Mohammad Salim 123
Ayn Jalut, battle of (1260) 76
Ayyubi, Allama 142
Al-Azhar 112, 122–3

Baderin, Mashood 25
Baghdad, fall of (1258) 75
Baha'iyya 116
Bahsul Masa'il (NU fatwa body) 159
al-Bajriqi, Jamal al-Din 94 n.23
BAKORPAKEM (Indonesian agency) 163–4
al-Baladhuri (d. 892) 62
Bangil (East Java, Indonesia) 166
al-Banna, Gamal (1920–2013) 47
Banu Hashim 56
Banu al-Nadir 20, 35, 41
Barelvis 132, 134, 136–7, 149
Barlas, Asma 180
al-Baydawi (d. 1286) 39
al-Bazzazi al-Kardari, Muhammad b. Shahab (d. 1414) 95 n.34, 139–44, 146
Behbahani, 'Abdullah (1840–1910) 201
Behery, Islam 115
belief 42–3, 88–9, 188 n.7
  as inner conviction 36–8, 47, 58
  see also arkān; *kufr*; orthodoxy
Bell, Daniel 205 n.41
Bellah, Robert 205 n.41
Bellver, José 64
Berg, Herbert 33
Bhatti, Shahbaz 1
Bibi, Asia 1–2, 133, 137, 178
bid'a 64, 76
Bielefeldt, Heiner 118

Bilad al-Sudan 55
Bilgrami, Akeel 205 n.41
Binori seminary (Pakistan) 145, 147
blasphemy
against Christians 115
as apostasy 22, 26–7, 60, 103, 138
as critique 4, 103
definition of 9, 24, 75, 79–80, 88, 95 n.29, 116
distinguished from political attacks 27
habitual and non-habitual 141–3
Ibn Taymiyya on 9
modern zeal for prosecuting 177
political power and 17–19, 25, 108, 113, 115, 159, 163, 179
punishments for 3, 8, 147
Qur'an and Sunna on 19–20, 26
terms for 6, 18–19, 93 n.4, 157
under duress or diminished responsibility 102, 107–8; *see also* apostasy, of married women
blasphemy and apostasy laws
calls for repeal 7
criticism of as blasphemy 28
development of 21, 112
discriminatory nature of 115–16, 133
generating conflict or cohesion 165, 169
groups targeted by 7, 9–10, 112–15, 165–6, 196, 199
as identity markers 177
justification 5
lacking legal safeguards 9, 109, 220
prevalence of 2–3, 48, 121
rethinking 25, 47, 200
sacredness claimed for 131, 134, 137, 148–9, 223
serving political or economic interests 1, 48
in specific countries *see* Egypt; Indonesia; Iran; Pakistan
stifling impacts of 1, 8, 25, 28, 105, 116, 124, 133, 148, 169
Bostom, Andrew 196
Brazil 184
Brunei 3, 12 n.6
Buddhists 163
Byzantine Empire 22, 40
Cairo Institute for Human Rights Studies (CIHRS) 111
capital punishment *see* death penalty
Ceuta (al-Sabta) 53–5
Charlie Hebdo 2
Chaudry, Ayesha 179
Christians 9, 35, 37, 39–40, 77, 113–15, 163–4
concept of blasphemy 12 n.13, 18
converting for divorce 118
crypto-Christianity 179
in Indonesia 25, 172 n.33
insulting God or the Prophet 60
missionaries 3
Muslim-Christian relations 55, 121
seeking martyrdom 188 n.7
use of 'Allah' by 24
see also People of the Book; *dhimmī*; non-Muslims
Cikeusik (Banten, Indonesia) 165
citizenship 150, 169
civil rights movement (US) 195, 201
clash within civilizations 201
coercion in religion 8, 34, 39, 228
incompatible with test of faith 37–8, 41–2
physical vs. by persuasion 40
referring to those who entered Islam after fighting 38–40
source of violence 121
cognitive dissonance 196, 202 n.6
colonialism 3–5, 41, 43
British (India) 179, 185
Dutch (Indonesia) 159
combating intolerance 7
comedy 103
communal boundaries/cohesion 92, 164, 177–9, 187
Companions (*ṣaḥāba*)
consensus of 86
insulting 21, 26, 60, 76, 90
compulsion in religion *see* coercion in religion
confession 220
Confucians 163, 202
consensus (*ijmāʿ*) 5, 135–7
authority of 132–3, 149
based only on hadiths (*ijmāʿ al-madrakī*) 224, 228

claimed despite conflicting evidence 9, 60, 82, 84–5, 87, 90, 92, 139, 145
Ibn Taymiyya on 75, 84, 90, 92
majority opinion as 84
on punishment 207, 228
Shiʿi view of 172 n.41
Constitutional Revolution (Iran, 1905–9) 201
constitutionalism 201
Convention on the Rights of the Child (CRC) 118
conversion 40, 117
averting punishment through 78–9, 82–3
of Christian women to Islam 186
in Egypt 112
from Islam 90, 120, 124, 192 n.68
as loss of identity 182
of Muslims to Christianity 119
public expression of 116, 122
as reversion to Christianity 118–21
of unbelievers to Christianity or Judaism 38
Córdoba caliphate 54
Córdoba martyrs 22, 72 n.107
Council of Indonesian Ulama *see* Majelis Ulama Indonesia
Council of Islamic Ideology (Pakistan) 152 n.10
counter-hegemonic struggle 200
counterspeech 8
Court of Cassation (Egypt) 112, 117
critique
as apostasy 197
based on human rights 133
from within tradition 133, 147–8
of religion 4
secular 131, 134
Crone, Patricia 34
Crusades 9, 23, 75–6, 92
cultural defence 11
cultural relativism 4
customary law 158

Dabbagh, Soroush 200
Damascus 76–7
Danish cartoon controversy 2, 7, 26, 65 n.1, 111, 113–14
darʿ 222
Dar al-Iftaʾ al-Misriyya 49, 123
Darul Arqam 162
ḍarūra 218
daʿwa 43, 46, 226
Dawkins, Richard 122
Dawud (prophet) 105
Daylami, Sallar 210
death penalty 3, 8–10, 28, 61, 88, 148
averting *see* conversion; doubt
contesting due to *wahn al-islām* 219
criticized 133
for apostasy 79, 82, 178, 207, 209, 228
for blasphemy 12 n.6, 17, 26, 65, 79, 83–6, 90, 92, 95 n.34, 132, 137–9
for breach of pact 87, 96 n.62
for transgressing sexual boundaries 182
in Iran 101, 105, 198
jurists cited in support of 59, 84
limitations on 109
opposition to as apostasy 140
in Pakistan 131, 134–5, 145
seldom applied in history 188 n.7
superseding other punishments 87
texts cited in support of 59, 85–6, 90–1, 105, 209–11, 222–3
see also punishment; *ḥadd*
defamation of religions 7, 114
democracy
majoritarian pressures in 158–9, 167
Muslim support for 4, 10, 128 n.76, 195–6, 200
Denmark 2, 13 n.17
denomination theory 158
Deobandis 132, 134, 136–7, 143, 147, 149, 185
Deringil, Selim 177, 182
desecration of religious sites 112
deviant groups 10, 24, 157–70
criminal prosecution of 158
determination of as identity politics 169
fatwas on 158
government authority over 163
groups so designated *see* Islam Jama'ah; Jama'ah Muslimin Hizbullah; Darul Arqam; Ahmadiyya (Indonesia); Inkar Sunnah; Eden group; Gafatar movement
MUI procedure for 160–1

Muslim 164
non-Muslim 172 n.33
rights of 158, 170
terms for 160
as threat to the state 163
Dewan Dakwah Islamiyyah 173 n.48
al-Dhahabi, Muhammad 33
dhimma (pact of protection) 141, 150
dhimmī (dhimmis) 22, 60, 86, 90, 143
blasphemy by 78, 82, 97 n.75, 138–9, 141
committing *qadhf* 85
conditions for protection of 71 n.94
criticizing Islam in public 86
repenting after blaspheming 87
vs. citizens 149–51
see also People of the Book; non-Muslims
dialogue and debate 7, 149
Dissolution of Muslim Marriages Act (India, 1939) 185
diversity
part of divine plan 47
divorce 10, 118, 178–9, 185–6, 192 n.64, 192 n.68
diya 104
doubt (*shubha*) 31 n.56, 72 n.108, 222, 230
in Iranian law 107–8
Dubois, W.E.B. 202 n.10
Dursteler, Eric 185, 192 n.68

Eden group 162, 167
see also Aminuddin, Lia
Egypt 1, 6, 9, 76, 111–24, 201
Upper Egypt 113, 126 n.21
Egyptian Constitution 112–13, 115, 120
Egyptian Initiative for Personal Rights (EIPR) 113
Egyptian Penal Law 112, 115
Egyptians against Religious Discrimination 121
Eje'i, Golamhossein Mohseni 198
El Cheikh, Nadia 186
epistemological crisis 202 n.9
Eshkevari, Hasan Yousefi 197–9
esotericism 63, 65
Ethiopia 46
Europe 7, 13 n.17, 167
European Commission 167
European Court of Human Rights 7
Evin prison 198
exclusivism 65, 158
extrajudicial violence 1, 3, 101, 103, 109, 131, 148, 166, 181, 200; *see also* *mubāḥ al-damm*; fatwas, legitimating
extramarital sex 178, 182
extremism 112, 124

al-Fadil al-Abi (d. 1291) 80–1
Faith for Rights initiative 8
al-Farisi, Abu Bakr (d. *c.* 960) 81, 84
fasād/ifsād fī al-arḍ see waging war and spreading corruption
Fatāwa ʿālamgīriyya (*Fatawa-e-Alamgiri*) 135
Fatima al-Zahraʾ 104–5
Fatima, Nisar 135
fatwas
declaring a group deviant 162
individual and institutional 159
influencing public discourse 157
legitimating extrajudicial violence 101, 103, 109, 200
non-binding 158–9
on apostasy 207
on blasphemy 147
politics of 10, 157, 162–5
and state law 158–60, 163
al-Fazari, Ibrahim 61
Federal Shariat Court (FSC) 132, 134–6, 144–5, 148, 152 n.10, 152 n.26
feminization of religious error 178–9, 185
feminists 10, 178
Festinger, Leon 196
Fez 54
Fierro, Maribel 64
fighting (*qitāl*) 37–8, 40, 42, 45–6, 48, 86
fiʿl al-Rasūl (Prophetic deeds) 211
fines 101, 104, 151 n.4
fiqh 5, 131
fitna 42, 45, 182
fiṭra 118
see also apostasy, *fiṭrī* and *millī*
flogging or beating 3, 12 n.6, 59, 101–4, 178, 226
Flora (d. 851) 178–9, 189 n.14

Franks 76
free will 37–8, 41, 44
Freedom and Justice Party (FJP) 114
freedom of expression 4, 7, 92, 109, 123–4
  in Arab world 111
  as Islamic right 25, 30 n.55
  limitations on 7, 114, 116–17; *see also* national security; public morals; public order
  Muslim acceptance of 29
  as threat 28
freedom of religion or belief 4, 6, 92, 109, 111, 123–4
  children's 118–19
  as Islamic principle 44, 47, 49, 212, 226, 228, 230
  protecting believers not beliefs 7
  right to change 7
  as threat 168
FSC *see* Federal Shariat Court

Gabriel (angel) 162–3
Gafatar movement 167
gender
  and divine attributes 179–80
  and Islamophobia 178
  and orthodoxy 177–9, 181–2, 186–7
  and prosecution of blasphemy 178, 189 n.10
  and theological error 179
Germany 103, 109
Ghabel, Ahmad (1954–2012) 200
al-Gharnati, Muhammad b. Ahmad b. Juzayy al-Kalbi (d. 1357) 37, 51 n.49
al-Ghazali, Abu Hamid (d. 1111) 72 n.121, 187
Gilʿadi, Avner 183
Gilani, Jamila 152 n.9
Gilani, Mohammadi 198
globalization 3, 101, 168
Golpayegani, Ayatollah Safi 103–4
Gramsci, Antonio 200
Granada 54–5, 61
group vs individual 181, 190 n.34

ḥadd (pl. *ḥudūd*) 5–6, 188 n.7
  suspending (Jaʿfari law) 229
  evidentiary standards of 135, 153 n.33, 220, 222, 230
  for apostasy 47–8, 81, 213
  for blasphemy 27, 60, 135–7, 139–40, 142
  Hanafi usage 81
  in Iranian law 104, 107–8
  modern zeal for 177
  and non-Muslims 82, 85, 134
  in Pakistani law 132
  popular approval of 196
  suspending (Jaʿfari law) 217–18
hadith
  authenticity of 210, 214, 216, 221, 223, 232 n.21, 232 n.26
  cited in support of coercion 40
  criticism of 57
  invalid if contrary to Qurʾanic dictates 223–6, 230, 234 n.53, 234 n.54, 234 n.55, 234 n.56, 234 n.57, 234 n.59
  rejecting 161, 171 n.20
  Shiʿi view of 172 n.41
hadith studies 56
Hafiz Imam Bukhsh 31 n.60
Hajj 76, 168
al-Halabi (d. 1517) 141
al-Halawani, Abu al-Fath (d. 1112) 85
al-Halawani, Abu Muhammad Abd al-Rahman (d. 1151) 85
Hamid, ʿAlaʾ 113
Hanafi school 5, 81
  and Ibn Taymiyya 81, 92, 149
  misrepresentation of 10, 137, 139–40, 142–5
  on averting *ḥudūd* 188 n.7
  on blasphemy 59, 80, 137–46
  on female apostates 185, 192 n.64, 208
  on female personhood 190 n.30
  on illicit sex 189 n.9
  on non-Muslim blasphemers 78, 84, 87, 142
  on repentance 21
  role of Egypt 117, 119
  role of in Pakistan 132, 134, 136–7
Hanbali school 5, 76, 80, 85, 89
  on repentance 21, 87–8
hanging 102, 105
al-Haskafi 143
hate speech 7–8, 166
Hawking, Stephen 122

Heli, Mohaghegh 105
heresy 23, 88, 160
    see also orthodoxy; *kufr*; *takfīr*; deviant groups
hermeneutics 6
    coherence-related 44
    contextual vs. dehistoricized 227
    ethical 44
    generalizing and particularizing 8, 48, 227
    Ibn Taymiyya's 9, 75, 86, 90, 92
    parallelism 91
    thematic 8, 37
Hezbollah 103
High Court (Pakistan) 131
Higher Council of Islamic Affairs of Egypt 45
al-Hilli, al-ʿAllama (1250–1325) 229
al-Hilli, al-Muhaqqiq (1205–77) 80–1, 217, 227, 229
al-Hindi, Safi al-Din 94 n.23
Hindus 3, 163, 192 n.68, 200, 202
ḥisba 6, 117
Hitchens, Christopher 122
Holocaust denial 114
honour 22, 28, 181–2, 223
HRCP *see* Human Rights Commission of Pakistan
ḥudūd see ḥadd
al-ḥukm al-ḥukūmī 218
human life 222–3, 230
human rights 6–8, 29
    advocates 101–2, 111, 121, 124, 152 n.10, 164, 219
    importance to Muslims 4, 123
    Qurʾanic concept of 168
    universality 4
    violated by blasphemy or apostasy laws 109
Human Rights Commission of Pakistan (HRCP) 148
humanism 196–7, 200–1, 205 n.34
Huntington, Samuel 201
Husam al-Din al-Razi, Chief Qadi 78
Hussein, Taha (1889–1973) 112, 125 n.5
hypocrites 21, 40–1, 86

Ibadis 5, 12 n.11
Iberian Peninsula 53, 55, 178
ʿIbn Abd Allah b. ʿAbbas 22
Ibn ʿAbd al-Barr (d. 1071) 80–1
Ibn ʿAbdullah Alghazi, Shaykh 142
Ibn ʿAbidin, Muhammad Amin (d. 1842) 135, 138–40, 142–3, 145, 147, 187
Ibn Ahmad b. Bassam, Muhammad (d. before 1440) 184
Ibn al-ʿAjami, Sadr al-Din 184
Ibn ʿAqil, Abu al-Wafa ʿAli (d. 1119), 85
Ibn al-ʿArif (d. 1141) 64
Ibn ʿAshur, Muhammad al-Fadil 33–4
Ibn ʿAshur, Muhammad al-Tahir (1879–1973) 44
Ibn Athir al-Jazari (d. 1337) 77
Ibn Barrajan (d. 1141) 64
Ibn Battuta (d. 1369) 94 n.15
Ibn Baz, Abd al-ʿAziz b. (d. 1999) 65 n.1
Ibn Furtish, Muhammad b. Ismaʿil (d. 1136) 61
Ibn Habib al-Sulami, ʿAbd al-Malik (d. 853) 59, 70 n.79
Ibn Habib, Harun 61, 70 n.79, 71 n.107
Ibn Hajar al-ʿAsqalani (d. 1449) 55
Ibn Hanbal, Ahmad (d. 855) 5, 40
    on belief 89
    on *dhimmī* blasphemer 87, 97 n.75
    on repentance 87–8
Ibn Hatim al-Tulaytuli (d. *c*. 1064–72) 61
Ibn Hazm 145
Ibn Hisham (d. 833) 62
Ibn Ibad, ʿAbdullah (d. 708) 12 n.11
Ibn Idris al-Hilli (d. *c*. 1201) 217
Ibn Ishaq (d. 768) 62
Ibn ʿIyad, Muhammad 55
Ibn Jaʿfar al-Sadiq, Ismaʿil (d. 755) 12 n.11
Ibn al-Jawzi (d. 1200) 70 n.70
Ibn al-Kamal al-Humam (d. 1457) 142, 144
Ibn Kathir (d. 1373) 39–41, 77–8
Ibn Khalaf, Dawud (d.884) 5
Ibn Khayr (d. 1179) 57
Ibn Madaʾ (d. 1196) 67 n.21
Ibn al-Maqdisi, al-Khatib Sharaf al-Din 94 n.23
Ibn al-Mundhir al-Nishapuri (d. 930) 22, 59, 84, 96 n.74
Ibn Nujaym, Zayn al-Din Ibrahim (d. 1563) 142
Ibn Qasi (d. 1151) 64, 73 n.140

Ibn al-Qasim (d. 806) 59
Ibn Qudama (d. 1223) 81
Ibn Rahwayh, Ishaq (d. 853) 59, 84–5, 89
Ibn Rushd (d. 1198) 26
Ibn Rushd al-Jadd, Abu al-Walid (d. 1126) 55, 82
Ibn Saʿd (d. 845) 62
Ibn Saʿd, Layth (d. 791) 84, 96 n.74
Ibn Safwan, Jahm (d. 746) 98 n.117
Ibn Sahnun, Muhammad (d. 878) 79–80, 84–5, 89, 95 n.34
Ibn al-Sahrawiyya, Yahya 54
Ibn Tashufin, Ibrahim (r. 1145–7) 54
Ibn Tashufin, Yusuf (r. *c.* 1061–1106) 54
Ibn Taymiyya, Taqi al-Din Ahmad (1263–1328) 26–7, 55, 75–92
  influence of 9, 77, 93 n.6, 135–6, 139, 144–5, 149, 156 n.80, 193 n.74
  jurisprudence of 90–2
  life of 75–6
  on theological boundaries 187
  polemical style of 77, 94 n.15
Ibn Tumart (d. 1130) 53–4, 62, 64, 72 n.121
Ibn Ubay Ibn Salul, ʿAbd Allah 21
Ibn Wahb, ʿAbd Allah (d. 812/13) 21, 70 n.75, 80–1
Ibn al-Wakil 94 n.23
Ibn Yusuf, ʿAli (r. 1106–43) 54, 64
Ibn Zahra al-Halabi (d. 1190) 80–1
Ibrahim, Meriam 2, 177–8, 189 n.14
ʿidda 208–9
identity documents 117–21, 158, 167, 173 n.60
identity politics 3, 11, 28, 147, 169, 229
idolaters 36, 39, 42, 45, 86
Ifriqiya 54
ijmāʿ see consensus
ijtihād 5, 123, 143, 223
  the Prophet performing 63–4
  ranks of *mujtahidīn* 138–9, 154 n.54
  traditional vs. constructional 218–21, 229
  women engaging in 187, 193 n.75
Ikatan Jama'ah Ahlul Bayt Indonesia (IJABI) 166
ʿIkrima (d. 723) 20
Ilkhan Ghazan 76
Imam Naghi campaign 102–4, 108
Imam Sadegh *see* Jaʿfar al-Sadiq
Imam, Adel 116
Imams, Shiʿi 172 n.41
  hadiths from 5, 210, 234 n.57, 234 n.58
  insulting 103–4
  sole authority to implement *ḥudūd* 217–18
Imanul Haq, Maman 172 n.32
imprisonment 59, 101, 103–4, 108, 134, 151 n.4, 188 n.7, 198–9
incitement *see* hate speech
independence of the judiciary 105
India 3, 179, 185
Indonesia 10, 157–70
  blasphemy law 24–5, 159, 163
  Constitutional Court 24, 164–5, 172 n.32
  Islamic organizations *see* Nahdlatul Ulama; Muhammadiyah; Majelis Ulama Indonesia
  progressive Muslim thinkers in 169
  state and religion in 158, 169
infallibility/sinlessness (*ʿiṣma*) 56, 62–3, 218
Inkar Sunnah 162, 167, 171 n.20
Innocence of Muslims (film) 114–15
insulting the Prophet 6, 88, 90, 111, 197
  claiming some of his unique characteristics 62
  death penalty for 79, 83, 135
  in Iranian law 104
  Montazeri on 219
  synonymous with apostasy 91
intent 89, 106–7, 208
International Covenant on Civil and Political Rights (ICCPR) 117–18
international law 92, 109
international organizations 167
international relations 2, 24, 92
intiqāṣ 89
Iran 9–10, 12 n.6, 101–9, 201
  apostasy trials in 3, 197–200
  legal contradictions in 197
  penal code (2012) 9, 101, 104–8, 197, 203 n.11
  press law (1986) 106, 110 n.17
  Supreme Court 102
Iranian constitution
  art. 23 ('Inquisition Article') 197, 199, 203 n.12

art. 167 (judging by uncodified law) 105–6
Iraq 201
enforcement of *ḥudūd* 196
Ireland 13 n.17
irtidād 214
see ridda
isaʾa 6
Isfahani, Ayatollah Gharavi (1879–1942) 200
ISIS 65 n.1
Islam Jama'ah 162, 167, 171 n.16
Islamic courts (Indonesia) 158, 160
Islamic dilemma 196, 200
Islamic law 3, 5, 19
as identity marker 177
objectives of 6, 123
schools of *see* schools of law
sources 5
terms of 4–6
as time-bound 197–8
traditional/uncodified 12 n.6, 101, 106, 109, 117, 192 n.66
varying ideas of 196
Islamic reformism 143, 205 n.35, 205 n.41
methodologies of 11, 221
motivating Qurʾan interpretations 34, 41, 43, 47–8
opportunities for 10, 197
recovering humanism from tradition 200–1
Islamic Research Academy 123
Islamic Revolution 109
Islamization of law 5, 123, 178
Islamists 5, 9, 112–15, 122–3, 126 n.21, 134, 137, 149
attitude to history 205 n.37
Islamophobia 11, 111, 196
Ismaʿilis 5, 12 n.11, 34
Istanbul Process 7
istiḥlāl 83, 89, 208
istihzāʾ 59, 89
istikhfāf 59, 61, 79, 89
istitāba see repentance or recantation, invitation to
iʿtibār 86, 91–2

Jaʿfar b. Abi Talib (d. 629) 58
Jaʿfar al-Sadiq (d. 765) 5, 105, 210, 225
Jaʿfari school 5–6, 11
on apostasy 209
on blasphemy 80–2
on female apostates 208–9
restricting punishments 216–19, 229
Jahangir, Asma 152 n.9
Jahmiyya 89
Jamaat-e-Islami 134, 137, 144, 146
Jama'ah Muslimin Hizbullah 162
Jamia Ashrifa 147
Jamia Madnia 147
Jamiat Ulema-i Pakistan 31 n.60
al-Jassas al-Razi, Abu Bakr (d. 980) 80
Jehovah's Witnesses 115
Jews 35–6
abandoning stoning punishment 200
concept of blasphemy 18
insulting God or the Prophet 60
in Medina 20, 59
Muslims' children nursed by 35, 39
see also People of the Book; *dhimmī*; non-Muslims
jihad 47
heading jurists treated apostasy/blasphemy under 95 n.33, 210
defensive 43–4
Ibn Taymiyya promoting 76
Qurʾanic verses on 9, 33
see also fighting
jizya 35–41, 43, 45–8, 82, 198
Jordan 3
Judaism *see* Jews
judicial discretion
to forgive 220, 229
'discernment' in Iranian law 108
JUI party 137
justice 9, 11, 101, 109
al-Juwayni, Imam al-Haramayn (d. 1085) 80–2
Jyllandsposten see Danish cartoon controversy

Kaʿb b. al-Ashraf 20, 59, 97 n.75
Kadivar, Mohsen 200
kāfir 38, 140, 160
kalām 56
as speech actions 89
Kalimantan 167

al-Kalwadhani, Abu al-Khattab (d. 1116) 85
Kamali, Mohammad Hashim 25
Kani, Mahdavi 198
al-Karaki, al-Muhaqqiq (1466–1534) 227
Karroubi, Mehdi 198
al-Kasani, ʿAlaʾ al-Din Abu Bakr b. Masud (d. 1191) 82, 138, 141
Katz, Marion 58
al-khabar al-wāḥid (pl. *akhbār al-āḥād*) 217, 223–4
  invalid in critical matters 221–3, 230, 234 n.47
  meaning of 234 n.47
Khadija 183
Khalidi, Tarif 53
Khamenei, ʿAli 102, 198–9, 233 n.38
Khan, Sayyid Ahmad (1817–98) 12 n.9
al-Khansari, al-Muhaqqiq 229
Kharijis (Khawarij) 21, 34
al-Kharkushi, Abu Saʿd (d. 1016) 57
Khatami, Mohammad 198–9
al-Khattabi, Abu Sulayman Hamd b. Muhammad (d. 998) 84–5, 97 n.75
Khawarij *see* Kharijis
al-Khiraqi, Abu al-Qasim (d. 945) 80, 85
Khomeini, Ayatollah (1902–89) 2, 197–8, 208, 218, 233 n.38
Khorasani, Akhund (1839–1911) 201
al-Khuʾi, Ayatollah Abu al-Qasim (1899–1992) 210
King, Martin Luther (1929–68) 201
Kufa, jurists of 95 n.34, 139
kuffār see kāfir
kufr 208
  Ibn Taymiyya charged with 76
  insult as 21, 60, 76, 88, 91
kufr mujarrad ('simple disbelief') 90

Lamptey, Jerusha 47–8
laʿn(a) 59, 79, 89
Lange, Christian 180
Lankarani, Ayatollah Fazel (1931–2007) 200
al-Layth (d. 971) 59
Loraux, Nicole 186

madhhab (pl. *madhāhib*) *see* schools of law
Madjid, Nurcholish 169
al-Maghrib 54
Magians *see* Zoroastrians
Mahdi 54, 62–4
Mahfudh, Sahal 166
Mahmoud, Abd al-Majid 118
Majelis Ulama Indonesia (MUI) 157–70
  expanding influence of 159, 164, 170 n.8
  Fatwa Commission 161
  on Ahmadiyah and Shiʿa 165–8
  on secularism, pluralism and liberalism 168–9
  on yoga and smoking 158
  relation to state and *ʿulamāʾ* 159, 164, 170 n.8
Majlis Tarjih *see* Muhammadiyah, fatwa body of
Majlisi, Mohammad Baghir 203 n.20
Malaysia 24
Malik b. Anas (d. 795) 5
  cited in *al-Shifāʾ* 57
  on blasphemy 21, 26, 59, 80, 84, 95 n.34, 96 n.74, 139
  on breach of pact 87
  on *dhimmī* blasphemer 97 n.75
  on repentance of *dhimmī* 87
Malik Mansur Lajin, sultan 76
Maliki school 5, 54, 80
  Almohad break with 53, 63–4
  on blasphemy 59–61, 80–2, 84
  on choice of religion 119
  on illicit sex 189 n.9, 192 n.64
  on repentance 21, 208
Mamluks 75–6
Mansoor Ali, Maulana 143
maqāṣid al-sharīʿa see Islamic law, objectives of
al-Maqdisi, Shams al-Din (d. 1362) 80
al-Marghinani, Burhan al-Din (d. 1197) 80, 82, 141
Marrakech 54, 64
marriage
  dissolved by apostasy 113, 178, 185, 192 n.64, 207, 209, 228
  enabled by conversion 192 n.68
  obstacles to registering 158
Mary the Copt 183
masculinity 179

maṣlaḥa (public good/interest) 6, 123, 218
invoked to suppress critique 146–7, 149
Mas'udi, Masdar F. 161
maternal grief 5, 10, 178–9, 182–6, 188, 193 n.72
Mauritania 3
al-Mawardi (d. 1058) 26, 71 n.94
mawlid 55, 58
Ma'arif, Syafi'i 169
MB *see* Muslim Brotherhood
Mecca 19, 27, 42, 45–6, 86
media 24, 101, 219
Medina 19, 27, 46, 86
Middle East and North Africa 48
migration 3, 24
miḥna 181
Ministry of Religious Affairs (Indonesia) 158, 163, 168
miracles 62
mob violence *see* extrajudicial violence
modernity 41, 121
Mongols 9, 23, 75–6, 92
Montazeri, Ayatollah Hussein ʿAli (1922–2009)
arguments of 200, 214, 218–21, 229
biography 233 n.38
supporting defendants 198–9
Moriscos 58
Morsi, Mohamed 9, 113, 115, 123
mourning
associated with Shiʿism 184–5, 191 n.57
as contesting God's decree 183–4
of widow 183; *see also ʿidda*
Muʿawiya b. Abi Sufyan 216
mubāḥ al-damm 6, 82, 86, 148, 182, 227
Mubarak, Hosni 113
al-Mufid (948–1022) 227
Mughals 132
Muhammad I (r. 852–86) 22
Muhammadiyah 157, 164–5, 167
fatwa body of 159, 164
Muhsin, Salah al-Din 113
muḥtasib 184
MUI 167
see Majelis Ulama Indonesia
mujtahid see ijtihād
Mulder, Niels 163
Mulia, Musdah 172 n.32
Mulla Khusru 95 n.34
multiplicity of legal truths (*taṣwīb al-mujtahidīn*) 64
Muluk, Tajul 164, 166
munāfiqūn see hypocrites
Muridun revolt 64
al-Murtada, Sharif (d. 1046) 82, 210
murtadd 6, 60, 215–16
murtadd al-mujarrad 88, 98 n.122
Muslim Brotherhood (MB) 112, 114–15, 122–4
al-muṣtafā 56
mutaʿakhkhirīn 143
mutawātir 211, 234 n.47, 234 n.66
Muʿtazila 34, 37
Muwaṭṭaʾ 21, 26, 59, 70 n.75, 95 n.33
Muzadi, Hasyim 165
Myrdal, Gunnar 10, 195

Naeem, Mufti 147
Nahdlatul Ulama (NU) 157, 159, 161–2, 164–5, 167
al-Nahr, Sahib 142
Najafi, Shahin 103–4, 109
al-Nasafi (d. 1310) 141
Nasir, Ammar 143
naskh see abrogation
national security 8, 25, 116–17
nationalism 182
al-Nawawi, Sharaf (d. 1276/7) 23, 81
Nekoonam, Mohammad Ibrahim 197
Nigeria 189 n.9
Nikbakht, Saleh 199
niyya see intent
non-Muslims 9, 41, 45, 60, 86
apostasy rulings misapplied to 144
blasphemy as violation of pact 22–3, 82, 86–7, 91, 139, 150
citizens not dhimmis 149–50
disbelief of 84, 90, 97 n.75, 138, 141
legal questions surrounding 79, 123
punishment for 27, 61, 83, 85, 92, 132, 134–7, 139–43, 148
restrictions on 22
see also dhimmī; People of the Book
normative dissonance 128 n.76, 196
NU *see* Nahdlatul Ulama

occasions of revelation 35, 39–41, 119, 212
official religion 121

OIC *see* Organization of Islamic Cooperation
Organization of Islamic Cooperation (OIC) 3, 7, 111
Orientalism 41–2
orthodoxy 10, 18, 23, 83, 158
  and gender *see* gender, orthodoxy and
Oslo Coalition on Freedom of Religion or Belief 2
Ottomans 132, 177, 182

Pakistan 1, 10, 131–51, 189 n.9
  Ahmadiyya in 167–8
  blasphemy laws 3, 12 n.6, 31 n.60; *see also* Pakistan Penal Code
  enforcement of *ḥudūd* 196
  UN initiatives of 7
Pakistan Penal Code 151 n.1
  art. 295c (insulting the Prophet) 95 n.29, 131–7, 140, 142, 145–6, 152 n.24
  art. 298 (wounding religious feelings) 95 n.29
Pakistan Supreme Court 136
Pancasila 24, 157–8, 169–70
Paracha, Fareed 144, 146
pardon 80–1, 84, 132, 136–9, 142, 153 n.36
  see also repentance; right of man
parental religion 118–19, 178, 189 n.12, 209
patriarchy 10, 178–80, 185, 190 n.34
penodaan agama (blasphemy) 157
People of the Book (*ahl al-kitāb*) 35–9, 41, 60, 86
  see also dhimmī; Christians; Jews; non-Muslims; religious minorities
Perfect Man, the 23, 28, 30 n.40
Persatuan Islam 165
pluralism 10, 158, 168–9, 202
Pole, the (*al-ʿamūdu, al-quṭb*) 62–3, 72 n.118
political Islam *see* Islamists
poll tax *see* jizya
post-colonial world 3, 202
post-Suharto era 157–8, 164–5
prisoners of war 87
property and inheritance rights 113, 208–9, 228
Prophet Muhammad
  (in)fallibility of 24
  assuming the characteristics of 163
  centrality of in Islam 75, 83, 92
  dealing with insulters or apostates 19–20, 59–60, 80, 86, 207, 211, 214–15, 222, 228, 232 n.21
  duties of believers towards 56
  faith (*imān*) in 57
  family and descendants of 58, 60, 105
  human or superhuman 23–4, 27, 56, 218
  insulting 7, 56, 59, 75, 131–2, 151 n.4, 153 n.36
  light imagery 27, 56, 58
  love for, devotion to, veneration of 4, 26–7, 55, 57–8, 62, 65, 69 n.56
  paternal grief of 182, 191 n.44
  prophetic lineage of 56
  qualities and attributes of 24, 56–8, 61, 65, 66 n.3
  rejecting as last prophet 161
  rights of 56–6, 80–1, 136, 153 n.36
  singularity of among the prophets 23
prophethood
  claims to 162
prophets
  characteristics of 56, 62
  denial of as apostasy 208, 219
  having no coercive authority 47, 212
  historical discussion of 60
  insulting 60, 104, 161
proportionality 116–17
proselytism 3, 166
protection of religious feelings 7
public good/interest 60, 158
public morals 111, 114, 116–17
public opinion
  helping the accused 199–200
  international surveys 2, 196, 202 n.7
  opposing harsh punishment 101–2, 204 n.31, 219
public order 25, 112, 114, 116–17, 121
  threatened by women's mourning 187, 193 n.72
punishment 27
  arguments for removing entirely 220–8
  cruel, inhuman or degrading 101
  disgracing Islam 9, 226–8; *see also wahn al-Islām*
  for *zināʾ* 192 n.64

forms of 101, 188 n.7, 227; *see also* fines; *taʿzīr*; *ḥadd*; death penalty; flogging; hanging; imprisonment
in front of the ruler 189 n.20
gender differences in 178
grounds for 79
in the hereafter 228
as individual duty 182
lacking textual basis 8, 17, 26–8
legitimate authority 6, 208, 217–18
Muslim support for 48, 128 n.76, 195–6, 202 n.7
purposes and actual effects of 109, 222

qadhf 79, 104, 107–8
Qadi Abu Yaʿla Muhammad b. al-Farraʾ (d. 1131) 85, 89
Qadi ʿIyad (d. 1149) 9, 26–7, 53–65, 139–40
claiming consensus 82
fahrasa of 55, 57, 66 n.6, 66 n.9
influence of 79, 136, 139, 144
life 54–5, 66 n.7
on belief 89
supporting death penalty 84
Qadri, Malik Mumtaz Hussain 133–4
Qadri, Turab-ul-Haq 135
Qalawun, sultan 76
al-Qaradawi, Yusuf 123
Qatar 3
al-Qayrawan 54, 61
al-Qayrawani, Abu Zayd (d. 996) 80
qiṣāṣ 81, 85, 104, 226
qiyās 6, 91–2, 149
qiyās jalī 92
al-Quduri, Abu al-Husayn Ahmad (d. 1037) 81, 141
Qum (Iran) 166
al-Qummi, Mirza 217
Qurʾan
createdness of 181
disavowing 60
ethical message of 46–9
exegesis of 4, 33–49, 145; *see also* hermeneutics
legal import of 5
Muhammad in 24
no temporal punishment 6, 8, 19, 21, 27, 90, 207, 213–14, 221, 225–6, 228
on harming God and His Prophet 59
support for freedom of expression 29
verses stressing choice 9, 33, 120, 211, 226
'deviant' positions on 161
Qurʾan and Sunna
contradicting consensus 207, 216
direct engagement with 63, 136
Qurʾan verses cited
2:190–5 42, 45–6, 81
2:217–18 86, 97 n.78, 213, 234 n.42
2:255 44, 189 n.20
2:256 4, 8, 33–49, 119, 211–12
3:21 91
3:33 69 n.40
3:72 234 n.42
3:86–90 213
4:65 86, 91
4:80 24
4:94 38
4:137 213
5:4–5 213
5:33 221
5:54 213
5:99 212
6:50 24
6:108 19
8:12–13 91
8:20 58
8:39 42
9:6–15 42, 86, 91
9:20 91
9:28–9 91
9:29–32 22, 86
9:36 45
9:58 86, 91
9:61–6 59, 86, 90–1
9:73 33, 37, 39, 212
9:74 213
9:101 86
9:123 40
10:99 33, 37–8, 41–2, 46, 212
10:108 212
11:28 212
13:40 212
16:106 213
18:29 33, 38, 41, 46, 212
21:107 24
22:39–41 46

24:4 86
24:35 56
24:63–4 86, 91
25:56–58 212
26:3–4 38, 41
27:91–93 212
33:6 234 n.56
33:40 24
33:53 59, 86, 91
33:57–8 59, 86, 91
33:60–61 86
39:41 212
47:4 97 n.94
47:25–28 213
48:13 57
48:16 40
49:1–5 91
49:13 51 n.55
50:43 212
53:4 63
55:1–4 25
58:5 86
58:20–1 86
58:20–1; 86
59:7 234 n.56
65:1 226
66:9 33, 40–1, 45
80:10 24
88:21–2 212
109:6 33, 46
Quraysh 20, 56
Qureshi, Haneef (mufti) 132
Qureshi, Muhammad Ismail 132, 140–1, 144–6, 152 n.18
al-Qurtubi (d. 1273) 39
Qutb, Sayyid (1906–66) 44

Rabat Plan of Action 7
racism 195, 201
Rahardjo, Dawam 172 n.32
Ramadan, Tariq 205 n.41
Ramali, Allama Khayruddin 142
rationality 65, 226
al-Razi, Abu Bakr al-Jassas (d. 1191) 141
al-Razi, Fakhr al-Din (d. 1209) 37–8, 41–2
Razini, Ali 198
reasonable people (*al-ʿuqalāʾ*) 221–3, 226–8, 230
rebellion 88
recognised religions
Egypt 112, 115–16, 124
Indonesia 163
Rehman, Sherry 152 n.9
religion/politics divide 43
religious authority 9
religious dominance/subordination 17–18, 22, 41, 43, 47, 115, 131, 187
religious establishments 4, 8–9, 25, 53, 63, 124
religious feelings 116
religious mainstream 158
religious minorities 1, 9
discriminated against 47
in Egypt 111–13, 115, 122
in Indonesia 164
in Pakistan 131, 133–4, 148, 150–1
see also Ahmadiyya; Christians; Jews; People of the Book; Shiʿa; non-Muslims
religious otherness 47–8
religious plurality 46
religious symbols 17–18, 23, 112
repentance or recantation 87, 208
in classical Islamic law 21, 27, 60, 81, 138, 143, 208
as grounds for pardon 79, 82, 102, 140, 220
invitation to (*istitāba*) 79, 81, 85, 87–8, 148, 208–9, 211
in Iranian penal code 107–8
in Pakistani law 136, 153 n.38
revelation 63–4
ridda (*irtidād*) 6, 21, 48, 60, 79, 142, 144, 197, 211, 216
as political offence 49, 215, 219
wars of 6, 215–16, 229, 232 n.25
see also apostasy
Ridwan, Cholil 166, 173 n.48
right of exit 186
right of God (*ḥaqq Allāh*) 181
right of man (*ḥaqq al-ʿabd*) 21, 80
Rippin, Andrew 33
Rushdie, Salman 2, 136

sabb 6, 19, 56, 83, 88
as emerging offence 22
meaning of 89

sabb allāh 19
sabb al-nabī 6, 79–80, 82, 93 n.4, 95 n.29, 95 n.33, 104–5, 107, 197
sabb al-rasūl 6, 19, 21, 95 n.29
sabb al-ṣaḥāba see Companions, insulting
Sabbah, Fatna 180
Saber, Alber 115
Sachedina, Abdul Aziz 47
al-Sadafi 64
Saduq 210
Sadzali, Munawwir 169
Saeed, Hafiz Akif 146
Safran, Janina 61
ṣaḥāba see Companions
Sahnun (d. 854/5) 21, 54, 57, 59, 79
Salafists 113, 123–4
salām greeting 38, 60
Salem b. ʿAwf 35
Sampang (Madura, Indonesia) 164, 166–7, 173 n.44
sanctities in Iranian law (*moghadasat*) 104
Saneʿi, Yousef (grand ayatollah) 198
al-Sarakhsi, Abu Bakr (d. 1096) 81–2
al-ṣārim al-Maslūl 9, 75–92
doctrinal context 79
influence 93 n.2
motivation for 76, 78–9, 83, 92
reception of 135, 139
studies on 93 n.9
Sassanid Empire 22, 40
Satanic Verses 136
Saudi Arabia 3, 12 n.6, 168, 173 n.48
al-Saydalani, Abu Bakr (d. *c.* 1044) 80–1
Scheper-Hughes, Nancy 184
Schimmel, Annemarie (d. 2003) 53
Schleifer, Aliah 184
scholarly authority
criticism of as blasphemy 24, 203 n.23
epistemic 53, 63–5
ʿIyad's *al-Shifāʾ* as defence of 63, 65
marginalizing unauthorized speakers 187
schools of law 5
adherence to 92, 143–4
agreement and differences 26, 78, 80, 132, 207; *see also* consensus
Sunni 208
sectarianism 118, 121, 171 n.15
secularism 122, 131, 133
dichotomies about 195, 205 n.41
fatwa against 168
objective vs. subjective 205 n.41
and religious law 160
as threat 146–7
Senghaas, Dieter 201
sepilis 168
sexual morality 181
sexuality and theology 177–8, 181
Shafiʿi school 5
on blasphemy 22, 59, 78, 80–1, 84
on *dhimmī* blasphemer 87
on repentance 21, 87
al-Shafiʿi, Muhammad b. Idris (d. 820) 5, 21, 26, 84, 90, 139
on breach of pact 82, 85, 87, 96 n.62, 96 n.74
on *dhimmī* blasphemer 97 n.75
on forced conversion 119
al-Shahid al-Awwal (1334–85) 227
al-Shahid al-Thani (1506–57) 227
Shahroudi, Hashemi 198–9
Shaltut, Mahmud (1893–1963) 44
Shams al-Din al-Aʿsar, Amir 77
Sharhabil b. ʿAmr 46
Shariʿa *see* Islamic law
Shariati, Ali 199
al-Sharif Abu Jaʿfar (d. 1077) 85
shatm 6, 79, 83, 88, 93 n.3, 93 n.4
see also sabb
al-Shawkani (d. 1839) 63
al-Shaybani, Hanbal b. Ishaq b. Hanbal (d. 886/7) 87
al-Shaybani, Muhammad b. Hasan (d. 805) 21, 81, 154 n.54
Shaykh Tusi (d. 1097) 80–1
al-Shayzari, ʿAbd al-Rahman b. Nasr (d. 1193) 184
Shiʿa 21, 115–16
challenge to Sunni rule 9
in Indonesia 25, 159–60, 163, 166–7, 169
legal thought *see* Jaʿfari school
mourning rituals of 185
Sunni controversy with 76, 172 n.41
targeted by laws 10, 112–13
al-Shifāʾ 9, 53–65, 80, 85
dating and transmission of 55, 62, 67 n.22

legal discourse in 61
mystical interpretations of 53, 66 n.3
reception of 55, 65, 139–40
socio-political context of 62
sources, structure, content of 56–7
Shihab, Quraysh 169
Shihab, Umar 166, 173 n.46
Shirazi, Abu Ishaq (d. 1003) 81
Shirazi, Ayatollah Naser Makarem 103, 198
shurafāʾ 58
Shurunbalali 142
al-Sijistani, Abu Dawud Sulayman b. al-Ashʿath (d. 899) 84
sin 89, 160, 226
Sion City of Allah 25
sīra 55, 57, 62, 211
Siradj, Said Aqil 164, 167
el-Sisi, Abdel Fattah 115, 124
siyar 95 n.33
siyāsa 41, 81, 85, 138, 141–2, 155 n.63
slavery 180, 185
social contract 150
social media 115, 219
socio-political context
shaping blasphemy/apostasy law 8, 11, 17, 26–8, 62, 75
shaping Qurʾanic interpretation 33, 48
Spain, Muslim 22–3, 27
Christian reconquest of 61
Special Court for the Clergy (Iran) 97–8, 203 n.15
State Council (Egypt) 119
stoning 101, 200, 218, 226
al-Subki, Taqi al-Din (d.1355) 55, 95 n.34, 135
Sudan 2–3, 12 n.6, 177–8
Sufis 27, 64, 73 n.140, 76, 162
al-Sughdi, Abu al-Hasan al-Sughdi (d. 1069) 80
Suharto, Haji Mohamed (1921–2008, r. 1968–98) 157, 159, 164–5
Suhaymi, Shaykh (b. 1925) 162
Sukarno (1901–70, r. 1945–67) 158, 163
Sunna 5, 8, 58
see also hadith; Qurʾan and Sunna; blasphemy, Quran and Sunna on
Sunni al-Bayyinat Foundation (Surabaya, Indonesia) 166
Sunni Ittehad Council 137
Sunni Tehreek 137
superiority of Islam 23, 28, 43, 47
Supreme Administrative Court (Egypt) 120–1
Supreme Court (Iran) 199
al-Suyuti, Jalal al-Din (d. 1505) 39, 55
Syamsuddin, Din 165–7, 169, 173 n.47

al-Tabari, Abu Jaʿfar Muhammad b. Jarir (d. 923) 35–6, 38–9, 62
Tabatabaʾi, Mohammad (1842–1920) 201
tafsīr 8, 33–49
Tagi, Rafiq 200
al-Tahawi, Abu Jaʿfar (d. 933) 80, 138–9, 141
tajdīf 6
Tajul Muluk 25
takdhīb 6
takfīr 3, 6, 160–1, 174 n.64
takhrīj 143–4, 155 n.79
takhṣīṣ (specification) *see* hermeneutics, generalizing and particularizing
takhyīr 6
talfīq 6
al-Tamimi, Abu ʿAbd Allah (d. 1111) 54
tanaqqus 89
Tanzeem-e-Islami 137, 146
taqbīḥ 89
taqlīd 92, 227
Taseer, Salman 1, 132–3, 137, 140, 147, 149, 152 n.9
tashbīh 59
taṭbīq 6
Tavana, Ruhollah 101–2, 107–8, 204 n.31
tawba see repentance
tawṣiya 160
taysīr 6
al-Tayyib, Ahmed 123
taʿzīr 27, 208
evidentiary standards for 220
in Iranian law 104, 107
non-Muslims liable to 90, 138
Tehreek e Tahaffuz Namoos e Risalat 137
Thanawi, Ashraf ʿAli 185
al-Thawri (d. 778) 59, 139
al-Tirmidhi (d. 892) 57
tohin 104
tolerance 46
tribal society 214

Tritton, A.S. 150
Tucker, Judith 177, 201
al-Tumartashi, ʿAbd Allah al-Khatib (d. 1596) 142
Tunisia 3
Turab-ul-Haq 145
al-Tusi, Shaykh al-Taifa (995–1067) 210, 215–16, 227

Uddin, Asma 25
ʿUmar b. ʿAbd al-ʿAziz (r. 717–20) 21
ʿUmar b. al-Khattab (d. 644) 30 n.55, 39–40
Pact of 150, 172 n.41
Umayyads 22, 27, 216, 221
al-Umm 26, 95 n.33, 96 n.62
UN Human Rights Committee 7, 116–17
UN Human Rights Council 8
United Arab Emirates 3
United Nations (UN) 7–8, 167
Universal Declaration of Human Rights (UDHR) 120
uṣūl al-dīn 160
uṣūl al-fiqh 5, 92, 139, 143
reconstructing 11, 220, 234 n.47
ʿUthman b. ʿAffan (d. 656) 172 n.41

vigilantism *see* extrajudicial violence

wadud, amina 180, 190 n.27
al-Wafd 122
waging war and spreading corruption (*muḥāraba, fasād*) 20, 91, 104, 107–8, 141, 197–8, 204 n.31, 221, 234 n.43
see also apostasy, as treason, rebellion or hostility
Wahid, Abdurrahman 169, 172 n.32
wahn 104
wahn al-Islām ('impairing' Islam) 218, 226–30
al-Wakidi (d. 822/3) 62
al-Walid, Khalid 166
Wansbrough, John 33
war, state of 83, 87, 92
West Africa 55
West, the
blasphemy in 4, 6, 12 n.13, 121
contemporary liberal views of 181
engagement of with the issue 2
Islamophobia in 111, 196
and legal change in Muslim world 5
Muslim reformers accused of serving 4, 28, 134
patriarchal norms of 190 n.34
and pluralist modernity 202
relations with 2, 4, 114, 168
Wibisono, Ahmad Fata 164
wifely restrictions 180
wives of the Prophet 26, 58, 60, 90, 105, 183
women
apostasy of 185–6, 192 n.64, 208–9
as blasphemers 27
experience of 182, 186–7
legal personhood of 180, 190 n.30
place of in tradition 187
protest of 186, 188
as scholars/thinkers 193 n.75

Yahya b. Zakariya al-Khashshab 71 n.107
Yayasan Pesantren Islam (YAPI) 166
Yazdi, Mohammad 198
Yemen 3
yoga 158
Youssef, Bassem 122
Yudhoyono, Susilo Bambang 170 n.8
Yusuf, Slamet Effendy 169

ẓāhir al-riwāya 138
Zahiri school 5, 67 n.21
zakāt (tax) 6, 215–16, 229
Zamakhshari, Abu al-Qasim Mahmud (d. 1144) 37–8, 41
zandaqa 6, 60, 71 n.86
Zanjani, Mohsen Amiraslani 204 n.31
ẓann 63, 223
Zayd b. Ali (d. 740) 12 n.11
Zaydis 5, 12 n.11, 34
Zayn al-Din al-Fariqi, Shaykh 77–8
zināʾ 81, 177, 192 n.64
zindīq 208
Zoroastrians (Magians) 36, 38, 141

www.ingramcontent.com/pod-product-compliance
Ingram Content Group UK Ltd.
Pitfield, Milton Keynes, MK11 3LW, UK
UKHW020856310326
469506UK00007B/175

9 780755 638826